BRITISH
GRAND PRIX

BRITISH GRAND PRIX

MAURICE HAMILTON

First published in 1989 by
THE CROWOOD PRESS
Ramsbury, Marlborough
Wiltshire SN8 2HE

Text: copyright © 1989 by Maurice Hamilton
Design: Steve Small

Jacket photographs of Stirling Moss *(front)* winning the
British Grand Prix in 1957 and Brooklands *(back)* are
courtesy of Quadrant Picture Library. The colour
photograph of Nigel Mansell is by Paul-Henri Cahier.

Illustrations in the duo-tone section *(pages 81-96)* are all
supplied by Quadrant Picture Library, except *page 93*
courtesy Eoin Young collection.

Illustrations in the colour section *(pages 161-176)* have been
provided by: LAT *(161, 162-3, 166-7, 175)*, Chris Willows *(164-5, 168-9, 170-1)*, Paul-Henri Cahier *(172-3)*, Steve Small *(174)*
and Nigel Snowdon *(176)*.

The bulk of the black and white photographs are courtesy of
Quadrant Picture Library with others contributed by Diana
Burnett, Michael Cooper, Nigel Snowdon, and the Eoin
Young collection.

Printed by BAS Printers Limited
Over Wallop, Hampshire

British Library Cataloguing in Publication Data
Hamilton, Maurice
    British Grand Prix.
    1. Great Britain. Racing cars. Racing. Races. Grand
Prix to 1988
    I. Title
    795.7'2

ISBN 1–85223–213–7

ACKNOWLEDGEMENTS

I am indebted to the many people who helped during my research and generally provided encouragement and guidance.

It is impossible to mention everyone but special thanks are due to Denis Jenkinson for looking over my shoulder and keeping me within the bounds of accuracy; any omissions or errors are mine. I am also grateful to the staff at Brooklands Museum, Quadrant Picture Library, the RAC Library, the British Newspaper Museum, Sandhurst Marketing in Horsham; to Nigel Roebuck for the loan of valuable archive material; to Eoin Young for the use of superb photographs and memorabilia from his collection; to David Tremayne, editor of *Motoring News*; to Peter Foubister, editor of *Autosport* for giving permission to use the many extracts culled from back issues; to Mike Cooper, Doug Gardner, Peter Lovering, Doug Nye and Chris Willows; to the drivers, past and present, who spent time recalling the British Grand Prix; and to Steve Small for applying his talent and zeal so generously.

Finally, a great deal of credit must go to my wife, Diane, and Christopher and Jo Forster for their inspiration, patience and infectious enthusiasm.

Maurice Hamilton
Ewhurst
Surrey
June 1989

CONTENTS

The front row of the grid before the start of the 1956 British Grand Prix at Silverstone. Stirling Moss and Fangio are lost in thought whilst Hawthorn and Collins are no doubt engaged in their usual banter.

To Dad

CHAPTER 1

A HESITANT START

Tootling along

Britain has its fair share of whimsical folk: people who collect lavatory chains or eat live frogs whole; that sort of thing. In 1926, however, there was a Southampton man who engaged in a much more hazardous pursuit while going about his everyday business.

He was known as 'The Tootler'. The sobriquet had been earned because, as one contemporary report put it, 'this man makes a habit of tootling a horn to warn motorists that he is about to cross the road'. He wouldn't last two minutes today; he probably didn't last much longer then, given the dubious stopping power of the vehicles of the time.

But it is an appropriate indication of the state of motoring in the mid-twenties and it goes some way towards explaining why Great Britain had been rather slow off the mark when it came to holding a Grand Prix. The first such race had been in France in 1906 but the idea did not take firm hold until Italy, Spain and Belgium staged Grands Prix in the early 1920s. Britain, though, did not rush to follow suit.

There was, quite simply, very little interest in motoring and the motorist. They were branded by 'The Tootler' and fellow pedestrians as something of a growing menace. Apart from Sunbeam and Aston Martin, the British motor manufacturers did not feel moved to enter the sport and the government of the day felt even less inclined to encourage them. All of which was a pity because, at the time, Britain possessed one of the finest automotive theatres imaginable; the imposing 2¾-mile banked track at Brooklands. But, as a circuit, it was not highly rated, at least, not when compared with tracks elsewhere in Europe.

The Madonie, a difficult and frequently rough road circuit of some 67 miles, hosted the *Targa Florio* in Sicily. In 1924, the Belgian Grand Prix was held on the magnificent Spa-Francorchamps road circuit, the practise of using public thoroughfares being widely accepted on the continent.

It was a victory for Major Henry Segrave in the San Sebastian Grand Prix in 1924 (following on the heels of his victory in France the previous year) which began to arouse interest at home. On top of that, Segrave, J.G. Parry Thomas and Captain Malcolm Campbell had each broken the world land speed record during the previous 18 months, all of which encouraged the idea of holding a British Grand Prix for the first time.

Britain was offered a Grand Prix in 1925 but nothing came of it; apparently a suitable venue could not be found. The following year, the Royal Automobile Club, after some deliberation and switching of dates, finally earmarked Saturday, 7th August. The venue: Brooklands Motor Course, near Weybridge in Surrey.

The building of Brooklands

Hugh Fortescue Locke-King was a man of considerable vision and enthusiasm. He was also a land-owner of considerable wealth. Part of the family estate embraced a meadow, marshy in parts due to the River Wey wandering through it, and bounded on one side by the London and South Western Railway. At one end lay a sewage farm serving Byfleet and Addlestone; at the other, a steep hill leading towards Locke-King's home (now part of Brooklands Technical College) and Weybridge.

In 1906, Locke-King conceived the idea of providing a motoring test centre and a suitable venue where racing could be held under controlled conditions rather than suffering from the haphazard organisation which attended road circuits in operation at the time. The fledgling British motor industry was in desperate need of a testing ground. Public roads in Britain could not be closed for the purposes of high-speed trials and, in any case, the Motor Car Act of 1903 restricted motorists to a beggarly 20 mph. Locke-King decided to put that right.

According to William Boddy's authoritative work *'The History of Brooklands Motor Course'*, it took 300 men to clear a way through the trees and level ground which would become the Railway Straight. Once the building operation got into its stride, as many as 2000

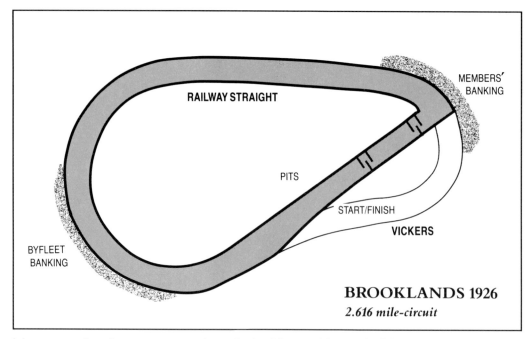

BROOKLANDS 1926
2.616 mile-circuit

labourers and craftsmen set to work on the banking at either end of the circuit. It was to be a remarkable feat of civil engineering.

The River Wey had to be diverted in two places but, more than that, the banking at the northern end had to be built across it. The curving bridge, which took about four months to complete, was eventually named after the Yorkshire Hennebique Co, the specialist contractors hired to undertake such a difficult and, at the time, novel operation. The Hennebique Bridge stood the test of time until it fell into disuse – and then into the river during floods in 1978.

When complete, the northern banked curve, known as the Home and Members' Banking, rose 28ft 8in. At the opposite end, the Byfleet Banking, the longer of the two, rose 17ft. The Railway Straight was the fastest part of the circuit. Roughly half-way along the return leg on the opposite side, the track divided and either became the Finishing Straight or, by forking right, the start of the Home Banking.

It required 200 carpenters to erect the fencing and sheds, plus seating for 5,000. Overall, facilities were provided for an anticipated 30,000 spectators, the main entrance being through a tunnel under the Members' Banking.

William Boddy wrote about his initial acquaintance with the track and the unforgettable sensation of 'emerging from the tunnel for the first time to encounter the breathtaking steepness of the banking behind one, and the Railway Straight spreading majestically away towards Byfleet on the right.'

Thanks to the efforts of Gallaghers (the present owners of the site) and Elmbridge District Council, a considerable portion of the Members' Banking remains and it is easy to understand how Boddy must have felt. Standing inside the circuit, the vast sweep of concrete forms the horizon. Although most of the site has since been redeveloped, the breath-taking proportions of Locke-King's scheme are still apparent.

But the thought of John Cobb urging one-and-a-half tons of Napier-Railton close to the upper edge of the banking at an average 143.44mph is more difficult to imagine. That record for the outer circuit (road courses were later constructed within the banked perimeter) remains etched in the minds of those who saw it in October 1935 – particularly as the track was damp in parts and the 24-litre leviathan was sliding under power.

Regrettably, there are few such stirring memories of the first British Grand Prix nine years earlier.

A ragged start

In 1926, an entry of 13 cars was considered by contemporary writers to be 'outstanding'. Grand Prix racing was beginning to suffer because of a lack of support from Fiat and other

A HESITANT START

manufacturers and, in view of the latest regulations, the RAC had indeed done well to attract such a number. Startled by the speeds achieved by the 2-litre cars, the rule-makers had reduced engine capacity to 1.5 litres and the minimum weight was pared from 1,433lb to 1,322lb.

It was enough to persuade Alfa Romeo, having enjoyed great success with the beautiful P2, to rest on their laurels. That left Bugatti (with the equally remarkable Type 35), Delage and Sunbeam (now known as Talbot or Talbot-Darracq). And precious little else. The likes of Fiat and Alvis had cancelled their racing plans early in the year and the entry lists, peppered with withdrawals as the season progressed, marked something of a low point in Grand Prix racing at the time.

The British Grand Prix suffered more than most. Nonetheless, three Talbots were entered for Henry Segrave, Albert Divo and Jules Moriceau. There were three Delages for Robert Benoist, Louis Wagner and Robert Sénéchal and a single works-supported Bugatti for Malcolm Campbell. The remainder of the field was a mixture of privately-entered machines, including two home-brewed Thomas Specials, built by Parry Thomas at Brooklands and driven by Clive Gallop and a gentleman revelling under the splendid name of 'Scrap' Thistlethwayte. Gearbox problems would lead to their withdrawal before the start.

Since Brooklands was open most days for testing, the official practice from 7am to 9pm on the Friday was a rather leisurely affair. By the following morning, the entry had been reduced to nine. But that did not prevent the *Daily Sketch*, in a moment of popular-newspaper excess, referring to the Grand Prix and Brooklands as 'The Derby' of the motoring world.

Taking a more serious line, 'Chiltern', the motoring correspondent of *The Daily News* (later to become the *News Chronicle*), described the cars.

'The Talbot,' he wrote, 'has registered 172bhp on test. Some of the cars are waistcoat pocket models with their aero windscreens no higher than the middle of a man of 5ft 8in.'

He went on:

'Benoist displayed a seemingly reckless cleverness which leaves one breathless in astonishment at his daring.'

In response to criticism that the circuit was a far cry from a road course, the RAC decided to place two chicanes on the Finishing Straight, one just after the pits and one on the gradient where the straight rose to meet the final section of the Members' Banking. After that, drivers picked up speed as they rushed onto the Railway Straight and careered round the Byfleet Banking before reaching the Finishing Straight once more. Hardly a challenge of Spa or San Sebastian proportions.

New pits were built on the finishing straight and a bridge erected to link the paddock with the public enclosure. The fact that one of the bridge supports was on the track itself not unnaturally caused some alarm, although the judicious placing of sandbags appeared to reduce the drivers' fears. The bridge, meanwhile, carried a banner advertising Delage cars and J. Smith & Co of Albemarle Street. It would prove to be portentous move by the London agents of the French manufacturer.

A. V. Ebblewhite, a musical instrument maker and the unofficial commander in chief of everything that went on at Brooklands, naturally assumed the role of official starter and raised his red flag (ironically, now the signal to stop a race) at 2pm. The nine cars roared off in a ragged fashion. Grand Prix racing had arrived in Britain.

Red hot racing

There would be three finishers. After four hours and 56 seconds of racing at an average of 71mph, perhaps it's surprising there were that many. The race was won by Sénéchal's Delage, but not without help from the veteran, Wagner. Theirs was a blistering pace in every sense of the word.

The Delage's exhaust pipe passed along the right-hand side of the car and, in no time, the bodypanels were scorched, as were the driver's feet, thanks to the pedals becoming like hotplates. Wagner, in trouble with a misfire in any case, called a halt when four pit stops failed to cure the problem, the Frenchman glad of the opportunity to bathe his feet.

Benoist and Sénéchal eventually took over the first two places for Delage, but the exhausts were giving trouble, Benoist stopping for repairs while taking on tyres and fuel – and not losing the lead in the process. In Sénéchal's case, the exhaust box had split and he was in agony, the soles of his shoes burned through. When he stopped on the eightieth lap, Sénéchal limped from the car and plunged his feet into a tray of cold water, an accessory which had become the most vital part of the Delage team's pit equipment. Wagner reluctantly took over, but now Benoist was in serious foot trouble.

The tray of water was called for once more and, in order to give Benoist respite, a Monsieur Dubonnet was asked to take over his car. M. Dubonnet had not had the benefit of practice and, just for good measure, he was wearing a blue lounge suit and a beret as he climbed into the simmering cockpit…

The Delages may have been in a shocking state, but at least they were running. As for the Talbots, the day had started badly when, on lap one, Moriceau went out with a broken axle, both front wheels leaning drunkenly towards each other. Segrave, having led briefly and enjoyed a spirited skirmish with Benoist, retired with a variety of engine-related problems and brake trouble, leaving Divo to fight for the lead with Sénéchal. The Talbot had the edge on speed and acceleration but the Delage had superior handling and scored heavily under braking for the chicanes. Any hopes Divo may have had of making the most of the Frenchman's *'mal de pied'* were scotched when his Talbot ruptured its supercharger casing.

Wagner led, while Dubonnet was taking time to learn the circuit, never mind the car, and his cautious drive allowed Campbell to move into second place, much to the delight of the vast home crowd. He would eventually finish almost ten minutes behind the Delage. But still second. The Benoist/Dubonnet Delage, a further eight minutes behind the Bugatti, was classified third simply because there was no one else running. Segrave, meanwhile, had the consolation of receiving a special trophy for setting the fastest lap, the Talbot averaging 85.99mph.

Neither of the French teams had covered themselves in glory, Delage being somewhat fortunate to win. Talbot's troubles had been many and varied; enough, it seemed, to have Divo and Moriceau engage in a heated exchange with the car's designer at an official function later that evening. Never let it be said that Grand Prix racing was all beer and skittles in the past. But, as William Boddy proudly proclaimed in his book, Brooklands on 7 August, 1926 had been 'a great day!' The national daily newspapers had yet to be convinced.

The following morning, the *Daily Sketch* carried a brief report under the heading 'Red Hot Racing' with a single photograph, run alongside shots of horseracing at Lewes and a ceremony known as 'Tilting the Bucket' at Cambuslang…

The Daily News, meanwhile, carried a front page advertisement, which said:

'The British Grand Prix won on British petrol. For Acceleration, Speed and Power, use BP.'

The report by 'Chiltern' was not on the sports pages, but alongside City news and an advert for a 'sensational hair-growing discovery'. Elsewhere in the paper, State Express 333 cigarettes were advertised at ten for sixpence (2½p). And you could buy a Ford for £125.

The ad, run by the Ford Motor Company (England) Ltd of Trafford Park, Manchester, explained that their 'Improved Manchester made Ford' included 'electric lighting and starting, five balloon tyres, rearview mirror, windscreen wiper, dual ignition, choice of three body colours, side curtains that open with the doors (rigid side curtains £5 extra). All prices net at Works, Manchester.'

In view of the agonies experienced by the Delage drivers, however, perhaps the most prescient advertisement appeared in *The Daily News* on the day of the race. Occupying most of the front page, the Dr. Scholls company implored:

'Look To Your Feet This Week'…

The right crowd

The British Grand Prix had merely been another day in the life of the Brooklands circuit. The track was in daily use for testing – available free of charge to members of the Brooklands Automobile Racing Club – and there were regular race meetings, particularly on Easter Monday, Whit Monday and August Bank Holiday. The programme would usually consist of bet

Chiron (Bugatti) and Divo (Delage) tackle the sandbank chicane in front of the packed Paddock Grandstand in 1927.

ween eight and ten short races, all run under handicaps devised by Ebblewhite.

The highlight of the season was a trio of long-distance races; the Six Hours Endurance Race, the British Racing Drivers' Club's 500 Miles Race and the Junior Car Club's Double Twelve Hours (so-called because noise limitations prevented the use of the track at night and precluded the running of a 24-hour race. The event was split in two and run for twelve hours on Saturday, followed by a repeat performance the next day).

But, in view of the pioneering role Brooklands was to play in another industry, 8 June, 1908 turned out to be a date of some significance when a Mr. A.V. Roe conducted his triplane at a height of two feet above the Finishing Straight for a distance of some 25 yards. Only the head-keeper and carpenter witnessed the 'flight' but it did mark the hesitant start of Brooklands as a major influence in the shaping of Britain's aero industry.

By 1910, space had been cleared on the inside of the Byfleet Banking and an aerodrome built. When war broke out four years later, the Royal Flying Corps immediately took over the ground and Brooklands swiftly became the hub of aviation.

In 1915, Vickers built what became known as the 'Vickers Sheds' by the outside edge of the track, at the point where it split into the Members' Banking and the Finishing Straight. It was from these hangars that the famous Vickers Vimy emerged to take Alcock and Brown on their historic first flight across the Atlantic. The Vickers Sheds, therefore, were a familiar sight for anyone working in the bustling complex of corporate and cottage industries.

Rather like the growth of race and preparation businesses around Silverstone today, the imposing clubhouse at Brooklands had become surrounded by various garages and work-shops. In the early thirties, one of the smaller sheds would be occupied by Charles Mortimer, a Dorking man who liked to think of himself as a 'racing motorist,' a contemporary term which, in Mortimer's case, covered a multitude of sins.

The main aim was to earn enough money to go racing. This Mortimer did by buying and selling, carrying out maintenance and offering a garaging facility – he could squeeze two motorcycles into the shed. But a prime source of income came from betting. Mortimer, in his splendid book *Brooklands and Beyond* recalls the methods employed in order to earn a swift bob or two:

> *'Most of the races at Brooklands were run on individual handicap basis, of course, and this was dealt with exclusively by the famous A.V. Ebblewhite who had undertaken the task since the very early days..... Ebby was an institution and his handicap system worked well, on the whole, despite the intrigue and manoeuvre of riders and car drivers to outwit it.*
>
> *In theory, with a field of riders whose abilities were known to the handicapper, the race should result in a dead heat for the entire entry and, again in theory, everyone sooner or later won a race. In fact, the latter did happen, but for many reasons the Brooklands finishes varied in their degree of excitement. One of the reasons, particularly in the car section, was the presence of bookmakers. Drivers did bet and many surprises upset the system. It was completely accepted in both car and bike racing that unless there was a little jiggery pokery, you could never make your racing pay as it should.'*

Mortimer was well-versed in the latest developments. He knew precisely what the lap speed should be for every competitor and, once the handicap was revealed, he could make an educated guess at the result. More than that, by keeping his ear to the ground, he could find out what the result might be in the event of collusion by competitors intent on making money for themselves. Much of this information could be gleaned in the café. Mortimer describes the social routine at Brooklands:

> *'There were two quite separate catering sections in the paddock, a very swish restaurant and bar for the car people and a rather tatty cafeteria for the bike boys. But certain drivers would nearly always use the café. These were the chaps who really got the tempo of the place, because while the restaurant was just like any other restaurant, the café was 'Brooklands'. Even when I switched from bikes to cars, I never used the restaurant. But more than once I had heard it said that you could dine there and never know a thing that was going on at Brooklands but couldn't have a cup of tea in the café without hearing something of interest.*
>
> *The menu was shocking and consisted almost solely of tea, bread and butter, toast and poached eggs. The tables and chairs were dilapidated, there were no table cloths and the cups were cracked and the saucers and plates chipped. But that wasn't the fault of the Brooklands Automobile Racing Club or its catering manager, Emery. It was the fault of the clientele, for a wilder lot never patronised an eating establishment anywhere.'*

1927 – A cold wind blows

Doubtless the entry list for the 1927 British Grand Prix came under serious discussion in the café. With 16 cars listed, the race looked to be extremely promising. But, once again, it did not work out that way. The second and final British Grand Prix at Brooklands was to be even more tedious than the first. Indeed, in William Boddy's weighty tome, it only merits a single paragraph, such was the fascinating level of activity throughout the rest of the Brooklands season.

There had been a fair amount of activity at the factories of the major Grand Prix teams during the winter of 1926–27 as modifications were carried out in preparation for the last year of the 1½-litre formula. The minimum weight limit had been raised from 1,322 to 1,543lb and the drivers were now allowed to sit centrally in the cars. (The previous year, riding mechanics had been banned but the cars had remained two-seaters. This latest amendment was an attempt to standardise European and American racing and tempt the latter across the Atlantic.) The cockpit, though, continued to have a minimum width of 31.5in.

Bugatti improved their engine performance; Talbot had, among other things, strengthened the front axles while Delage threw themselves into a major revision of the engine installation. By altering the cylinder head porting they were able to redirect the exhaust system along the nearside of car and away from the driver's feet. A revised straight-8 engine gave an official

Benoist's victorious Delage after nearly four hours of racing.

170bhp but those in the know reckoned the figure to be conservative. The new Delage looked every inch a winner.

They swept to victory in the French Grand Prix with such authority that the Sunbeam-Talbot-Darracq group decided to withdraw from motor sport. Bugatti had been a non-starter and they withdrew from the Italian Grand Prix, leaving Delage to run the race as they pleased. They entered just one car for Benoist. He won by 23 minutes.

Benoist won again at San Sebastian, but not before Bugatti had led for most of the Spanish race. That, at least, offered some promise for the British Grand Prix on 1 October.

There were six Bugattis in total, including three works entries from the Molsheim factory for Louis Chiron (who had made his Grand Prix debut earlier in the season), Emilio Materassi and Count Conelli. A private entry was to be shared by the Englishmen, George Eyston and Sammy Davis, while Malcolm Campbell turned out once again in his Type 39.

A pair of Thomas Specials were entered but the Brooklands-based team were struggling along without their guiding light, Parry Thomas having lost his life the previous March while

attempting to regain the land speed record on Pendine Sands in Wales.

An Alvis was withdrawn, as were three cars from Fiat, the Italians preferring to concentrate on their aero-engine programme for the Schneider Trophy – or so they said. Fiat had entered a single car for the Milan Grand Prix, the brand new Type 806 walking away from weak opposition. Word in the Brooklands café was that Fiat had only managed to build one car, and in any case, they did not want to face the might of Delage.

There were three cars from the French firm for Benoist, Edmond Bourlier and Divo. And that's the order in which they finished. The rest were nowhere.

There had been a token resistance but the biting north-easterly wind, carrying light rain, seemed to sap everyone's enthusiasm, particularly when, in the space of a handful of laps, all three Delages had swept past Materassi's Bugatti to take a lead which they would never lose.

Apart from easing the sandbag chicanes slightly, the circuit was the same as the previous year. And, once again, the field of eleven starters (the first occasion on which double figures had been reached in the 1.5-litre formula!) simply crumbled away during the course of 326 miles of racing – if that's the right word.

The Thomas Specials went out with clutch and transmission failures; Materassi's Bugatti began to gush water; the Bugatti of Eyston and Davis was troubled by a misfire and a seized supercharger; and Campbell paid the price of running smaller brakes in order to accommodate his preference for wire wheels. In between, there was light relief in the pits when Prince Ghika, frustrated by a gasket failure on his Bugatti, attacked the pit counter with a hammer...

But unlike the previous year, the mood in the Delage pit was serene. The drivers were urged to slow down and Divo, who had led for most of the way, was called into the pits to attend to what seemed to be a perfectly sound exhaust. That let Benoist into the lead, a fitting place for the European champion. Divo then rejoined his team-mates for the final lap and an impressive clean sweep which summed up the team's season – and the 1927 British Grand Prix.

Meanwhile, journalists wondered what to write about.

A fiasco and a free gift

On Monday morning, the *Daily Sketch* carried a brief nine-line report, dwarfed by the paper's fashion column which explained that the 'short skirt is still with us – and long may it remain,' an observation which was not as contradictory as it sounds. The writer, Florence Roberts, went on the explain that 'short' meant a rather daring line somewhere between the knee and the top of the calf...

'Chiltern' meanwhile had grasped his pen and set-to with a vengeance in *The Daily News*. Under a heading of 'Motor Race Fiasco,' he wrote:

'Thousands of motor enthusiasts visited Brooklands in the rain on Saturday to see a race for the British car Grand Prix, with a prize of £1,000 to the winner, £300 to the second man and £200 to the third.

What they saw was a travelling car 'mannequin' parade demonstrating the high speed reliability of French engines and cars, a free gift of world prestige from the British trade.

The three Delages, contemptuously indifferent to the other machines on the track, ran the race as if they were tied together like camels in a convoy, 200 yards between each, two of the cars changing places near the end.

The race travesty was won by R. Benoist (Delage), with E. Bourlier (Delage) second and A. Divo (Delage) third. Benoist, in winning four out of five world championship Grands Prix in one year has created a record which will stand for many years.

The only thing the British trade has to pride itself on in the race is that the three Delages were all fitted with British tyres, which were about the only things upholding British motor prestige in this so-called British Grand Prix.

The only entry by a British firm, an Alvis, did not start, having had trouble in a test; two other British cars, Thomas Specials, entered privately, faded off the track after about 70 miles; and six Bugattis (French), two driven by three Englishmen, for, say, 150 miles, gave the event a shadow character of a race.

The ignoring by the British car trade of Saturday's racing gave the French makers the right to tell the world that they are supreme in high-speed reliable motor cars, whereas they are not, for British brains, British workmen and British drivers can beat them if given the chance by makers.'

Such unbridled patriotism was supported a few days later when the same newspaper, presumably as a prelude to the forthcoming motor show at Olympia, carried an advertisement which said:

> 'Own a British Car. British Cars for British Folk. A British Car is a car made entirely in the British Isles of British materials, fitted with British made tyres and accessories and completed with a British "finish".'

Try placing an ad like that today....

In view of the patriotism evident at the time, 'Chiltern' was clearly frustrated by what he saw at Brooklands. He was, after all, a serious motoring journalist. Very serious, in fact. The previous year, legislation had been passed calling for cars to be fitted with rear illumination. 'Chiltern' took it upon himself to stand on the Portsmouth Road between 10 and 11pm on a Sunday evening and note that, of the 329 cars which passed by, 'only 41 had a rear number plate which could be read at 50 paces on a grass verge'.

'Chiltern's' race report is likely to have found reluctant favour in the Brooklands café. It was to be the beginning of a particularly low period in Grand Prix racing in general as the sport's governing body dithered over suitable regulations during the next few years.

Certainly Grand Prix racing would not return to Brooklands even though the circuit continued to flourish. It was the outbreak of World War II in 1939 which not only brought racing to a halt but sealed, just as dramatically, the fate of Brooklands as a motor racing centre. Brooklands became a major centre of aviation and research, the motor racing circuit being damaged and hacked about as a matter of expediency at a time when the war effort came first.

The banking may have been bumpy and not particular popular among the drivers. But there were compensations. Charles Mortimer reflects on an idyllic existence:

> 'It was different from any other circuit I have known. Every day brought its own highlight. It was a happy, carefree place, exciting and completely unorthodox – always fun. The ten years I spent there as a tenant in the paddock live with me now and, like many others, I really loved the place. And the people too. There were more characters there who were "larger than life" than any other community I've known.'

More's the pity, then, that the British Grands Prix in 1926 and 1927 did not match the ambience inherent at Brooklands. All was not lost, however. In 1937 and 1938, Britain ran two races of such outstanding quality that they were worthy of the title 'Grand Prix.' Unfortunately, the RAC did not see fit to confer the prefix 'British.' But the contribution to Britain's motor racing heritage cannot be doubted.

Meanwhile, down on the Riviera....

CHAPTER 2

ECURIE JACKBOOT

Memories in Monaco

'They have the most astounding audacity in some parts of Europe. For instance, there is going to be a Grand Prix at Monaco – a Grand Prix, mark you, in a Principality which does not possess a single open road of any length, but has only ledges on the face of a cliff and the ordinary main thoroughfares that everyone who has been to the Casino knows so well.'

Presumably, the indignant writer in *The Autocar* assumed that his readers made a habit of nipping down to Monte Carlo. Mind you, given the status associated with owning a motor car in 1929, that was probably the case. But the irony was that the race had been conceived as a means of attracting visitors to the Principality, particularly in the off-season. It required a remarkable degree of forbearance by the inhabitants since the track cut a swathe through a country no larger than Hyde Park; it would be the first race to be run inside a town.

The inaugural *Grand Prix de Monaco*, held on 14 April 1929 was, according to Charles Faroux, a 'veritable triumph.' Not surprisingly, they made the French motoring critic the Director of the Race after such a generous remark. Nonetheless, Faroux was right. It marked the birth of a Grand Prix classic.

The race was won by an expatriate Englishman, William Grover, or 'Williams' as he was known. With his cap turned back to front, Williams and his Bugatti 35B more or less dominated the race during the 3 hours and 56 minutes it took to complete 100 laps.

As the years went by, balconies overlooking the circuit would become prized possessions during the five days in May when the motor racing world swept imperiously into Monte Carlo. And, for almost twenty years, a particular apartment on *Boulevard Albert 1er* would provide a warm welcome for the British press. Up until 1982 there would be a fight for places on the guest list of Mr and Mrs E.R. Hall.

Joan Hall had acted as team manager while her husband, Eddie, played the part of a highly successful amateur racing driver in the thirties. Once they had moved to Monaco not long after Eddie's retirement, Joan would use her organisational skills to mark out places on their balcony overlooking the course during race weekend.

There was rarely a spot left for Eddie. But that didn't matter. He would sit in his armchair until minutes before the start, then struggle to his feet, poke a youth – usually a distant relative – on the backside with his walking stick and tell him to answer the door. While the youngster scampered off to deal with the imaginary caller, Eddie would take the child's place on the balcony and no-one, least of all the boy, dared argue. In any case, the position would soon be vacated again. Several noisy and processional laps were usually enough for the old Titan and he would happily return to the comfort of his armchair.

Hall was never one to talk at length about the past. There was no need. The apartment was tastefully decorated with memorabilia which told of success at Brooklands and in the Tourist Trophy. There were photographs of that cheery, chubby face sipping champagne, Joan by his side. And, among the drawings by contemporary artists, one picture, by Brian de Grineau, told of a minor victory which was to have historical significance for British motor sport as a whole. It showed Eddie Hall's supercharged MG Midget winning the very first race at Donington Park in the Midlands.

Donington delivers

In fact that race, for cars up to 850 cc, was one of several events on that perfect spring day in late March 1933. But it marked the opening of the first licensed road circuit in England at a time when interest in motor sport was on the increase and plans for private tracks were being announced at frequent intervals.

Donington Park succeeded where other circuits either failed to reach fruition or faded into early obscurity. And the fact that Hall and his colleagues were able to exercise their racing cars in the midst of such a splendid parkland was thanks to J. G. Shields, the owner of the land, and Fred Craner, the energetic secretary of the Derby and District Motor Club.

Motor-cycle racing had started there in 1931, or thereabouts, by utilising the gravel paths and farm roads on the estate. Craner had suggested that a road circuit could be laid out by upgrading the existing 'track.' A scheme to resurface where necessary cost £12,000 and the result was a demanding and picturesque circuit measuring 2.25 miles.

Narrow in places, it had more than enough to keep the drivers busy. Swooping downhill, twisting through woods, passing between gate-posts, the circuit had a good balance of fast and slow corners. At one point it ran between farm buildings and this was designated a 'no-over-taking' area, a large notice to this effect being positioned on the farmhouse roof.

There were four race meetings in 1933 and, appropriately, E.R. Hall also won the last race that year in an MG Magnette. It had been a productive season for Eddie. He won the Brook-lands 500-mile race and then went on to persuade Rolls Royce to build a special racing Bentley sportscar for 1934.

Hall would use the massive car to great effect in the Tourist Trophy on the Ards circuit in Northern Ireland, a race which ranked as Britain's leading motor sport event in the early thir-ties. Bentleys and sports cars were in vogue; winning the Le Mans 24-hrs endurance race was the high-point of the season as far as the British were concerned.

Grand Prix racing was in a confused state, having reached its nadir between 1928 and 1930. The constant chopping and changing of the regulations prompted many organisers to simply hold formula libre events, the plus-point here being that the absence of many factory teams allowed the independent drivers to flourish. Thus, anyone who could lay their hands on a Type 35 Bugatti had a a reasonable chance of winning, the spoils in 1930 being shared by the French manufacturer and Maserati, whose 2.5-litre straight-8 won seven of the more impor-tant races that year.

Bugatti produced the twin-cam Type 51 for 1931 and did the lion's share of winning in races which lasted for a minimum of ten hours. The following season, however, saw the arrival of the sleek 'Tipo B' Alfa Romeo Monoposto, so-called because of the single-seat central driving position. Introduced in June, it went on to win all but two of the races entered. Satisfied with that, Alfa Romeo decided not to compete the following year. The cars were acquired by a former driver who had been running a team of Alfa Romeos from premises in Modena, Italy. His name: Enzo Ferrari.

Thus, while *Scuderia Ferrari* had just taken another step towards international acclaim, there were developments in Germany which were to have a more immediate and profound effect on the Grand Prix scene – not to mention the world at large.

Nazi power

Germany, with six million unemployed, was in a state of near-financial collapse. When the Nazis came to power in January 1933, Adolf Hitler saw Grand Prix racing as a powerful prop-aganda weapon, one which could provide the world with dramatic proof of German technical skills and superiority. He offered an annual grant of £40,000 to the German firm which pro-duced the most successful racing car for the 1934 season. Auto Union – represented by four interlinking circles symbolising a recent merger between Audi, DKW, Horch and Wanderer – and Daimler-Benz A.G. accepted the challenge and, in the end, it was decided that the grant should be shared between the two. No matter, since £40,000 would have been but a small part of each team's budget, even in 1934

Mercedes-Benz and Auto Union worked to a new set of regulations, known as the 750 Kilogram Formula, with an initial life span of three years. The AIACR, the governing body of motor sport, concerned about speeds of up to 150mph attained by the Alfas, Bugattis and Maseratis, figured that a weight limit of 750kg would be the answer. They worked on the theory that manufacturers would find it difficult to go on increasing the size of the engine. It was about as much use as asking the drivers if they wouldn't mind driving more slowly.

The two German firms were to produce the most powerful and dramatic Grand Prix cars ever seen. Their devastating performance, encouraged by intense rivalry between the two makes, would leave the world in no doubt about the quality of German engineering and man-agement, not to mention the simplistic thinking of the misguided souls within the sport's gov erning body. Some things in Grand Prix racing never change....

The W25 Mercedes-Benz was produced in less than a year. Designed by Dr Hans Nibel, the 3,360cc, straight-8 engine developed at least 300bhp. All four wheels were independently sprung and, overall, the car was graceful and conventional in appearance.

Not so the Auto Union. Designed by Dr. Porsche, this machine represented a complete breakaway from traditional racing car design. The 4.4-litre, 16-cylinder engine also developed in excess of 300bhp. But it was mounted in the rear, along with the fuel tank, to give the car a menacing appearance as the massive engine cowl dwarfed the driver, perched near the front.

While development of these cars took place, the *Scuderia Ferrari* 2.9-litre Alfa Romeos dominated the early races in 1934 and, even when Mercedes-Benz and Auto Union turned out in force for the French Grand Prix, teething troubles meant that Ferrari inherited the first three places. But the writing was on the wall; a new, dramatic age was dawning.

Ring out the old

Tazio Nuvolari
Arguably one of the greatest drivers of all time; certainly, one of the most determined. Relished taking on the major teams, the wiry little Italian humbling them frequently. Signed for Auto Union in 1938 and his victory in the Donington Grand Prix was a classic example of how to tame such a brute of a car.

Just one look at the starting grids in early 1934 said everything about the mixture of the old and the new: Hans Stuck, crouched low in the cockpit of the bullet-like Auto Union; Achille Varzi, perched high at the rear of the Alfa Romeo; the Bugattis, with their drivers in an off-set position, looking more ancient still, particularly when compared with the smooth, stream-lined shape of the Mercedes-Benz. It was clear from the speed of the German cars that no one could live with them.

They possessed an impressive quality, enhanced by the silvery appearance of the aluminium paintwork. The Auto Unions had worn this colour scheme from the outset, but originally the Mercedes were painted white, the national racing colour of Germany. That plan had been changed when the Mercedes-Benz team arrived for their first race, the Eifel GP, at the Nürburgring. The meticulous men from Stuttgart were stunned when the W25s were weighed and found to be one kilo over the 750kg limit.

Searching for a remedy, Alfred Neubauer, the imposing team manager, ordered the paint to be stripped, taking with it a fair amount of filler made necessary by the uneven surface of the hand-beaten aluminium bodywork. The cars were weighed again – and deemed to be legal.

It is difficult to imagine an organisation such as Daimler-Benz making such an elementary mistake in the first place. That, at any rate, is how the story goes. It is clear, however, that the phrase *Silberpfeile*, or Silver Arrows, quickly became a popular term among members of the motoring press.

Everything about the German effort seemed *right*. And that included a driving force which, in the case of Mercedes-Benz, included Rudolf Caracciola, Manfred von Brauchitsch and Luigi Fagioli. Auto Union were less well-endowed with driving talent, but Stuck was to score a significant win for them when he beat the rugged Fagioli in the all-important German Grand Prix. It was the start of a German landslide; no one would get a look-in for the next four years. There was, however, one notable exception.

The Great Little Man

Tazio Nuvolari was, arguably, the greatest driver Italy ever produced. Certainly, he was one of the most determined. His early career on racing motor-cycles seemed to produce success and broken bones in equal amounts. His ambition was to race cars and, ironically, a trial at Monza in 1925 ended in disaster. The gearbox of the P2 Alfa Romeo seized, spinning the hapless Nuvolari into the trees. He was removed to hospital, where medical opinion suggested a convalesence of at least 30 days. Riding his Bianchi in the Italian Grand Prix in six days' time would be out of the question.

Nuvolari would have none of it. He persuaded the doctors to bandage him in such a way that he could adopt a riding posture. The sight of the little man shuffling towards his machine and being lifted on board lent weight to the theory that he was quite mad. But those who knew Nuvolari quickly realised that this was merely an extension of a remarkable determination to compete and succeed.

When he won the race, there was no further discussion. And the home crowd loved him for it. There was to be a similar episode in Britain 13 years later.

Clearly, Nuvolari was not the sort of driver to be depressed by the German onslaught. In

1935 he joined forces with Enzo Ferrari (still running Alfa Romeos on behalf of the factory) partly motivated by the news that his great Italian rival Achille Varzi had been signed by Auto Union. It was also said that certain Auto Union drivers, Hans Stuck among them, had conspired to keep the little man out of the team. This seems unlikely as Stuck and Nuvolari were good friends and Nuvolari always tried to avoid working with large organisations. He preferred to be his own man and take on the big teams head-to-head. He was about to have the perfect opportunity.

Nuvolari's Tipo B Alfa Romeo may have been three years out of date but he dearly wanted to defeat the Germans. And he could think of no better place to do it than the Nürburgring *Nordschleife*, a 14-mile masterpiece twisting and squirming its way through the Eifel mountains in West Germany.

The full 17.58-mile Nürburgring had been built in the mid-1920s to alleviate unemployment and boost tourism; now Hitler saw it as the perfect showcase for Germany's technical and sporting expertise. After all, Mercedes-Benz had won seven races thus far in 1935 and Varzi had taken victory for Auto Union in Tunis. Even the most optimistic members of *Scuderia Ferrari* knew their chances against such mighty opposition were slim.

It took Tazio Nuvolari a shade over four hours to humble the silver cars. In damp conditions, he took the challenge to Mercedes-Benz and Auto Union, led briefly, but then lost valuable time with a lengthy pit stop for fuel and tyres. Whereas the well-drilled Germans had their drivers under way in a minute, sometimes less, a blocked pressure pump meant Nuvolari's fuel had to be poured into the tank by churns. The agitated driver leapt from the cockpit and danced round the car, swearing and shouting at all and sundry. It was typical Latin theatre. But it also took more than two minutes.

Rejoining in sixth place, Nuvolari urged the ageing Alfa around the 14.17 miles of the North Circuit and moved into second place. On the last lap, he overtook Manfred von Brauchitsch when the Mercedes-Benz driver pushed too hard and destroyed a rear tyre.

The Germans were stunned. In fact, such was their confidence that no one had thought to prepare anything other than the German national anthem at the finish. The Italian version could not be found! In a final masterstroke, Nuvolari produced his own copy, which he always carried for good luck, and handed it over. Total collapse of the stout party....

The Nürburgring was one of the few circuits which allowed a driver's skill to overcome the deficiencies of his car. Or, in the case of the rather unwieldy Auto Union, permitted a driver to use his natural reflexes and bravery to tame a recalcitrant machine. And there was no better example than a bright young star who emerged in 1935 and, in fact, briefly held second place in the German Grand Prix.

Rosemeyer

Bernd Rosemeyer was completely without fear, which perhaps accounted for the fact that he was one of the few drivers to master the Auto Union, beginning in 1935, his first season not just in the Auto Union, but in *any* racing car. At the *Eifelrennen* early in the season, he used a knowledge of the Nürburgring gained by racing motor-cycles to finish two seconds behind Caracciola's Mercedes-Benz. It seemed only right that he should end the season with a victory at the Masaryk Ring at Brno, Czechoslovakia, albeit without opposition from Stuttgart.

In 1936, however, Bernd Rosemeyer really made his mark. He won six races and the European championship, the equivalent then of the world championship today. Such was the furious struggle for honours at home that Mercedes-Benz and Auto Union had developed their cars further, both sides now claiming more than 520 bhp. Unfortunately, the latest car to bear the Mercedes' three-pointed star could not cope with the power. The Auto Union, on the other hand, was changed in detail only in order to deal with an increase in engine size to 6-litres.

Bugatti and Maserati had by now given up the struggle, but Alfa Romeo continued, Nuvolari remaining on their driving strength. Louis Chiron, meanwhile, had been tempted by Daimler-Benz to leave *Scuderia Ferrari*; a bad move as it turned out, given that the former pace-setters were to score just two wins (Monaco and Tunis). Auto Union on the other hand won six, while the remarkable Nuvolari beat the Germans four times. Clearly, there would be serious discussion in the boardroom of Daimler-Benz A.G. over the winter of 1936-37.

For chief engineer Hans Nibel, it was the end of the road and he was succeeded by Rudolph Uhlenhaut. It was decided that the engine capacity should be increased to 5.6 litres. The suspension was heavily modified and the 1937 car, known as the W125, appeared with a new tubular chassis. Caracciola, von Brauchitsch and Hermann Lang (who had made his debut in the 1935 German Grand Prix) were retained – and joined by Richard John Beattie-Seaman, the only world-class driver Britain was to produce in the thirties.

Der Englander

Dick Seaman
Britain's only world class driver of the thirties. Raced abroad in order to attract the attention of the continental teams; signed for Mercedes-Benz in 1937. Had mixed fortunes in both Donington Grands Prix but caused a stir by winning the 1938 German Grand Prix. Died of burns received when he crashed while leading the Belgian Grand Prix in June 1939.

It was true that Dick Seaman enjoyed the benefit of a wealthy background, education at Rugby and Cambridge and an MG, followed by a Bugatti, on which to indulge in his passion for fast cars. But he quickly developed a flowing style and the belief that he had it in him to race for a Grand Prix team.

He achieved moderate success at home and abroad, but for 1936 he sought the advice of Giulio Ramponi, a former racing driver and *Scuderia Ferrari* mechanic who tended Seaman's car. If Seaman wanted to win races in the 1,500cc class, said Ramponi, he should buy a Delage, the type of car which had dominated the British Grand Prix at Brooklands ten years earlier. Seaman had his doubts. Earl Howe, the owner of the car they had in mind, wanted a top price. But he also had a spare engine and numerous spare parts. Seaman, reluctant at first, finally agreed to purchase.

Ramponi was right. The Delage, which Ramponi stripped completely, modifying and reducing weight where he could, proved to be the perfect tool, particularly in Seaman's skilled hands. He was invited to drive, among other worthwhile cars, a Maserati and an ex-*Scuderia Ferrari* Alfa Romeo. Then at the end of the season he received an offer to test drive for Mercedes-Benz.

Apart from recognising Seaman's potential, the telegram from Alfred Neubauer was also indicative of the almost desperate need for Daimler-Benz to find a winning driver after a disastrous season. Neubauer had employed Italians in the past but entertaining the thought of having an Englishman race for Germany was something which did not sit well with Hitler's nationalistic instincts. The tests, however, showed that the 23-year-old was quick enough to win races. And, it was pointed out to the Führer, this was a neat piece of public relations work at a rather delicate time....

It was a difficult start for Seaman. He crashed during a test session at Monza and had to face the first race of the 1937 season in Tripoli with very little experience of the powerful Mercedes-Benz. Nonetheless, he held second place before supercharger trouble dropped him to seventh. The race was won by Hermann Lang, who also took the honours for Mercedes-Benz at the Avus, the 12-mile blast up and down a dual carriage-way being enlivened by the addition of a steeply banked turn at one end. Lang's winning average in 1937 was 162 mph!

But for the sheer exuberance and skill of Rosemeyer in an Auto Union which had been changed very little since the previous year, Mercedes-Benz would have had the upper hand during the rest of the season. By the time they reached the final round they had won seven races to Auto Union's four. Seaman had finished second once and claimed a couple of fourth places. But he had also crashed twice. The final Grand Prix of the season, however, was to be held at Donington Park. Clearly, there was much to play for.

Extending a welcome

British enthusiasts relished the thought of seeing, for the first time, 600bhp Grand Prix cars which were capable of accelerating from 0-60mph in five seconds. It would be ten years exactly since the last British Grand Prix had been held at Brooklands. A lot had happened since then – not least in the grounds of the magnificent circuit in the Midlands.

Such was the energy and enthusiasm of Fred Craner and the Derby and District Motor Club that Donington underwent continual improvement from the moment it opened for car racing in 1933. For the following season, the elimination of an S-bend on Starkey's Hill, and an extension at the end of it, increased the length of the circuit by 644 yards. It was in this loop that the pits were located, even though the paddock was to remain near the site of the previous start-and-finish line on the downhill approach to the old hairpin. By May of that year, the installation of telephones at various points around the circuit allowed the commentator to be kept in better touch with progress during the seven races which were a typical mixed bag of events at Donington.

The increasing competence and status associated with Donington saw the appearance of

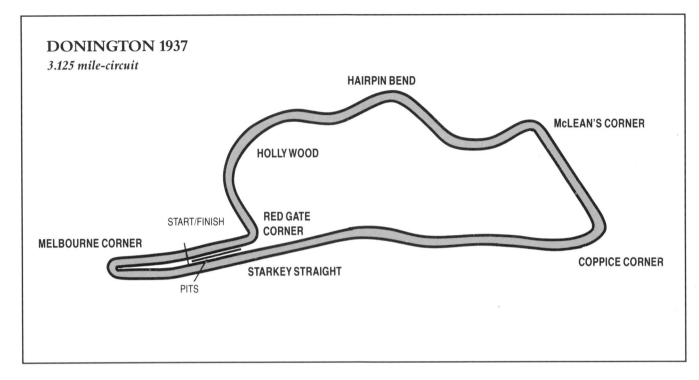

DONINGTON 1937
3.125 mile-circuit

HAIRPIN BEND

McLEAN'S CORNER

HOLLYWOOD

START/FINISH

RED GATE
CORNER

MELBOURNE CORNER

STARKEY STRAIGHT

PITS

COPPICE CORNER

'Grand Prix' cars in the hands of British privateers and, by the end of 1935, the introduction of the Donington Grand Prix, a 300-mile race, marked another milestone for the organisers.

This became an annual event and prompted the construction of a paddock nearer to the pits and the doubling in size of the starting area. And it was close by the start line that they erected a Belisha Beacon, named after Mr Hore-Belisha, the then Minister of Transport who had introduced the pedestrian crossing sign in 1934. The black and white striped pole, with the orange globe on top, marked locations where pedestrians were supposed to have the right of way. Someone in the Derby and District Motor Club had a keen sense of humour.

Covered stands were in evidence, with a number of footbridges allowing access to vantage points, both inside and outside the track. New clubrooms were built and there were detail touches such as the marking of drivers' names above the pits. The circuit had a mature look about it and the annual programme of events would include anything from short sprint races to the Nuffield Trophy and, of course, the Donington Grand Prix. In 1937, however, the Leicestershire circuit really made its mark on the international scene.

With the Northern Ireland Ards circuit now declared unsafe, it was decided to run the classic Tourist Trophy event for the first time at Donington, but first the circuit had to be lengthened. Fred Craner duly arranged for the pit loop to be extended over an abrupt brow (and into Derbyshire) towards a new 180-degree bend to be known as Melbourne Corner, after the nearby village of the same name. The return leg climbed a 1-in-8 rise before reaching the existing circuit again just before the pits. A lap now measured 3 miles 220 yards instead of 2 miles 971 yards.

Having captured the TT, there seemed no reason why Donington could not attract a grid of 'continental' drivers for its Grand Prix in October. This was eventually achieved thanks to hard work by the motor club, J. G. Shields and Fred Craner. But, in the background, Richard Seaman, a 'businessman racing driver,' was to play a vital role in negotiating start money with Mercedes-Benz. Figures were not made public, but at the time it was believed to be about £500 per car.

The date was finally set for Saturday 2 October.

Sipping and smiling

'Make a note of that date,' warned 'Grande Vitesse,' writing in *The Motor*. 'It will be a sight never seen in this country before.'

'Grande Vitesse', alias Rodney Walkerley, knew what he was talking about. *The Motor* would frequently dispatch Walkerley abroad to cover the Grands Prix, a task he completed with relish if his wonderful reports are anything to go by. Walkerley knew he was witnessing a spectacle which went beyond the wildest dreams of the most avid enthusiast back in Britain. His written word successfully attempted to convey the message. This is how he opened his account of the 1937 Monaco Grand Prix:

> *'This afternoon I saw the most breath-taking exhibition of motor racing that it has ever been my fortune to witness in many years devoted to watching the sport....It is difficult to convey in words the terrific spectacle of these cars racing.'*

Then, a few months later, Walkerley reported from the town of Adenau as he watched preparations for the German Grand Prix and the arrival of 300,000 spectators.

> *'If 100,000 arrived at Brooklands, the organizers would have three fits, each more convulsive than the last, although their delight would know no bounds. Yet if such a number turned up at the Nurburg Ring for a German Grand Prix the authorities would weep tears of blood and wonder what on earth was keeping people away...*
>
> *...Every day the teams are out on the circuit, and sitting sipping one's beer on the veranda of a cafe, the thin wail of the superchargers can be heard drifting down the wind, and the good people of Adenau stop and listen, smiling.*
>
> *...The military sappers move in and build a pedestrian bridge a few days before the German Grand Prix, when the narrow streets are chock-a-block with thousands of cars and pedestrians go to the wall.*
>
> *And 20,000 people is a good crowd at Brooklands....'*

Small wonder, then, that Walkerley urged his readers not to miss the Donington Grand Prix. 'Go and see this race,' he implored. 'Those present will see such motor cars as have never before turned their wheels on English soil'.

And he was absolutely right.

CROSSING OUR PATHS WITH SILVER

The Germans have landed

The British motor sport fans could hardly believe their luck when the details were revealed. And neither, for that matter, could William Boddy, the Editor of *Motor Sport*.

Boddy's enthusiasm took him to Croydon aerodrome on a wet, dismal evening on the Monday of race week. There, he greeted the *Lufthansa* Junkers Ju52 tri-motor from Munich as members of the Mercedes-Benz team stepped onto British soil. Boddy, while delighted by the array of talent before him, was not impressed by the rather pathetic welcome. In his column, Boddy wrote:

> *'That so few people were present.... made me very sad. Charlie Martin, who had landed about half-an-hour earlier by D.H. Express, stayed with Mrs. Martin and some friends who had met him in his Aprilia Lancia, Tommy Wisdom was there, in spite of his story in* The People *that the drivers had arrived the day before, and I had gone out to meet several planes beforehand with John Eason-Gibson, as the Mercedes-Benz people in Park Lane could not, or would not, tell us when the team was due. I suppose one cannot hope that the British public will show the enthusiasm or curiosity for racing aces that they show for long-distance aviators or sex-appealing film stars, but I do think that the Mercedes-Benz racing team should have had a warmer reception on their first arrival at these shores.'*

Four Mercedes-Benz 230s were waiting to take Lang, von Brauchitsch and Seaman (Caracciola was travelling by ship and train, on his wife's insistence) to the Dorchester Hotel in London, and then on to The Black Boy Inn in Nottingham, Alfred Neubauer personally supervising the loading of luggage into the fourth car and the general welfare of his drivers.

Most of the Auto Union team arrived at Croydon the following day. Joining Rosemeyer were Hermann P. Müller, a former motor-cyclist who had been called upon as reserve earlier in the year, and Rudolph Hasse, a most unlikely, bespectacled character, winner of the Belgian Grand Prix who was also the leader of the fire brigade in his home town in Germany.

According to Boddy, the reception committee for the Auto Union team was just as sparse as it had been for Mercedes-Benz. Their luggage was loaded into a lorry, the personnel then travelling by the Leyland coach of Imperial Airways. Even at this early stage, the subtle differences in organisation could be seen.

The cars, of course, were already in place at the circuit and prepared for a day of testing on the Wednesday, the Mercedes-Benz (reckoned by Tommy Wisdom of *The People* to be worth £20,000 each) garaged overnight in the barn at Coppice Farm. *The Leicester Mercury*, covering their local event with great interest, reported that the German teams had brought 10½ tons of tyres, 2½ tons of inner tubes and several thousand gallons of their own special fuel.

Something in the air

Spectators would soon catch a whiff of this 'special petrol', a potent mixture of alcohol, benzole and gasoline. Admission to practice cost 1s 3d (6p), and it was to be a bargain. Before the cars so much as turned a wheel, the bellow of the exhausts and the pungent smell of the fuel announced a new and wonderful aspect of the sport. And, once on the move, the top professionals quickly got down to learning the circuit and lapping at an average of 80mph.

But, more than that, they were reaching 160mph on Starkey Straight and becoming airborne as they crested the rise where the new loop joined the pit straight. This was *real* motor racing. British enthusiasts had not seen the like before. The silver cars used every inch of the narrow park roads, the fearsome power causing wheels to spin, tyres to smoke and the trees to seem very close as the drivers frequently got out of shape. It was a wide-eyed William

Boddy who stood, notebook in hand, his horizons considerably broadened by this new experience. he wrote:

> '…it is very difficult adequately to express one's enthusiasm. Those of us who saw the German cars in action for the first time….were soon almost raving with enthusiasm and astonishment.
>
> It was noticeable that even after a few laps at speed the drivers were perspiring freely, and appeared tired, drawing coats around their shoulders while adjustments were made. Verily, these German aces take their medicine, lifting the throttle-foot only occasionally, and then momentarily, when the cars look quite out of control.'

Watching from the pits, he also noted:

> 'The Mercedes had 5.50 in x 19 in Continental tyres on the front wheels and 7 in x 19 in on the rear. For the training, Müller wore bright blue overalls and helmet, Rosemeyer, changing in full view of onlookers at the pits, a shirt and pullover, but no jacket, Lang had white overalls and helmet, Hasse likewise and Seaman his customary blue kit. Caracciola wore dark-lensed goggles. A complete spare engine unit was noticed in the Auto Union depot.'

In the midst of such seriousness, however, there was time for a spot of humour. One enthusiast tied a banger to the ignition lead under the bonnet of Neubauer's road car. The Mercedes-Benz team manager apparently took the jape in good part when there was a loud report as the ignition was switched on.

When the drivers had arrived at Croydon, Boddy had noted that von Brauchitsch 'was in extremely good spirits, even performing a little dance out in the rain…' Manfred's good humour continued for the rest of the week and he took an immediate liking to Donington, 'flying' higher and driving faster than anyone else to give his team pole position.

Mercedes-Benz, having dominated a major part of the 1937 season, were keen to end it on a high note and they seemed to be in a strong position to do so when Lang and Seaman joined von Brauchitsch on the front row.

But there was one snag. Sitting alongside von Brauchitsch would be Rosemeyer in the Auto Union. With their ace driver in such fine form, Auto Union were not quite so worried when Müller and Hasse were split by Caracciola's W125 on the second row.

Hasse, incidentally, had been called in to replace Varzi. The Italian had gone into sudden decline the previous year, an addiction to morphine destroying the ice-cold demeanour of this once immaculate man. Having rid himself of the habit, he attempted a return for the final three races in 1937. The natural ability was still there, but the previous excesses had taken their toll. Varzi no longer had the stamina to conduct a Grand Prix car for three hours and more at a place like Donington.

The remainder of the grid was made up by a gallant band of private entrants, led by 'Bira' in a Maserati 8CM. Otherwise known as HRH Prince Birabongse Bhanubandh of Siam (now Thailand), 'Bira' had lapped in 2 minutes 25 seconds, a worthy time indeed, but one which was almost 16 seconds slower than von Brauchitsch. A second Maserati 8CM, driven by A.B. Hyde, had been withdrawn when the Englishman felt rather humbled by the powerful presence of the silver cars blasting past him.

There was a 1.5-litre Maserati for Robin Hanson and a Riley for Donington stalwart, Percy Maclure; the rest of the field being made up of ERAs, the British cars which were the life-blood of the domestic scene. Leading the way would be the works car of Raymond Mays, followed by Earl Howe, Arthur Dobson, Charlie Martin and Peter Whitehead – 15 starters. But, in truth, the Donington Grand Prix would be all about the imposing ranks of German armoury at the front. They were not about to let the expectant British public down.

Good news, bad news

Crowd figure reports varied between 38,000 and 50,000. But whatever the number, they were drawn to Donington by a sunny, crisp autumnal day and startling reports on practice in the national and local media. *The Derby Evening Telegraph* had carried front-page pictures of the cars arriving, and subsequent news of practice. On the Friday before the race, the front page also carried the headline 'Warning Of Grave European War Risk,' issued at a National Council of Labour debate. There was also news of an Imperial Airways flying-boat having come to grief while landing at Athens.

On the same page as the practice report, it was recorded that a motorist had been fined £1 for not producing his licence and a further pound for not having his insurance certificate. According to the report, when warned that he was causing an obstruction, the motorist 'got out of his car in a towering rage and said he was not going to be badgered about...' Refusing to give his address to the police officer did not exactly help matters either...

On race day, there was a story of a more serious note. A light plane had crashed, killing the pilot and two passengers as they tried to land at Breedon-on-the-Hill, near Donington. Given the traffic chaos, the idea of flying to the Grand Prix was sound. *The Leicester Mercury* reported that there was a 'rush-hour going on' and that it took a tramcar three times longer than normal to travel from Victoria Park to the Clock Tower.

Once actually inside the park, the spectators soon became aware that this was a very special event. Certainly Boddy seemed to have caught the flavour. He wrote:

'As the mist lifted and gave way to brilliant sunshine we saw a moving sight at our premiere road-racing circuit. Cars filled every park until finally they were left in the roads outside while their occupants hurried to the course.'

Then, he added an extraordinary observation – extraordinary, that is, by today's standards:

'Mercedes-Benz models of all ages thundered into the grounds and owners of lesser marques moved their cars that these Mercs. might be parked in the front rows...'

Not a move which Mercedes or, indeed, Honda owners would be advised to try at Silverstone today....

Community singing perhaps nullified the ominous sight of a German official giving a Hitler salute as he arrived at the Mercedes-Benz pits. Certainly, worries about events in the rest of the world were obliterated when the Mercedes mechanics applied the portable electric starters and the engines fired into ground-shaking life.

The thundering noise of the multi-cylinder cars was phenomenal; the rasping British entries pathetic by comparison. *The Light Car* had likened the exhaust note of the ERAs and Maseratis to the tearing of calico but, on this occasion, they noted that 'the gentle unravelling of a piece of knitting' would have been a more appropriate analogy...

A moving sight

As the flag fell, Lang snatched the lead while Caracciola caught von Brauchitsch, Seaman and Rosemeyer by surprise as he barged through from the second row. Deafened officials standing at the back of the grid peered through the smoke and haze as the pack jostled into the tight left-hander at Red Gate before disappearing into Holly Wood. Then followed the swoop down towards the so-called Hairpin Bend, in fact, a medium speed right-hander with a notorious bump on the apex. (The term 'hairpin' was a throw-back to the days when Donington's loose surface track was used purely for motor-cycle racing and there was, in fact, a hairpin near this point.)

Then, on towards the narrow arch of the stone bridge, sweeping left before negotiating the right-hander at McLean's Corner. Into Coppice Wood now before changing down for the narrow Coppice Corner and accelerating hard past the farm buildings, blasting out of the dense woodland, under two footbridges and past the packed grandstands on Starkey Straight.

Flat out now, Lang reached 165mph as he rushed towards the slope leading down to Melbourne Corner. The drum brakes were worked to the maximum as they pulled almost one ton of racing car down to 25mph. Then a Teutonic right foot fed the power in gently before slamming the throttle against the stop, Lang gripping the steering wheel firmly as the W125 bucked into the air as it crested the rise before the pits. The race was well and truly on. The spectators were awe-struck.

Mercedes-Benz occupied the first four places as Caracciola, von Brauchitsch and Seaman followed their team-mate across the line. But Neubauer had his eye on the Auto Union in fifth place. Sure enough, on the second lap, Rosemeyer moved past Seaman and there was to be further bad news for the crowd when the British driver was promptly punted from behind by

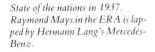

State of the nations in 1937. Raymond Mays in the ERA is lapped by Hermann Lang's Mercedes-Benz.

the Auto Union of Müller as they braked for Coppice Corner. Seaman slid towards the trees but managed to rejoin in sixth place, his off-side rear suspension damaged as a result of the collision.

There were further changes as Caracciola, not in his usual sparkling form and apparently not at home with the close proximity of the trees and grass verges, began to drop back, allowing von Brauchitsch and Rosemeyer to chase after Lang. After ten laps, at an astonishing average of 82.96mph (the previous mark had been around 75mph), Lang's lead had been cut to 3.4 seconds while Rosemeyer was a similar distance behind von Brauchitsch.

A decison by the BBC 'to interrupt programmes and give a commentary' was paying off as this fierce three-way fight continued at an unrelenting pace. On lap 14, von Brauchitsch took the lead and Rosemeyer began to close on Lang. Then the order changed yet again as the pit stops began, von Brauchitsch taking on fuel and fresh rear tyres in 30 seconds.

Neubauer, controlling operations in his usual meticulous and highly individual manner by using flag signals, brought Lang in next. Rosemeyer took the lead and stayed there until his pit stop, which took 31 seconds on lap 32. That let Caracciola into the lead, but he had not yet been into the pits. Von Brauchitsch, lying second, had made his stop and the German aristocrat, having set the fastest lap of the race, duly took the lead when his team-mate received the call from Neubauer on lap 40.

Rosemeyer was second – and closing on von Brauchitsch. The race would be a thrilling contest between these two. Mercedes-Benz v Auto Union. This was exactly what the crowd had come to see – except that they had rather hoped Seaman would be showing the way. In fact, the Englishman had retired on lap 29 when a rear damper, damaged in the early incident, finally gave way. Seaman rolled to a halt on the grass opposite the pits and parked behind the similar W125 of Lang, an early retirement with a similar suspension problem at the front of his Mercedes. Both cars were duly covered over in sombre fashion....

With Seaman gone, the home crowd had little else to cheer. The British contingent of ERAs and Maseratis were miles behind, albeit engaged in their own personal battles. 'Bira', driving in his familiar smooth fashion, led while Howe and Dobson fought all the way, the Englishmen paying heed to the flag marshals and moving courteously to one side each time a German car bore down on them. And, in the case of Maclure, that had occurred for the first time within the space of five laps. Whitehead had retired after 11 laps with engine trouble and Martin would stop not long after with a broken piston.

Raymond Mays, in brake trouble, had clouted the bank near the stone bridge, Rosemeyer doing likewise, although the German driver's excursion had more to do with over-enthusiasm than any problem with the car. Mays eventually found that the brakes had given up completely and he retired just after half-distance and, by then, Dobson had lost 14 minutes in the pits while a broken magneto rotor was replaced.

Indeed, the routine pit stops were leisurely in comparison with the efficiency shown by the works teams. Mays had required over a minute to take on fuel; Dobson needed 41 seconds for oil and water while Howe, coping with a number of fuel churns, managed to pour the last one all over the back of the car. This was but a side-show in every sense.

The leaders were now due to make a second stop for tyres, von Brauchitsch giving up a 26-second lead when he came in on lap 52. He rejoined in second place, knowing that Rosemeyer had yet to stop. But that did not prevent a continuation of the exuberant style which had marked the progress of the Mercedes-Benz.

Unfortunately, it all came to a dramatic end not long after. Von Brauchitsch's left-front tyre exploded as he hammered down Starkey Straight but, despite the car slewing dangerously across the grass, he managed to slow down without incident. On limping into the pits, a new tyre was fitted in 28 seconds – but Rosemeyer was long gone. The Auto Union driver held a 31-second lead, with 18 laps to go. Driving at his most brilliant best, Rosemeyer did not let up for a second and managed to make a final stop without losing the lead. It was all over, bar the shouting.

And there was plenty of that at the finish. Once a semi-exhausted Rosemeyer, followed by von Brauchitsch, Caracciola (whose car was later discovered to have a rag stuck inside the supercharger, an uncharacteristic lapse in Daimler-Benz preparation which perhaps contributed to a lacklustre performance), Müller and Hasse, had taken the flag after three hours of flat-out racing, the crowds stormed across the track, thus preventing the 'second division' from completing the required distance. As a result, 'Bira' – sixth on the road, plus Earl Howe, Dobson and Hanson (Maclure had retired with a back axle failure) were not classified.

Ah'm doomfounded

The motoring correspondent from the *News Chronicle* (formerly *The Daily News* and no longer staffed by our friend 'Chiltern') was not impressed. His headline read: 'The biggest and worst behaved crowd at a motor race in England.'

Mind you, certain members of the public had due cause to be enraged when they discovered that many of the course bookies, having given 5-1 on Rosemeyer, had simply fled. It was hardly surprising, since their 'expertise' had led them to offer exactly the same odds on Raymond Mays! The vacant betting stalls were reduced to matchwood by the angry crowd. Among those short-changed by such sportsmanship were a number of German officials but the Derby and District Motor Club raised the outstanding £50. This was duly handed over that night at the prize-giving at the Friary Hotel in Derby.

As for the spectators, their senses were still reeling. 'Grande Vitesse' knew exactly how they felt. In his report the following week, Walkerley recalled a quote from one befuddled man who, upon watching the three hour's worth of spectacle, declared in a stout Midlands accent:

'Ter think that they can make iron and braas and roober stand up to it, eeh, well, Ah'm doomfounded!'

On Monday morning, news of the German walkover was treated in a rather subdued manner by the national press. The headlines carried reports of serious disorder in Bermondsey when 111 people were arrested at a Fascist march, led by Sir Oswald Mosley. The *Leicester Mercury*, apart from covering the race, also had a picture of the wreckage of the light aircraft being removed by horse and cart from the field near Donington.

Elsewhere, though, there was heartening news for British motoring, the Austin Motor Company claiming another successful year with a 24.9 per cent increase in home sales and a gross profit of £1,665,125, an increase of £168,429 on the previous year.

For anyone suitably enthused by the Grand Prix, it was possible to go out and buy a new Hillman 14 'with Evenkeel independent front springing' for £248, or a 3½-litre Jaguar drophead coupe for £465. On the other hand, The Light Car Company of Derwent Street, Derby, were offering a 1935 Jowett Sun saloon for the princely sum of £78.

There were two cars on show in London which were definitely not for sale. Auto Union made arrangements to have Rosemeyer's car on display at the Great Portland Street showrooms of Auto-Union Sales Ltd. Predictably, though, Daimler-Benz had a more lavish presentation when they wheeled Seaman's car into their Park Lane premises. Either way, it was a slap in the face for the British motor industry. William Boddy summarised:

> *'The outstanding impression....is one of profound respect for the thorough way in which Germany goes about this serious business of motor racing – and that, in turn, reflects very favourably on the entire outlook of the Germany of today.'*

It is easy to understand what Boddy meant but, with the benefit of hindsight, it was a propitious, if unfortunate, choice of words. Before Europe was thrown into turmoil, however, Britain would have one final chance to witness the sustained drama and spectacle provided by this epic struggle for Grand Prix supremacy. If anything, the 1938 Donington Grand Prix would be even better than its predecessor. Sadly, though, the star of the 1937 race would be missing.

A pointless business

Bernd Rosemeyer was killed on 28 January 1938. He died as the result of a massive accident on the Frankfurt-Darmstadt autobahn. His Auto Union had been travelling at close to 270mph at the time.

Record-breaking had become another instrument in Hitler's quest to demonstrate Aryan superiority to the world. The south side of the autobahn running from Frankfurt to Mannheim, although only two lanes wide, provided the location for speed attempts which produced a limited amount of technical feedback for Mercedes-Benz and Auto Union. But once the crazy merry-go-round had started in 1934, neither company could afford to jump off. Or so their publicity departments told them. And, in the background, the government actively encouraged the pursuit of national prestige.

By 1937, the performance of these cars had gone beyond the facilities provided by a stretch of motorway, complete with bridges, trees and unseen enemies such as gusts of wind bursting through the clearings. And yet an official Record Week had been designated in October, Rosemeyer becoming the first man to exceed 250mph (400kph) through the measured mile and kilometre on this stretch of road. Daimler-Benz were not best pleased and, anxious not to wait for another year, they asked for the autobahn to be closed the following January. Caracciola raised the record to an average of 268mph.

Auto Union responded immediately, Rosemeyer keen to have the matter dealt with, despite the fact that the morning was cold, a stiff breeze freshening. Caracciola had warned of a mounting cross-wind but Rosemeyer made one run, coming close to the latest record.

On the next, at the point where there was a clearing to allow the Langen-Morfelden road to bridge the autobahn, the streamlined Auto Union was caught by a freak gust. Wreckage was scattered everywhere and they found Rosemeyer lying among the trees. He died minutes later. A small but neatly maintained memorial, near the Morfelden crossing, marks the location today.

It was a devastating blow to Auto Union, not to mention the sport as a whole. Rosemeyer had been the darling of the crowds, his impudent brilliance stirring the blood. No one else had managed to wring the neck of the rear-engined Grand Prix cars with such skill. Now, Auto Union were left with Rudolph Hasse and H.P. Müller; two competent drivers but not in the same class as Rosemeyer. At one point, the company actually considered withdrawing.

There was the additional complication of a change to the regulations, announced in 1936. Still vainly attempting to harness the performance of these monsters, the AIACR had decided on a sliding scale of weight limits in relation to engine capacity. This would be restricted to 4.5 litres unsupercharged, or 3 litres supercharged.

Of course, it made not one jot of difference. Indeed, the 3-litre Mercedes-Benz W154 would lap faster than the previous year's car, which had an engine twice the size. Mind you, Daimler-Benz had put a considerable amount of work into the new car, major alterations to the location of the transmission allowing the driver to sit much lower. The V12 engine also revved more freely, 450bhp being quoted at 7,800rpm.

Auto Union had to get along without Dr Porsche, who had left to concentrate on the production of the Volkswagen. Like their rivals, Auto Union chose the supercharged route, and a V12. Alfa Romeo had returned in an official capacity, Enzo Ferrari continuing to run cars which had 3-litre engines, but in a variety of configurations; straight-8, V12 and V16. Maserati had an eight-cylinder 3-litre car with twin superchargers while France was represented by Talbot, Delahaye and, occasionally, Bugatti. But the running, as ever, would be made by the German cars.

After an unexpected win at Pau, in the south of France, for René Dreyfus in a rather ungainly 4.5-litre unsupercharged Delahaye, Lang, von Brauchitsch and Caracciola scored a clean sweep for Mercedes-Benz in the blazing heat at Tripoli. The French Grand Prix, switched for the first time to the fast triangle of roads at Reims, provided another 1-2-3 finish for Mercedes-Benz, being aided in part by Kautz and Hasse crashing their Auto Unions on the first lap. The fourth car, a Darracq, was ten laps behind.

For the Germans, though, the home Grand Prix at the Nürburgring remained the pressure point of the season. And, for both teams, the 1938 race was a veritable *tour de force*. A fourth W154 was readied for Seaman, who had remained idle thus far in his capacity as 'junior' driver. Auto Union brought in Hans Stuck, and then pulled off a major coup by signing Tazio Nuvolari. He spun off early in the race while attempting to remove oil from the windscreen, and then took over Müller's car to finish fourth.

The race had looked like belonging to von Brauchitsch until his car caught fire in the pits. Seaman, who had pulled in behind his team-mate, managed to rejoin without harm and go on to become the first Briton to win a Grand Prix since Segrave in 1923. The result was a difficult one for the strutting Nazis to swallow while, for his part, Seaman appeared slightly bemused after achieving a major ambition.

There were five races left. Mercedes-Benz won the next three, at Livorno, Pescara and Berne, but Auto Union were gradually getting their act together and Nuvolari scored a magnificent and, as usual at Monza, highly emotional victory in the Italian Grand Prix. And, to please the Italians further, Alfa Romeo showed an encouraging turn of speed when Guiseppe Farina finished second. It was the perfect prelude to the final race of 1938: the Donington Grand Prix.

Crisis? What crisis?

The date had been set for 1 October but, a few weeks before, gloom descended on Europe when Hitler threatened to invade Czechoslovakia. The German teams arrived in England, the RAC holding a lunch in Seaman's honour to celebrate his victory at the Nürburgring. The political situation deteriorated and the Germans were recalled, Daimler-Benz being prepared to destroy their cars if they could not get them out of England. They got as far as Harwich by train and the tension eased when Chamberlain met Hitler in Germany.

The so-called Munich Crisis was over. 'Casque', writing in *The Autocar*, summed up the general feeling by quoting from a short poem published in *Punch*:

> '*I want to sit down*
> *To my lunch or my tea*
> *And not have a crisis*
> *Come bothering me.*'

Not exactly John Masefield, but the message was clear.

The race was rescheduled for 22 October and the fleet of Horch lorries carrying the Auto Unions returned to Donington on the weekend before the race, Nuvolari lapping inside the record on Monday – before hitting a stag which had wandered out of the woods.

Nuvolari was found stroking the poor animal but there was nothing which could be done. He asked to have its head stuffed and mounted, and placed alongside his other mementos and trophies in his study in Mantova – all of which merely contributed to the mystique surrounding the little man.

The Mercedes-Benz team flew in the same day, Hermann Lang reporting that the captain of their Junkers Ju52 had flown round the Nürburgring in their honour while *en route* to Croydon. The following day, Lang improved upon Nuvolari's time, the W154 lapping in 2 minutes 11 seconds. Despite the change to the regulations, and the smoothing out of the vicious bump leading onto the pit straight, the progress of these cars was as spectacular as ever. The stage was set for another electrifying confrontation.

Mercedes-Benz had four entries, Walter Baumer, previously the reserve driver, joining Lang, von Brauchitsch and Seaman in the absence of Caracciola, who had burned his foot during the Italian Grand Prix and was not particularly enamoured with Donington in any case. Interestingly, Rudolf Uhlenhaut, the technical director at Daimler-Benz A.G., was then nominated as reserve, such was his competence at the wheel as well as the drawing-board.

There were four Auto Union D-Types for Nuvolari, Müller, Hasse and Kautz (the handsome Cambridge undergraduate who was formerly the reserve with Mercedes-Benz). Ulrich Bigalke, a qualified doctor, was brought along as the back-up driver. Racing under the banner *Ecurie Bleu*, Delahaye entered two of their V12 cars for Dreyfus and one Raphael Bethenod de Las Casas (otherwise known as 'Raph'), while Maserati brought along an 8CTF for Villoresi.

Once again, a band of stalwarts from the British scene gathered at the back of the grid. Three ERAs, for Arthur Dobson (who qualified ahead of Dreyfus), Ian Connell and bandleader Billy Cotton, outnumbered Cuddon-Fletcher's MG, the Riley of the indomitable Maclure and Hanson's Alta. And according to *The Autocar*, Earl Howe would not be racing because 'naval duties still claim him.'

There was not a hope of the British cars doing anything other than get in the way, but not everyone in the public enclosure understood that. *The Autocar's* Sports Editor, S.C.H. Davis, felt obliged to issue a warning in a bid to halt the uninformed criticism which had surfaced after the previous year's Grand Prix.

'A reminder that British Small Cars are Competing Against German Big Cars Tomorrow,' the headline said, and Davis added: 'Nothing less than a miracle can give the British entries any chance of outright victories whatsoever.'

Yes, well, that seemed fairly clear. But, to anyone with the mildest interest in Grand Prix racing, it was a matter of no consequence. The German teams were back and that's what counted.

Ever since Chamberlain had brandished his piece of paper at Croydon airport, optimism took grateful hold and the Grand Prix adopted a mood of reconciliation. The Duke of Kent, in his role as President of the British Racing Drivers Club, agreed to start the race. There were a number of German dignitaries present, including *Korpsfuhrer* (Sports Leader) Hühnlein, members of the German Embassy in London, and the President and Vice-President of the ONS, the German equivalent of the RAC.

Dick Seaman took the Duke of Kent on a conducted tour of the circuit in a Lagonda, the second of two laps apparently being fairly swift. General Hühnlein (tactfully not wearing his Nazi uniform on this occasion) was driven round rather more slowly in a Bentley. Fred Craner, his toothbrush moustache neatly trimmed, rushed hither and thither; A. V. Ebblewhite, resplendent in three-piece suit and trilby hat, took charge of affairs on the starting grid.

All was in order. There did, indeed, seem to be peace in our time.

News of the spectacle generated by the previous year's race had obviously spread. 60,000 spectators turned out on a day which dawned misty, but rapidly became warm and sunny. The traffic chaos encountered in 1937 prevailed once more.

The cars slowly emerged from the paddock (located on the outside of Starkey Straight) and made their way to the pits, von Brauchitsch (without his red helmet) driving alongside Nuvolari, kitted out in his customary red helmet, blue trousers and bright yellow short-sleeved jumper bearing his interlocking initials. The cowling of von Brauchitsch's car was painted red; green on Seaman's car, blue on Lang's and white on the W154 of Baumer.

The Duke of Kent, on a signal from 'Ebby,' dropped the flag. By the time the field had rounded Red Gate, Nuvolari was beginning to pull away, and at the end of the first lap the Auto Union led from Müller, von Brauchitsch, Seaman, Lang, Baumer, Hasse, Kautz, Dreyfus, Dobson and Luigi Villoresi. Kautz, no more at home with Auto Union than he had been with Mercedes-Benz, felt even more unhappy after a few laps when his throttle jammed open at the end of Starkey Straight. The Auto Union charged straight on before coming to a halt, nose into a bank, the rest of the car straddling a ditch. The Swiss walked away, unhurt.

After ten laps, Nuvolari had pulled out a 14.6-second lead but Seaman had moved into third behind Müller. The progress of Villoresi was just as spectacular. Anxious to make up for a poor start, the Italian had overtaken Dobson and Dreyfus and was reeling in Hasse and Baumer. He passed them both and, just as he was coming to terms with von Brauchitsch, a piston failed and his Maserati was out.

Nuvolari was untroubled. Six laps later he had lapped Dreyfus – who was in ninth place, ahead of the British contingent, now without Maclure (broken axle – a repeat of the previous year) and Cuddon-Fletcher, who left the road at Melbourne Corner. And it was to be the departure of another British driver which would have a major influence on the outcome of this race.

A pit stop for a change of plugs had dropped Nuvolari to fourth place at the 20-lap mark, Müller now leading from Seaman and Lang. As Nuvolari left the pits, he followed Hanson, who had been in more serious trouble with the Alta. All was not well with the British car and on the fast swerves before the hairpin the engine suddenly blew up, dumping a vast pool of oil on the track. Hanson managed to cruise round the corner before stopping, thus leaving few obvious signs of something amiss.

Nuvolari, sensing the danger, just had time to back off before the Auto Union lost grip and began to slide gracefully onto the grass. He let the car take its own course, a typically cool reaction which allowed him to regain the track with little further drama. Others were not so lucky.

Von Brauchitsch came storming down the hill and the Mercedes-Benz suddenly went into a series of wild slides, onto and off the grass, before spinning and then miraculously getting round the right-hander. Hasse was next, the Auto Union sliding onto the grass on the right before shooting back across the track and tearing down 15ft of fencing around a programme kiosk on the opposite side. The car narrowly missed a tree and then a hut, inside which sat Mrs Fred Craner, happily minding her own business. Hasse was almost thrown from the car before it finally came to rest against a safety bank. Hasse's first reaction was to exhort the officials to provide warning for other drivers.

Too late. The yellow flag went out just before Seaman arrived and he didn't see it, the business of keeping one ton of Mercedes-Benz on the road at 150 mph more than holding his attention at the time. Suddenly the graceful movement of the big car became a series of unpredictable swerves and Seaman almost followed the path taken by Hasse, except that the car came to rest on some soft ground, more or less undamaged.

Urging marshals and officials not to offer assistance lest he be disqualified, Seaman struggled in vain to free the car. The rules stated that in such instances a driver should restart the car unaided; a difficult enough manoeuvre when it called for the use of a starting handle. The

Donington organisers, however, had amended that particular rule and an official indicated that help would be in order. Seaman, to much cheering, was eventually pushed back into the race. But he had lost a lap in the process.

Müller now held a five-second lead over Lang with Nuvolari further back in third place. After a series of pit stops the lead changed, Lang pulling out a 23-second advantage and feeling confident that he could win. Nuvolari, of course, had other ideas. 'Grand Vitesse' described what happened next in his own inimitable style:

> 'Nuvolari rolled up his sleeves and, roaring with laughter, set about motor racing in earnest. He came through the bends with his arms flashing up and down like pistons, the steering wheel jerking quickly from side to side – and yet all the time the car ran as if on rails, the front wheels always pointing dead on the line of travel. Maestro.
>
> There's no doubt little Tazio was on top of his form. He is 49 years of age. He was driving a car, he said, last year was unmanageable. And yet he was driving as he drove 15 years ago, doing things no one else can do, and slowly catching up after his two pit stops to his rivals' one.
>
> At 43 laps Baumer came in with the engine on fire and retired. Dobson, driving better than I have ever seen him, was 2½ minutes ahead of the next ERA and sixth in the race. Magnificent.
>
> And then Nuvolari pulled out a fastest lap at 82.72 mph, just to show them. At 50 laps he was 58 seconds behind leader Lang, 17 seconds behind Muller. At 53 laps, he passed Muller. At 54 laps, he was 39 seconds behind Lang.'

Lang, in fact, was in difficulties. A stone had smashed his windscreen, leaving his face exposed to a blasting from the chill October air. He was finding it difficult to breathe and focus properly. But he did not give up, despite the growing menace from behind. Walkerley takes up the story:

> 'Nuvolari drew closer and closer, still smiling all over his face, never making a mistake, changing down and braking at exactly the same spots on every corner every lap. At 56 laps he did 82.96 mph – fastest lap of the day. At 60 laps, he was 21 seconds behind, Lang averaging 80.01 mph. At 63 laps Nuvolari went faster still – 83.71 mph and closed to 12 seconds. Lap by lap the lead vanished – 10 secs., 6 secs., 3 secs. – and at 67 laps, the little Italian caught the Mercedes-Benz on Starkey Straight, pulled out, slammed his foot down, and shot past on maximum speed – about 160 mph.'

When the flag fell shortly after four o'clock, Seaman had passed Müller to take third place behind the brave Lang. Von Brauchitsch finished fifth while Dobson drove brilliantly to take sixth place, the ERA leading home the similar cars of Cotton and Connell. The next edition of *The Autocar* would carry a letter from a British enthusiast, praising the home drivers for their splendid efforts. (Interestingly, the same correspondence column would also carry a letter of complaint from an Ilford man, outraged at having been asked to pay 1s 10d (9p) for two teas, two portions of cheese and two rolls and butter at the infamous Brooklands Cafeteria the week before Donington.)

Dobson received £100 (and the dubious honour of meeting Hühnlein on the rostrum) while Auto Union and Nuvolari took away £250. But the race meant much more than mere financial reward, the Italian appearing to be quite overwhelmed by the reception from the crowd. He spoke neither English nor German but the look of delight as he was carried shoulder-high said all there was to be said.

If he appeared to wince slightly it was because the accident involving the stag earlier in the week had caused Nuvolari to fracture a rib. Fearful of hospitals and the trappings of medical aid, he had told no one of his injury, preferring to make a 'corset' by applying bandages tightly. Nonetheless, the bumps of Donington Park must have extracted their dues during the course of three hours and six minutes of a virtuoso performance. The Great Little Man had won the hearts of his audience once again.

Out of the shadows, into the darkness

When *Deutschland Uber Alles* rang out over Donington, the crowd momentarily ceased their invasion of the track and stood to attention. There was confident talk of another Grand Prix in 1939 and British enthusiasts relished the thought.

The Auto Union team packed up as international tension grew prior to the original date for 1938 Donington Grand Prix.

Not everyone adopted such a benevolent attitude towards the German domination of Grand Prix racing. The Italians were heartily fed-up with it all and made a unilateral decision to hold all their races to a 1,500cc formula in 1939. And that included the Tripoli Grand Prix in Libya, then an Italian protectorate.

The 8.14-mile Mellaha circuit staged one of the fastest road events in the Thirties. It was also one of the richest, funds being raised through the proceeds of a lottery. It was a very popular race with excellent facilities. But, with the 1,500cc formula in force, it seemed the German teams would be obliged to miss it, thus leaving Alfa Romeo, with the new 158, and Maserati to collect the prize money.

The Italians were shaken rigid when a ship docked in Tripoli and unloaded two brand new Mercedes-Benz cars, more or less scaled-down versions of the 1938 cars with, of course, 1.5-litre engines, in V8 form. Code-named W165, they had been built in total secrecy. Lang and Caracciola ran away with the Grand Prix and these little gems of racing cars were never raced again. It was the motor sport story of the season.

For the British, though, there was another story to tell, albeit a much sadder one. On 25 June 1939, Dick Seaman died from burns received when his car crashed during the closing stages of a very wet Belgian Grand Prix at Spa.

Seaman had taken the lead and, although the rain had eased and the track was beginning to dry in places, it remained treacherous in parts. He lost control on the left-hander at Club House Corner, just before the hairpin at *La Source.* The W154/163 struck a tree, knocking Seaman unconscious. He was not seriously injured but, because the car had recently made a pit stop, the contents of the full fuel tank spilled onto the hot exhaust and the car caught fire. By the time he had been extricated from the blaze, Seaman's chances of survival had gone. He died that night.

It was the end of a particularly traumatic period. Seaman had fallen deeply in love with Erica Popp, the daughter of the managing director of BMW. They had been married the previous December but it was a move which had not found favour with Seaman's mother. And the family tension had been exacerbated by the threatening activities of Adolf Hitler as the Spring of 1939 moved into a nervous, uncertain Summer.

In one respect, Richard Seaman's story was merely another intriguing aspect of a classic period of motor racing, perhaps one of the most thrilling and compelling we have seen. It had everything; wealth, international tension, stunning racing cars, intense rivalry, romance, drugs, scandal and heroes. But, throughout this period, there were menacing overtones; the crunch of the jackboot on the simplistic pleasures of sport.

On 3 September 1939, war was declared. A Golden Era had ended. And Donington Park, such an admirable theatre for the sport, would be given over to fighting a nation which, perversely, had provided the British enthusiasts with such pleasure not twelve months before.

CHAPTER 4

POST-WAR

The Mutton Grand Prix

It's amazing how far you can go on a pint of bitter. In September 1947, the brew served up in the Mitre Oak, at Ombersley in Worcestershire, was strong enough to prompt the idea of a trip to a village in Northamptonshire the following day. Beer and adrenaline had been flowing readily as the lads, fired up by a day's competition on the nearby Shelsley Walsh hill-climb, looked for alternative methods of motoring combat.

There was very little on offer. In fact, there were no motor racing circuits at all. Brooklands had been sold to the Vickers aircraft company and Donington was littered with military vehicles, relics of the war which had ended in August 1945. There was a circuit at Crystal Palace in south London, but this was now in need of major renovation. So, where could a motoring chap go to exercise his racing car?

An enthusiast called Maurice Geoghegan lived in the Northamptonshire village of Silverstone and he mentioned the nearby airfield. This had been occupied by 17 Operational Training Unit, their prime function being the training of crews for Wellington bombers. Now it was more or less redundant and would shortly become, in RAF parlance, 'a surplus, inactive station.'

Geoghegan said that during the summer of 1946 he had wanted to test a rebuilt Frazer Nash and the airfield seemed as good a place as any. He had found a fairly respectable two-mile 'course', starting at, as we now know it, Club Corner and running anti-clockwise along the perimeter road to Stowe, down to Becketts before returning along one of the runways to Club. He had been back a couple of times since then, in fact. So why not go tomorrow? Very little persuasion was needed. Another round was ordered to celebrate.

After a hearty breakfast, the owners of 11 Frazer Nashes and a Type 51A Bugatti set off, accompanied by their mates. Upon arrival, they set up a base at Maggotts and, so the story goes, the pilot of a passing Tiger Moth landed on the runway and joined in the fun. William Court, writing some years later in his colourful and highly individual style for the now defunct magazine *Speed World International*, describes what happened next:

> *'The perimeter was used anti-clockwise, first for practice then a race of sorts. During practice, agriculture struck a blow at the invaders when someone ran over an old garden fork which jumped up and stabbed him in the arm. Apparently no less than four doctors were present, but none of them were admitting it and the wound eventually stopped bleeding by nature, thus anticipating the health service.*
>
> *The race itself, who won it and how long it was are very properly lost in the mists of time: its name however is not. One of the cars, appropriately carrying Maurice himself, had rounded Club and was going up to Stowe when agriculture made its second intervention in the shape of a well-nourished and slothful sheep. The resulting impact inverted the sheep and caused it to out-accelerate the Nash up the straight with its legs in the air and very dead. The race for Geoghegan was over as the Nash bowed down at the front and threw its axle after the deceased. Later, folding money changed hands in the best traditions of pioneer motoring and the party finished at the Saracen's Head, Towcester.'*

The race was henceforth known as the Mutton Grand Prix. But it was by no means the first post-war event, official or otherwise, to bear the title 'Grand Prix'.

No sooner had the fighting in Europe ceased than Charles Faroux, whom we met at the inaugural Monaco Grand Prix in 1929, busied himself with an urgent return to motor racing in France. On 9 September 1945, a race was held in the Bois de Boulogne, just over six years after the last Grand Prix had been run in Yugoslavia when the war was actually several hours old. That race, the Grand Prix of Belgrade, had been won by Tazio Nuvolari's Auto Union. Naturally, German industry had matters other than motor racing on its mind in the autumn of 1945.

But, elsewhere, the need to return to normality and indulge in some of life's pleasures quickly filled the post-war vacuum. You raced wherever you could, with whatever you could lay your hands on. If it had four wheels and an engine, and you were willing to have a go, then the race was on. Accordingly the Fédération Internationale de Automobile (FIA) – successor to the AIACR – initially authorised *Formula Libre* Grands Prix, open to any Grand Prix cars which had survived and were fit to run.

For 1948, the FIA rationalised matters by recognising a formula which embraced the pre-war 4.5-litre unsupercharged cars and a division known as *Voiturettes* (in effect, Formula 2). Limited to 1.5-litre supercharged engines, the *Voiturettes* were seen, competitively speaking, to be more in line with the 4.5-litre cars. Certainly, lessons had been learned and there was no intention of returning to the pre-war 3-litre supercharged formula with which Mercedes-Benz and Auto Union had annihilated the 4.5-litre unblown brigade. In fact, this would have been the way of the regulations in the early Forties, had not war intervened.

Exit Germany; enter Italy

Sick and tired of the Auto Union/Mercedes-Benz monopoly, Alfa Romeo had decided in 1937 to concentrate on *Voiturette* racing. It had been the idea of their racing manager, Enzo Ferrari, and from this emerged the 158, or Alfetta; a motor racing classic if ever there was one. The supercharged 1.5-litre straight-8 was designed by Giaocchino Colombo at Ferrari's workshops in Modena, but all was not well between Enzo Ferrari and the Alfa management. Following a major disagreement over the manner in which the marque's future racing plans should be handled, Ferrari went his own way. Plans for the first Ferrari Grand Prix car were laid by the end of 1939.

That was the year the Alfa Romeo 158 suffered its only pre-war defeat when Daimler-Benz wheeled out their secret weapons at Tripoli. Until then, the slim red cars had turned many a head, Emilio Villoresi doing the majority of front-running until hostilities brought racing to an end. Nonetheless, development continued apace and, indeed, work was carried out spasmodically until 1943, when the cars were left in garages at Monza. There was a hasty piece of clandestine removal work when the Germans took control of Northern Italy, the cars and equipment being spirited to the village of Melzo where, legend has it, the 158s were hidden in a cheese factory.

Thus, when racing resumed in 1946, Alfa were able to speedily regroup and place a stranglehold on the *Formula Libre* events from the moment the Italian team appeared at the Grand Prix des Nations at Geneva.

This was almost inevitable, given the comparatively advanced state of development of these cars and the talent available to drive them. Alfa Romeo were represented by Dr Guiseppe 'Nino' Farina, Jean-Pierre Wimille, Count Carlo Felice Trossi – and Achille Varzi, making an extraordinary comeback. Speaking of which, Tazio Nuvolari, now a sick man, finished fourth in a Maserati in this race.

In 1947, Alfa restricted themselves to four appearances – naturally, they won all four – giving the independent drivers a chance to take the honours in the rapidly increasing number of races which were being held elsewhere in Europe.

This, however, was not the case in Great Britain, except for the aforementioned Mutton Grand Prix of course. But there were unofficial plans by members of a recently-formed club to take this impromptu event a stage further.

Pipsqueaks

The 500 Club developed from an idea, first mooted at a meeting sponsored by the Bristol Aeroplane Company Motor Sports Club on 10 December 1945. Before the war, enthusiasts had stuck motor-cycle engines into home-built chassis as a form of cheap and cheerful racing. Now, in a time of austerity during the aftermath of the war effort, it seemed worth exploring these spindly little cars as a means of going motor racing.

It was reckoned that a 500cc car, capable of 80-90mph, would probably cost less than £100 to build. In the interests of economy, the engines would be limited to two cylinders, supercharging would not be permitted and the cars would carry no more than two gallons of fuel, the latter also ensuring the need for pit stops.

Those who had 'real' racing cars deplored the growing presence of these 'pipsqueaks' with their snorting engines and megaphone exhausts. But the 500 men did not care about that. The movement flourished; they were game for anything. Thus, when news spread of an illicit meeting at the Silverstone airfield on 25 October 1947, there was no stopping them.

Unfortunately, the enthusiasm of the 500cc racers took an excessively strong hold and they arrived, along with a coach-load of enthusiasts from Bristol, at the airfield before the official caretaker had left for the weekend. This man was not impressed and forced the party to adjourn to Towcester racecourse, where they had been invited by Lord Hesketh whose son, Alexander, would enter a Grand Prix car for James Hunt at Silverstone and win the International Trophy 27 years later. But more of His Lordship anon.

The altercation at the gates of Silverstone airfield did at least draw the attention of the RAC to the site. A race committee, led by Colonel F. Stanley Barnes, had been searching for a suitable venue. There had been a growing feeling of frustration, shared by the British Racing Drivers' Club (BRDC) at the complete absence of a motor racing circuit in Britain at a time when the sport was being swiftly redeveloped abroad.

Attempts to buy shares in the Brooklands company in order to have a say in the future of the banked track had failed, and the government refused to release Donington following its requisition by the War Office almost ten years before. Indeed, the RAC had been in touch with Field-Marshal Montgomery but 'Monty' wrote back, saying that he had to agree with the War Office view that handing Donington back to motor racing would invoke too great a loss to the State.

There were fleeting moments of hope, however. Desmond Scannell, the secretary of the BRDC, met members of the Corporation of Barrow-in-Furness and there seemed to be no objections to holding a race meeting on nearby Walney Island.

In the meantime, the RAC continued searching elsewhere. Clearly, the money was not available to build a new track and the answer increasingly seemed to lie with one of the many airfields scattered across the country. Indeed, almost as soon as the war had ended, there had been speed trials on the runway of Elstree aerodrome, 30,000 spectators turning up to watch a massive entry despite the limitations imposed by petrol rationing. There had also been two serious race meetings on the site of Gransden Lodge airfield in Suffolk.

With the closing of public roads prohibited by law (except in the Channel Islands, the Isle of Man and Northern Ireland; hence the continuing growth of classic road circuits in these parts) the conversion of an airfield was indeed the only alternative. There had been talk of using Snitterfield, near Stratford-upon-Avon, but the escapades of the bandit racers suddenly brought Silverstone into the reckoning. More than anything, its central location had great appeal.

On 21 July, 1948, Earl Howe, Chairman of the RAC Executive Committee, reported that a short-term lease for one year could be obtained from the Air Ministry for Silverstone Aerodrome. But they would need to act quickly particularly if they wished to use Silverstone for the RAC Grand Prix, which had been reserved on the international sporting calendar for 2 October.

With the need to find a motor racing circuit reaching almost desperation level, you would think the Silverstone venture would have received full and immediate approval. But it wasn't that easy. We speak here of government departments and committees – and the fundamental issue of who would actually take responsibilty for converting the airfield into a temporary circuit and running the race. This certainly had not been the brief of the RAC in the past; they did not have the mandate to become involved with the financial implications of such a scheme. And there was the question of time, with just two months available to organise a Grand Prix from scratch. But, the more they thought about it, the more the idea appealed.

At the end of July 1948, a temporary lease was arranged; the RAC Grand Prix would be held at Silverstone on 2 October. And, happily, the 500cc men were invited to provide a supporting race.

The shaping of Silverstone

Silverstone had been built as an airfield as late as March 1943, but when the RAC visited the site to weigh up the task before them the place had the forlorn look familiar to abandoned aerodromes of a greater vintage: rotting wood, faded paintwork, weeds and grass sprouting freely in the concrete runways, the odd broken pane of glass allowing the chill wind access to deserted buildings and hangars. Everywhere had a layer of dust and grit. It was clearly a place that no-one had been sorry to leave. An unhappy era was about to be replaced by one with a similar sense of tingling anticipation which came from a more acceptable source.

Before then, however, the RAC had to wade through an administrative nightmare. A sub-committee to help organise the race consisted of many distinguished figures, including General A. H. Loughborough, who had won the first RAC Rally in 1932, S.C.H. Davis, John Morgan of the Junior Car Club and Captain A.W. Phillips of the RAC.

Dealing with one county council would be difficult enough but with the Northamptonshire-Buckinghamshire border bisecting the airfield, the problem immediately doubled in size. On top of that, the war had caused havoc with the various government departments and the race organisers had to deal with the Ministries of Air, War, Town and Country Planning, Agriculture, Supply, Transport, Fuel, Works and, just for good measure, the Board of Trade. As *The Autocar* noted sagely, it was a 'Gilbertian situation.'

On a more practical front, motor clubs weighed in with labour when it came laying out the track itself. The aim was to simulate a road circuit as best they could, a requirement which obviously ruled out the use of the perimeter road alone since, regardless of the direction of travel, one particular type of medium-speed corner would dominate. By utilising the runways as well, it would not only be possible to add to the length of the circuit, but there would also be the opportunity to include hairpin bends.

The races would be run in a clockwise direction. It made sense to place the pit and paddock area near an access point. There was a particular spot close to Luffield Abbey Farm, so-called because of the nearby ruins of Luffield Priory. Thus, the name Abbey Curve was given to the sweeping left-hander which led onto what would now become the pit straight.

The first corner, a fast right-hander, was to be known as Woodcote, named after the RAC's country club at Woodcote Park, near Epsom in Surrey. The perimeter road then ran towards Copse (so-called because of the nearby Seven Copses Wood) where the track then swung onto a runway for the first time and headed along Segrave Straight. A sharp left turn would take competitors back towards the perimeter road, rejoining it at a point on the short straight between Maggotts Curve (in deference to another local landmark, Maggotts Moor) and Becketts Corner. The ruins of the Chapel of Thomas à Becket lent its name to this right-hander, and Chapel Curve, which followed in quick succession.

Onto Hangar Straight now, a name derived from two large aircraft hangars, now demolished, on the left-hand side, before reaching Stowe Corner, a link with the local school of the same name. A sharp right-hander at Stowe meant a return to the same runway – now called Seaman Straight – and the prospect of motoring flat-out towards competitors racing along Segrave Straight. The erection of screens perhaps blanked out the drivers' fears but it did nothing to lessen the risk of a potentially serious incident if drivers failed to negotiate the left-handers at the runway intersection.

By doubling back, competitors rejoined the perimeter road for the last time at Club Corner (named after the RAC Club in Pall Mall) before charging through Abbey Curve to complete a lap measuring 3.67 miles.

Worth waiting for. The sound and the smell of international motor sport returns to England as the 1948 Grand Prix gets under way.

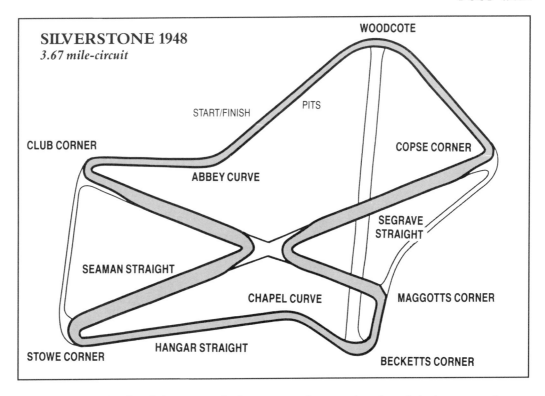

SILVERSTONE 1948
3.67 mile-circuit

WOODCOTE

START/FINISH   PITS

CLUB CORNER

COPSE CORNER

ABBEY CURVE

SEGRAVE
STRAIGHT

SEAMAN STRAIGHT

CHAPEL CURVE

MAGGOTTS CORNER

STOWE CORNER   HANGAR STRAIGHT

BECKETTS CORNER

There would be detail changes to the layout over the years but the original names and most of the track remain part of Silverstone today. And with the advent of private travel by air, the runways have been returned to the use for which they were originally intended.

In the meantime, Earl Howe had visited Europe in a bid to persuade international manufacturers and racing drivers to enter the RAC Grand Prix.

Enter Ferrari

His efforts met with some success but it was a major blow to the race committee when they did not succeed in tempting the Alfa Romeos to England. And neither did they manage to attract a significant newcomer, the Ferrari 125.

True to his angry word in 1939, Enzo Ferrari had produced his own Grand Prix car. In fact, his first private foray had been made at the 1948 Monaco Grand Prix with what, in essence, was a converted Ferrari sportscar. But there was no doubt about the 125. Powered by a V12, this Colombo-inspired car looked and sounded like a genuine Grand Prix racer. Three were entered for the Italian Grand Prix, then run through Valentino Park in Turin, for Farina, Raymond Sommer and Prince 'Bira'. Sommer finished third. Farina did win the *Grand Premio Autodromo* at Monza a few weeks later but the rest of the season was a succession of teething troubles, coupled with the fact that the car, with its short wheelbase, was something of a handful, particularly in the rain. There was disappointment, but no real surprise, when entries for Farina and Sommer were withdrawn from the RAC Grand Prix. Ferrari, though, would more than make their mark at Silverstone in the decades to come.

There would, however, be a strong Italian presence at the 1948 Grand Prix. Maserati sent along two of their latest cars, the 4CLT, a heavily modified version of a well-established design which first saw the light of day in 1939. The 4CLT won first time out in the 1948 San Remo Grand Prix, a significant feat in itself. But, with hindsight, just as important was the fact that the Maserati was driven by a man who would become the performance yardstick during the next eight years. His name; Alberto Ascari.

Maserati, through their works-assisted team, *Scuderia Ambrosiana*, entered Ascari and Villoresi for the Silverstone race although the marque was well represented by 4CLTs for 'Bira' and the British driver Reg Parnell, plus various earlier models driven by Baron Emmanuel de Graffenried, Duncan Hamilton, Sam Gilbey, Roy Salvadori and Bob Ansell.

There was a strong Gallic influence too, *Ecurie France* entering four of their stately Lago-

Speedy pit stop as Villoresi's Maserati is refuelled with the aid of a pressure hose in 35 seconds.

Talbots. The blue cars were a development of their pre-war models, the big 4½-litre engines throbbing along at 5,000rpm, reliability and superior fuel consumption being their main assets. The team was led by Louis Chiron, now something of a veteran at 48, and Phillippe Etancelin. Louis Rosier and the Italian Gianfranco Comotti drove the other two.

Elsewhere in the paddock, 1.5-litre ERAs were thick on the ground, the six-cylinder British cars, despite a design heritage stretching back to 1933, proving more than their worth at a time when decent racing cars were hard to find. There were ten in all, led by Bob Gerard and Raymond Mays, the man who had conceived the English Racing Automobiles project in the first place.

That left an Alfa-Aitken (originally a pre-war Alfa Romeo *Bimotore*, a fearsome device with twin engines, but now only running with one at the front) driven by Tony Rolt, and an Alta – of which we will learn a little more at a later stage. An Emeryson Special, powered by a 4.25-litre Clemons engine, had been entered by Bobby Baird from Belfast but this rare machine was not permitted to start, the scrutineers declaring that the eight carburettors were prone to flooding and the fire risk was too great.

Practice began on Thursday with no sign of the 'works' Maseratis, but Leslie Johnson, driving a 1939 E-Type ERA, gave the organisers a boost by recording the fastest time. Friday, though, saw Chiron knock a couple of seconds off that. And there was still no sign of the *Scuderia Ambrosiana* cars. The lorry eventually puffed into the paddock towards the end of the day and Ascari and Villoresi were immediately sent out to establish which way the circuit went. During the course of just four laps, Villoresi unofficially knocked more than a second off Chiron's best; Ascari, in turn, was only four-tenths slower than the Talbot. The Maseratis would have to start from the back of the grid – but the form for the race was clear.

Basic – but better than nothing

A dishevelled wartime aerodrome it may have been but, on Saturday 2 October, it was a Grand Prix circuit. And, after the deprivations of war and a 10-year break since the last major motor sport event in Britain, *anything* was welcome. 100,000 spectators flocked to Silverstone that day, the queue of traffic reportedly stretching several miles beyond Towcester. If they expected a repeat of the Donington classics a decade before, they were to be disappointed.

Two grandstands, each holding 750 spectators, had been erected. It cost £2 to sit in the covered stand opposite the pits and £1 10s (£1.50) for the uncovered version. It cost another £1 10s for a car, regardless of the number of occupants, and £5 for a 20-seater coach. A 10s (50p) charge was levied on motor-cycle combinations while those on foot parted with 7s 6d (37½p); charges which Mr. G.C. Tysoe of Worcestershire considered to be 'extremely reasonable' in a letter to the press the following week.

It had to be said that the facilities were nothing like those which had been established by Fred Craner and the Derby and District M.C. – very basic lavatories, haphazard car parking, barbed wire and bits of aircraft scattered here and there, mud everywhere, no spectator fencing – just a rope and straw bales.

But that didn't matter. The rasp of racing engines and the smell of racing oil and rubber was in the air. It was an *event*. And the 'Continentals' were present to add some credibility to the proceedings.

A roll in the hay. Geoffrey Ansell was lucky to escape serious injury when his ERA rolled at Maggots.

First, though, a bit of flag-waving. The previous September, John Cobb had taken his Railton-Mobil Special to Bonneville, in Utah. Despite the local salt flats not being in perfect condition, the London stockbroker managed to raise his own land speed record to 394.196mph – a single run having been recorded at over 400 mph. It was just the sort of boost Britain needed and that record would stand for 16 years. Cobb was present at Silverstone and he opened the course at the wheel of a Healey Sportsmobile, escorted by motor-cycle TT winners Artie Bell, Freddie Frith and Maurice Cann.

Earl Howe briefed the drivers before they returned to the cars, spread in rows of five-four-five down the grid. There were 25 starters, including the two Maseratis at the back. The question was, how long would it take the red cars to work their way to the front?

As soon as Earl Howe had dropped the Union Jack, the Maseratis began carving their way through the buzzing ERAs. Making the most of their temporary absence from the front, Louis Chiron had thrust his Talbot into the lead, with Leslie Johnson giving the crowd their money's worth by challenging the Frenchman strongly. The ERA got as far as Maggotts, where Johnson thumped a marker tub and broke a drive-shaft.

It was a bad start for the English contingent. Raymond Mays had stalled on the line, Salvadori oiled a spark-plug, Rolt's Alfa Romeo would soon begin to misfire and, on lap two, Parnell spluttered to a halt, his Maserati out of fuel. A solid-looking drain plug had been dislodged from the bottom of the tank, one report suggesting that flying stones had been the culprit; another saying that the Englishman had caused the damage when he ran over a landing-light. The latter would seem to have been the most likely reason, although Parnell had indeed been showered with stones as he pursued Chiron's leading Talbot.

The sister car of Etancelin would not get that close although the Frenchman was keeping an eye out for the rapidly advancing Maseratis as they moved 'Bira' out of third place. Villoresi, shadowed by Ascari, quickly dealt with Etancelin but Chiron was rather more difficult to shift. Eventually, though, the Maseratis were through and by quarter distance they had the race to themselves.

There was, however, a slim hope that the Talbots might be able to make the most of their fuel economy, the blue cars being scheduled to make just one pit stop as opposed to two refuelling halts for the Maseratis.

In the event, it made little difference. The Italian mechanics may have been in a state of excitable confusion but their performance was slick when compared with the chaos elsewhere. Pit crews simply went to pieces under pressure and plans went out the window; some teams appeared to have no plans at all. After the rigid discipline witnessed in the Auto Union and Mercedes-Benz pits at Donington ten years before, this was a retrograde step.

Gilbey had fuel slopped down his neck; others left the pits with their cockpits awash. 'Bira' and Gerard were notable exceptions, the Englishman taking on oil, water and 30 gallons of fuel in just 43 seconds, a superb effort which received a rousing cheer from the grandstand opposite. Ascari, by comparison, had taken 1m 27s – not that it affected the positions at the front.

The only concern now was the state of the track, rubber and oil combining with soft tar to make the going treacherous, particularly on the tight corners on the infield. Geoffrey Ansell had slithered into the straw bales at Maggotts, his ERA then somersaulting and throwing the driver out: Fortunately, his injuries amounted to no more than cuts and bruises. Even Villoresi had managed to nudge the bales at Seaman Corner. Perhaps it was that incident which caused

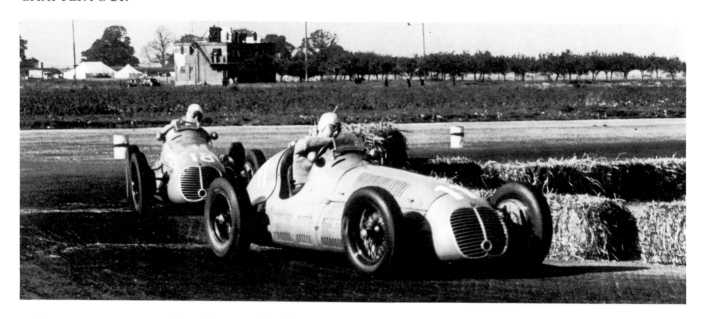

Ascari leads Villoresi at Segrave Corner with the control tower in the background and, beyond that, the pits.

the rev-counter to come loose, but certainly the instrument fell out of the dash-panel later in the race and then lodged under the clutch pedal, forcing clutchless gearchanges – not a serious problem for a man of Villoresi's experience.

The final pit stops came and went without incident. Ascari, in trouble with a fractured exhaust pipe in any case, took longer than his team-mate, thus putting the result beyond doubt. Chiron had retired with a seized gearbox and, with Comotti and Etancelin out with brake trouble and a cracked cylinder head respectively, that left Rosier as the sole Talbot representative in fourth place. The Frenchman did not put up a struggle when Gerard displaced him, and when 'Bira' experienced brake trouble, the Englishman, driving impeccably, moved into third place.

The final piece of drama occurred when de Graffenried, having struggled with overheating trouble, spun into a potato field, only to emerge with a commentator's microphone cable attached to his car. Unfortunately, the announcer was not aware of this until the microphone was suddenly whipped from his hand and the cable almost throttled the poor chap. Ironically, this little diversion ensured sixth place for John Bolster, a larger-than-life character who would soon become better known as a commentator than a driver.

The race had been about as exciting as the surroundings had been attractive, but that did not prevent the crowd from swarming over the straw bales and onto the track. At least they had witnessed an international motor sporting event on British soil. Little did they know that they had been present at the birth of what would become the home of one the best organised and, frequently, the most dramatic Formula 1 races in the world series. Silverstone had begun to move on from the Mutton Grand Prix of 1947. And the RAC Grand Prix of 1948 had one other significant point to make.

Before the main race had started, the 500cc men had taken their turn. Among their number was a 19-year-old by the name of S.C. Moss. He had set the fastest lap in practice and then retired when the JAP engine in his Cooper blew up. But we would hear more about Stirling Moss just as surely as we would become very familiar with the sight of nimble racing cars with their engines mounted in the back.

Alfa withdraw

Alfa Romeo, meanwhile, had been busy. Development on the engine had increased the power output; everything pointed to further success. Once again, they won the four races entered, but emotions were mixed.

The first outing had not been until early July, when four cars were entered for the European Grand Prix on the *Bremgarten*, a superb road course at Berne. The latest car was entrusted to Varzi during practice. For some inexplicable reason, the car got away from him and he crashed. With only a linen helmet for protection, the head injuries proved fatal. He died instantly. It was only the second major accident in a long and spectacular career for Varzi – both in and out of the cockpit. Victory for Count Trossi, with Jean-Pierre Wimille second and Consalvo Sanesi fourth, was scant consolation for Alfa Romeo.

They finished 1-2-3 in the French Grand Prix; Wimille won in Milan, and, a month later, Alfa Romeo filled the first four places at Monza, Piero Taruffi making up the numbers. It had not been as easy as it appears on paper, however, the Alfa coming under threat from Maserati and, of course, the new Ferrari. A few months later, in January 1949, the brilliant Wimille was killed while practising a Simca for the Peron Cup races in Argentina. Such had been his contribution to the honour of France that he was awarded the Cross of the Legion of Honour.

The, shortly after the loss of Wimille, Count Trossi finally succumbed to cancer, an illness he had fought bravely for several years. All of this, plus a difficult financial situation and the pressure of work putting into production their new saloon car, prompted Alfa Romeo to withdraw from racing in 1949. At least they went out with honour, the 158 Alfa Romeo having won 16 times - including ten one-two-three victories – in the 19 events entered between 1938 and 1948.

That left the way clear for Ferrari and Maserati. Ferrari immediately struck a mean blow when he signed Ascari and Villoresi, and that fairly took the wind out of Maserati's sails even before the season had started. Of course, the fact that Ferrari already had Farina and Sommer on his books did not seem to be a matter of any consequence. It was, perhaps, the first sign of Ferrari's cunning when it came to manipulating his drivers in order to keep everyone on their toes.

Despite continuing development and a search for reliability on his car, Ferrari also managed to sell two of them to private teams which, presumably, he did not see as a direct threat. Both cars came to England, Peter Whitehead taking delivery of one while the other went to Tony Vandervell, the engine–bearing magnate, who intended to use the Ferrari as a test bed for his products. This car became known as the 'Thinwall Special'. It was the first step towards the magnificent British-built Vanwalls which, several years later, would give Enzo Ferrari's cars a serious run for their money.

Ferrari, in fact, formally entered Whitehead for the Jersey Road Races (a race meeting which was the necessary product of the inability to close public roads on the mainland). It rained hard and the skittish handling of the 125 prompted Whitehead to finish a conservative seventh, the race being won by Bob Gerard and his splendid 12-year-old ERA. Gerard would enjoy even more fame a few weeks later at Silverstone.

Let's do it again

In the aftermath of the first Grand Prix in 1948, Silverstone continued to be viewed as nothing more than a stop-gap measure, pending either the release of Donington or the construction of a 'proper' circuit elsewhere. But, one thing was sure. Having set the ball rolling, the RAC was not going to let 1949 pass without Great Britain holding a Grand Prix, regardless of the shortcomings and the insecurity of the tenancy at Silverstone.

A day in May was seen to be more favourable from every point of view, not least the expiry of the leasing agreement the following August. Of more importance, however, was the granting of official Grand Prix status by the FIA, thus putting the Silverstone race on a par with classics in France, Italy and Monaco. The RAC immediately renamed the event the British Grand Prix. But the tricky question of financing, not just the Grand Prix but motor racing in general, remained.

Desmond Scannell of the BRDC had raised the subject in casual conversation with Basil Cardew, motoring correspondent of the *Daily Express* who, in turn, discussed the matter with Tom Blackburn, the general manager of the newspaper. It was quickly agreed that the *Daily Express* would lend its considerable weight to motor racing at Silverstone, thus beginning a liaison which would last for at least 40 years.

The first thing the *Express* wanted to know was the quality of the entry for the British Grand Prix. The news was not good. Once again, there was not enough 'starting money' on offer for the likes of Ferrari; the £1,500 prize fund alone was insufficient. But, at least Maserati had agreed to be present once more, albeit in a semi-works capacity. That meant the mixture had changed little since the inaugural race seven months before. The track, though, was different.

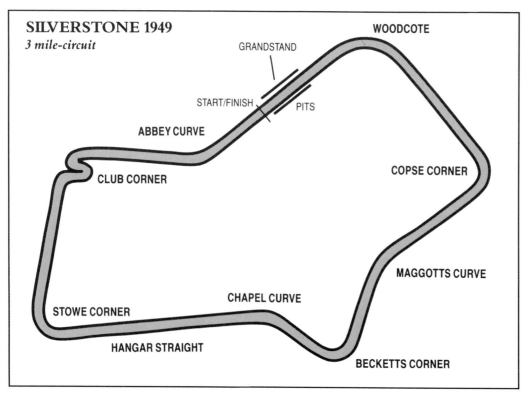

SILVERSTONE 1949
3 mile-circuit

WOODCOTE

GRANDSTAND

START/FINISH

PITS

ABBEY CURVE

COPSE CORNER

CLUB CORNER

MAGGOTTS CURVE

CHAPEL CURVE

STOWE CORNER

HANGAR STRAIGHT

BECKETTS CORNER

The runways were abandoned since spectators had been prevented from getting close enough due to the cultivation of strips of land on the infield. Thus, the track now followed the perimeter road, duly widened and resurfaced in places, for its entire length. And, in the interests of variety, a ludicrously tight chicane, marked out by straw bales, was introduced at Club Corner to slow the cars. There were now two grandstands 'out in the country': the East stand at Becketts and the South stand at Stowe. And, in an attempt to speed up the traffic flow and make the points of access more understandable, the various parking areas had been given different colours. The scaffolding representing the pits was shifted further away from the exit of Abbey Curve and the lap distance now measured three miles exactly.

Villoresi, back in a Maserati for this event, mastered the new track better than most when he urged the 4CLT round in 2 minutes 9.8 seconds on Friday, the second day of practice. The previous day had belonged to the ERA of Peter Walker, but the Englishman had to be satisfied with an eventual third-fastest time behind Villoresi and the 4CLT of 'Bira.' The privately-entered Maserati of 'Bira's' team-mate, Baron 'Toulo' de Graffenried, was just four-tenths slower than Walker and they were joined on the five-car front row by the immaculate ERA of Bob Gerard.

The second *Scuderia Ambrosiana* Maserati was entrusted to Reg Parnell, the doughty Englishman nearly half a second slower than Gerard, although that was not a true reflection of Parnell's ability. This time, Talbot were represented by five cars, the Belgian driver Johnny Claes and Yves Giraud-Cabantous (cutting a dash of sartorial elegance with a beautiful knitted helmet) joining Rosier, Chiron and the effervescent Etancelin. Ferrari may not have been entered officially but the British privateers were present, Whitehead on the outside of the third row in his 125 while Tony Vandervell had entrusted his 'Thinwall Special' to Raymond Mays. As usual, Mays' pride and joy, the ERA, was well represented but, on this occasion, the classic upright machines would be rattled by the more advanced Alta of George Abecassis.

A Briton leads!

It was clear that the primitive facilities evident the previous year had not deterred the enthusiasts; this time an estimated 120,000 choked the narrow roads leading to Silverstone. If they thought the amenities would have improved in the intervening seven months, the spectators were to be disappointed, but for most, it was the sport which mattered.

Once again, there was a 500cc supporting race, the 'vivid little projectiles' (as *The Autocar* referred to them) taking a rolling start behind Col. Barnes in an Austin A90 Atlantic. And this time Moss won.

There was, however, little chance of a British victory in the main event. But with Gerard on the front row in a very reliable car, you never knew, although 100 laps at an average of around 80 mph would be a tall order and, in the event, 300 miles would prove too much for over half of the 25 starters.

Indeed, the race had barely started when Roy Salvadori pulled into the pits for a change of plugs on his Maserati 4CL. His early absence would scarcely have been noticed since there was a battle royal going on at the front. 'Bira' had stormed into the lead, chased strongly by Villoresi, the Italian forcing his way through after two laps. But that was not the end of the story. 'Bira' gave chase and retook the lead, only to have Villoresi regain the initiative a few laps later. Then the lead changed hands again on lap 24 but, this time, the *Scuderia Ambrosiana* car was in trouble and Villoresi made a pit stop to investigate sagging oil pressure. Eleven laps later, the previous year's winner was out.

That left 'Bira' with a massive lead over Parnell but, once again, the Prince was in trouble with fading brakes. It was almost inevitable that if trouble were going to strike, it would occur under heavy braking for the Club chicane and that's exactly what happened on lap 47, the blue and yellow Maserati ploughing into the straw bales and hitting a marker tub. Unfortunately, the 'tub' was an oil drum filled with concrete. The front of the 4CLT was badly damaged and, even though 'Bira' managed to limp into the pits, nothing could be done.

There was little dismay in the enclosures since this meant that an Englishman was leading the British Grand Prix for the first time in 23 years! Driving with his familiar blend of determinated aggression, Parnell seemed comfortable as he maintained a 25-second gap over the 4CLT of de Graffenried. The excitement lasted for about 15 minutes. An oil plug worked loose from the back axle of the Maserati and Parnell was forced into the pits. He returned to the track but, after stopping a few more times, Parnell's race was run. De Graffenried was in the clear.

Further down the field, there was a heroic drive of truly British proportions as Abecassis pushed the Alta round Silverstone at a pace which even surprised members of the team. The one exception was Alf Francis, a Polish-born mechanic completely devoted to his trade. From the minute he had joined H.W. Motors Limited at Walton-on-Thames the previous summer, Francis had been impressed by their Alta which, in effect, was the only purpose-built Grand Prix car made in England at the time.

Alf Francis would prove to be one of the greatest improvisers in the pit lane at a time when racing teams could not afford to discard faulty parts and simply replace them with new ones. Alf could seemingly keep a car running on sheer ingenuity alone. He would go on to become chief mechanic to Stirling Moss and, in association with the journalist Peter Lewis, he later wrote the book *Alf Francis. Racing Mechanic.*

Francis described George Abecassis as 'one of the pre-war gentlemen drivers who has not acquired his style of driving from anyone....on one of his good days, he is a difficult driver to catch and a pleasure to watch in action.' 14 May 1949 was one of George's good days.

After 10 laps, he was in fifth place, the Alta, as Francis described it, 'going like a bomb.' Then carburettor trouble meant a four-minute pit stop as Francis lay on his back in the pit lane and reached inside the engine compartment, plugging off the miscreant carburettor by feel. The bodywork was so low that he could not get his head underneath the engine.

Abecassis, *really* fired up now, rejoined and began carving his way through the field. There would be a routine stop for fuel, and not even a broken exhaust pipe would deter the Englishman. It was the most satisfactory sight a hard-working mechanic could wish to see. Francis describes the moment in his book and, along the way, he unconsciously sums up a classic chauvinistic view of motor racing.

'We were all so excited about the prospects of the flying Alta getting to grips with the front end of the field that James Tilling (who was managing the pit) agreed with my suggestion to speed up Abecassis even more. This was the first time our pit had been really well organized and our code was a simple one : F. for faster.

Twice we showed the chalked message to Abecassis and then, much to the disgust of Mrs. Abecassis, I added the plus sign.

"Do you want to kill my husband?" she said.

"Madame," I replied, "we are motor-racing."'

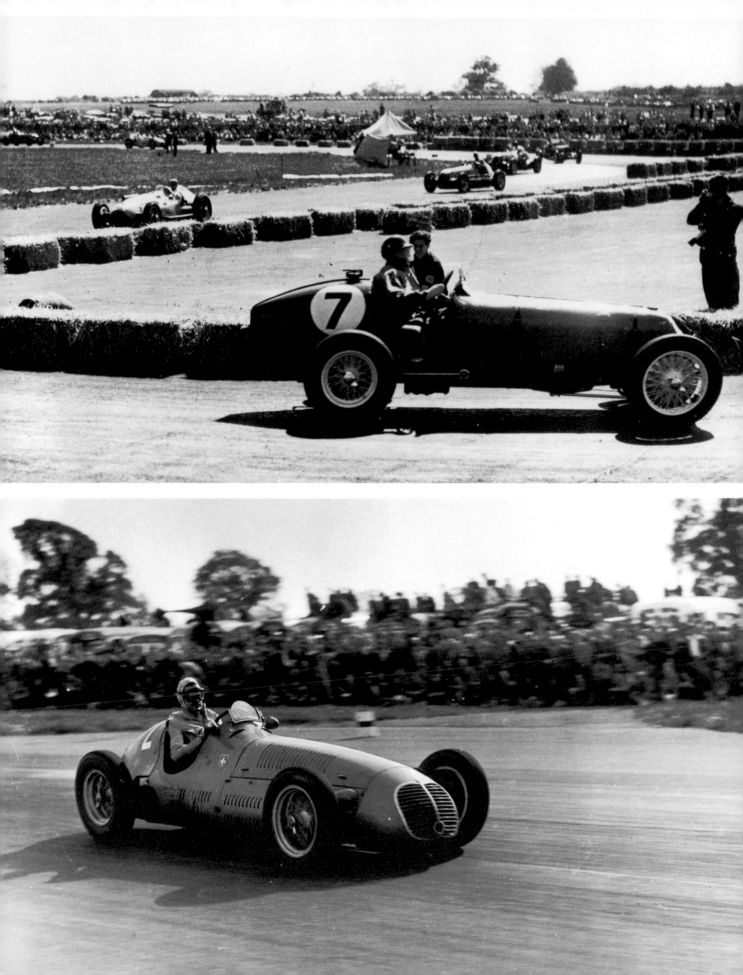

Mr Bob's big day

While George Abecassis was doing his bit for Britain in the mid-field, the hopes of a home victory rested with the steady 'Mr Bob'. Gerard's ERA was some three minutes behind de Graffenried. The only hope was that the Swiss would go the way of Giraud-Cabantous, who had retired with a piston failure, or Walker, whose ERA had been forced out by brake trouble, or Chiron, a victim of transmission failure on the Talbot.

Bolster had been injured very badly when his ERA left the course at Stowe but there was an incident of an even more serious nature when Ken Richardson, having taken over the Thinwall Ferrari from Mays, proved that the handling of the short-wheelbase car really was as bad as Mays had claimed. Coming through Abbey Curve, the inexperienced Richardson lost control and spun backwards into the crowd, injuring several spectators. Whitehead's Ferrari was in trouble too when Dudley Folland spun wildly at Maggotts shortly after taking over from the car's owner.

With 20 laps to go, Gerard rose to the occasion and stepped up the pace. It was asking a bit much from a 12-year-old car however and he eased off enough to maintain his second place ahead of Rosier, who ran the race non-stop, and the ERA driven by Billy Cotton and David Hampshire.

For de Graffenried, though, this was almost too difficult to believe. The immaculate 'Toulo' would go on to become adviser to Philip Morris when they introduced their 'Marlboro' brand to motor sport as tobacco sponsorship truly got into its stride in the Seventies. De Graffenried also became Chairman of the *Club International des Ancient Pilotes de Grand Prix* and, doubtless, he was grateful for the Silverstone success as a means of counting himself as a Grand Prix winner.

When recalling that race forty years later, however, de Graffenried did not embellish the story behind his victory.

'I had my chance and my luck,' he said. 'It was a long race and the thing was to wait during the first half and see what happened. For instance 'Bira', who was now my team-mate, went out when he hit that oil drum; then Villoresi's Maserati went out. The aim was to finish, obviously, but you always set out expecting to win – even if you eventually finished last. But just to finish was vital because the prize money was more important than anything else if you were a private team.

'The Maserati was owned jointly by me, a friend, and the chief mechanic, Enrico Platé. In fact, the team was called *Scuderia Enrico Platé*. Things were very different in those days you know! It was not uncommon for the driver to take his turn at driving the lorry so that the mechanics could rest while we travelled to the circuit.

'We had genuine hopes of a good finish and it looked good when 'Bira' disputed the lead with Villoresi. When they both went out, it was up to me to do something for the team and I chased Parnell's Maserati. Then I noticed his car was spilling oil and I wasn't surprised when he had to stop. 'After that, I had to worry about Gerard, even though he was quite a long way behind me. I knew his car was likely to finish but I kept getting encouraging signs from the pits. In fact, I remember that Villoresi was standing with my team and helping with the pit board. I can't imagine that happening today! Anyway, once Gerard began to ease off, I knew I could do the same. But those last few laps were very worrying. The car was okay – but I kept checking the oil pressure gauge just in case.

'It was to be my first victory in an international Grand Prix and it meant a lot to me. Winning that race meant I was engaged in all the Grands Prix and my sporting career began to improve from that point.

'For me, the British Grand Prix was, and still is, a great name. I was lucky, yes. But, my God, it was a nice feeling…'

Bob Gerard's ERA tackles the highly unpopular chicane, marked out by straw bales, at Club Corner.

A nice-feeling. Baron de Graffenried heads towards victory in his privately-entered Maserati 4CLT.

CHAPTER 5
DREAMS AND NIGHTMARES

Life begins at 38

No one had heard of Balcarce, never mind the stocky gent who claimed to live there. His first race had been 20 years before, at the wheel of a Ford special in Argentina. Now, here he was in San Remo, Italy, claiming to be a Grand Prix driver. At the age of 38.

In South America, they knew all about this man. He had won their admiration for his stamina and car control during long distance races on dirt-surfaced tracks which barely passed as roads. Some of these marathons would last for two weeks, take the competitors from Buenos Aires to Peru and back, with not a back-up vehicle in sight. If your car broke down, you had to fix it yourself. Character-building? Certainly. But Grand Prix racing? Never. And yet, here was this man venturing into Europe with that in mind.

There were certain anomalies. His team was known as *Equipe Achille Varzi*. It was said that the Italian maestro had been greatly taken with this shy Argentine driver. It was also said that Jean-Pierre Wimille had seen the same potential and taught him all he knew about how to develop a 'feel' for the modern Grand Prix car. Apparently the poor man, greatly saddened when Varzi died, was devastated when Wimille lost his life, right there in Argentina.

And yet, here he was in San Remo, with the blessing of Balcarce and the *Automovil Club Argentino*, at the wheel of a Maserati 4CLT. He was on the front row, alongside 'Bira'. But no one was particularly bothered. Then he won the race. Now they made a note of the name on the side of the car. But a film crew, unfamiliar with this chap 'J. M. Fangio,' missed him as he walked to the victory rostrum.

A few weeks later in Pau, France, he won again. They didn't miss him this time. Now it began to dawn that Juan Manuel Fangio might just be someone special. He went on to win at Perpignan and Marseilles. The competition was not top rate but the man's instinctive ability was impressive. Being 38 was clearly no obstacle. Fangio's arrival in Europe was to be the high point of 1949.

With Alfa Romeo lying low, it gave a hollow ring to victories earned by Maserati, with their ageing 4CLT, and Ferrari, with a car which was far from perfect. Nonetheless, the records show that once Villoresi had switched to Ferrari, he won a mixture of Formula 1 and Formula 2 races at Rome, Luxembourg, Zandvoort (the first international event for the Dutch circuit), Garda and Brussels. Ascari took his turn in the European, Swiss and Bari Grands Prix.

The supercharged Ferraris, though, were drinking their fuel at a prodigious rate and a non-stop run by Rosier in the unblown Talbot gave the French firm victory in the Belgian Grand Prix. Chiron, using a similar tactic, scored an emotional win for Talbot at Reims, although the French Grand Prix was notable for the fact that, but for a gearbox problem, the race would have gone to Peter Whitehead's privately-entered Ferrari. The Englishman did, however, win at Masaryk in Czechoslovakia after the Maseratis of Farina, 'Bira' and Parnell had all crashed at the same corner.

The talking point of the 1949 season, though, was the arrival of Fangio. He won six of the ten European races he entered. It was easy to predict a great future for the man of 38 from the Argentine.

If only the same could have been said of the rise and rapid fall of the British Racing Motor (BRM). Fangio was to bring Argentina honour and pride but, sadly, the disastrous BRM V16 was to be the butt of British music hall humour. And whereas Fangio had arrived quietly on the scene, the BRM was hailed as a world-beater almost before it had turned a wheel in anger. That, of course, was the indirect cause of much of the grief which was to follow. The trouble started in earnest on 15 December 1949.

A patriot's game

Folkingham lies nine miles north of the town of Bourne, in Lincolnshire. A disused airfield near the village was used for a demonstration run which would inflame the belief that Britain

Juan Manuel Fangio
The surprise is that the legendary Argentinian claimed the British Grand Prix just once (1956) but he shadowed Moss across the line the previous year. World champion no less than five times and yet did not begin Grand Prix racing until he was 38; a suitable indication of a supreme natural talent.

had produced a Grand Prix car which could take on the world. On the old motor racing premise that, if it looked and sounded right then it must be right, the BRM was indeed ready to grind the opposition into the dirt – or at least, that was the view of some of the so-called experts. Those with a more critical eye could see one shortcoming straightaway; there were no louvres in the bodywork to allow air from the radiator to escape. What other follies lay beneath the bonnet?

Certainly, the V16 engine assaulted the eardrums of the watching pressmen. It was the most ferocious sound imaginable. At long last, here was evidence of a project which had been talked about but, with each passing month, never seemed likely to be fulfilled. It had, in fact, been the dream of Raymond Mays for ten years and more.

In 1933 Mays and his friend, Peter Berthon, had, with assistance from Murray Jamieson, modified a Riley with such effect that Humphrey Cook, a wealthy motor racing enthusiast, suggested they should build a car to, as Mays put it, 'represent England in international races.' Thus ERA – English Racing Automobiles – was born with Cook as Managing Director, Berthon as designer and Mays the number one driver. A piece of land at the back of Eastgate House, the Mays family home in Bourne, was sold for the purposes of building workshops. It was to be a hugely successful project which, ironically, encouraged Mays and Berthon to become even more adventurous in their thinking when they split with ERA in 1939.

The ERA had been a *Voiturette*. Now Mays wanted to build a Grand Prix car that would not simply be a larger ERA. This car would be on the scale of Mercedes-Benz and Alfa Romeo; a machine with the backing of the nation; a car financed and built by Great Britain and racing for Great Britain.

Mays and Berthon formed a company called Automobile Developments Limited but their plans were put on hold by the advent of World War II. No sooner had it ended than Mays was circulating British industry in an effort to raise finance for a scheme to 'remove England from the back seat in which she languished all too long in pre-war competitive motoring.'

The first two replies – from Joseph Lucas Limited and Alfred Owen, the head of the Rubery Owen Organisation – were positive. Mays went to see Lucas first. He put his case and was caught unawares when the board enquired how much he would need. Maintaining a positive approach, but calculating off the top of his head, Mays asked for the free manufacture of parts such as magnetos – plus £1,000. He was immediately asked to whom the cheque should be made payable.

Later that day, Alfred Owen agreed to a similar amount, plus the supply of parts worth around £4,000. It was a remarkable start. Other companies, including motor manufacturers, followed suit, the Standard Company alone contributing £5,000. Within 12 months, Mays had collected £25,000, with the promise of a similar amount in parts.

It was not enough. Post-war inflation made a mockery of the budget, but with more than 100 firms now involved there was no turning back. In order to handle the mushrooming business on a proper basis, the British Motor Racing Research Trust was formed in July 1947. Members of the Trust were individuals or firms who had subscribed £100 or more. It was agreed that the car would be known as the British Racing Motor, or BRM for short.

Berthon had been at work on the car from the moment Mays had returned with the first two cheques. Perhaps feeling that they had to give their backers value for money, Mays and Berthon opted for a complicated and highly ambitious supercharged V16. Whatever the reason for such a curious choice, the engine would be of 1.5 litres to conform to the Grand Prix regulations of the time.

The centrifugal supercharger would be developed by Rolls Royce, based on their experience with aero engines, and the object of the entire exercise was the pursuit of power. Berthon talked of 500bhp, a massive improvement over the 425bhp enjoyed by Alfa Romeo, who were then dominating Grand Prix racing. But it was all too much in every respect.

The engine-build programme was hamstrung by supply problems as the well-meaning manufacturers, now 350 strong, struggled to get their houses in order before worrying about a racing car being built in Lincolnshire. The design had been completed in the spring of 1947 but the delivery of parts took from April 1948 to May 1949! And, when the car finally reached completion the following December, it would prove very difficult to drive. But it would sound glorious.

Mays and Berthon, however, were dead against giving the car a public airing at Folkingham. There were fierce arguments, but the men who knew most about the project were overruled. Such were the drawbacks of going motor racing by committee. The investors wanted to see something for their money. The Press Day was set for 15 December.

On a cold, wet and windy morning, Earl Howe removed a Union Jack to reveal a striking pale green car. Zipping up his windcheater and donning a crash helmet and visor, Mays climbed aboard and started the V16. The ground shook; the reporters were stunned. Mays set off for three laps of the improvised test track. Ironically, in view of what was to come during the next 12 months or so, the car ran beautifully.

The press immediately proclaimed that Britain had a world-beating car. Those inside BRM knew that the work had barely begun. In the midst of the congratulations and back-slapping, Mays did his best to reduce the rampant expectation as tactfully as he could. But to no avail. And, into the bargain, Mays was suffering from influenza; he had a temperature of 104. It would not be the last headache he would endure in the company of the BRM V16.

More for your money

At one stage, there had been talk of entering the BRM for a race at Silverstone the previous August, but it soon became apparent that such an idea was out of the question. The race meeting, to be known as the *Daily Express* International Trophy, was the direct result of the enthusiasm generated by the British Grand Prix a few months before. The *Daily Express* had been overwhelmed by the public interest in motor racing and, naturally, they could see that by associating themselves with the sport they might sell one or two extra newspapers along the way.

Taking matters a stage further, it was agreed to provide a more attractive race-day package for the spectators. The International Trophy meeting would include a number of races to be run in quick succession. It would put the organisation to a stiff test. They would now be dealing with a 500cc event (won by Eric Brandon, despite his crash helmet almost falling off) and production sportscars (a popular innovation, won by the 3.5 Jaguar XK 120 of Leslie Johnson), as well as laying on demonstrations by Bob Berry (aboard a JAP-Brough which was due to attempt to break the motor-cycle land speed record) and 'Goldie' Gardner. And then there would be two 20-lap heats and a 30-lap final for the International Trophy itself.

It was every bit as successful as the Grand Prix. The hunger for motor racing had not died down in the least and the crowd, estimated to be in excess of 100,000, witnessed a full day's entertainment, the highlight being the Formula 1 race, won by Ascari at the wheel of a Ferrari. Farina, in a Maserati, was second with Villoresi third in his Ferrari.

Ascari had averaged more than 89mph, thanks to the removal of the abhorred chicane at Club Corner. It was now accepted that Silverstone should be noted for its high speed, just as Monaco was known for a plethora of tight corners. This layout, measuring 2 miles 1,564 yards, would endure for 25 years. And so, too, would the *Daily Express* International Trophy.

The BRDC were, with some justification, able to describe that meeting as one of the most successful ever held in Britain. Even Donington at its best could only attract half the number of spectators. And as for Brooklands....

There was, however, a sad note. St. John 'Jock' Horsfall, a talented and popular British competitor, died from injuries received when his ERA crashed at Stowe. It was noted that the accident had been aggravated by the straw bales causing the car to overturn; not the first time this had happened. The BRDC, who organised the race meeting, were also rather startled when marshals on the spot offered widely differing opinions as to the cause of the accident. An immediate step was the introduction of Observers (usually senior police officers) around the track, and a look at new ways of defining the outline of the corners.

This, of course, assumed that Silverstone would become a permanent part of the British motor racing scene. The RAC had managed to obtain agreement from the Ministry that the land could be leased again in 1950, the rental being £900 plus rates, estimated at £450. Plans went ahead for a British Grand Prix. And, this time, the race would reach new heights in terms of recognition and status.

Grand Prix d'Europe

A memorable 1950 began when the FIA created the world championship for drivers to consist of seven races – the first of which would be the British Grand Prix at Silverstone. On top of that, it was also decided to confer the title *'Grand Prix d'Europe'* on the race; something of an honour even if the appellation was purely a nominal one which switched from Grand Prix to

Grand Prix at the FIA's discretion. Indeed, as the race programme pointed out, the *Grand Prix d'Europe* had not been awarded between 1931 and 1946. But, as far as the British were concerned, the title had a splendid ring to it.

The media, however, would soon coin an even better name. When it was announced that King George VI and Queen Elizabeth would attend, the event immediately became known as 'Royal Silverstone'. This would be the first time a reigning monarch had attended the Grand Prix. It was the ultimate accolade and elevated Silverstone and Grand Prix racing into the socially acceptable realms of Ascot and Wimbledon. Nonetheless, it did not disguise the fact that, beneath the bunting and brass bands, this was still a airfield race track built from straw, scaffolding and yards of rope. But who cared. It was international motor racing. And there was an excellent entry to prove it.

Alfa Romeo were back. After a year's absence, a 158 had been entered for the San Remo Grand Prix and nothing seemed to have changed; it won with ease. Mind you, it was driven by Juan Manuel Fangio, the Italian firm wisely snapping up the Argentine driver after his remarkable season in 1949. Fangio joined Farina and the remarkable Fagioli, who seemed, at 52, be enjoying an Indian Summer. The trio were known as the 'Three Fs.' And they were out in force at Silverstone.

As a concession to the British, and as a token of respect for his driving, Alfa brought along a fourth 158 for Reg Parnell. In fact, this car should have been entrusted to Consalvo Sanesi but the Italian was recovering from injuries received in the *Mille Miglia*, a daunting race for sportscars around 1000 miles of public roads in Italy.

Parnell fully justified his inclusion by giving Alfa Romeo a 'full house' on a front row, now reduced from five to four cars wide. The remaining 17 runners were outgunned from the moment practice began. 'Bira', almost two seconds slower than Farina, led the 'second division', the Prince entered as usual by Enrico Platé, who brought along a second Maserati for the previous year's winner, Baron de Graffenried. In fact, Maseratis outnumbered even the venerable ERAs. There was a 4CLT for Chiron; *Scuderia Ambrosiana* entered two for the Davids, Hampshire and Murray, while Joe Fry found a place on the back of the grid with an older 4CL.

Talbot were out in force once more with the familiar 4.5-litre unblown 'sixes' for, in starting order, Giraud-Cabantous, Eugene Martin, Rosier, Etancelin and Claes (now entered by *Ecurie Belge*). Of the various ERAs, Walker put his 'E'-type on the third row, ahead of Leslie Johnson, Bob Gerard and Cuth Harrison. Two Altas for Geoffrey Crossley and Joe Kelly completed the entry.

Farina set the pace throughout practice on Thursday and Friday, the cherry-red car lapping at an average of 93.85mph. With the remainder of the team just a second or so slower, the outcome of the race was obvious. But, like the surroundings, that was of little consequence. Saturday 13 May 1950 was a major occasion.

That being the case, it was hardly surprising that members of the British Motor Racing Research Trust had been applying pressure on Raymond Mays. The call to enter the BRM for the Grand Prix had been resisted but Mays, understandably, could not find an excuse when asked to demonstrate the car at Silverstone. With Royalty present, of course, it amounted to a command performance.

The car had reached 190mph (according to Mays) during tests at Folkingham not long before but, as ever, time was short and the demonstration was yet another unwanted intrusion. None the less, Mays completed a few laps and, of course, the fabulous sound of the green car merely raised expectations even further.

The King and Queen, accompanied by Princess Margaret, showed great interest in the BRM, all of which must have made Mays feel uneasy. Even so, he promised to compete in the International Trophy meeting three months later.

A Royal Flush

The appearance of the BRM contributed to the sense of occasion and there was no doubt that the presence, at long last, of the world-beating Alfa Romeos gave Silverstone that final touch of credibility.

The Italians had requested their pits to be at the top end of the row, the grass area immediately to the rear being neatly cut and roped off in their honour. And, on race morning, there was great excitement when mechanics drove the four 158s from their base at Banbury to the circuit; all highly illegal, of course, but nobody dared halt such a splendid procession. On a lesser note, the GPO created mild curiosity by bringing along a mobile post office. According to *Motor Sport*, 'Chiron, in racing attire, was one of the first to use it'.

The King and Queen took their places in the royal box after a tour of the circuit in the company of Earl Howe. And, with the BRM now on display in the paddock, yet another demonstration, courtesy of *Alfa Corse*, began at 2.30 pm.

William Boddy was watching the royal box intently, and with due deference, as his report in *Motor Sport* would subsequently show:

> *'Earl Howe, sat between the King and Queen, and as the flag was about to fall the King looked up from his programme and eagerly down towards the starting grid. As the cars roared away he appeared to be heavily interested, but the noise and the smoke took the Queen a trifle unawares, as the mass-start of a race does to those close to the course.....Princess Margaret seemed to want to concentrate solely on what was happening, and to regard conversation as merely incidental. But this is to anticipate.'*

Farina led from the start and such was the superiority of the Alfa Romeos that the drivers laid on a rather unconvincing mock battle, Fagioli moving ahead at the 10-lap mark, Fangio taking his turn five laps later with Farina returning to the front five laps after that. The rest of the field, meanwhile, was falling rapidly apart in a bid to keep up.

Walker and Johnson were soon out with gearbox and supercharger troubles while de Graffenried's race did not have such a happy ending this time, a broken con-rod bringing the Maserati to an expensive halt just before Abbey Curve. Chiron retired with a broken gearbox, and the very slim hope of a challenge from 'Bira' ended when fuel starvation stopped the Maserati on Hangar Straight.

The Alfa Romeos, meanwhile, were running like clockwork, the different coloured bands on the nose cowlings breaking the red monotony. Farina (white) maintained a narrow lead over Fangio (yellow) and Fagioli (blue) as the veteran and the 39-year-old 'new boy' swapped places at a furious rate. Parnell (green), the front of his 158 showing evidence of a collision with an errant hare, maintained a steady fourth place, untroubled by either Cabantous or Rosier.

Then came the pit stops. And still the Alfa armada ran imperiously on, all four cars getting away in 30 seconds and less. After 50 of the 70 laps had been completed, Fangio was in front but Farina, leaning back from the wheel in his beautifully composed style, was hovering close by. Ten laps later he was back in front, although whether by accident or design is not clear since Fangio had slowed momentarily.

The Argentine then put on a spurt but a patch of oil at Stowe caught him out, the 158 clouting one of the omni-present straw bales as Fangio spun off. Damage to an oil line would lead to an engine failure. And that was the end of the excitement, such as it was. It did, however,

Majestic. Farina makes his imperious way towards the chequered flag with the all-conquering Alfa Romeo 158.

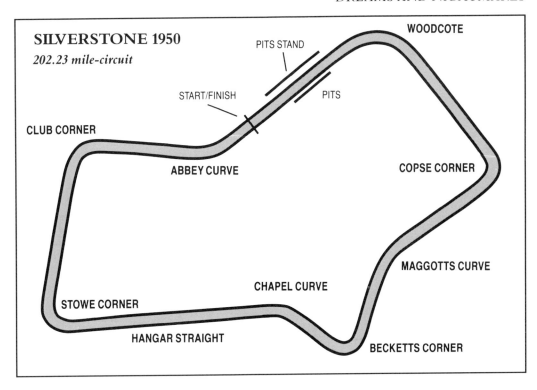

SILVERSTONE 1950
202.23 mile-circuit

PITS STAND

WOODCOTE

START/FINISH

PITS

CLUB CORNER

COPSE CORNER

ABBEY CURVE

MAGGOTTS CURVE

CHAPEL CURVE

STOWE CORNER

BECKETTS CORNER

HANGAR STRAIGHT

mark the beginning of a period of intense rivalry, the rather aloof Farina not taking kindly to the intrusion by the upstart from South America.

Towards the end of the race, Farina eased off and allowed Fagioli to close to within three seconds as they passed the time-keeper's bus, parked at its usual angle to the finishing line. Parnell received warm applause for his steady third place, almost a minute behind.

The rest, led by the rumbling Talbots, were nowhere. Gerard took sixth place behind Cabantous and Rosier, the ERA driver collecting the Fred Craner Memorial Trophy for the first British driver in a British car. Although he was three laps behind the leaders, Gerard had been made to work very hard by Harrison's ERA, the two changing places in the early stages, and Gerard claiming the place by a car's length after a late pit stop for a precautionary churn of fuel.

It had not been a classic race by any means and there were signs that the patience of the spectators, not to mention certain sections of the press, was beginning to run out. Mr. A. P. Bird wrote to *Motor Sport* to say that the 'lavatory accommodation was nothing short of disgusting'. And, judging by the following rather stiff summary of the race meeting, the magazine's editorial staff were none too pleased either.

'The R.A.C. Grand Prix de L'Europe, then, was no better than preceding races in the series, a sentiment with which we feel sure those who arrived late because of traffic congestion, those who spent four hours or so getting out of the car parks, those who received the wrong passes and those honorary club marshals who had to sleep the Friday night in old tents because R.A.C. patrols had taken the beds in the huts, will readily concur.'

Well, quite. Still, there was always the International Trophy to look forward too. The BRM would show those continentals a thing or two...

The first world champion

It had not been a classic race by any means and soon the Grand Prix teams moved on to Monaco for the second round of the 1950 championship. The street race had been struggling to make ends meet and the prospects of raising the necessary starting money in 1949 had caused the Monegasques to abandon the Grand Prix. Now it was back, albeit on an unsteady financial footing.

Etancelin's lumbering Talbot sits it out with Kelly's Alta through Woodcote.

So, too, were Ferrari, after missing the British Grand Prix in an attempt to regroup during a period of change at Maranello. Plans had already been laid for a switch from supercharged 1.5-litre to unblown 4.5-litre engines, Ferrari's new chief engineer, Lampredi, rightly arguing that there was potentially more power, and certainly lower fuel consumption, to be had from the unsupercharged route. As a result, development of the blown 125 had not been quite so intensive but, nonetheless, two such cars, equipped with a long wheelbase and a modified V12, were entered for Ascari and Villoresi. Interestingly, Maserati were represented by Chiron and Franco Rol, while *Scuderia Achille Varzi* had brought along two cars, one of which was for yet another unknown Argentine; José Froilan Gonzalez. We would also hear a lot more of this man.

For a start, Gonzalez put his 4CLT on the front row, alongside Farina – with Fangio on pole. Straightaway, the Alfa Romeo drivers were hard at it, Farina taking the lead through *Ste Devote*, Fangio moving ahead on the climb towards the Casino. The Argentine maintained his advantage as they swept down past the station, onto the sea front, through the tunnel and weaved through the chicane before powering along the quay. Safely through the left-hander at *Tabac*, Fangio raced on, unaware that there was mayhem behind him.

He had noticed that the wind had carried spray onto the quayside at the exit from *Tabac*. Farina, following closely, had not seen it. The Italian spun across the track, only to be hit by Gonzalez. Some cars got through but several did not, each collision blocking the track even further. And all of this was out of Fangio's sight as he accelerated out of the chicane for the second time. He seemed destined to crash into the wreckage yet, for no apparent reason, he slowed, motored gently around the corner and carefully picked his way through the disaster area.

In the absence of the warning flags which would be in evidence today, how had he known? He had noticed something about the crowd overlooking *Tabac*. There was movement, and the general colour of the scene did not seem right. Then he realised he was seeing the backs of the spectators' heads; they weren't watching him and yet he was leading the race. Clearly, some thing was holding their attention. So he backed off.

Such a remarkable example of cool awareness not only helped Fangio win the race but it also accounted for a major part of the genius which would make him one of the greatest drivers of all time.

That victory made it one race apiece as Fangio and Farina lined up on the front of the grid for the Swiss Grand Prix. They left the rest for dead. The lead changed hands continually as they lapped the field, but a broken valve would ultimately mean retirement for Fangio.

He made up for that in Belgium and France, leaving everything to play for in the final race at Monza. (The FIA in trying to control racing in the USA had included the Indianapolis 500 in the world championship as a sop to the Americans, but none of the Grand Prix teams participated in such a widely divergent race.) Fangio retired, leaving Farina to win the Italian Grand Prix. That meant three wins each but Farina became the first world champion thanks to his third place in the Belgian Grand Prix. Fangio would have his day, five times over in fact.

There was no question that Alfa Romeo were the pace-setters in 1950 but they had received a severe jolt at Monza; there was serious competition on the horizon. After continuous development work, Ferrari had begun to make their unblown V12 work, two 4.5-litre versions being entered for Ascari and top motor-cyclist, Dorino Serafini (replacing Villoresi, who had been injured during the Geneva Grand Prix).

Farina had led the race and, while he had the measure of Ascari, he could not pull away. Quite simply, that meant Alfa would lose since the unblown Ferrari would only need to make one pit stop compared with the two made necessary by the thirsty supercharged 158. In the event, Ascari's Ferrari retired with engine failure but he took over Serafini's car and climbed back to second place. Alfa may have been celebrating their championship, but the writing was on the wall. And it wasn't talking about the BRM.....

Mind-battering pressure

A great day had dawned a few weeks before on a showery August afternoon. One contemporary magazine had hailed it as 'the most important in the history of British motor racing.' They were referring, of course, to the long-awaited debut of the British Racing Motor in the International Trophy race at Silverstone.

Raymond Mays was still a worried man. The V16 had been misfiring and bending connecting rods at regular intervals and there was a deep sense of foreboding at Bourne. The high-speed misfire could not be traced despite endless modifications and nights without sleep – Berthon had gone so far as to make himself a temporary flat in the control tower at Folkingham. The car had been tested by Raymond Sommer, a big-hearted driver who gave his services free simply because the BRM, with its enormous power, excited him like no other car. Reg Parnell had been asked to drive the second entry at Silverstone and, like Sommer, Parnell felt that, on the basis of a brief test at Folkingham, the car had enormous potential. But still the engine trouble persisted.

It was decided not to attend the first official practice session so that further tests could be carried out. Then came the really bad news. A dawn run at Folkingham on the final day of practice had resulted in cracked cylinder liners on both cars. There was no way the BRM, could race.

Mays, in his book *BRM*, recalls what happened next:

> '*I explained the situation to the race authorities and the* Daily Express *who were the sponsors. I said: "let me speak over the microphone and tell the crowd the complete truth. It will be less of a disappointment for everybody than if we appear and fail."*
>
> *But naturally the organisers were extremely keen that BRM should run. They had advertised its appearance heavily. They did not want to lose their crowd-pulling star attraction. "Surely it is possible to get at least one car on the starting grid for the race tomorrow," they pleaded.*
>
> *The Trust Committee agreed with the organisers but, although I was in full sympathy with them and very conscious of the difficulties we were causing, I stood out firmly against risking a breakdown on our first appearance.*'
>
> *I was desperately tired. I had not had time to shave. I was nearly frantic with worry. The noise of the Ferraris at practice outside battered my mind. Alone I argued until the last possible minute and finally I was overruled by the Trust Committee. I was to produce a BRM the next day. I said: "You'll regret this day!" I was furious.*'

He was also right – but not quite for the anticipated reason. The engine would not get the chance to break.

The exhausted BRM mechanics had been hauled from their beds for another night's work. In the early hours of race morning, the *Daily Express* sent a Silver City Airways Bristol freighter to collect the car at nearby Cranwell and fly it to Bicester, where it was loaded onto a van (provided by the Austin Motor Company) and driven to Silverstone under police escort.

Now the pressure was really on. The *Daily Express* had produced a booklet entitled *BRM, Ambassador for Britain. The story of Britain's Greatest Racing Car*, while even the BBC had been presumptuous enough the previous evening to broadcast a programme under the title of 'British Achievement. The story of the BRM.'

Amid wild cheering, Sommer completed three laps to qualify for Heat 2. He took his place on the back of the grid, the engine revved beautifully, the flag dropped – and he travelled no more than a foot. A drive-shaft had snapped; ironically, a totally unexpected failure due to the wrong specification of steel.

The cheering immediately became jeering, some spectators cruelly tossing pennies into the cockpit as the car was wheeled into the paddock. Mays and his exhausted team neither knew nor cared that Farina and Fangio would each win a heat, with the champion-elect taking the 35-lap final. It was a total disaster for BRM.

Out on Friday

The International Trophy was notable on two further counts. The final had been run in continuous rain but Stirling Moss made the most of the treacherous conditions by finishing sixth. He was driving an HWM; a 2-litre Formula 2 car produced by the workmanlike team from Walton-on-Thames and tended by Alf Francis.

It was yet another feather in the cap of this promising young star and his efforts were recorded in *Autosport*, a new magazine launched at Silverstone and due to last much longer than the BRM whose cause it embraced with much patriotic fervour.

A few weeks later an editorial rightly called for 'a Dictator to put BRM on a business like footing, with someone at the top of the tree to make the decisions'. There was also the call for a public demonstration of the car as soon as possible.

On the opposite page, *Autosport* carried a report of the Italian Grand Prix, written by Gerard Crombac, their French Editor. 'Jabby' Crombac would become a well-known figure in Grand Prix circles as Editor of *Sport-Auto* and a friend and confidant of Colin Chapman and Team Lotus. In 1950, however, the introduction to his report of a meeting, where the first World Championship was finally settled no less, adequately sums up the priorities of the time. Crombac wrote:

> '*Man of the moment at Monza on 3rd September was Enzio Ferrari (sic), known to his intimates as "Al Capone". Signor Ferrari produced, not the expected 4,040 cc Ferraris, but a couple of brand-new 4,500 cc cars.*'

Then, in the final paragraph, tucked away on the back page of *Autosport*, the report says that 'Ascari just failed to catch Farina, whose win gives him the World Championship.' End of story. There is no mention of the fact anywhere else in the magazine. The cover shows a picture of an MG TD motoring gently through the Devon countryside and talks of the Brighton Speed Trials and a track test by John Bolster of the Sports Cooper.

Compare all of this to the hype which surround the conclusion of the World Championship today. On second thoughts, maybe they had their priorities right after all. These were indeed gentle times.

Raymond Mays probably didn't think so as he tried to motivate his demoralised workforce. On the day after the Silverstone fiasco, the *Sunday Pictorial* had carried the banner headline:

> '*Four Years, 18 Men and £160,000 – and much of it in Half-crown subscriptions – went to build the car that would not start.*'

In fact, the *Sunday Pictorial* was wrong. The half-crown subscriptions had nothing to do with the Trust. They were subscriptions from members of the BRM Association, a group of supporters who remained faithful to the project despite the many problems. And doubtless

Team-work. The well-drilled Alfa Romeo mechanics, under the guidance of team-manager Guidotti (dark glasses, right), refuel Parnell's car. Note the cover over the exhaust to reduce the risk of fire.

they were relieved to hear that, in a spirit of true British grit, Mays and his colleagues made enough progress with the car to venture into competition

It didn't happen until later in the year in pouring rain at the Goodwood circuit in Sussex, where Parnell won two races of five and twelve laps respectively. Even so, *this* news made the cover of *Autosport*. And, given the vicious response of the V16, Reg Parnell deserved all praise for driving the thing in appalling conditions.

Suitably encouraged, BRM entered two cars for Parnell and Peter Walker in the Penya Rhin Grand Prix at Barcelona. Both cars retired but not before they had shown a flicker of promise.

The Grand Prix had been a walkover for the Ferraris of Ascari, Serafini and Taruffi. Alfa Romeo were absent since this race did not count towards the world championship. In any case, they had, as one observer put it, 'been very roughly handled by Ferrari at Monza!' As the season drew to a close, there were rumours that Alfa were on the point of withdrawing once more. Fortunately, that would not be the case. But the 1951 British Grand Prix would prove to be a major turning point in another memorable year.

WITHDRAWAL SYMPTOMS

'I have forgotten many races.
But always fresh in my mind is 14 July 1951;
the British Grand Prix.'

Froilan Gonzalez

It was the motor racing equivalent of being called before the headmaster. Froilan Gonzalez had been told that Enzo Ferrari wanted to see him, and the humble Argentine did not know what to expect. He was confused and unsure of himself; the life of this straightforward man had taken one or two strange turns recently.

He had not enjoyed a particularly noteworthy season in 1950 but the Argentine Automobile Club had maintained their faith and he was given another year with *Equipe Achille Varzi*. At times like this, he said to himself, you wonder if anyone notices your efforts; whether the big break will come.

Then, shortly before the French Grand Prix, Gonzalez was approached by the Ferrari team-manager, who told him that Piero Taruffi, who had been standing in for the injured Serafini, was unwell himself; would Gonzalez care to take the drive? He would be a substitute, but no matter. He would be racing alongside Alberto Ascari and Luigi Villoresi. This was Froilan's chance to show the world. He jumped at the chance.

He led the race briefly. Then, when he stopped to refuel, Gonzalez was asked to hand over to Ascari, whose car had broken down. This he did without question although, inside, Gonzalez wondered what he had done wrong. Ascari finished second but nothing much was said to Gonzalez. And now Ferrari wanted to see him.

Gonzalez was led into Enzo's office which, even then, possessed a hallowed image. Or, at least, it did if you were, as Gonzalez described himself, a simple country boy. Ferrari asked him if he would like to sign a contract with the team. It was the motor racing equivalent of being asked to sing at La Scala. Gonzalez, who had dragged his feet going in, left the room walking on air

Apart from the prestige of being chosen by Enzo Ferrari, Gonzalez was excited by the fact that the team from Maranello was on the verge of breaking the Alfa Romeo stranglehold. The momentum which had begun at Monza the previous September had slowly gathered strength during the first few races of the 1951 season.

The supercharged Alfa Romeos were now developing around 410bhp from 1.5 litres, but Ferrari had been working on a twin-plug version of the 4.5-litre V12. It was not as powerful as the Alfa – but it was much more frugal, the straight-8 returning as little as 1.6 miles per gallon thanks to the need to run rich in order to keep the engine internals cool. And that meant

Sheer brute force. Froilan Gonzalez hustles the Ferrari through Stowe towards a historic victory.

Farina's overcooked Alfa Romeo at Abbey.

the fitting of additional fuel tanks. With the Alfa's capacity increased to 66 gallons, it still meant two refuelling stops would be necessary in a 300-mile race.

While Ferrari seemed intent on entering every race under the sun (non-championship Formula 1, Formula 2 and sports cars) Alfa Romeo confined themselves mainly to the world championship events in 1951.

The opening round, the Swiss Grand Prix at Berne, had not proved much. Ascari had been off form thanks to a nasty burn received on the arm during a Formula 2 race and Villoresi slid off the road in the very wet conditions which characterised this event. Taruffi had managed to keep Ferrari's name in the frame by finishing second between the Alfas of Fangio and Farina. At Spa, a jammed wheel at a pit stop had cost Fangio his second win in succession but Farina had been there to take the honours for Alfa Romeo.

The French Grand Prix turned out to be a furious battle which, after a change of cars for both Ascari and Fangio, was eventually settled in favour of the Alfa Romeo – Fangio taking over from an emotional Luigi Fagioli, now a brave veteran no longer physically able to deal with such a punishing pace in the broiling heat at Reims.

It had not been an easy victory for Alfa Romeo by any means. The British Grand Prix was next and, in the intervening few days, Froilan Gonzalez would have his painless interview with Enzo Ferrari.

100 mph!

Such had been the speed of the negotiations at Maranello, the programme for the British Grand Prix (price 2s [10p]) did not contain a portrait of José Froilan Gonzalez. It did not even mention his name on the entry list. Not that many people would have noticed, given the galaxy of stars signing on for a potentially thrilling confrontation.

Alfa Romeo had four cars (Fangio, Farina, Sanesi and Bonetto) while Ferrari brought along three of the type 375s for Ascari, Villoresi and, of course, Gonzalez. There would also be support from Peter Whitehead in Tony Vandervell's green 'Thinwall Special'. This was still the 125 from the previous year – but heavily modified and now powered by a single-plug 4.5-litre V12. And, on paper, this car had beaten the Alfa Romeos at the International Trophy a few months before! In fact the final, run in a downpour, was stopped after just six laps and Reg Parnell was leading at the time, the Alfas having sucked a fair amount of water into their superchargers.

Talbot returned to Silverstone with their familiar 4.5-litre cars for Rosier, Chiron, and Claes – who had sold his previous Talbot to Duncan Hamilton, the burly British driver bringing it along for his home Grand Prix. (Etancelin continued to be a member of the works team but his car had been damaged at Reims). The Maserati representation was now reduced to ageing 4CLTs for David Murray and John James while Philip Fotheringham-Parker was battling on with an even older 4CL.

The British Grand Prix would not have been the same without an ERA, Bob Gerard and Brian Shawe-Taylor now the sole representatives of the English marque while Joe Kelly was soldiering on with his Alta. And finally, still living in hope, BRM had entered two cars for Reg Parnell and Peter Walker.

Financial problems had seriously delayed the BRM's winter development programme – engine bench tests had to be stopped at 5.30 each evening simply because, according to Mays, BRM could not afford the overtime payments – and the entries for the Swiss Grand Prix had been withdrawn.

Mays did manage to secure additional backing but a recurrence of the high-speed misfire meant further failures and BRM's subsequent absence from Reims. The team were working their socks off but they knew that no excuse would be acceptable when it came to the British Grand Prix.

Their horror can be imagined, therefore, when a new problem with the oil system arose a week before the race. They even went so far as to run a car one evening by the light of hurricane lamps – and still the trouble persisted. Mays and Berthon had no alternative but to scrub practice at Silverstone.

Not that they would have had time to appreciate it, but the BRM team missed an epic battle during practice on Thursday as Alfa Romeo and Ferrari came out of their corners fighting. John Bolster, writing for *Autosport*, described the scene:

> *'Thursday found me walking round the circuit, trying to work out how on earth these boys get round the corners in the way they do.*
>
> *My stopwatch was busy in my hand, and I had a conversion table, so it was with immense excitement that I observed that Froilan Gonzalez had lapped at 99mph. His next tour looked even faster and, yes, the magic 100mph had been topped at last!*
>
> *The interesting thing is that he brakes later than anybody else, actually enters the corner faster, and gets through in an immensely long drift. In this he is abetted by the roadholding of the latest Ferrari, which does not slide its tail to the extent that the rival Alfas do. He has none of the ease in the cockpit that Farina exhibits, and certainly does not follow the same path every time. Unlike all the other drivers, he changes down without gunning his motor, and yet there is no clash of gears and the box stands up to the treatment. John Wyer and I listened to this for lap after lap at Woodcote, and were fair amazed. A phenomenon, this Froilan!*
>
> *Fangio was trying really hard, too, and once nearly came unstuck at Woodcote. Like his friend, he has an astonishing sense of balance when his car is in a slide, and is a master of the use of power, and bags of it, in getting through a curve mighty quick.'*

But not quick enough, it seemed. At the end of Thursday's practice, Gonzalez had lapped Silverstone in 1 minute 43.4 seconds, a full second quicker than Fangio, the lack of a comparatively long straight preventing the Alfa Romeo from really stretching its legs. And with the track being damp on Friday, those times would remain. In fact, honours were evenly divided across the front row, with Farina's Alfa Romeo beating Ascari, the number 1 Ferrari driver being two seconds slower than his novice team-mate. And just for good measure, Ascari knew that Gonzalez did not have the benefit of the latest twin-plug engine.

The absence of the BRMs during practice had a detrimental effect on the attendance, one or two newspapers forecasting that they were not going to turn up at all. It was reckoned that around 50,000 spectators arrived on Saturday, many of them choosing to travel by train. British Railways offered a return ticket from Euston to Blisworth for 19s (95p), including admission, but not the connecting bus fare between Blisworth and the circuit. Or, if you preferred, the Grey-Green coach company would make the round trip from London for 12s 6d (62½p). And, for those who stayed at home, the BBC had regular broadcasts on the Light Programme, Raymond Baxter providing the commentary, aided by Robin Richards at Stowe and John Bolster in the pits.

Doubtless the first piece of news imparted by Baxter was that the BRMs had finally arrived on race morning. And doubtless many an armchair critic would have passed a derisory comment or two concerning the lack of effort by the British team. If only they had known…

At 1am that morning, there had been a power failure at Folkingham. It was almost the last straw. Drawing on their last reserves of energy and enthusiasm, the mechanics completed their work by the light of the headlamps of the transporters driven up to the windows and small cars brought into the workshop. They reached Silverstone at 7am and the RAC stewards agreed to waive the necessity for practice laps. Both cars would start from the back row.

In the meantime, there was a runaway win for Stirling Moss in the 500cc race and, in 10th place, a Cooper-Norton driven enthusiastically by a certain B.C. Ecclestone. It was a name which the Grand Prix world would come to know only too well in 20 years' time…

Moss was later called upon to join Peter Walker and Peter Whitehead on a lap of honour in the Le Mans-winning C-Type Jaguar. Except that it wasn't the actual winning car. On the same day, an eagle-eyed *Autosport* reader had spotted another Jaguar, purporting to be the Le Mans winner, on display at the South Bank Show in London. His subsequent letter to the magazine forced the admission that the Silverstone car was not quite all it had been cracked up to be….

> *'For my money, the British Grand Prix of 1951*
> *rates high in the list of Great Races of History.'*
> William Court *(Speed World International)*

Patriotic sporting fevour had been pumped up a few days before when Randolph Turpin took the world middleweight title from Sugar Ray Robinson on a points decision at Earls Court in London. There seemed little chance of a British driver causing such an upset at Silverstone, at least not while the Ferrari and Alfa Romeo drivers were eyeing each other with such intensity. Poor Gonzalez was in a terrible state, as he recalled in the book *My Greatest Race.*

'I was very tense, very anxious. I had to rush to the toilet about five minutes before the start and I remember I was talking to myself all the time! There were some people there from Argentina trying to calm me, but I couldn't talk to them. I was thinking about nothing but this race and I didn't even hear what they were saying. Of course, I didn't speak English, so I didn't understand anything else that was going on all round me. I seem to have been in a trance.'

The reverie was broken by the horn as the minutes were counted down. Glad to be doing something positive, Gonzalez lowered his considerable bulk into the cockpit of the 375 Ferrari and looked across at the remainder of the front row: Fangio, Farina, Ascari; the cream of Grand Prix racing. No wonder poor Gonzalez was in a state.

As it turned out, he was not alone. So anxious were the occupants of the front row to reach Woodcote first, that all four drivers spun their wheels excessively and were immediately engulfed. Bonetto led the field on the opening lap and it was soon apparent that the carefully planned team tactics were no longer of any use. It was every man for himself. Just what Gonzalez wanted. He put the hammer down and took the lead on the next lap. Fangio gave chase.

'I knew it was important not to do anything stupid,' said Gonzalez. 'I also knew, of course, that the Alfa Romeo would need to take on extra fuel. So I let Fangio overtake me.'

During the next 15 laps, Fangio built up a lead of of five seconds, but Gonzalez hung on. It was an awe-inspiring sight, the hard-working Fangio being pursued by this man crouching over the steering wheel, the Ferrari indulging in glorious power slides at every corner. It was not elegant by any means and, indeed, Gonzalez had one or two anxious moments as he visited the edge of the track – and sometimes went beyond it.

Such was their pace that the Argentines had pulled out 44 seconds on the third-placed Farina who, in turn, was engaged in an equally fierce tussle with Ascari, these two having drawn clear of Bonetto and Villoresi. Alfa Romeo, Ferrari, Alfa Romeo, Ferrari, Alfa Romeo, Ferrari. It was delicately poised. Could Ferrari finally defeat the Alfas? The fuel stops would settle the

Farina raised the lap record to 99.99mph but he could do nothing about the furious competition at the front. Gonzalez, living up to his image of 'the Pampas Bull,' seemed to be trying to tear the steering wheel from its roots as he grasped the rim and appeared to physically push the car faster than it cared to go. Having lost time with a barrel and straw-bale bashing moment at Becketts, he gradually closed on Fangio and retook the lead on lap 39. The crowd loved it.

Fangio stopped at the end of lap 48, Gonzalez coming in 13 laps later. By now Ascari had retired with gearbox trouble, and Gonzalez climbed from his car and graciously offered it to his team-mate. Ascari would have none of it and urged Gonzalez to continue. The stop took 23 seconds. Fangio had taken 49 seconds to have his rear wheels changed and, of course, a full load of fuel added. The gap between the leaders as Gonzalez rejoined was 1 minute 19.2 seconds. Despite a superb effort from Fangio the race had been settled, Gonzalez relaxing his pace towards the end.

They had left the rest far behind. Villoresi, two laps down at the end, took third place after Farina had pulled off at Abbey Curve, smoke pouring from the engine compartment. Bonetto was a further lap behind the Ferrari but there was a rousing cheer for Reg Parnell as he brought the BRM into fifth place ahead of Sanesi. And, for good measure, Walker was seventh, the two Englishmen deserving medals for their guts and perseverance.

In the hurry to complete the cars, the BRM exhaust pipes had not been properly insulated and the drivers had been roasted. They had been placed in a considerable dilemma because each time they accelerated it meant their right foot was nearer the source of the discomfort and, of course, the exhaust would become even hotter. It was so bad that Parnell and Walker had wanted to retire at their pit stops but they were persuaded to continue after their legs had been wrapped in cotton wool soaked in burn dressings. There were further complications caused by fuel vapour swirling around the cockpit, yet somehow Parnell and Walker managed to race on despite being badly burned and blistered.

The Talbots had shown their age, Rosier struggling home 10th ahead of Gerard's ERA and Hamilton, who had spun more than once in his enthusiasm to keep the big Talbot under control. Whitehead, meanwhile, had lost three minutes while having the brakes adjusted, the Thinwall Ferrari finishing ninth.

When Froilan Gonzalez finally came to a halt, he was lifted bodily from the car; not a simple feat by any means – but such was the Ferrari team's delight that Alfa Romeo had finally been beaten. And Gonzalez had done it single-handed. He memories of the minutes which followed were somewhat blurred.

'It was very confusing,' he said. 'But very exciting. Everyone was shouting and talking; the mechanics saying over and over again that the Alfa Romeos had been beaten. Then I was taken to meet the Queen and I was given a laurel wreath. Of course, I understood little of what was said but it was a very nice feeling to have all those people congratulating me. On the winner's podium I was embraced warmly by Fangio. That meant a lot to me. Then they played the Argentine National Anthem. I had never experienced anything like this before. When I saw my country's flag being hoisted, it was just too much for me and I cried. That moment will live with me for ever.'

José Froilan Gonzalez
Only won two Grands Prix – and both of them were at Silverstone. The first, in 1951, was an historic occasion, the burly Argentinian giving Ferrari their first world championship victory. 'The Pampas Bull' made impressive viewing as he man-handled his car during a comparatively brief stay in Grand Prix racing.

Out on a high note

A fortnight later, Gonzalez impressed even more by lapping the Nürburgring two seconds slower than the fastest man, Ascari. It was the first time Gonzalez had seen the place. The first post-war German Grand Prix for Formula 1 cars turned out to be a three-cornered fight between the two Ferrari drivers and Fangio, the Alfa Romeo finishing second behind Ascari.

The battle continued at an average of more than 120 mph during the Italian Grand Prix but it was to be a disastrous day for Alfa Romeo. Two of their four cars retired after nine laps, Fangio burst a tyre, and then his engine, while a brilliant comeback by Farina in Bonetto's car was foiled by a bungled pit stop and a leaking fuel tank and he eventually finished third. Ascari won again, with Gonzalez second.

BRM, meanwhile, had left the paddock in disgrace, both cars being withdrawn after another catalogue of disasters and management muddles. It was the last time that the V16 BRM would be seen at a major Grand Prix.

With one round to go in the drivers' championship, Fangio had 27 points, Ascari 25, Gonzalez 21 and Farina 17.

There was a tremendous tussle during the Spanish Grand Prix between Ascari and Fangio but tyre trouble for Ferrari meant Fangio went on to win and claim his first world championship. And this time, *Autosport* would carry an autographed photo of the great man on their cover the very next week...

Alfa Romeo may have taken the title for the second year in succession but they knew as well as anyone that the British Grand Prix had been a major turning point. The days of the fabulous 'Alfetta' had, at long last, drawn to a close. There were plans for a replacement, but an application for a five-fold increase in their government grant was refused and Alfa Romeo withdrew from Grand Prix racing on the spot.

Giv'us a job

'Please Mr. Mays give me the chance to show you how I can drive. I have just been released from prison. I pinched a Jaguar for a smash and grab and the police nearly caught me by the BBC. I accelerated like hell and touched eighty down Regent Street and never hit a thing. Give me a try and I'll show what sixteen cylinders can do.'

The young man didn't get the job. But this letter to Raymonds Mays summed up the passions which continued to be aroused by BRM. And, almost predictably, the company was to become embroiled in even more controversy in 1952.

The first sign of trouble could be traced back to the previous year when the FIA announced a change of Formula, due to come into force in 1954. Their reasoning – as much advanced warning as possible – was perfectly sound but there were disastrous side-effects due to a number of unforeseen circumstances.

When Alfa Romeo withdrew, it more or less cut the feet from under any hopes of competitive racing in 1952. Ferrari would be there, of course, but who would provide the competition for such a first-rate car? It was immediately evident that race promoters faced the prospect of a Ferrari whitewash as they walked all over the shambling BRM outfit and a number of ancient and windblown ERAs, Maseratis, Talbots and the like.

Much to the alarm of Raymond Mays, one by one the race organisers began to apply for

Reg Parnell forces himself and the BRM to finish fifth.

Formula 2 races and the governing body nailed the lid on Formula 1 when they granted these Formula 2 events world championship status.

There had, however, been a slim hope of Formula 1 maintaining its prestige. The Valentino Grand Prix, a non-championship race in Turin, was scheduled for the early season and everyone looked to this for an indication of how BRM would fare against Ferrari.

BRM withdrew; Ferraris finished 1-2-3, and that was that.

Of course, BRM took a considerable amount of stick – but then they were becoming used to that. Indignant letters to *The Times* were now the norm, although during this period BRM were also stoutly defended by their chairman, Alfred Owen, and Lord Brabazon of Tara. Even so, it seemed that there were few events of distinction in which the BRM could race. In which case, Ferrari would be in the same boat.

Well, not quite. Formula 2, introduced for the 1948 season, was for cars up to 2 litres unsupercharged (or 500cc supercharged, although no one bothered with this alternative). And Ferrari happened to have a perfect car in the '500' model. This had been developed throughout 1951, the in-line 4-cylinder engine being uncomplicated, powerful – and light.

One attractive aspect of Formula 2 was the variety of competitive cars springing from many a workshop. Gordini in France and Maserati and Osca in Italy had new cars in the pipeline. But, from a British standpoint, there was tremendous interest in a busy little area to the south-west of London. Here, within about 10 miles of each other, were HWM, Connaught, Alta and Cooper, all busily preparing serious campaigns for the coming season. Then there were cars from Frazer Nash and ERA, each company responding vigorously to the added stimulus of being associated with the front line of motor racing.

The future, though, looked less promising when Alberto Ascari kicked off with three consecutive wins for Ferrari at Syracuse, Pau and Marseilles. Ferrari did not enter the *Daily Express* International Trophy at Silverstone, leaving the Gordinis to fight it out with the British teams, HWM taking a most popular and well-deserved 1-2 in the final.

Ferrari did not miss the Swiss Grand Prix since it marked the start of the championship proper. Farina, made redundant by Alfa Romeo, had joined his former rivals but he had to retire, leaving Taruffi to give Ferrari the anticipated win as Ascari was competing at Indianapolis.

Ascari was back in time for Monza, a race which would have far-reaching effects despite its non-championship status. This was seen as the point when the Ferrari's threatened monopoly would cease since they would have to deal with new 6-cylinder Maseratis handled by Fangio, Gonzalez (dropped by Ferrari for 1952) and Bonetto.

It was a disaster for Maserati. Fangio, having competed in the Ulster Trophy the previous day, had been grounded in Paris, leaving him with no alternative but to drive to Monza. Exhausted, he started from the back of the grid without practising and crashed heavily on the second lap, suffering neck injuries which would keep him out of action for the rest of the season. It was a salutary lesson for the great man. It also blew a hole in the Maserati attack, which then crumbled and Ferrari filled the first three places.

Ascari won in Belgium and France, the latter race held for the first time at a very fine road circuit near Rouen. The crowd flocked there in huge numbers, Gallic pride having been pumped up the previous Sunday by a brilliant win for Gordini in the non-championship Reims Grand Prix.

The impoverished little team had provided France with a hero in Jean Behra, a former motor-cycle racer who drove with great fire and passion. Ascari had tried everything he knew to get by and, contrary to all expectations, it was the Italian car which broke under the strain.

The victory for the little blue car gave hope not only to France, but to the rest of the motor racing world. And Gordini had entered for the British Grand Prix in three weeks time which, despite its Formula 2 status, was shaping up to be a very fine race indeed.

In at the deep end

When Fangio crashed on that fateful morning at Monza, he had been racing the previous day at Dundrod, a fearsome eight-mile course on a plateau to the north of Belfast. And to make matters even more interesting, he had been driving a BRM. Taming the beast on a flat airfield was one thing, but pointing it down long narrow roads, broken by blind brows and lined by grass banks, gate posts and telegraph poles was a different proposition entirely. Dundrod was strong meat and it would claim it dues during a regrettably brief period on the motor racing

Anyone who raced there was unlikely to forget the experience and a victory at Dundrod was worth savouring.

In the previous summer of 1951, Farina had won the Ulster Trophy at the wheel of his trusty Alfa Romeo and, on the same day, the supporting races were carried off by two bright young Englishmen, the 10-lap handicap going to the Riley of Mike Hawthorn while a dashing 19-year-old by the name of Peter Collins had won the five-lap scratch race for 500cc cars at the wheel of a JBS-Norton. They were both entered for the 1952 British Grand Prix. And so, for that matter, was Stirling Moss. All told, it would be the best field of British drivers and cars yet assembled for the home event.

Pride of place on the entry list, of course, went to the three works Ferraris for Ascari, Farina and Taruffi, backed up by three similar but privately entered 500s for Rosier (who would eventually be a non-starter), Rudi Fischer from Switzerland and Roy Salvadori, in a car owned by the Belfast newspaper proprietor Bobby Baird. There were also two unblown 2-litre V12s for Peter Hirt and Peter Whitehead.

Gordini entered cars for Robert Manzon, 'Bira' and their star driver, the suave Maurice Trintignant (Behra was recovering from one of the many accidents which marked his all-or-nothing approach to racing). The Gordinis were the latest six-cylinder models, an older 'four' being entered by *Ecurie Belge* for Johnny Claes. De Graffenried was back with a Maserati 4CLT heavily modified by Enrico Platé, this great enthusiast (the Fifties equivalent of Enzo Osella) giving his second car to a promising young American from Paris by the name of Harry Schell. More up-to-date versions, the so-called A6 GCM, were to be driven by the South Americans, Bianco and Cantoni.

That accounted for nearly half the field. The rest was made up of British entries of varying degrees of competence – but the front runners really did carry a great deal of promise, even if the thought of giving the Ferraris a run for their money was pushing optimism a bit too far. The problem lay with a comparative lack of finance to match the sheer devotion of these teams. That and the fact that most of them had no alternative but to develop engines which had sportscar derivations.

Connaught, for example, used an engine based on a four-cylinder Lea-Francis to power cars for Dennis Poore, Eric Thompson, Kenneth Downing and Kenneth McAlpine. It was McAlpine's enthusiasm for the first Connaught sportscars, built in the late 1940s, which encouraged him to sponsor the construction of a Formula 2 car. Gradual development over the past season had led to a neat and competitive machine, one which was capable of taking on the HWM team, a known and respected quantity in this formula.

John Heath and his team from Walton-on-Thames brought along three of their latest single-seat HWMs for Duncan Hamilton, Lance Macklin and the promising Peter Collins. Mike Hawthorn, meanwhile, was part of a five-car entry of Cooper-Bristols for Alan Brown, Eric Brandon, Murray and Parnell.

ERA were still competing and Stirling Moss had the latest G-type, which featured the same 6-cylinder Bristol engine found in the Coopers. Alta, apart from supplying the engines in the HWMs, were represented by Graham Whitehead. There was a Frazer Nash Le Mans Replica sportscar (with the wings and lamps taken off) for Tony Crook while Bill Aston entered his rather specialised and extremely slow Aston-Butterworth.

It promised to be an intriguing race, and in all the excitement it was easy to forget that, for a time, it seemed there might not be a British Grand Prix at all. Or, at least, not at Silverstone.

Alberto Ascari
Considered to be one of the greatest drivers of the fifties. A perfectionist with a precise style, he won the British Grand Prix in 1952 and 1953, the years he became world champion. Quiet and modest, the Italian drove mainly for Ferrari. Died of injuries received when he crashed inexplicably while testing at Monza in 1955.

A new lease of life

'The RAC has announced that it will not renew the lease on Silverstone airfield circuit after the present year. Whilst the Club is most anxious for such facilities as have existed at Silverstone and elsewhere to continue, it has come to the conclusion that it is most inappropriate that it should continue to remain lessee of a motor racing circuit, and that in retaining the lease, it may deter other interested and suitable bodies, who would be acceptable to the authorities, making arrangements of a more permanent character there or elsewhere.'

Autosport 25 May 1951

Clearly, the time had come for the RAC to stand down. By taking on the lease at Silverstone, they had made a major contribution towards the revival of post-war motor racing in Britain. Running a race track was not a responsibility to be undertaken by the governing body of the sport and, besides, they were sensitive to uninformed accusations that the RAC were using Silverstone to make a profit. So, when they did not renew the lease, the future of Silverstone as a race track seemed very uncertain.

There was talk of the London County Council reviving the Crystal Palace track, but even if they did the narrow circuit would be far from suitable for a Grand Prix. Certainly, the Boreham airfield in Essex had proved that it could cope with Formula 1, but at the time it did not seem possible to take the necessary measures to build a permanent Grand Prix facility there.

Desmond Scannell and the BRDC could see that there was no alternative but to take over the Silverstone lease. It was a major undertaking for what was essentially a small club but the members – and the *Daily Express* – responded magnificently. Motor racing and the Grand Prix would continue at Silverstone in 1952.

In order to invest a degree of permanence, the first move had been to construct brick-built pits, rudimentary by today's lavish standards but a necessary luxury then. A new site was chosen just after Woodcote corner and this had the advantage of allowing the use of the nearby runway (later to become the Club circuit) as a paddock. In addition, many of the corners had been slightly modified and the lap distance now measured 2.926 miles.

Thinking on a more commercial basis, the BRDC built a walkway along the top of the pits and, at the Grand Prix, charged £2 10s (£2.50p) for admission to the balcony and the paddock, the whole area being known as the Stewards Enclosure.

Anyone spectating from the top of the pits would have had an excellent view of the Ferraris powering out of the very fast Woodcote corner on their way to the first three places on the grid. Manzon, fourth fastest in the Gordini, was five seconds slower than Farina's pole position time...

Downing led the charge of the British brigade, with Parnell and Hawthorn placing their Cooper-Bristols alongside the Connaught on the second row. All told, there were nine green cars spread across rows two, three and four. But everyone knew that the red Ferraris at the front would be untroubled.

Dull and slightly overcast

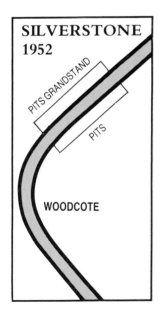

SILVERSTONE 1952

PITS GRANDSTAND

PITS

WOODCOTE

At the 1952 Grand Prix new pits had been built after Woodcote Corner.

And so it proved. Ascari led all the way; there was not even the hope that he might lose ground in the pits since the Italian would run non-stop. Indeed, he was a lap ahead of Taruffi at the finish, Ascari's team-mate having spent some time making up for a poor start. It took Taruffi 14 laps to work his way past the Connaughts and Cooper-Bristols to claim third.

Thirteen laps later, Taruffi assumed second place when Farina stopped to attend to a misfire. The change of plugs cost three minutes, and even then the problem was not cured completely, although the Ferrari appeared to revive in the closing stages and Farina narrowly missed catching Thompson's fifth-placed Connaught.

The British cars could not hope to keep up and the Connaught challenge had been severely dented by the need to stop and take on fuel. All of which let Hawthorn, driving with the press-on enthusiasm which would catch Enzo Ferrari's eye, move his little Cooper-Bristol into third place, helped in part by a pit stop which was vastly superior to the chaotic efforts of the Connaught team. Collins and Moss, meanwhile, had retired with ignition and engine problems. And the Gordinis were nowhere, Manzon and Trintignant running into transmission trouble.

It had been a dull, overcast day and that, in some ways, summed up the race. Certainly, the final straw had been the retirement of both BRMs from the *Formula Libre* race – but not before Gonzalez had the crowd on its feet with his efforts to stay on terms with Taruffi in the victorious Thinwall Ferrari. Moss, however, had won a superb wheel-to-wheel contest with Don Parker in the 500cc race, but only after Parker's driving chain had snapped half-way round the last lap.

It would make up for Moss's tribulations later in the day with G-type ERA, a project which Moss would later describe as 'making an awful lot of fuss about doing very little.' Certainly, he must have felt extremely frustrated as he spun while trying to compensate for overheating problems, only to watch Hawthorn sail into third place with the infinitely more straightforward Cooper.

It was enough to make a man want to take up smoking, the last thing Stirling would do, of course. At least, that's how we see Moss today. But in 1952, the Grand Prix issue of *Autosport*

carried a half-page ad under the heading:

'"When I smoke – I'm choosy," says speed-merchant Stirling Moss.' The ad went on to say:

'For Motor Racing, like most sports, one has to keep in strict training. "I'm a light smoker," says Stirling Moss, "and that makes the taste of a cigarette an important consideration. Craven 'A' give me all I want of a smoke – and nothing I don't!"'

And there, alongside the copy, was a picture of the speed-merchant, helmet on, cigarette in hand, looking the part.

Certainly, the smooth image created by the ad was a far cry from the sight of Alberto Ascari washing the grime of 85 laps from his face with the aid of water from a tap at the back of the paddock. Not a motor home or a physio in sight. Judging by today's standards, one wonders how Ascari and his colleagues survived…

Proof that Ascari thrived on such a seemingly spartan existence was demonstrated during the next three championship Grands Prix. He won them all and carried off the world title. Looking at the year overall, it was no contest although, towards the end of the season, development work on the Maserati began to show dividends, Gonzalez turning in some magnificent performances.

But, when the record books are examined, they show Alberto Ascari was behind the wheel of the winning car on 11 occasions, six of them counting towards the championship. Because of such monotony and the fact that the Formula 2 cars were less spectacular than their Grand Prix predecessors, 1952 was hardly a classic year. Indeed, there were a mere five Formula 1 races. A Ferrari won them all. And BRM did not register a single finish.

By this stage, even the loyal *Autosport* had abandoned the cause, a strongly worded and well-reasoned feature coming out in favour of winding up the project and saving the country from further embarrassment.

On 4 September 1952, an Extraordinary General Meeting of the BRM Trust agreed to sell. Mays, when asked to estimate the worth of his cars, reported that they could only be valued as scrap – about £500 each.

The following month Alfred Owen took over the assets and liabilities of this sadly troubled company, although in many ways it was a relief to Mays and Berthon since they were more than happy to continue with the project under the auspices of the Owen Organisation. Better days were ahead. They could hardly have got any worse.

Accidents during practice are never serious

Britain's attention now switched from cars to drivers, particularly when it became clear towards the end of 1952 that Enzo Ferrari was keen to sign Mike Hawthorn.

Matters seemed so much simpler then; none of the furtive meetings and wrangles over money and contracts which characterise every move the modern-day Grand Prix driver makes. Compared with the ballyhoo surrounding Nigel Mansell's signature on a Ferrari contract for 1989, Hawthorn's approach, as outlined in his book *Challenge Me the Race*, is almost beyond belief. Hawthorn says Tony Vandervell had 'kindly spoken up for me' and Ferrari had shown interest. Hawthorn wrote:

> *'Ferrari's asked if I would like to drive one of their cars (in the Modena Grand Prix). I said I would, but first of all I would like to try my Cooper-Bristol round; it was a twisty circuit and the Cooper had good acceleration and cornered quite well on that sort of track.*
>
> *They said: "Yes, try it by all means, and if you think you can do it better with the Cooper, drive that, but we would like you to drive the Ferrari."*
>
> *I said: "I don't think the Cooper will be quicker but I would like to try it." They took me out one day and we unloaded the Cooper, but it was not quite ready so they asked me to try the Ferrari.'*

Hawthorn duly tried the Ferrari, liked it and immediately agreed to race it at Modena. Ferrari said they would bring one along for official practice.

On the appointed day, Hawthorn's car was not quite ready and he went out for a few laps with the Cooper. Forgetting he was no longer in the Ferrari, he braked later than the Cooper wanted to know about, locked his brakes and slammed into straw bales and concrete posts at around 80 mph. There were no broken bones but the accident made an impression on Hawthorn in every sense:

> *'There were no ambulances or doctors there – nobody bothered with that sort of thing as this was only practice, not the race. I had only been wearing a jersey and where I had hit the deck it had been torn off; all one shoulder and my back had had the skin taken off and were covered in dirt and grit and so on.'*

Hawthorn was confined to bed for a few days. While his relaxed negotiations had merited the occasional line in *Autosport*, the accident was not worth much more. Today, it would be half a page, with bland quotes from the driver's battery of public relations people and personal physicians, all of whom would have been on the spot within seconds of the car having come to rest.

Indeed, at the beginning of December 1952, tucked inside the magazine, there was a picture of Hawthorn sitting in a Ferrari, the caption saying matter-of-factly that he had signed. It was, in many ways, to be the saving of the 1953 season.

Wheel to wheel

The championship opened in Argentina, Ascari leading Villoresi home to signal a repetitive year. But Maserati had been hard at work. An improved, sleeker version of their six-cylinder car was wheeled out in May and they had signed three hard-charging drivers; Fangio (now fully recovered), Gonzalez and Onofre Marimon, a protégé of Fangio. They went on the attack almost immediately.

Ferrari won the Dutch Grand Prix but Gonzalez forced his Maserati into a 49-second lead at Spa – then his accelerator pedal broke and Fangio retired, leaving Ferrari with another 1-2.

On to Reims and one of the classic motor racing encounters of the fifties. It was between just two drivers; Juan Fangio and Mike Hawthorn. They ran neck-and-neck for lap after lap, a powerful duel with the young Englishman forcing Fangio to use every trick he knew to stay on terms. Hawthorn described the battle thus:

> *'We would go screaming down the straight side by side absolutely flat out, grinning at each other, with me crouching down in the cockpit, trying to save every ounce of wind resistance. We were only inches apart and I could clearly see the rev. counter in Fangio's cockpit.'*

Hawthorn could also see that Fangio had lost first gear. On the last lap, Hawthorn braked very late, took a tight line through the final hairpin, shoved the car into first and floored the throttle. The extra impetus from the initial acceleration gave Hawthorn the edge he needed for that final sprint to the line. And Fangio, apart from struggling without first gear, also had to deal with a very late challenge from Gonzalez!

It was that sort of race. It was also the first Grand Prix win by an Englishman since Dick Seaman's victory at Nürburgring in 1938. Silverstone rubbed their hands with promotional glee; the British Grand Prix was next on the agenda.

A repeat performance

Maserati and Ferrari were out in full force. There were 500s for Ascari, Hawthorn, Farina and Villoresi while Maserati entered Gonzalez, Fangio, Marimon and Bonetto. The Italian teams dominated the front two rows, Ascari claiming pole, with Gonzalez and Hawthorn on identical times (the timing was to the nearest second!) and Fangio redressing the balance for Maserati by taking a place on the outside of the front row. Farina, Villoresi and Marimon were next, three seconds covering the first seven cars.

The competition, if you could call it that, ranged from the Gordinis of Trintignant, Schell and Behra through the now familiar collection of Connaughts, HWMs and Coopers to sundry Maseratis and Ferraris from continental privateers. Peter Collins was in an HWM but the Cooper-Alta for Stirling Moss was withdrawn following an engine failure at Reims. And, interestingly *Ecurie Ecosse* entered a Cooper-Bristol for Jimmy Stewart, elder brother of the wee Scot who, in 16 years time, would be the talk of Silverstone.

In 1952, however, one of the main points of discussion concerned the erection of small towers of scaffolding at various points around the track. BBC Television had arrived. Unfortunately, the race would make very boring viewing.

In a repeat of the previous year, Ascari led from start to finish although, in the early stages, the Maseratis were determined not to let him get away with it. Fangio gave chase, forcing Ascari to break the lap record on lap two and, next time round, Gonzalez had pushed past his Maserati team-mate and had equalled Ascari's lap record.

While all this was going on, the crowd were naturally hoping for some fireworks from Hawthorn. The chap with the red helmet, windcheater jacket and bow tie would not let them down.

Having made what was becoming a customary poor start, Hawthorn had just overtaken Marimon for fifth place when he arrived too quickly into Woodcote. Going wider all the time, the Ferrari then started to spin as Hawthorn reached the exit, a small wooden fence being shattered as he charged backwards onto the broad grass verge. Scattering photographers as he went, Hawthorn continuing to gyrate at high speed, fortunately in the general direction he wanted to travel. Maintaining great composure, he kept the engine running and finally caught the car before accelerating back into the race, almost without losing momentum. The packed grandstands rose in spontaneous applause.

The rough ride had popped the fuel filler cap open, but otherwise the car was unharmed. After a quick pit stop to have the cap shut, Hawthorn rejoined, now in last place.

Ascari and Gonzalez had continued to circulate at the same pace but the prospects of a close finish took a knock when the race officials spotted oil spraying from the back of the Maserati and leaving a treacherous trail on the road. They immediately informed Gonzalez's pit, who acknowledged – but did nothing. With cars now sliding on the oil, there was no alternative but to reach for the black flag and display it, along with the number 24.

The driver of car 24 was far too busy to bother with minor details such as reporting to the pits. Gonzalez pressed on, the agitated officials now almost leaning into the cockpit each time he passed the start line.

Gonzalez, realising the officials were pretty angry now, finally arrived at his pit in a towering rage himself. The oil leak had stopped and, after telling the officials what he thought of them in colourful Spanish, Gonzalez roared back into the race, the Argentine now fourth. A local journalist, meanwhile, was busy dusting himself down, a well-meaning attempt to act as interpreter and take the heat from the fracas merely resulting in the scribe being bundled against the pit counter. For many observers, it was the highlight of the race.

Indeed, from here on, Hawthorn's climb back through the field would be the only point of interest. That and the fact that a brief shower of rain in the closing stages caused cars to spin

Losing his shirt. Roy Salvadori presses on with the Connaught.

in all directions. But Ascari was too experienced to be caught out like that. With almost a minute in hand over Fangio, he reduced his pace by several seconds a lap and came home an easy winner.

The British contingent, apart from being destroyed by Ferrari and Maserati, had been decimated by mechanical failures, literally from the word go, McAlpine and Crook failing to get off the start line! Nonetheless, Tony Rolt had worked his way into a steady sixth position when a half-shaft broke on Connaught. Jimmy Stewart, the youngest driver in the field, immediately inherited the place – only to spin off in the wet at Copse. At the end of the day, the best-placed 'local' combination turned out to be the Cooper-Bristol of Ken Wharton in ninth place. He was 10 laps behind Ascari.

With Hawthorn working his way into fifth place behind Gonzalez, the finishing order read Ferrari, Maserati, Ferrari (Farina), Maserati, Ferrari and Maserati (Bonetto).

It would take Maserati until the penultimate round, the Italian Grand Prix, to finally score a long-awaited victory, and this came only after an extraordinary two-car battle, Fangio and Ascari often grinning at each other as they swept side-by-side round the autodrome. The outcome was settled when Ascari spun at the final corner. But, no matter; by then, the championship was already safe in Ascari's hands for a second successive season. And the Formula 2 world championship interlude was drawing to a close.

In 1954, Formula 1 would return to the front line. And so would Mercedes-Benz.

CHAPTER 7

BACK TO THE BLITZKRIEG

Fresh formula; familiar faces

It was like the arrival of the school bully in the playground; you wanted to tell him to go away, but knew you couldn't.

As the 1953 season reached its conclusion at Monza, a familiar portly figure, stop watches slung around his neck, had appeared in the pit lane. The preceding 15 years had done nothing for Alfred Neubauer's waistline, but neither had it impaired his sharp eye for detail. The Mercedes-Benz team-manager had turned up at previous races, frequently accompanied by Rudolph Uhlenhaut, the chief engineer unashamedly measuring and noting the dimensions of any car which took his fancy. The pre-war domination by Mercedes-Benz had not yet faded into the mists of time. The presence of these German gentlemen could only mean one thing; trouble.

The Daimler-Benz organisation had, in fact, made no secret of their wish to return to Grand Prix racing. There had been a touch of *déjà-vu* in 1951 when three 1939 cars were brought back to life to fill the front row of two non-championship races in Argentina. They were beaten on each occasion by Froilan Gonzalez, performances which would bring the Argentine driver to Enzo Ferrari's attention and cause Daimler-Benz to go away and have a re-think.

In fact, Mercedes-Benz knew exactly what they would do as soon as the FIA announced the change in formula, due to come into force in 1954. Engines would be limited to 2.5 litres unsupercharged; the 750cc supercharged alternative having no appeal to anyone, least of all Daimler-Benz.

They set to work on a straight-8 fuel-injected engine of an advanced design. The chassis would also bristle with innovation; a necessary measure given the work going on in the Ferrari and Maserati factories in preparation for the new season. And yet, despite time – and Juan Manuel Fangio – being on their side, the German cars were not ready for the start of the season in Argentina.

Ferrari began by developing a 2.5-litre version of their highly successful four-cylinder engine and dropping it into the previous year's Formula 2 cars, now suitably dubbed '625.' A new chassis, known as the 'Squalo' (shark), appeared at Monza but the signs were that this rather tubby car was in need of further development. Drivers were Farina, Hawthorn and Gonzalez.

Encouraged by their narrow victory at Monza the previous September, Maserati had produced a 2.5-litre, heavily-revised version of their six-cylinder engine and a new chassis to put it in. This very sleek car, one of the first to feature a wrap-round windscreen in place of the traditional aeroscreen, was known as the 250F and would become one of the most successful designs of the 2.5-litre era. Maserati had taken Fangio ('on loan' while Daimler-Benz completed their cars) and Marimon onto their driving strength and they made a promising, if rather lucky, start to the season when Fangio won in the wet in Argentina.

It was, in a way, a bad omen for Ferrari. Work on the new car was stepped up. But there was a fundamental problem when the drivers, almost to a man, found it difficult to feel comfortable with the car's handling; there was an alarming tendency for the Ferrari to spin out of control without warning once the limit of adhesion had been reached. Ferrari entered both the old (625) and the new cars (553) for the non-championship races and matters took a turn for the worse in Syracuse.

Hawthorn's car (a 625) burst into flames after the Englishman had glanced a wall, the impact causing the filler cap to pop open and fuel to slop onto the hot exhaust pipe. Hawthorn managed to evacuate the car, hurdle a wall and extinguish his burning clothing by rolling in a field.

Gonzalez, seeing the blaze, assumed Hawthorn was trapped and stopped to give assistance even though the full tank of fuel could have exploded any second. He was relieved to spot Hawthorn eventually, but the brave Argentine was not so happy when he turned round to see

Moss, his hand raised, coasts in after an impressive performance with the Maserati. Officials at the leader-board struggle to keep up since Moss (number 7) had passed Fangio (number 1) a few laps before.

his Ferrari rolling down the slope towards the blaze. Both cars were burnt out.

Hawthorn was confined to hospital while he recovered from second-degree burns to his legs and hands. Fortunately it was several weeks before the first European round of the championship in Belgium.

Fangio won again for Maserati and Ferrari's misfortune continued, Gonzalez suffering from engine trouble on the opening lap and Hawthorn being badly affected by gases from a cracked exhaust pipe. Nonetheless, Ferrari were gradually licking the new car into shape and they felt reasonably confident upon reaching Reims for the third round. Then they saw the Daimler-Benz transporters from the *Rennabteilung*.

Inside were three silver cars which simply took the breath away. Not only did these W196 models have the very latest engine and chassis technology from Stuttgart, but they were clothed in all-enveloping aerodynamic bodies for this very fast circuit. By comparison, the Ferraris and Maseratis seemed to be from a different era. And not only did the Mercedes-Benz look sensational, they had performance to match. The only drawback to be seen at this stage was the political necessity to employ German drivers although, wisely, they made an exception in the case of Fangio, now returned from Maserati. But it had to be said that Karl Kling, a former motor-cyclist, and the young Hans Herrmann were not top-rate.

Even so, the Mercedes-Benz team laid on a demonstration which sent rivals into despair. Such was the pace that cars blew up right, left and centre, only six of the 21 starters surviving.

Herrmann's Mercedes suffered a massive engine failure after setting the fastest lap. But Fangio and Kling finished first and second. Already the *Daily Express* was looking at ways of tactfully playing down the thought of a German wipe-out in the British Grand Prix.

Over a barrel

History held at least one consolation. Mercedes-Benz had not won a Grand Prix in England, despite being expected to do so in 1937 and 1938. So the previews talked about that and the healthy number of British drivers on the entry list.

Hawthorn was the centre of attention, of course, although Stirling Moss was worth more than a passing mention. He had, after all, a Maserati 250F at his disposal. But this was a production rather than a factory car and it had cost £5,500. It was probably one of the best investments Moss would make in his career.

He had been prompted to take such an adventurous step by Neubauer's refusal to consider Stirling for the Mercedes-Benz team in 1954. Neubauer had pointed out that this chap Moss, whoever he was, had yet to prove himself in Grand Prix terms.

It was clear to Stirling that there was no way he could manage that in a British car. The only alternative was to fork out for a 250F, regardless of Moss's wish to drive a home product. He found the Maserati a joy to drive from the moment he first sat in it.

After taking part with mixed success in one or two non-championship races, Moss finished third in the Belgian Grand Prix but missed out Reims because he had a commitment to drive for Jaguar in the 12-hour race which preceded the Grand Prix. In any case, the break would allow Tony Robinson and Alf Francis (now Moss's chief mechanic) time to prepare the Maserati for the all-important race at Silverstone.

In fact, Moss ended up lending the car to the works team for the French Grand Prix, a shrewd move as it turned out since they later rebuilt the 250F and incorporated the latest modifications – at no cost. Matters financial were always close to Moss's heart...

Maserati were in some disarray on the driver front following Fangio's call from Daimler-Benz. They still had the relatively inexperienced Marimon of course and a temporary solution was to 'borrow' Ascari and Villoresi since both Italians were kicking their heels waiting for the arrival of a new Grand Prix car from Lancia. All three were entered for the British Grand Prix.

There had also been changes at Ferrari. Farina was out of action following an accident in a sportscar race, Maurice Trintignant joining Gonzalez and Hawthorn to drive the older 625, now updated to take the latest engine from the 553. The car was a compromise, but it pleased the drivers.

There were privately-entered 625s for Parnell and Rosier, while Maserati's policy of selling their 250F meant strength in numbers, the works entry and Moss being joined by Salvadori (entered by Syd Greene's Gilby Engineering), 'Bira' and Wharton (entered by Alfred Owen, a stop-gap measure while BRM worked on a new 2.5-litre car – with a more manageable four cylinders instead of 16).

There had also been policy changes within Tony Vandervell's racing team. Plans to build their own Formula 2 car, using a 4-cylinder engine based on the Norton racing motorcycle engine, and a chassis produced by Cooper, had been seriously delayed. With the arrival of the new Grand Prix formula, Vandervell had the engine enlarged to 2.3 litres and carried on as before. The car, now called a Vanwall Special and featuring a surface cooler mounted on the nose, was to be driven by Peter Collins.

Gordini had enlarged their six-cylinder engine and it was clear that Behra, André Pilette and Clemar Bucci had little hope of finishing, never mind figuring in the first six, although such pessimism appeared to play no part in Behra's energetic plans. It was the same for Harry Schell

Behra's Gordini swoops round the outside of Parnell's Ferrari as they leave Club Corner.

in the older Maserati, a similar A6GCM being entered by Roberto Mieres.

Then came the usual plethora of British Formula 2 machines; five Connaughts, one of which was entered by a very fine gentleman by the name of Robert Ramsay Campbell Walker, and three Coopers, two with Bristol engines and one running a 2.5-litre Alta.

Practice on the Thursday proved little apart from illustrating to visitors from abroad that the British summer can often take a turn for the worse. The grey clouds returned the following day, but this time it did not rain. And Mercedes-Benz did not shine either. Or, at least, not straightaway.

To the delight of a large and knowledgeable crowd, Hawthorn and Moss set the early pace with Gonzalez, showing his usual enthusiasm for Silverstone, getting in among the Britons. It was towards the end of the session that Neubauer's decision to have Fangio on the driving strength was fully vindicated, the Argentine wrestling the big German car, running a minimal amount of fuel, onto pole position.

By today's standards, Silverstone is considered to be a 'fast' circuit. In 1954, when compared with Francorchamps, Pescara, Reims and Albi with their long straights, it was referred as 'twisting' and Fangio would have agreed with that, the nose of his W196 severely dented after contact with the barrels defining the corners. The streamlined bodywork was all very well on the long straights at Reims but it was nothing but a hindrance when it came to placing the car through Copse, Becketts and Stowe.

All of which made Fangio's best lap, one second quicker than anyone else, even more remarkable. Kling, out of his depth here, was three seconds slower and consigned to the second row behind his team-mate. (Herrmann's entry had been withdrawn by Daimler-Benz following the engine failure at Reims). That made it silver, red, red and green on the front row. The *Daily Express* rightly pointed out that this would not be an open-and-shut case for Mercedes-Benz.

> *The defeat of Mercedes-Benz at Silverstone last Saturday was one of the best things that could have happened*
>
> 'Autosport 23 July' 1954

Quite a few of the drivers must have read the sponsor's newspaper. In *Autosport*, Gregor Grant reported that the starting grid was 'occupied by serious-looking drivers who realized that everything possible would have to be done to prevent a repeat of the Reims sort out. In fact, I cannot remember ever having seen the conductors of G.P. machines looking so grim and determined.'

Certainly, Moss was feeling confident. For once, he knew that he could rev the Maserati to its maximum without worrying about a blow-up; or, to be more precise, the cost of a replace-

ment. When Maserati had heard that financial constraints had been forcing Moss to use 400rpm less than the works cars, Omer Orsi, the Managing Director, had promised to pick up the bill if Moss's engine failed. Maserati were keenly aware of the importance of the British Grand Prix, both for themselves and Stirling.

Maserati had also fitted an extra-low first gear and Moss was able to make good use of it at the start as he took second place behind Gonzalez. Hawthorn and Fangio quickly moved ahead but Moss was pacing himself and allowing the race to settle down.

Not so Marimon, Ascari and Villoresi. Thanks to the late arrival of their cars (the transporter had gone to the wrong channel port in France), the works Maserati drivers had missed official practice and were forced to start from the back of the grid. On the first lap, the young Argentine driver had passed no less than 20 cars. Ascari, trapped on the inside at the start, had only managed to take 17! Villoresi, with a mere 12 to his credit, was almost leisurely by comparison. Marimon's enthusiasm got the better of him, however, and he lost a couple of places by spinning at Abbey on lap three.

Two laps later and Fangio had taken second place from Hawthorn, leaving the Ferrari to fend off an immediate attack by Moss. It was a duel which the 90,000 crowd wanted to see; this might go some way towards settling disputes about who was the top British driver. Alf Francis, working in the Moss pit, had no doubts about the answer to that question.

For almost an hour, Francis watched Moss and Hawthorn set identical lap times as they changed places on at least four occasions. Then Moss went ahead once more and Francis placed a red marker on top of the signal board, a sign that encouraged Moss to take the Maserati to the limit. His times tumbled by a couple of seconds and, for five consecutive laps, Moss went round in 1m 50s. Hawthorn equalled that time just once and his challenge was effectively broken.

Now Moss had his sights set on Fangio. Gradually he caught the Mercedes as Fangio struggled with a car battered by the oil drums and hobbled by gears jumping out and brakes which were fading badly. But Fangio being Fangio, he refused to give up.

On lap 55, the world champion was overtaken by Moss. It was an important moment for the Englishman. If Alfred Neubauer had not been fully aware of Stirling Moss's capabilities before, he sure as hell knew about them now.

Making up the 20 seconds or so on Gonzalez was out of the question and Moss backed off slightly in order to make sure of finishing second. Certainly, there were no immediate challengers threatening. Fangio had been overhauled by Hawthorn and Marimon while Trintignant was some way behind in sixth place. Ascari had stopped with engine trouble, only to retire for good when a connecting rod broke after he taken over Villoresi's 250F.

Kling, not at all happy on a circuit made even more difficult by rain, was running in the midfield, four or five seconds off the pace. Indeed, at one point he had been passed by Collins, only for the Vanwall to retire not long after with a leaking cylinder-head joint.

As the final ten laps beckoned, the rain fell even harder, but the finishing order seemed settled. Then Moss went missing. A gear-wheel had come loose in the transmission, leaving the Maserati with no drive and Moss with a walk back to the pits. It was the first time the Maserati 250F had suffered such a failure. And it had to happen to Moss. None the less, he had made his point.

Gonzalez, on the circuit where *he* had made his mark three years before, ploughed on towards a most worthy victory, Hawthorn making it one-two for *Scuderia Ferrari* with Marimon finishing an impressive third. Fangio struggled home fourth – it was quite a day for Argentina.

In fact, it was quite a day for Britain too. Apart from the performances of Moss and Hawthorn, there had been a fine win for the Aston Martin of Peter Collins in the sportscar race and Moss had partially made up for his earlier disappointment by leading the Formula 3 race (for 500cc cars) from start to finish.

In the race for smaller capacity sportscars, there had been a hint of things to come. The 17-lap supporting event had been won by Colin Chapman. The manner of his victory, beating Hans Herrmann in the works 550 Porsche, was impressive enough. But it was Chapman's car, a Lotus Mark 8, which really caught the eye. The beautifully streamlined body covered an advanced spaceframe chassis which required the 1,500cc MG engine to be partially dismantled before it could be removed! That disadvantage aside, the fleet little car clearly worked well. In less than four years, Colin Chapman would be applying his fertile mind with equal success to Grand Prix racing.

Brooklands in October 1927. The Bugattis of Materassi and Chiron take an immediate lead at the bleak-looking start of the 1927 British Grand Prix.

Right: *Don't know how to cure overheating? I know a man who does.' George Eyston's mechanic, Gillow, adopts a fairly direct method of dealing with high temperatures on the Aston Martin at Brooklands in 1926.*

Even in 1926, chicanes blighted the racing landscape. A fine view of the Finishing Straight at Brooklands, with the splendid Clubhouse to the right and the Byfleet Banking sweeping across the background. Campbell's Bugatti leads Divo's Talbot onto the Home Banking.

*The might of Germany thunders
into Red Gate at the start of the
1937 Donington Grand Prix. The
Mercedes of Lang, Caracciola and
Seaman lead Rosemeyer's Auto
Union.*

Right: *State of the art. Von Brauchitsch has a front wheel changed in 28 seconds following a tyre failure; a swift piece of pit work at Donington which was considered to be a 'fine art' by* The Autocar *in 1937.*

Below: *The bravest of the brave. Tazio Nuvolari tames the powerful Auto Union on his way to victory in the 1938 Donington Grand Prix.*

Above: *New horizon for Silverstone aerodrome. The field sets off towards Woodcote at the start of the 1948 RAC Grand Prix.*

Right: *All action at BRM.
Parnell's car is refuelled while
Raymond Mays (hand in pocket)
watches Walker accelerate away
towards Woodcote. John Bolster
stands to the left of the policeman
while an elegantly dressed lady
photographer records the fact that
the BRMs are still running during
the 1951 British Grand Prix.*

Above: *Wash and top-up. Grime
is removed from Bob Gerard's visor
while fuel is added to the ERA at
Silverstone in 1949.*

Right: *Start – and the finish at Silverstone in 1952. Ascari makes one of his stunning starts and is not troubled for the rest of the afternoon. The Ferrari streaks past the new pits, now positioned between Woodcote and Copse.*

Above: *A bit of a bash. The previously smooth lines of Fangio's Mercedes-Benz show signs of contact with the Silverstone's oil drums whilst (right) Herr Neubauer prepares to inform Fangio that Gonzalez, Moss and Hawthorn are ahead of him during the 1954 British Grand Prix.*

British driver; German car; Argentine courtesy? Fangio chases Moss to the line after keeping the Englishman on his toes all the way. But where is everyone? Note the sparsely populated pit lane at Aintree in 1955 and compare it with the scenes of mass hysteria which greet the winner today.

Left: 'Look ol' boy, sorry to bother you but your car's not quite the ticket…' John Eason-Gibson, Clerk of the Course for the 1956 British Grand Prix, explains to de Portago that he has been black-flagged because his damaged Ferrari is considered to be a hazard. In which case, it is to be assumed that the pipe of the Deputy Clerk of the Course is not lit….

Below: The cup that cheers. A.G. Vandervell, flanking by Moss and Brooks, holds aloft the trophy that says he's beaten 'those bloody red cars' at Aintree in 1957.

Right: Plenty to smile about. Mike Hawthorn poses with the Ferrari Dino 246 in the Silverstone paddock in July 1958, the year he became the first British driver to win the world championship.

Left: *Jack Brabham opposite-locking his way to victory at Silverstone in 1960.*

Bottom left: *The glamour of Grand Prix racing. Von Trips splashes to victory against the backdrop of industrial Liverpool in 1961.*

Below: *Sheer all-round brilliance: Jimmy Clark and the Lotus 25 on their way to victory at Silverstone in 1963.*

Jim Clark's Lotus leads Graham Hill's BRM along Bottom Straight during their race long duel at Brands Hatch in 1964.

In the meantime, the day had belonged to Froilan Gonzalez. He had driven with such commanding authority that more victories seemed certain to follow. In fact, Gonzalez would never win another Grand Prix. His outlook on motor racing would be changed considerably two weeks later at the Nürburgring.

Argentine anguish

Onofre Marimon was killed during practice for the German Grand Prix. The pressures of being the nominal leader of the Maserati team had weighed heavily on his young shoulders when Moss set a typically brilliant time in his privately entered car. Marimon, still unfamiliar with the tricks of this awe-inspiring circuit, had tried to keep up with Moss during the final practice session. The Argentine had left the road on the descent to *Wehrseifen*, his Maserati plunging through a hedge and rolling down a steep slope.

Fangio and Gonzalez, two giants of Grand Prix racing, wept openly in the pits. It took some time for Neubauer to persuade Fangio to return to his car, but once on board, he shut off his emotions. He won the race the next day but his sombre expression could not hide the fact that his performance had also been a remarkable victory of mind over matter. Gonzalez, still overcome with grief, had been forced to stop and hand over to Hawthorn, the Englishman finishing second.

Mercedes-Benz had dispensed with the streamlining, the W196 now clothed in an angular body which exposed the wheels. Fangio's win at the Nürburgring proved that this was the answer and, when he led from start to finish in the Swiss Grand Prix, his championship tally had gone beyond the reach of Gonzalez and Hawthorn.

Fangio, back in a streamlined W196, won again at Monza, but not before he had given second best to Ascari and then Moss, the Englishman actually leading for 19 laps. Ascari's Ferrari went out with engine trouble, and nine laps from the finish Moss's oil tank split. When Alfred Neubauer walked over and patted Moss sympathetically on the shoulder, it was clear that the 250F had more than served its purpose. The Mercedes-Benz team chief had seen all he wanted to see.

A horse for every course

Stirling Moss was now a very marketable commodity; a fact of which he was only too aware. The cigarette advertisements had made way for a more appropriate invocation to drink Lucozade. 'Its valuable Glucose content supplies energy when you need it most,' beamed Moss from the half-page spread in *Autosport*. 'So,' the ad went on, 'keep some by you, *always!*'

Of course, having agreed to be associated with such an exhortation, Moss had to set an example. And Alf Francis knew all about that. In the midst of frantic preparations to drive to Italy and collect the Maserati 250F at the beginning of the season, Francis had been given an extra chore, as he recalled in his book:

> '*One way and another, I had a very busy time. There were travellers' cheques to sign, documents and authorizations to obtain and a spares list to be worked out. I also had to pick up two gallons of paint from the offices of Stirling Moss Limited, in William IV Street, as Stirling is very particular about his colours and was anxious that the Maserati should be painted in true British racing green. At the same time I loaded a set of off-white seat covers for the cockpit and a set of metric tools.*
> *Then, in the sacred cause of publicity, four cases of Lucozade had to be collected for Stirling so that we had a permanent supply in the lorry.*'

Alf Francis gave the impression that Stirling's commercial activities created the odd headache from time to time, but he could forgive Moss anything once he got into the car. Certainly, Francis was a proud man on 29 May 1954. That was the day Moss and the Maserati came home first in the Aintree 200, the first time that a car prepared by Francis had won a major event.

It was also the first time that Aintree had been used for a motor race. This was the culmination of a year's work by Mirabel Topham, owner of the famous Grand National steeplechase course. It took some time for Mrs Topham to sort out various problems with licences, roads, footpaths and parish councils, but once under way, the contractors completed most of the

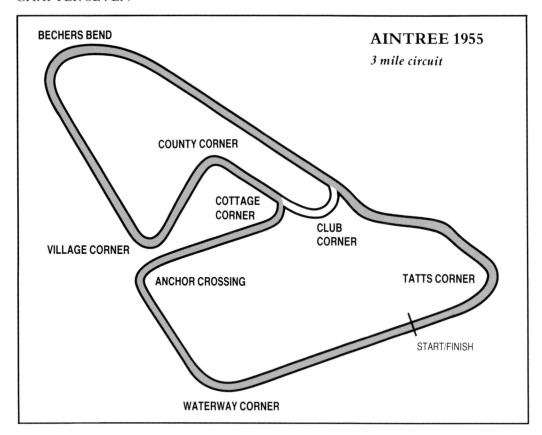

three mile course in as many months. The cost was around £100,000.

The benefit for the spectators, though, was enormous. Not only was this a purpose-built race track, as opposed to a converted airfield, but the splendid stands and facilities associated with horse racing were automatically available for motor sport. It made the tents and scaffolding of Silverstone seem second-rate. Or, at least, that was the major selling point. The correspondence columns would prove otherwise the following summer.

The inaugural meeting had been run in pouring rain. It had also been run in an anti-clockwise direction. Both the weather and the direction of travel were reversed for another major Formula 1 race in the autumn of 1954. And, by now, the RAC were showing more that a passing interest in the circuit since it would give enthusiasts living in Scotland and the north of England a fairer crack of the whip should the British Grand Prix be moved to Aintree.

British sporting achievement had been to the fore in the newspapers that summer. In May, a 25-year-old medical student by the name of Roger Bannister had become the first man to run the mile in under four minutes. British technology, though, was undergoing a difficult period as Comet airliners continued to crash for no apparent reason. Meanwhile, a few days before the British Grand Prix, Boeing had given their 707 its maiden flight from Seattle with the boast that it could carry 219 passengers at 600 mph.

In motor sport, attention turned to Lancia in Italy. On 5 November 1954, *Autosport* carried a brief description of the brutish D50 which, at long last, had made an appearance in the Spanish Grand Prix, the final race of the season. Ascari had been fastest in practice and he led until sidelined by clutch trouble. The race was won by Hawthorn's Ferrari (now the 'squalo') but the raucous V8 Lancia had given Mercedes-Benz something to think about over the winter.

And tucked away at the bottom of the *Autosport* report was a note to say that the 1955 British Grand Prix would be run by the British Automobile Racing Club – at Aintree.

A few weeks later came not altogether unexpected news: Stirling Moss had signed a contract to race for Daimler-Benz AG. 'Told you so' crowed the media. In fact, Moss had given serious thought to signing for Maserati; after all the 250F was a fine car. But the offer to test a Mercedes-Benz was an invitation he could not refuse. The experience made a major impact. This team was *serious*.

From the moment Moss, his father and manager arrived at Stuttgart airport, the methodical Mercedes-Benz system purred into action. There were three cars to meet them; one was purely for luggage. There was an army of technicians waiting at Hockenhiem and Moss was given a 220 saloon and then a 300SL sportscar for exploratory laps on that damp and misty morning.

Then he climbed into a W196. It was quite difficult to drive at first but the engine and gearbox were very impressive. In fact, the entire operation was mind-blowing. When he returned to the pits for the first time, a mirror was held in front of him, along with a bowl of hot water, a sponge and fresh towel – just in case he wanted to remove the dust created by the inboard front brakes.

Later that day, Karl Kling and Rudolph Uhlenhaut both drove the car; neither could improve upon Moss's time. Moss, of course, would rather have driven a car painted in British Racing Green. Mercedes said they would be more than happy to place a Union Jack on his car. Moss signed five days later. One wonders why he waited that long.

It seemed certain that Britain would, at long last, have a world champion; 1955, said the experts, would be a season to remember. In fact, it would turn out to be a year most people would rather forget.

The death of Alberto Ascari

At first, everything seemed to go according to plan. Mercedes-Benz won in Argentina, Fangio being the only driver capable of tolerating the insufferable heat. The asphalt bubbled and an egg could have been fried on the silver bodywork of the W196. At one stage Moss, briefly overcome by the heat, had stopped by the trackside to catch his breath. Marshals went to investigate and suddenly Moss found himself being pulled from the car, layed on a stretcher and carted off to the medical centre.

Moss tried to get off the stretcher but, the more he shouted his innocence, the more convinced the medical men became that he was suffering from acute sun-stroke. It took the intervention of an English-speaking doctor to quickly effect Moss's release from his well-meaning captors.

Moss felt light-headed again at Monaco after following closely in the wheel-tracks of Fangio. The silver cars appeared to be walking off with the Grand Prix until engine trouble brought Fangio to a halt on lap 50, Moss losing the lead 31 laps later.

That left Ascari in front with the Lancia D50, the only car that had any hope of offering Mercedes-Benz some sort of challenge in 1955. But the race was reaching its closing stages and the brakes on the red car had passed their best. Coming into the chicane – on the very lap he had inherited the lead – Ascari arrived too quickly, ploughed into the straw bales, the Lancia then plunging into the harbour. Ascari emerged from the Mediterranean with nothing more than a broken nose. The race was won by the Ferrari of Maurice Trintignant and, all told, it was a spectacular story with a happy ending.

Four days later Alberto Ascari was dead. He had crashed inexplicably while testing a Ferrari sportscar at Monza. The motor racing world, and most of Italy, went into deep shock. There was disbelief because the accident, occurring as it did on a Thursday, caught most people unawares. In any case, Ascari was not due to be at Monza, never mind drive the car. And he was not the sort of driver to make mistakes.

It soon emerged that Ascari had turned up to watch Eugenio Castellotti test the car which they were due to share in a sportscar car race at Monza the following weekend. Ascari did not even bring his lucky pale blue crash helmet. When he suddenly asked to drive the car, Ascari surprised those present even further by happily borrowing Castellotti's white helmet.

On the third lap he crashed and, to this day, no one knows why. It was clear, however, that the world had lost one of its greatest drivers. Milan came to a standstill on the day of his funeral and, by now, uncanny facts were emerging. He had died exactly 30 years after his father, Antonio, had been killed in the French Grand Prix – another crash for which there had been no logical explanation. Both men were 36 years old and they met their deaths four days after surviving potentially serious accidents. Motor sport legend has fed on the story ever since.

At the time, though, young Eugenio Castellotti suddenly found himself burdened with responsibility. He had been recruited by Lancia as number 2 driver to his hero, Ascari, but in the aftermath of the great man's death, the team withdrew. (Perhaps it was no coincidence that the team were also running short of funds at the time.) They did, however, release one car for Castellotti to enter privately for the Belgian Grand Prix.

The effect on the emotional Italian can be imagined. With one inspired lap, he took pole position at Spa-Francorchamps, but on race day gave best to Fangio and Moss until the Lancia's gearbox gave up, many people seeing the failure as a merciful intervention.

The tragic loss of Ascari was something with which the motor racing world could cope. But when a Mercedes-Benz 300 SLR sportscar crashed into the crowd at Le Mans, killing more than 80 people, the sport suddenly became public property. Bad news sells newspapers and motor racing was raw meat tossed into the headline writers' den. The season, instead of flowing with anticipation, degenerated into a daily diet of uncertainty and apprehension. The French, German, Swiss and Spanish Grands Prix were cancelled. Would the British Grand Prix follow suit?

The RAC quickly reaffirmed their support, and in the meantime the Dutch held their race as planned, Moss dutifully following Fangio home in yet another Mercedes-Benz demonstration. Would Moss be allowed to reverse the order at Aintree on 16 July?

First among equals

The preparations appeared to be lavish. Spectators could chose seats on the roof of the famous Tatts, Aintree and County stands for between £1 15s and £2 5s (£1.75 and £2.25). Inevitably, though, there were complaints in *Autosport*, S. G. Miron writing from Banbury to point out that these prices were 15s (75p) more expensive than Silverstone.

He received short shrift the following week when a letter signed 'M.D. Topham (Mrs)' pointed out that admission to the paddock was free and spectators would have the benefit of fixed assets worth more than £1 million. Certainly it was true that Silverstone could boast neither 'cloakrooms' nor 'luncheon and dining rooms'. But, as Mrs. Topham was soon to discover, Aintree as a Grand Prix venue had one or two shortcomings.

The same could not be said of the entry list. Mercedes-Benz had cars present for Fangio, Moss, Kling and Taruffi, plus a spare car. Maserati, now led by Jean Behra, had carried out very little development work on the 250F but at least they were well represented at Aintree. The remainder of the works cars were to be driven by Roberto Mieres, Luigi Musso and André Simon. The Owen Organisation entered their car for Peter Collins while Lance Macklin had

'They're off!' Grand Prix racing comes to Aintree. Fangio and Moss chase after Behra, out of view in the Maserati.

reached agreement to drive the familiar 250F belonging to Stirling Moss Limited. Roy Salvadori (still in the Gilby car) and Horace Gould (driving the model which formerly belonged to 'Bira') completed the Maserati line-up.

Ferrari were in some disarray. Continuing development with the 553 had seen the code number changed to 555 and the name upgraded to 'Super Squalo.' It made little difference and Ferrari arrived at Aintree with three of the rather tired and hopelessly inadequate 625 models for Hawthorn (returned to the fold following a brief and rather unhappy spell with Vanwall at the beginning of the season), Trintignant and the former Lancia star, Eugenio Castellotti. Vanwall had cars for Ken Wharton and Harry Schell. while Gordini struggled on with entries for Robert Manzon, Hernano da Silva Ramos and 'Mike Sparken' (real name, Michel Poberejsky).

Indeed, the French cars were put to shame by the standard of preparation of many of the British teams. Connaught had been experimented with streamlining since the previous year, the result of their endeavours being an impressive all-enveloping bodywork on cars for Kenneth McAlpine, Jack Fairman and Leslie Marr. The Rob Walker entry for Tony Rolt remained in open-wheel form. And, at the very back of the grid, a rear-engined Cooper sportscar with a central seating position for the driver, an Australian by the name of John Arthur Brabham.

The Grand Prix was sponsored by the *Daily Telegraph* and news of pole position for Stirling Moss doubtless helped swell the crowds. The official figure was 150,000 and while some observers had cause to doubt that estimate, those caught in the massive traffic jams stretching back to the Mersey Tunnel were ready to agree.

On a glorious summer's day, there was many a boiling radiator as cars struggled into the car parks, but the atmosphere around the circuit quickly made up for trials and tribulations on the way in. *Autosport* sets the scene:

> *'Hot-weather dress was the rule everywhere, and practically every woman wore sun-tops, brightly hued skirts and, of course, sunglasses and plenty of lipstick. Some of the men wore pyjama tops that looked like shirts, and others donned shirts that looked like pyjama tops. There was even a Scotsman in the paddock area wearing a kilt, no shirt, and a broad sombrero.*
>
> *Hundreds of husky men carried crates of beer and lemonade to the bars, and, within a few minutes, carried empty ones back again to the waiting lorries. Ice cream vendors could hardly keep pace with the demand.'*

Autosport did not mention the rather sinister overtones evident that weekend in 1955. On the day before the race, Ruth Ellis had been hanged in Holloway Prison. She had been found guilty of murdering her lover, a racing driver by the name of David Blakely, outside a pub in Hampstead. The trial took a mere two days. The jury had reached their verdict in 25 minutes. It was the talk of the nation – and nowhere more so than in the paddock at Aintree.

Meanwhile, there was business to be done. The BARC initiated a welcome method of introducing the drivers to the crowd. Instead of following the familiar procedure of walking behind their cars to the starting grid, the drivers were taken round the course in a cavalcade of white-painted Austin Healeys bedecked with the national flags of the occupants. Announcements, made in English, French and Italian, identified the drivers. Moss and Hawthorn received a tumultuous reception and there was generous applause for Schell, who had managed to put the Vanwall onto the third row, five places ahead of Hawthorn and the rest of the Ferrari team!

Schell was an effervescent Franco/American and there must have been colourful language in the cockpit of the Vanwall when he threw away a splendid effort in practice by fluffing the start. And he was not alone in his misery, Marr also stalling on the grid.

There had been no such mistake by Fangio as he took the lead into the first right-hander, Waterway Corner. By the time he had reached the next right-hander at Anchor Crossing, in readiness for the in-field loop, it was clear the Mercedes-Benz team were about to lay on another demonstration. The silver cars held the first four places, Kling and Taruffi already dropping back slightly from Fangio and Moss.

On to the left at Cottage Corner, down the short straight to Country Corner, then another quick burst of acceleration before Village and the run towards the top of the circuit at Bechers Bend. The tightly-packed crowd on the embankment watched as Fangio led the field through the right-hander and onto Railway Straight, preparing himself for the very tricky left-right flick over Melling Crossing and the short run towards the final right-hander at Tatts Corner.

Not a particularly demanding circuit, Aintree, but for 90 laps Moss knew he could not afford a single error while racing with a master such as Fangio.

There had been speculation that Behra, having disrupted the silver monopoly during practice by thrusting his Maserati onto the front row, would give the Mercedes-Benz drivers something to think about. That hope took a dive at the start when the Frenchman spun his wheels but, as ever, such a setback was only temporary and he was soon ahead of Kling and Taruffi and desperately trying to stay in touch with Fangio and Moss. His brave effort lasted for nine laps, the Maserati straight-6 suddenly crying enough.

By then Moss had taken the lead of the British Grand Prix. Fangio had not put up a struggle but was now shadowing the young Englishman. Further back, Schell was providing just as much entertainment as he carved through the field, his progress almost being matched by Collins, who had started his Maserati from the back of the grid. Both drivers overhauled Hawthorn, badly affected by the heat, but then the Vanwall went out with a broken throttle pedal, followed not long after by Collins as his 250F suffered a clutch failure.

But what about Moss? Any thoughts that Fangio had been looking after Moss's interests were soon dispelled when the Argentine moved back in front and set a furious pace, Moss having to work hard to keep up. A couple of times Moss had tried to retake the lead but Fangio was not about to wave him through. At least, not yet.

On lap 26, however, Moss was back in front, Fangio sitting on his tail. The world champion made no attempt to overtake which, perhaps, was even more unsettling; Moss simply did not know what to expect. But he did appreciate that the slightest slip would allow his teammate through and Fangio was not the sort of driver to be charitable a second time round.

This internal dispute had pulled them well clear of the rest of the field, now led by Kling and Taruffi, all four Mercedes-Benz drivers lapping a couple of seconds faster than anyone else. Moss gradually eased ahead of Fangio, the Englishman then dutifully obeying signs 'Pi' ('Piano') to slow. With three laps to go, however, he cut loose and went round Aintree in 2 minutes 00.4 seconds to match his pole position time. On the penultimate lap, Fangio responded and, as Moss slowed slightly on the final lap, the Argentine powered through Tatts and began to draw alongside Moss as they crossed the line. An Englishman had won the British Grand Prix for the first time. But had it been staged?

'I honestly don't know,' says Moss. 'If Fangio was playing, then all I can say is he played damned hard! Sure, I was driving well that day but the Old Man seemed to be able to catch me whenever he liked. There were no team orders and nothing had been said between Fangio and I before the race. Before receiving the slow-down signal, I had managed to pull away from Fangio by leaving him a backmarker to pass just before a corner.

'Everybody says that the Mercedes-Benz were unbeatable and so on and that it must have been easy. But I tell you, while those cars performed beautifully, they were hard work. You really had to concentrate – the pattern of the gearchange was the reverse of what I was used to, for example – and, with someone like Fangio on your tail, it was no easy ride I can tell you. I had won the Mille Miglia a few weeks before, but winning a Grand Prix in front of your home crowd really is something very special.'

A faller at the first

It had, on the face of it, been a splendid day for Aintree and the BARC. But not everyone was happy. The report in *Motor Racing* – a magazine affiliated to the rival British Racing and Sportscar Club – went straight for the throat. The opening paragraph ended:

> '..... *This was the first time the British* Grande Epreuve *had been run at Aintree, and if some people have their way it will also be the last. There is some justification for the public and private criticism which has been levelled at this Aintree meeting, but it was the first major event to be held there and many of the faults can be rectified if the owners are willing to go to the trouble of satisfying the wishes of the paying public. In the main the criticisms were were mostly connected with the amenities provided for the prices charged, particularly those 'out in the country.' The paddock arrangements at Aintree are bad, the dust-laden atmosphere caused by cars and people moving over the loose ash surface is not popular with anybody but most particularly with mechanics trying desperately to keep oil and fuel and carburetters (sic) clean. The paddock is also too far removed from the race track from which it is completely isolated.*
>
> *Other disturbing complaints came from those who had paid the most money, and whose view*

from the permanent stands was limited to only a few yards of the finishing straight. Then there was a general complaint, which must be accepted in the right spirit by Aintree, if they are to encourage motor racing there, and that is the alleged officious manner of the officials. We must have order and control, we know, but if, as it seems, motor racing enthusiasts are sensitive, then their peculiar temperament must be studied if big gates are wanted at Aintree.

The complaints levelled at Aintree as a circuit may have been influenced, and made more pronounced, by Liverpool's treatment of visitors. Throughout the Liverpool area it seemed that visitors were no longer welcome. Good food was not obtainable, good service did not exist, good manners by the hotel and restaurant staffs was something that we should apparently not expect.'

Other reports, if rather less trenchant, did back that up, although William Boddy ploughed his own furrow, the Editor of *Motor Sport* commenting that 'Aintree showed up well....and rose to the Grand Prix occasion.'

But they all agreed on the result. With Kling and Taruffi finishing third and fourth, the Daimler-Benz AG *blitzkrieg* had been total. Small wonder that there were few regrets when the German firm announced their intention to withdraw at the end of the year.

It was the close of another remarkable chapter in the history of Grand Prix racing and, appropriately, Mercedes-Benz went out on a high note, Fangio winning the final round at Monza (now featuring a banked section) to take his third world title. Moss, a retirement with engine failure in the Italian Grand Prix, was runner-up in the championship. It was a position with which he would become frustratingly familiar during the next few years.

The red or the green?

There was mild disbelief in January 1987 when Martin Brundle invited members of the motorsport press to join him for an informal lunch in London. Grand Prix drivers simply did not do these things and cynics wondered what the ulterior motive would be.

There was none. Brundle simply wanted to outline his plans for the forthcoming season and to say thanks for the support he had received in the past. Journalists, battered by the blandishments of sponsorship and sickly-smooth public relations firms, were in a state of shock and in need of the medicinal libations at the end of the meal.

In the fifties, however, driver/press relationships operated along similar lines. There were, of course, certain parties who could not stand the sight of each other but, by and large, it was a friendly and uninhibited atmosphere. And, in December 1955, Stirling Moss gathered together one or two of his 'press mates' for a meal at the RAC Club in London's Pall Mall. He wanted to talk through his options for the 1956 season, now that he had been made redundant by the Mercedes-Benz withdrawal.

The dilemma boiled down to whether to drive for Britain or Italy. In the green corner were Connaught, Vanwall and BRM. In the red, Maserati and Ferrari. There was also a blue corner but no one seemed to be taking Gordini and the resurgent Bugatti firm too seriously.

The sudden burst of interest in the 'green' party had been prompted in part by two fairly significant events at the end of 1955. The Oulton Park circuit in Chesire, opened in August 1953, had hosted their Gold Cup meeting, for which BRM had finally entered their latest creation, the P25. Driven by Peter Collins, this 4-cylinder car had been challenging for the lead when the oil pressure gauge suddenly zeroed. Collins pulled off, only to find that the gauge had been at fault. But a point had been made.

Then, at the very close of the season, Connaught beat the works Maserati team to win the Syracuse Grand Prix. The Alta-engined car was driven by C.A.S. Brooks, a young dental student from Manchester, and it was the first Grand Prix win for a British car in a very long time. That sort of thing held great appeal for Stirling Moss.

Ferrari had not approached him but Maserati had offered Stirling the number one drive with Behra as number two. BRM, on the other hand, had said he could be their leading driver for which, according to the magazine *Motor Racing*, he would receive £200,000 and a full Grand Prix programme. And if the car let him down after two races, then BRM would be willing release him.

In typically thorough fashion, Moss had tested all three British cars at Silverstone – on the same day! Such co-operation by teams would be unthinkable now and it says much for Moss's standing that the teams were happy to comply.

Moss found the handling of the BRM did not match the impressive power. The Connaught

Stirling Moss
One of the world's truly great drivers. Won 16 Grands Prix – including the British in 1955 and 1957 – but never claimed the world championship despite coming desperately close on two occasions. A thorough professional and at his peak when an accident at Goodwood in 1962 ended a brilliant career.

had been not too bad – but not too good either, whereas the Vanwall was beautifully balanced, but less powerful than the BRM.In any event, Moss confided that his choice lay between Maserati and Vanwall. What should he do?

The specialist press suggested that he would wiser to drive for Maserati, win the championship – and then worry about doing it in a British car. The popular press, however, took a typical British line by telling Stirling that he would achieve popularity if he drove a British car yet lost the championship!

Fortunately, wise council prevailed and Moss signed for Maserati. There would be time enough to drive for a British team; these were early days in the promising development of Vanwall and, to a lesser extent, BRM. Connaught, for all their clever chassis and bodywork design, were hamstrung by the lack of a decent engine. The 4-cylinder Alta was now long in the tooth and, indeed, Connaught were fortunate to have the continuing support of Kenneth McAlpine, his flagging enthusiasm buoyed by the win in Syracuse.

Tony Vandervell had taken the right step by choosing to build his own engine. More than that, Vandervell had also realised that the Cooper chassis was all very well but, if he was to compete seriously against the 'continental' opposition, he needed to have something much more sophisticated. Vandervell had not been alone in admiring Colin Chapman's handiwork and he commissioned the Lotus boss and his collaborator, Frank Costin, to design a new chassis and bodywork for 1956. Thus, the seeds for the eye-catching teardrop shape and elaborate spaceframe chassis were sewn.

It also prompted a proper little punch-up between the *Daily Express* and *Motor Racing* magazine. As soon as the Vanwall had been completed in March, but before it had been painted, Vandervell, dressed in a suit, but no hat of any description, had driven the car at Goodwood.

Motor Racing published a picture in their May edition (published on 19 April). The *Daily Express*, as a lead-in to the International Trophy at Silverstone, had run a picture of the car, complete with paint finish, on 26 April – and claimed this was the 'first published picture of the secret Vanwall Special.'

When *Motor Racing* took issue with this, the Express boldly declared that 'the picture which you published was, in fact, that of an unfinished car.' Exit *Motor Racing*, spluttering with indignation.

They did, however, run a glorious front cover shot the following month, showing Stirling Moss taking the Vanwall (the word 'Special' had been dropped by this stage) to victory in the International Trophy. For the championship proper, of course, he would return to Maserati.

Italian supremacy

When the championship season had opened in Argentina, the shuffling of driver seats and contracts had finally ceased. Fangio had gone to Ferrari, and so too had Peter Collins and Musso. Vanwall had signed Trintignant and Schell, while Hawthorn, unable to stay with Ferrari because they would not agree to him driving for Jaguar (such was the importance of sportscar racing to a driver then), had gone to BRM. He was joined by the promising Tony Brooks.

In effect, the season was a Maserati-Ferrari battle. There had been a considerable amount of political and financial manoeuvring in Italy following the withdrawal of Lancia halfway through the previous season. The Lancia D50 was seen as car with great potential and, following lengthy negotiations between Lancia, Fiat and Ferrari, it was agreed that Ferrari would take over the Lancia project, lock stock and barrel. After a number of rather rough modifications had been carried out, the Lancia-Ferraris appeared in Argentina with the yellow Prancing Horse badges by the cockpit – and they won.

It had not been a straightforward victory for Fangio, and neither was a splendid win for Moss at Monaco, but that made it one each to Ferrari and Maserati. The former team-mates were at it again in Belgium until the Maserati lost a wheel and Fangio's transmission broke. That allowed Peter Collins to win for Ferrari, the Englishman then scoring an even more emphatic victory at Reims.

Three wins in a row for British drivers; a previously unheard-of statistic. And there had been yet another encouraging sign in France of the swing towards Britain as Harry Schell, driving out of his skin on the very fast track, moved the lofty Vanwall in among the leading cars until the fuel injection pump gave trouble. The net result of all this was that Peter Collins was leading the world championship as the teams moved to Silverstone for the British Grand

Drivers' Briefing. Left to right: Fangio, Castellotti, Fairman, Brooks, Halford, Salvadori and Scott-Brown.

Prix. Patriotism was at an all-time high. So was frequently ill-informed talk of the terrible dangers of motor sport.

The 1955 Le Mans disaster had rightly brought the question of spectator protection into sharp relief worldwide but Silverstone had started to think along those lines some time before. In 1952, the BRDC had begun work on the provision of a ditch between the track and the enclosures. That was quite acceptable, but the additional construction of an earth bank was not well-received by spectators. Initially, the two-foot bank was placed in front of the more heavily populated spectator areas but the Le Mans tragedy accelerated the need to have the bank cover the entire length of the circuit. From the driver's point of view, the tatty marker barrels had finally been replaced by a low concrete wall on the inside of most corners, with the occasional potted ever-green placed here and there for the sake of appearances.

And, speaking of green, there was a splash of that on the front row of the grid, plus a larger dash on row two while the third rank was dominated by Britain's national racing colour. The editorials previewing the British Grand Prix spoke earnestly of a home win. They even mentioned BRM in glowing terms. But then we had heard that sort of talk before and, when the heat was on, not a lot had changed at Bourne.

I told Mother this would happen

Mike Hawthorn knew all about BRM, 1956-style. In fact, he had nobody but himself to blame. When he first tested the car, he tried it on a wet day 'and found it very frightening indeed.' But he felt the potential was there – and the offer was very acceptable.

Hawthorn had driven the Owen Maserati 250F and a Vanwall in various races while waiting for the BRM to be put right. During the Easter Monday meeting at Goodwood a rear universal-joint had seized as he travelled through Fordwater at around 100mph. The BRM went into a series of rolls, Hawthorn momentarily trapped by the ankle before being mercifully flung clear.

During a test session at Silverstone, the bonnet had come loose, smashed his visor and almost knocked Hawthorn unconscious. Then, at Aintree, the brake pedal fell off because there had not been a split-pin to hold the clevis-pin in place. Hawthorn had come to no harm this time but he motored slowly back to the BRM pit to deliver a thousand words on what he thought about it all.

A BRM leads! Hawthorn makes the best start while Brooks (24) prepares to pass Fangio (1) and support his team-mate.

Raymond Mays walked over and said to Hawthorn: 'It's a funny thing; I was saying to my mother this morning "Mike has had two bad crashes, one when the car turned over at Goodwood and one when the bonnet flew off in his face. There's usually a third, and I hope it isn't going to be a bad one."'

Hawthorn's reply to that is not printed in his book. But he did wonder why BRM did not have proper signalling gear, relying instead on an ancient blackboard on which the new signs frequently became mixed up with traces of the old ones....

But, at Silverstone for the British Grand Prix, he was on the front row of the grid! The wheelbase of his car had been lengthened in a bid to cure the very nervous handling. Brooks, meanwhile, was on the third row with the original set-up, while a third car, in the hands of the Scot, Ron Flockhart, was even further back.

But the really good news was that Stirling Moss was on pole, albeit in a red Maserati. He was streets ahead of his team-mates Behra and Cesare Perdisa who, in turn, had been shown up by Salvadori, on the second row with the Gilby entry, and Gould, alongside Behra on the fourth row. Elsewhere, there were six more privately entered examples of the 250F for Villoresi, Bruce Halford, Umberto Maglioli, Francesco Godia, Rosier and Brabham.

Ferrari were in with a shout, of course, Fangio and Collins placing their D50s on the front row with the fourth car for the dashing Spanish nobleman, Marques Alfonse de Portago, lining up on the row four, directly behind Castellotti. Vanwall had invited Gonzalez, now in semi-retirement in Argentina, to join Schell and Trintignant at Silverstone, while Connaught, struggling along as best they could on limited finance, had cars for Jack Fairman, Desmond Titterington, an accomplished sportscar driver from Belfast, and Archie Scott-Brown, a gritty little Scotsman with one arm. There were a pair of Gordinis for Manzon and Ramos while Bob

Gerard (Cooper-Bristol) and Paul Emery (Emeryson-Alta) shamed one or two of the Maserati owners at the back of the grid. But, in truth, professionalism and the big team effort was spreading further down the British Grand Prix grid with each succeeding year.

There was good news and bad news for Britain within seconds of the start. The BRMs of Hawthorn and Brooks shot into the lead while Gonzalez's Vanwall broke a drive-shaft on the line. It had been a long way for the Argentine to come, only to enjoy a few feet of racing.

By the end of the first lap, Hawthorn and Brooks were pulling away, Schell was in fourth place, just behind Fangio, while Salvadori was sixth and chasing Castellotti, with Collins and Moss (a poor start) bringing up the rear of the group. Fangio began to close on Brooks, the Lancia-Ferrari taking second place on lap seven. It didn't last long. An uncharacteristic spin by the world champion at Becketts allowed Brooks, a fast-moving Moss, Salvadori and Collins to slip by.

Brooks was finding the BRM very hard work and he could do little to prevent the two Maseratis from overtaking on successive laps, Moss then setting after Hawthorn at a prodigious rate. By lap 16 he was in front and the BRMs were about to slide into their more customary sad state.

Hawthorn, on feeling a vibration from the transmission, correctly diagnosed a failing universal joint. Rather than go cart-wheeling down the track once more, he pulled into the BRM pit and retired. Shortly afterwards, Brooks called in for repairs to a broken throttle cable. Some years later, he recalled the events which followed in an interview with motor sport writer, Nigel Roebuck:

'On paper, that car was a flier. A good development team could have sorted out its problems, but they didn't have a good development team. That car was lethal. You had to corner it geometrically. If you tried to drift it, it would just fly off the road. But the big four-cylinder engine had loads of torque, and we were very quick in a straight line. Once I had the cable repaired, I went back out because I wanted all the experience I could get. BRM raced very seldom that year.

'The throttle was sticking a bit but I was very naive and inexperienced. Before the stop, I'd been going through Abbey flat – believe me, I don't know how! – so I thought I could carry on doing that, even if I were wary of the sticking throttle at other corners. The trouble was that during my long pit stop, a lot of oil had been put down at Abbey.

'The car started to go wide and I lifted off momentarily to get the nose to tuck back in. It made no difference, and I came off the corner three or four feet on the grass. Being that car, it just went completely out of control, spun into the bank, somersaulted and threw me out. Finally it landed upside down on the track again, and set itself on fire, which was the only thing it could reasonably do...'

It was the last Brooks would see of BRM that year and he counted himself very fortunate to have got away with no more than a chipped ankle bone.

After that, it was downhill for the British. Moss made two pit stops before finally retiring with a broken rear axle; Salvadori was also a frequent pit visitor before dirt in the fuel tank ended an excellent drive; Collins came in with no oil pressure but at least he was back in the hunt thanks to de Portago handing over his Ferrari (a British driver receiving preference; a sign of the times); the remaining two Vanwalls retired, as did two of the Connaughts – but at least Jack Fairman was still out there, the only local driver in a British car in the top four.

Connaught stayed the distance, finishing three laps behind Fangio's winning Lancia-Ferrari, two behind Collins and one lap behind Behra's Maserati.

In one respect, it was a satisfactory result since no one would wish to deny Fangio his first victory in the British Grand Prix. On the other hand, there was an air of despondency over the collapse of the British effort, particularly after Hawthorn had taken off into the distance – in a green car, no less.

During the previous year or so, the blond-haired lad from Farnham had caught the imagination of the public, what with his rakish good looks, distinctive bow tie and a penchant for the odd pint or two of bitter. Indeed, one gent's outfitters from Regent Street had seen fit to carry a half-page advert in the press showing an immaculately dressed and groomed Hawthorn peering beneath the bonnet of a Riley! Under the heading 'Internationally acclaimed..' it said Hawthorn wore a short coat and cavalry twill trousers, perfectly tailored, ready to wear, for 18 guineas (£18.90p) and 5½ guineas (£5.12½p) respectively.

As things turned out in 1956, however, the man they should have used was the debonair Peter Collins. His result at Silverstone kept him in serious contention for the championship.

Peter Collins
The Italians have never forgotten the unassuming Englishman for handing his Ferrari over at Monza in 1956 so that Fangio might win the championship. Totally dominated the British Grand Prix for Ferrari two years later and lost his life shortly afterwards at the Nürburgring.

A gentlemanly act

A shot of lubrication into the oil tank in the tail of Behra's Maserati 250F.

Fangio was on the attack at the Nürburgring, the Ferrari leading all the way, Moss finishing second while Collins, having run into mechanical problems, eventually spun off after taking over de Portago's car. Once again, the final round at Monza would settle the issue.

Monza, of course, was all about full throttle and bravery and Harry Schell was at his work again as he hustled the green Vanwall among Moss, Fangio and Collins as they disputed the lead. This time, it was a broken oil pipe which would end Schell's heroism.

Fangio, meanwhile, appeared to have said farewell to the championship when his steering broke. Musso declined to hand his car over, understandable perhaps since he would take the lead of his home Grand Prix after Moss had run out of fuel. Interpretations of what happened next vary. Certainly, Collins promptly came into the pits and handed his car over, thus effectively ending the Englishman's chances of winning the championship and presenting it to Fangio at one and the same time. The British press hailed it as the act of a supreme gentleman. Others saw it as the response to a pit signal. Either way, Collins had not hesitated and he leapt from the car the minute it came to a standstill.

Moss, meanwhile, had been nudged into the pits by a helpful private entrant and he was back in pursuit of Musso, with Fangio closing on them both. Then, with three laps to go, the ferocious bumps on the banking took their toll on Musso's steering and he was out. Moss, now nursing a badly worn rear tyre, just made it to the finish. Second place, plus the generous actions of Collins, gave Fangio his fourth world title.

Peter Collins would be fondly remembered by Fangio and Enzo Ferrari after that. It did a great deal for the image of British sportsmanship. But it brought us no nearer a Grand Prix victory for a green car. Messrs. Vandervell, Moss and Brooks were about to change all that during a momentous day at Aintree in 1957.

WEARING
THE GREEN

'Let's get one thing straight. Basically, these three marques (BRM, Vanwall and Connaught) are the hobby-horses of three wealthy men, and public appeals for financial assistance are unwarranted and an admission of failure.'

Extract from letter to *Autosport*, February 1957

That fairly set the correspondence columns humming with indignation. And leading council for the defence was John Webb, later to become management supremo at Brands Hatch, but in 1957 the guiding light behind the Connaught Grand Prix Car Club.

Operating from offices in London's Trafalgar Square, Webb had asked if anyone was interested in supporting this hard-pressed team. He received 2,000 applications for membership. This was, after all, the celebrated period when Prime Minister Harold Macmillan had said: 'Let's be frank about it. Most of our people have never had it so good'.

The annual subscription for the Connaught Club was 10s 6d (52½p) with members being asked 'to make further donations, according to their means and feelings,' the idea being to raise perhaps as much as £10,000 as a contribution towards the team's welfare.

It was an idea which received the full support of *Autosport* – if not all of its readers. Mr Douglas O. Ingram, of Twickenham, the irate correspondent mentioned in the introduction to this chapter, finished his letter thus:

'I, too, have been bitterly disappointed at the failure of a green car to receive the chequered flag; have borne in mind that their disappointment must be so much greater; have thrilled with them in their moments of glory and will continue to applaud when warranted. I will not believe, however, that this great sport can be supported by the shoe-strings of ethusiasts. (If those that disagree will each send me a fiver, I will do my best to prove them right!).'

How many five pound notes he received is not recorded, and with the benefit of hindsight Mr. Ingram had a valid point. None the less, that did not stop the Connaught Club from chartering a plane to fly to Syracuse (cut-price charge £35; scheduled fare £62).

This was the first Grand Prix of the 1957 European season and, in the event, the Connaught supporters had very little to get excited about. The B-series chassis had almost become as outdated as the engine, but there was no alternative but to plug on.

It was a bad omen when the very car which claimed that momentous victory in Syracuse in 1955 was burnt out during practice. The driver, Les Leston, had suffered a drive-shaft failure, the flailing shaft then cutting into the fuel tank with disastrous consequences. One Connaught, driven by Ivor Bueb in his first Grand Prix, finished fifth. An Italian reporter, wrestling with the unfamiliar name, apparently referred to Bueb as 'Igor Bulb.' All told, it had not been a particularly encouraging day.

Then, on the way back to the airport, the club's bus developed a serious water leak. The only source of supply was a stream, far below the mountain road on which the bus was stranded. Motor racing people are nothing if not enterprising, and a human chain, using Sicilian wine jars, soon had supplies reaching the bus. Interestingly, in these days of private jets and helicopters, that chain included Stirling Moss, his father Alfred, Rob Walker, Peter Walker and Jack Brabham.

Presumably the contents of the wine jars had been dealt with in the appropriate manner before the delay occurred but, sadly, the efforts of the Connaught Club would come to nought. A £500 contribution to the team's kitty had helped send a car to Monaco for Stuart Lewis-Evans, the gallant little Welshman going on to finish fourth.

There had been encouraging performances in other non-championship races (Lewis-Evans running second between two Ferraris at Naples until a front hub fractured) but in the end the money simply ran out. In May 1957, Kenneth McAlpine and Rodney Clarke announced the closure of the racing side of Connaught Engineering. It merited but a brief paragraph in *Auto-sport*.

Rationing success

There was, however, good news for Stuart Lewis-Evans. He was immediately snapped up by Vanwall as Tony Vandervell continued to mount a serious attack on 'those bloody red cars.' He had already signed Moss and Brooks, and development continued apace with the beautiful 'teardrop' machines.

Vanwall had missed the opening round of the championship, held as usual in Argentina. Fangio had switched to Maserati and as soon as Mike Hawthorn heard the news he contacted Ferrari. His telegram is reputed to have said something to the effect of 'I'm willing, if you are.' Knowing Hawthorn's devil-may-care attitude, the story probably has some substance.

This time, there was no disagreement over the contract (Ferrari being more than grateful that Jaguar had allowed Mike to help Maranello out on occasions in 1956) and Hawthorn joined what appeared to be a cast of thousands, including Collins, Musso, Castellotti and de Portago.

Fangio kicked off by winning at home to give Maserati a clean sweep, Jean Behra finishing second ahead of another local driver, Carlos Menditeguy.

Vanwall were out in force for the Monaco Grand Prix and looked hopeful of a spectacular maiden victory when Moss took the lead. On the fourth lap, however, brake trouble sent Moss careering straight on at the chicane, a harmless enough incident – except for the fact that there was a wall, built of telegraph poles and sandbags, placed across the entrance to what could have been an escape road.

In the confusion which followed, Collins and Hawthorn crashed their Ferraris, thus wiping out most of the British interest at a stroke. And of course, sailing serenely through the middle of it all came Fangio, the Argentine motoring on to win the race and build up a healthy lead in the championship.

If Fangio had been rather fortunate in Monaco, he totally dominated the French Grand Prix with a truly masterful display of throttle control as he hurled the 250F through the sweeps of the Rouen circuit. It had almost been two months since the Monaco race, a sign of financial and political difficulties in Europe.

Monetary problems had caused the cancellation of the Dutch and Belgian Grands Prix while, in Britain, there had been talk of reducing the motor sport calendar in the aftermath of the Suez Canal crisis the previous year. This had brought severe petrol shortages and led to rationing which would last for five months. The future for motor sport looked bleak simply because spectators would not be able to travel to the races.

The events themselves had received some protection when, in March, the Ministry of Power had agreed to allocate petrol to a strictly limited number of races. The list had been drawn up by the RAC on the understanding that these events 'ought to be maintained in the interests of the motor car industry.'

That schedule, of course, included the RAC British Grand Prix at Aintree on 20 July. The race had been granted the title '*Grand Prix d'Europe*', an accolade which was neatly summed up by *Motor Sport* when they said:

> '*It is a rather pointless title which carries no significance with it and is given to one of the major Grand Prix races in the World Championship each year by the FIA and allows the organisers to pretend that their event is the most important of the season.*'

Certainly, the RAC and the BARC made full use of the promotional windfall and, as things turned out, the British Grand Prix would be one of the most important events of the season.

Casualty ward to pole position

During the preceding weeks, however, it seemed that Britain's premier race would be without two of its star attractions; Stirling Moss and Tony Brooks.

Horses for courses; the four-wheel Grand National gets under way.

Moss had been water-skiing with his fiancée, Katie Molson (a member of the Canadian brewing family), when an attempt to perform a complicated manoeuvre resulted in a plume of spray shooting straight up Stirling's nose. The resulting sinus infection meant Moss had missed the French Grand Prix but he was discharged from a London clinic at the beginning of race week at Aintree.

Moss was lucky. Tony Brooks was in hospital right up to the day before practice was due to commence. He had been fortunate to escape without broken bones when he overturned an Aston Martin during the Le Mans 24 Hours but abrasions and a thigh injury were serious enough to keep him out of action. As a result, he was at less than peak fitness when he climbed onto the rear wheel of the Vanwall and stepped into the cockpit. And yet, withal, he managed to set third fastest time and take a place on the outside of the front row.

It almost went without saying that Stirling Moss was on pole. It was as if the nation expected him to be there and it took no account of either his fitness or the fact that the Vanwall, although powerful, had to be driven to very precise limits.

This car could not be thrown around like the Maserati 250F, and there was one of those, the works car of Jean Behra, splitting the Vanwalls on the front row. It had been another dazzling effort which saw the Frenchman a full five seconds quicker than Menditeguy, one second faster than Schell – and a couple of tenths ahead of Fangio, the leader of the championship sharing the second row with Hawthorn's Ferrari.

This had not been a good year for Maranello. Apart from receiving a drubbing by Fangio and Maserati, Ferrari had suffered the loss of Eugenio Castellotti during a test session at the Modena autodrome. There was further turmoil in Italy when the dashing Marquis de Portago crashed while competing in the *Mille Miglia*, the Ferrari ploughing into the crowd, killing the Spanish nobleman, his passenger and eleven spectators.

Ferrari had employed Maurice Trintignant as a replacement for Castellotti and the Frenchman was on hand at Aintree to take a place on the fourth row alongside his team-mate, Luigi Musso. A great deal of development had been carried out on the V8 engine but the Lancia-Ferrari D50, despite being built around a new chassis frame and having the distinctive side-tank fairings removed, continued to be comparatively difficult to drive. Indeed, Hawthorn could

go no faster than Lewis-Evans, although that should not denigrate the Vanwall driver's burgeoning talent.

And what of BRM? Well, the 1956 fiasco – as opposed to the fiasco of any other year you care to mention – had produced a rethink involving someone who could think in racing terms. During the winter months, Colin Chapman had received the Ferodo Trophy for work with his Lotus sportscars and the Vanwall chassis. He was then asked to advise on the BRM P25 rear suspension; which he duly did and, predictably, transformed the cars, although not without one or two other problems arising in other areas as a result.

Nonetheless a BRM, in the hands of the American driver, Herbert Mackay Fraser, was seen rocketing though the field at Rouen before the transmission failed. In fact, the French Grand Prix was bitter-sweet, Ron Flockhart putting himself in hospital after spinning on oil and writing off his car. Then, not long after, Mackay Fraser was killed at the wheel of a Lotus sportscar. So BRM arrived at Aintree with mixed feelings and two fresh drivers – Les Leston and Jack Fairman.

Fairman was beaten during practice by a pair of Coopers designed for Formula 2 – which came into force that year. Formula 2 was for 1,500cc unsupercharged engines but the works car (for Roy Salvadori) and Rob Walker's entry (for Jack Brabham) had 1.9-litre Coventry-Climax 4-cylinder engines on board. There was a third Cooper, a 2.2-litre Bristol-engined special, adapted by Bob Gerard and completed just in time for Aintree. Indeed, the British Grand Prix would not have seemed complete had the name F.R. Gerard been absent from the entry list.

Once Gerard's Cooper took to the track, its progress was marked by an ever-increasing trail of smoke. When the car eventually caught fire, it was only saved by the intervention of Horace Gould, who was passing in his Maserati. Unfortunately, during the course of the drama, Gould suffered the indignity of Gerard's car running over his foot, putting Horace out of action for race day. There were, however, two more privately-entered Maseratis for Joakim Bonnier from Sweden and the Gilby 250F for Ivor Bueb.

Nose up, head high. Moss displays the graceful lines of the Vanwall under fierce acceleration at the start of a proud day for the British.

As ever, Jean Behra gave his all but the Maserati could not stand the pace.

The dream result

There was a strong breeze on race morning. The good news was that it eventually blew away the heavy rain. The bad news; it brought with it an unpleasant smell from the nearby factories. Some spectators had other things on their minds. A bus and coach strike had made life difficult – but not impossible, judging by the massive crowd braving the poor weather. And anyone walking to the circuit early that morning would have been treated to the sight of Bertocchi, Maserati's chief mechanic, taking the Gilby 250F for a test run along Preston Road, a spare works engine having been borrowed by the British team and fitted during the night. Later on, all four factory cars would be driven in convoy to the track.

The clouds began to clear, the odd shaft of sunlight illuminated the industrial backdrop and the track dried rapidly in the breeze. The drivers were marshalled for a lap of the circuit in Austin-Healeys before returning to the grid.

Two green cars on the front row. They had been close to victory before. Would they be reliable enough this time? Could Vanwall do it for Britain at last?

Not if Jean Behra had any say in the matter. The red Maserati shot into the lead but Moss had surged to the front by the time the field reached Tatts Corner. For 22 laps he stayed there, building up a nine-second lead over Behra.

Then the Vanwall engine began to misfire and lose power. Immediately Behra began to close the gap. Moss rushed into the pits, an earth wire was ripped out on the assumption that the problem might be magneto trouble, and he rejoined in seventh place. But it was no good; the misfire was worse than ever and Moss was back again almost immediately.

From the outset, Brooks had known that he was not fit enough to last the full 90 laps. It had been agreed that he would keep his car running and hand over to Moss or Lewis-Evans if necessary. Finding the going difficult, Brooks was relieved to receive the call after 26 laps. He was helped from the car while Moss, agile as a cat, sprang onto the rear wheel, dropped into the cockpit and was away. He was in ninth place. The race was on.

Ninth became eighth when Schell slowed, soon to retire with overheating. Then Moss caught and passed Menditeguy and set after Fangio. Apart from Behra pressing on relentlessly at the front, the Maserati attack was crumbling rapidly. As Menditeguy pulled in with transmission trouble, Moss took sixth place from Fangio's 250F and, five laps later, Musso's Ferrari succumbed to the rapid Vanwall. The atmosphere was electric. Moss was fifth. But the next bit would be more difficult.

Behra held a comfortable lead over Hawthorn, with Lewis-Evans doing a magnificent job in third place, keeping everyone busy while Moss made ground on Collins. By lap 47, Moss was fourth. And still the task seemed impossible since Behra was 59 seconds ahead.

The Maserati driver lowered the lap record; Moss responded by shaving a second off that to lap Aintree at an average of 90mph. With just over 20 laps to go, Moss was 22 seconds behind Behra. It was a lot to ask. Then the complexion of the race changed entirely.

The strain had been to much for the clutch/flywheel assembly on Behra's car. It suddenly shattered and deposited pieces of metal onto the track – and Hawthorn, about to inherit the lead, ran over one of them and punctured a tyre. And at the same time, Moss passed Lewis-Evans to take the lead! The grandstands erupted.

What an incredible turnaround. Given Moss's usual luck, it would have been the Vanwall which had picked up the puncture. But there he was, in the lead. Vanwalls first and second.

Next question: would they last?

Hearts sank when Lewis-Evans suddenly coasted to a halt. The throttle-linkage, the Achilles heel of the Vanwall, had come apart. Moss pressed on, now feeling vulnerable even though the next man, Luigi Musso, was over a minute behind. There was time for a quick pit stop to take on a precautionary few gallons of fuel, Moss hurtling back into the race still with more than 40 seconds in hand.

The car simply had to keep going – not an easy task considering that Brooks, having bravely continued in Moss's car, had finally stopped with a broken fuel pump while Lewis-Evans had struggled for some time to reconnect the throttle linkage. Having rigged up a temporary repair, he motored back to the pits for a permanent one, leaving the bonnet behind on the grass. That would cost him seventh place, the officials administering a rather severe disqualification.

As Moss headed towards an emotional victory, a disastrous day for Maserati was capped when Fangio retired with engine trouble. Ferrari, though, would take second, third and fourth places, Hawthorn finishing behind Musso after rejoining with a fresh tyre. Collins, having stopped with a water leak, took over Trintignant's car to finish fourth.

Brabham's spirited drive had been ended by clutch failure while Salvadori, having made the BRMs look foolish and caused havoc against Trintignant's Ferrari, rattled to a halt with gearbox trouble. He pulled up just before the finishing area and would claim fifth by pushing his Cooper across the line once the chequered flag had been shown. With Gerard about to be classified sixth, there was a healthy representation of British drivers on the scoreboard.

But the crowd only had eyes for one man. The majestic grandstands lining the finishing straight erupted in a wall of sound as Moss accelerated out of Tatts Corner for the last time, raised his right arm in the air and swept past the chequered flag. It was a truly heart-warming victory, not least for the man himself:

'It was something I had dreamed about for years; winning a Grand Prix in a British car. Then, to do it at home into the bargain; you know, Tony and I being the first British drivers to win a Grand Prix since Segrave and Sunbeam back in 1923. And also to be the first all-British winners of the British Grand Prix. Fantastic experience.'

Never to be repeated

There was, of course, muttering abroad about luck having favoured the British. Moss and Vanwall would silence the sceptics before the season was out. There were three rounds of the 1957 championship remaining. And each one would be a classic of its kind.

Next on the agenda, the Nürburgring; a place which you either liked or loathed. And Fangio loved all of its 14.2 miles. He had been strangely off form at Aintree but the opposition realised they were in for a hard time in Germany when the great man put his Maserati on pole by almost three seconds. It would be a battle between the Argentine and the Ferraris of Hawthorn and Collins; Vanwall, never having been to the Nürburgring before, took time to become attuned to the bumps, twists and turns. In any case, this circuit would play havoc with Brooks's injury.

Fangio took the lead and, running with less than a full tank of fuel, he pulled away from the Ferraris. When the Maserati stopped to refuel, the Ferraris swept by and, at the end of the next lap, they were 45 seconds ahead. At the end of the following tour, the gap had increased

Tony Brooks
One of the most talented and under-rated British drivers of all time. Drove for Ferrari but achieved greater success with Vanwall, winning convincingly at classic tracks such as Spa-Francorchamps and the Nürburgring. Will be best remembered for sharing a Vanwall with Moss to win the 1957 British Grand Prix.

slightly. Hawthorn and Collins had it in the bag, so much so that they arranged between themselves who should finish first. Fangio, meanwhile, had gone to work.

The Maserati 250F may not have been the most powerful car, but it was beautifully balanced; the perfect tool for a man of Fangio's skill on a circuit such as this. But, even then, he took the car to its absolute limit. All the way. He cut 15 seconds off the lap record. Hawthorn and Collins were stunned when their pit board showed the gap had shrunk to 35 seconds. Casting aside gentlemanly arrangements, they put the hammer down. And Fangio went quicker still.

On the next lap he went round the Nürburgring eight seconds faster than he had managed during practice. It was, he would say later, a lap he would never forget. He had never driven like that before. The chances he took made him shiver at the very thought. It was a supreme effort – but one he would not care to repeat. As a the result of this stunning performance, he had the Ferraris in his grasp with two laps to go. Of course, Hawthorn and Collins put up a stern fight, but on a day like this nothing would stop Juan Manuel Fangio. After perhaps one of the greatest drives in the annals of motor sport, he won the race and, appropriately, the championship.

Vanwall had their revenge at Pescara, a very fast road circuit on Italy's Adriatic coast. There was a rule that each country should host just one championship Grand Prix per season but the cancellation of the Dutch and Belgian races had allowed the FIA to make an exception at Italy's request. Moss simply outpaced Fangio's Maserati to score the first championship victory by a British car on Italian soil. And Monza was next. The Italians could put up with a lot – but not defeat at the Holy of Holies.

With Ferrari no longer in serious contention with the Lancia V8, Maserati threw everything they could into this race. A glorious V12 car had appeared during practice at Monaco, and raced at Rouen. It had plenty of power at the top of the rev range and it was thought this might be the answer at Monza. Fangio, after trying the car during practice, opted for his trusty 6-cylinder, leaving Behra to race the V12. But they were struggling. The green Vanwalls, led by Stuart Lewis-Evans, with Moss next, then Brooks, occupied the entire front row.

Well, not quite. This was more than the Italians could bear and overnight they changed the grid from 3-2-3 formation to 4-3-4, thus allowing Fangio's red Maserati onto the front row!

The first 20 laps were enthralling, the lead being carved up between the Vanwalls and the two Maseratis. Then Brooks went out, followed soon after by Lewis-Evans. Behra's V12, meanwhile, was rapidly consuming its rear tyres and he dropped back leaving Moss and Fangio to fight it out. In the end, not even Fangio's sheer determination and sublime skill could match the combination of Stirling Moss and the powerful Vanwall on this very fast track – then without the chicanes which strangle the circuit today.

It was yet another wonderful moment for Messrs S.C. Moss and A.G. Vandervell as they scored a convincing win on the doorstep of 'those bloody red cars.' And it had been done without the shoe-string support of motor sport enthusiasts. All told, 1957 must have thrilled Mr Douglas O. Ingram of Twickenham.

A likely lad

Easter Monday, 1958. Mike Hawthorn had been competing in the Glover Trophy International 100, a 42-lap race for Grand Prix cars at Goodwood. It was a non-championship event, of course, but in those days, time and the Grand Prix teams were not so precious. Ferrari had sent along a car for Hawthorn and he duly won the race. Then he flew his Vega Gull, a single-engined four-seater, to his base at Fairoaks airfield – and promptly drove back towards Goodwood. Hawthorn being Hawthorn, he did not want to miss the routine which had become a Goodwood tradition. He describes it in Champion Year, his account of the 1958 season:

'We always have a set run home. A drink at the Bricklayers in Midhurst and then one or two at the Spread Eagle. Then down to the Coal Hole for a few and sometimes for blotting paper we go to Bows, a fish-and-chip joint run by a splendid character. The party is usually the same, some of the drivers and a group of friends

....I left Goodwood in the Gull at the same time as some of my chums left for Midhurst by car and I flew back, collected the car, drove back and joined them not very long after their arrival. From Midhurst we went on to another of our ports of call, the Duke of Cumberland at Henley-on-the-Hill, just outside Midhurst. It is an old pub, very small, where we played darts, drank beer and enjoyed a meal of steak and chips. Then we all went home after a pretty good day.'

It's hard to imagine such a life-style being anything other than 'pretty good'. Hawthorn's spirits must have been uplifted by that win since it marked the first victory for what would turn out to be another Grand Prix classic; the Ferrari Dino 246.

This car had not been produced overnight. The original design brief had been for a car to comply with unsupercharged 1.5-litre Formula 2 which had been introduced as a stepping stone between the 500cc Formula 3 class and Formula 1.

The V6 engine was the work of Vittorio Jano, with a certain amount of input from Enzo Ferrari's only son, Dino, during the early stages of design in 1955. At the time Dino was fighting a losing battle with muscular dystrophy, and when he developed nephritis the following winter his health went into serious decline. Dino's death, a few months later at the age of 24, would mark the greatest tragedy in Enzo Ferrari's life. From then on, most V6 Ferrari engines would carry his son's name. The Dino 246 would provide a fitting epitaph to the man who had been groomed to run his father's empire.

In fact, the Formula 2 car had raced infrequently and it gradually evolved into a 2.4-litre Grand Prix version which would re-establish Ferrari's reputation. It was neat and powerful. And it ran on pump petrol. In the winter of 1957/58, this was a major point of discussion.

When the 2.5-litre formula was given an extension until the end of 1960, it was decreed that straight petrol should be used. Until now, engines had run on special alcohol fuels and petrol companies such as Shell, BP and Esso wanted to see a return for their investment in the form of advertising. It was difficult to boast that your fuel had been used by the winning car when that brew was not available to the public.

Pressure had been brought to bear on the FIA and alcohol fuel was banned in favour of pump petrol. The FIA soon wished they had not bothered when Mr G. A. Vandervell stormed into their Paris headquarters and demanded to know which particular petrol pump they had in mind. The variation in the quality of straight petrol was such that it was impossible for engine designers to work to a clear set of parameters. Eventually it was agreed that aviation fuel should be used, which meant the petrol companies were no better off and the design departments at Vanwall and BRM had to start again from scratch.

This was too much for Maserati and they withdrew, leaving Jean Behra and Harry Schell free to join BRM. Fangio, meanwhile, opted to take life at a more gentle pace, a reasonable decision considering he had just won the championship for the fifth time. He could not afford to miss his home Grand Prix of course, which was just as well for the organisers since they had very little to shout about, the confusion over fuel having forced BRM and Vanwall to give the opening round of the championship a miss.

That, in turn, allowed Stirling Moss to accept the offer of a drive in a Cooper owned by Rob Walker and powered by a Coventry Climax engine enlarged to 2 litres. A further change to regulations suited the smaller car since the race distances had been reduced from 500 to 300 km – or from three hours to two. As an important aside, drivers were no longer permitted to change cars during the races and share the points gained, as had Moss and Brooks at Aintree the previous year. In Argentina, however, Moss was not considered a major threat to the four Dino Ferraris of Hawthorn, Collins, Musso and the German, Count Wolfgang von Trips.

The blue Cooper with the white noseband won by 2.7 seconds from Musso's Ferrari, Moss having nursed his car through without changing tyres. And still the rear-engined Cooper was seen as nothing more than a novelty.

Then it won again at Monaco, although Maurice Trintignant's victory only came after representatives of Vanwall, BRM and Ferrari had led before running into trouble. Status seemed to have been restored when Moss's Vanwall won the Dutch Grand Prix with the rapidly improving BRMs taking second and third.

Then Brooks took a splendid win at Spa-Francorchamps for Vanwall while Hawthorn finally gave Ferrari success in the French Grand Prix, a race which brought sorrow and joy to Italy since the nation lost their only driver in Formula 1 when Luigi Musso crashed and died of his injuries. And, although it was not known at the time, the race at Reims would mark the last appearance of Juan Manuel Fangio, the Argentine finally retiring after a remarkable career.

Who would take his place? After the French round, Mike Hawthorn and Stirling Moss held joint first place in the championship. And the British Grand Prix was next.

The Grand Prix returned to Silverstone and, if the contemporary reports are anything to go by, there had been little change to an already high standard of organisation. Indeed, the only reference in *Autosport* concerned an enclosure and refreshment tent for members of the BRDC: 'a popular innovation,' it said.

Moss briefly heads for the British double with the Vanwall but Collins (1) is about to power between the BRM of Schell and Salvadori's Cooper (10) and Walk off with the race.

On a more serious note, *Autosport* devoted two and a half pages to a preview of the 'Moss-Hawthorn struggle for World Championship Points.' Ferrari brought along three Dino 246s for Hawthorn, Collins and von Trips to counteract the Vanwall entries for Moss, Brooks and Lewis-Evans. Cooper had a 2.2-litre model for Salvadori, with support from the 1960cc versions for Brabham and Ian Burgess, plus the Rob Walker entry for Trintignant. Lotus, encouraged by the reduction in race distances, had produced what appeared to be a mini-Vanwall, the Mark 16, in time for the French Grand Prix. There were two at Silverstone for Alan Stacey (making his Grand Prix debut) and a determined gent who would make a major impact on the Grand Prix scene: Graham Hill. Cliff Allison, meanwhile, was entrusted with the older Mark 12 from 1957.

BRM had P25s for Schell, Behra and Masten Gregory, a bespectacled American who suffered another of his many spectacular accidents during practice for the sports car supporting event and was whisked off to hospital. Maserati may not have been present in an official capacity but the 250F lived on, Joakim Bonnier, Gerino Gerini and Carroll Shelby doing the driving for the various private entrants. The Connaught name survived too, thanks to the enthusiastic efforts of B.C. Ecclestone, the former 500cc driver. Bernie entered the 'toothpaste tube' for Bueb and a more conventional car for Fairman.

The Ferraris were in trouble from the start of practice, handling problems making Woodcote, in Hawthorn's words, '....a very shaky do.'

Hawthorn was horrified during the first practice session (3.15 to 4.30 pm on the Thursday) when Salvadori managed to equal his time in the little Cooper and it became even more embarrassing between 11 am and 12.30 pm the following day as Salvadori improved further. Moss was on pole, with Schell second quickest, then Salvadori and Hawthorn. That made it four different makes on the front row; three of them British with three of the drivers from home soil. And Allison had urged the Lotus onto the inside of the second row, ahead of Collins and Lewis-Evans. It seemed this would not be a clear-cut battle between Moss and Hawthorn after all.

As an interesting aside, the organisers allowed Ferrari an extra 20 minutes of practice in which to try out the new Dunlop RS5 racing tyre. Hawthorn was forced to squeeze his lanky frame into von Trips's car since the Englishman's Dino had already returned to the team's garage in Northampton. Hawthorn was able to ascertain that the Dunlops were an improvement although the team would be obliged to revert to Engelberts for the race. Try asking FISA for an extra practice session today. And wait for your existing tyre company's reaction in the unlikely event that you are given permission to sample the rubber of a rival firm.

Jobs for the boys

There must have been brisk trade in the BRDC refreshment tent on race day as the sun beat down strongly. And, heaven forbid, a girl dared to walk through the paddock, clad only in a bikini! One report suggested, half-heartedly, that the lady in question had been sent forth by the Italians in an effort to throw the British mechanics off their stroke. Certainly, there was a healthy representation of British Racing Green on the grid. Among the 20 starters were 14 British cars and 13 British drivers. But which one would win?

It had to be Stirling. Sure enough, Moss took the lead into Copse, but by the end of the lap Collins had forced his way through from the second row to pass the Vanwall with ease. There was nothing Moss could do about it and Collins would not be troubled for the rest of the afternoon.

Within ten laps, Collins had established a lead of seven seconds. Moss chiselled some of that back during the next ten laps but, coming through Woodcote at the end of lap 26, the Vanwall broke a connecting rod. Hawthorn was now second. Moss free-wheeled straight into the paddock, convinced his championship was run. He had set the fastest lap but the point awarded for it would be taken from him in the closing stages by, of all people, Hawthorn.

The highly publicised struggle between the two may have ended prematurely but there was a right royal battle going on elsewhere as the Coopers and Lotuses created havoc among their more lofty rivals. Hill had worked his way past von Trips, Schell and Brooks before retiring, and a bad day for Lotus was completed when Stacey and Allison went out before half-distance. Behra's wretched luck continued when he struck an equally unfortunate Silverstone hare, a bone from the poor animal puncturing a rear tyre.

Harry Schell on his way to fifth place in the BRM.

Salvadori, meanwhile, was in tremendous form as he moved the Cooper into third place ahead of Lewis-Evans, engine problems with the Vanwall making it difficult for the Welshman to fight back effectively. Brooks was in similar difficulties in seventh place and had no hope of getting on terms with a battle between Schell and the Cooper of Brabham, Schell taking the opportunity to break free from the Australian by nipping behind Collins as the Ferrari lapped the BRM.

Collins was driving magnificently. Before the race he had agreed to help Hawthorn in his quest for the championship, but the 'Farnham Flyer' was more concerned about finishing, never mind winning. From an early stage, Hawthorn had noticed puffs of smoke from the exhaust and a gradual fall in oil pressure. Fearing that an engine failure might be imminent, he stopped to replenish the oil and still managed to return in second place, a position he held to the end. Then, on the slowing down lap, he stopped to take on liquid of a different kind, as he recounts in his book:

> '*I remember the last few laps of the race very well because I was very hot and thirsty and every time I went through Becketts the marshals on that corner, Tony Rolt, Bill Ruck-Keene and David Phillips, were standing there drinking beer from pint mugs and taunting me by swigging the stuff as I went through – it made me even thirstier. On the last lap I signalled to them that I would like a drink myself, so after I got the flag I kept going fairly fast until I reached Becketts where I stopped and was given a pint of shandy. Then I drove on sipping the shandy. I had my crash hat off and drove in with the drink – it foxed a lot of people.*
>
> *A friend of mine overheard a couple discussing this. One chap said that he wondered how I had got hold of the beer. His friend, obviously out to impress, said: "Oh, that's just a gimmick. He's had it with him all through the race."*'

Shandy indeed. It's hard to imagine Hawthorn drinking the stuff but, either way, it had been another 'pretty good day' for the Englishman. The six points, plus one for the fastest lap, gave him a seven-point advantage over Moss with four races to go. And, to round off the celebration in the BRDC tent, Mike's mate Collins had won at a canter. As the report in *Motor Racing* concluded, 'Nobody who witnessed his performance could have dreamed that this was to be his last victory.'

Bitter–sweet ending

Hawthorn took pole position at the Nürburgring and the German Grand Prix developed into a furious battle between the Ferraris and Vanwalls. Moss went out with magneto failure on the fourth lap, leaving Brooks to carry the Vanwall challenge to the Ferraris. This he did in style, finally moving to the front after a lengthy dispute.

Collins gave chase but, in a moment of enthusiasm, he went into the right-hander after *Pflanzgarten* a shade too quickly. The Ferrari hit the bank and overturned. Hawthorn, following closely, saw it happen. Mike subsequently retired on the far side of the circuit and it was not until much later that he discovered that his 'mon ami, mate' was dead. The news rocked the entire British motor racing scene just as, earlier in the year, the world of football had been stunned by decimation of Manchester United in the Munich aircrash.

During the three-week gap between the German and Portuguese Grands Prix, Hawthorn had to brave the funeral of his friend in Worcestershire and the hysterical outbursts in the national media which usually accompany the death of a racing driver. In a way the next race, on the bumpy 4.6-mile Oporto circuit, came as a relief.

Moss won, Hawthorn finished second – and was surprised to do so. The brakes on the Ferrari had almost failed completely, and on his last lap Hawthorn spun. Moss, having taken the chequered flag, stopped to aid Hawthorn in warning off would-be helpers as Mike restarted his engine on an incline. He was amazed when told he had still managed to finished second – and astonished when it was made clear that he had also gained a point for fastest lap.

Hawthorn felt sure Moss would have taken care of that detail, and indeed Moss would have done so had he read his pit signs correctly. Mistaking 'HAW-REC' (Hawthorn has the fastest lap) for 'HAW-REG' (Hawthorn Regular – there's nothing to worry about), Moss had simply maintained his lap speed as before.

That made it Hawthorn 37 points; Moss 32. And the irony was that Moss had come to Hawthorn's aid during a Stewards' Inquiry after the race. The officials had tried to exclude

Hawthorn on the grounds that he had motored along the track in the opposite direction while re-starting his car on the incline. Moss argued that Hawthorn was not on the track at all, but on the pavement. The officials relented and Hawthorn collected his points.

At the penultimate round at Monza, Moss retired with a seized gearbox and Hawthorn nursed his car, complete with damaged clutch, into second place behind Brooks in the Vanwall. Once again, he was fortunate to collect the six points since the next car also happened to be a Ferrari, driven by a young American by the name of Phil Hill. Hill had distinguished himself in sportscar racing and this was the chance he had been waiting for. Fortunately he saw Hawthorn's urgent signal not to overtake during the closing stages, otherwise it might have been his last Grand Prix for Ferrari. So, Hawthorn now had an eight point lead with the Moroccan Grand Prix to come.

The mathematics were simple. If Hawthorn finished second or higher, he had the title no matter what Moss did. Stirling, of course, drove brilliantly, won the race and set the fastest lap; he could do no more. But Hawthorn finished second. He won the title by a single point and became the first British world champion. Vanwall, on the other hand, had accumulated enough points to take the very first constructors' championship.

Those were the facts. The records also showed that Stirling Moss had won four Grands Prix to Hawthorn's one. It made a mockery of the drivers' championship and polarised opinion at home. Many believed that Moss should have won it; after all, he was driving a British car. Others, who preferred Hawthorn's more relaxed style out of the cockpit, said he was a 'good lad' and deserved any success which came his way.

As for the man himself, he decided that enough was enough. The sport was changing onto a more professional footing and, in truth, Hawthorn saw himself as a garage owner who happened to go motor racing. Then, the death of Peter Collins had finally tipped the balance and Mike decided to retire.

All told, it had been a season which had seen more than its fair share of sadness. In Morocco, Lewis-Evans had crashed, the Vanwall catching fire and inflicting serious burns before the driver could escape. Hawthorn flew home in the same chartered aircraft as Lewis-Evans and Mike, along with the rest of the motor racing world, was distressed to learn a few days later that the young Welshman had succumbed to his injures. It had been an appalling year in that respect. Lewis-Evans's name was added to a list which included Archie Scott-Brown, Luigi Musso, Peter Collins and Peter Whitehead.

A few months later, in January 1959, Mike Hawthorn lost control of his Jaguar on the downhill approach from the Hogs Back to Guildford. The car smashed into a tree. Hawthorn was killed instantly. He was 29.

Denis Jenkinson, the motor sport writer who knew Hawthorn well, summed him up best when penning a profile some thirty years later for the book *The Grand Prix Drivers*. Jenkinson wrote:

> '*As British as the Royal Family and roast beef, Mike was a "super bloke"…His sense of fun at all times was natural and infectious…His death in a road accident after he had retired from racing was tragic, but it was the result of his competitive spirit and willingness to "have a go" at all times. I often think that Mike's last words were before his Jaguar hit the tree must have been "Oh F…".*'

Mike Hawthorn
The archetypical Englishman who wore a bow-tie while racing and enjoyed a pint of bitter and a pipe while relaxing. Never won the British Grand Prix but, while driving for Ferrari in 1958, became the first Englishman to win the world championship. Died in a road accident at the beginning of 1959.

CHAPTER 9

FRONT TO BACK

A bit of a do at the RAC

One of Mike Hawthorn's final duties had been to advise the FIA and its sporting arm, the Commission Sportive Internationale, of his views on which path Grand Prix racing should take when the current formula ended on 31 December 1960. The general consensus had favoured a move to 3 litres and Hawthorn, along with Moss and Trintignant, had supported the suggestion. The CSI were left to mull this over and make their announcement at their annual prize giving, to be held on that December evening at the RAC Club in Pall Mall.

When it was revealed that, from 1 January 1961, Formula 1 would be for cars with a maximum cylinder capacity of 1,500cc unsupercharged, there was uproar in the house. The speaker was scarcely able to make himself heard. The general view was that the French were determined to screw the British.

On 13 January 1959, Tony Vandervell announced that he was withdrawing his team from Grand Prix racing. Vandervell cited ill-health, the strain of building up his team having taken its toll. On top of that, it was believed he had been deeply troubled by the death of Lewis-Evans, the only driver to come to serious harm in a Vanwall. But for the purposes of the press announcement, Vandevrell said he was acting on doctor's orders.

Colin Chapman, interviewed by Independent Television News, was more outspoken. When asked if he thought the proposed changes to Formula 1 had influenced Vandervell's decision, Chapman replied:

'Well, yes, I do. I think that he was a profoundly disappointed man to see these changes brought about which he was convinced were purely political moves because of his supremacy in Formula 1 racing, as we know it at the present time. He very deeply resented the fact that the amount of effort that had gone into it over the past years would come to nought in two years' time, merely because of administrative changes in the sport.'

The interviewer then asked if this meant the end of Grand Prix racing. Chapman was adamant.

'Oh no,' he said. 'Definitely not. I think it will continue but we look to people like BRM and Ferrari to provide the major spectacle.'

With the benefit of hindsight, we can now see one glaring omission in that last statement – the Cooper Car Company of Surbiton, Surrey. Indeed, looking back to January 1958, the most significant announcement in the motoring journals had been the launch of the Cooper Formula 1 car.

Modifications and improvements to the rear-engined machine had continued apace. In 1959, of the 13 Formula 1 races entered, Cooper would win eight, Moss kicking off the season by winning at Goodwood on Easter Monday. And you can be sure that he did not fly to Fairoaks and then drive back to Sussex for a couple of pints with the lads...

Which to choose?

Moss, of course, had to look elsewhere once Vandervell announced his retirement. He enjoyed the prospect of taking on the works teams in privately entered cars run from Pippbrook Garage, in Dorking, by Rob Walker. The question was, which car should they race?

Coventry Climax had enlarged their twin-cam four-cylinder engine to 2.5 litres and Moss had been impressed by development with the BRM 4-cylinder. An abortive attempt to mate the BRM with the Cooper chassis failed and, in any case, progress was seriously compromised by a decision to use what would become a notoriously unreliable Colotti gearbox although there was little else available to the Walker team. Inbetween times, Stirling would drive a BRM P25, on loan to the British Racing Partnership and painted a pale shade of green.

Meanwhile, *Autosport* reported that Tony Brooks was 'going foreign' by joining Jean Behra and Phil Hill at Ferrari. Brabham would continue with Cooper and there was a hint of things to come when Jack won the opening round of the championship at Monaco.

British Racing Green continued to dominate at Zandvoort where victory, at long last, went to BRM as Jo Bonnier won the Dutch Grand Prix in the face of stern opposition. Moss had led before the Colotti gearbox gave trouble, but at least the Cooper name was kept in the frame as Brabham and his works team-mate, Masten Gregory, finished second and third respectively. And into fourth place, at the wheel of a front-engined Lotus, came an ex-Rolls Royce apprentice by the name of Innes Ireland.

Ireland had made an impressive Grand Prix debut, and during the same period the motoring press had been recording the meteoric progress of another Scot. Indeed, while Moss was giving the Cooper its successful outing at Goodwood on Easter Monday, the man who would become his successor in the eyes of the British public was winning four races at Mallory Park. His name: Jim Clark.

In the meantime, though, Moss remained the national idol and, somehow, his struggle against the odds increased the attraction – and a growing army of critics.

In the French Grand Prix, for instance, he drove the BRM into second place before spinning off on tar made treacherous by scorching conditions. Try as he might, Stirling could not push-start the car, but at least he had the satisfaction of lapping Reims faster than anyone else. His average had been a shade over 130mph and there was consolation for the British when Brooks took a stylish win in the Ferrari.

Unfortunately, though, a 'metal workers strike' at Maranello meant the red cars would not be present at Aintree for the next round of the championship. Indeed, for the first time in many years, there would not be a single factory car from Italy taking part in the British Grand Prix. And it would have a predictable effect on the quality of the racing.

Cooper were numerically the strongest. There were works cars for Brabham, Gregory and Bruce McLaren, a 21-year-old New Zealander who had created a favourable impression on John Cooper in Germany the previous year. Driving a Formula 2 car, young Bruce had won that category in the German Grand Prix and finished fifth overall. Cooper and Jack Brabham did their best to persuade Bruce not to go home and continue his engineering studies. Their arguments were strong enough to convince him to join the Formula 1 team for 1959. It was the start of a long and distinguished association between the name McLaren and Grand Prix racing.

Rob Walker, still not happy with the reliability of the Colotti gearbox, persuaded Moss to run the pea-green BRM once more while Trintignant took charge of the Cooper-Climax. There were Maserati-engined Coopers for Hans Herrmann and Ian Burgess, neither of whom posed a serious threat to the works cars. The opposition would come from the BRMs of Schell, Bonnier and the Scot, Ron Flockhart backed, of course, by Moss in the BRP example. And the British presence was strengthened further by the arrival of the Grand Prix Aston Martins with their six-cylinder engines.

With Cooper enjoying so much success, it was clear that the front-engined Aston Martins were almost obsolete before they had started. None the less, Roy Salvadori put his on the front row, between the pole position Cooper of Brabham and Schell's P24. The second Aston Martin of Carroll Shelby qualified on row three, alongside Moss and McLaren, and ahead of Bonnier.

Graham Hill was the fastest Lotus driver, Ireland taking a place on the fifth row, just behind his team leader. Innes was far from fit however, injuries received at Rouen the previous weekend prompting him to hand his car over to Alan Stacey. Brooks, unemployed this weekend, had accepted the offer of a drive in a Vanwall, dusted down for the occasion by the works. He would have been better off staying at home. It was a far cry from 1957 as Brooks struggled to beat the Maserati 250F of Fritz d'Orey and failed to improve on the time set by Brian Naylor in his JBW-Maserati special.

In all, there were 24 starters, the maximum permitted by the BARC. Sixteen runners (from Aston Martin, BRM, Cooper, Walker-Cooper, Lotus, Vanwall, and the two Cooper-Maserati teams) had been guaranteed places on the grid, leaving the rest, mainly Formula 2 entrants, to fight it out. It meant that Jack Fairman (Cooper), Trevor Taylor (Beart Cooper), Keith Greene (Gilby Cooper), W.F. Moss (Cooper), Mike Parkes (Fry-Climax) and Denis Taylor (Lotus-Climax) would be spectating on Saturday afternoon.

It turned out to be a race of tactics. Before the start, little attention had been paid to tyre wear, but this would play a large part in deciding the outcome.

Motor Racing reported that Harry Schell had asked Brabham to let the BRM go first because he 'only wanted to go fast for a few laps.' If it's true, then Schell clearly did not know Brabham very well. As soon as the flag fell, Jack shot off the line, never to be seen again by his pursuers.

Jack Brabham brings on the rear-engined revolution with the Cooper-Climax.

Bruce McLaren hangs on grimly to the BRM of Stirling Moss. (Note the front of the Cooper, still bearing the shot-blast scars of the previous slip-streaming race at Reims.)

The only hitch in his plan began to emerge after half-distance, when the left-front tyre began to wear badly. This is what the opposition had hoped for since a pit stop for the Cooper, with its bolt-on wheels, would be a time-consuming disaster. Brabham's team kept showing a spare wheel but, as Jack continued to drive with just enough caution to stay in front, it became clear that the spare wheel was perhaps a ruse to throw the competition off the scent.

Moss had been driving with his usual brilliance, smashing the lap record time and again as he closed to within 10 seconds of Brabham. He would pay a price for such a furious pace. A tyre change was inevitable and Moss spent 31 seconds in the pits at the end of lap 49 as the left-rear wheel was changed. Moss, still in second place, returned to the fray and set about the almost impossible task of catching Brabham. Then, with nine laps to go, the BRM dashed into the pits for fuel. Brabham was able to slow right down and still finish with more than 22 seconds in hand.

In any case, Moss was too busy dealing with McLaren. The New Zealander had been in the thick of things from the start. There had been an early bonus when Shelby and Salvadori rushed their Aston Martins into the pits to see if anything could be done about fuel spilling from the overflows. McLaren gradually moved through the field to take third place, Trintignant and Schell being startled by his bold moves under braking for the slower corners as Bruce made the most of his agile little car. Then he equalled the lap record as he fought to keep in touch with Moss and, when Stirling made his second stop, McLaren gratefully, if briefly, accepted second place.

Moss soon surged ahead but the youngster was not about to give up, the BRM and the Cooper slashing the lap record further as they made a race of it to the finish. With a handful of laps to go, Moss recorded 1minute 57.6 seconds. Then he went round in 1:57.0. In a frantic effort to deprive Moss of second place, McLaren equalled that time on his last lap. The BRM and the Cooper, the only cars not lapped by Brabham, crossed the line 0.2 seconds apart.

With the rear-engined Coopers showing such form, the old order was clearly changing in every respect. At times like that, critics begin to examine the 'old hands' in the light of energetic performances by the new boys. Moss's failure to win was seen as another example of his decline. He became the 'Aunt Sally' of the editorial and correspondence columns. L.F. Hill of RAF St. Mawgan, launched into the attack in *Autosport*.

> '…I am strongly inclined to put forward a blunt and to-the-point argument concerning Stirling Moss's apparent inability to finish a Formula 1 race…It can hardly be considered pure ill-luck for Stirling each and every time and just simply good fortune for Jack Brabham that the latter has amassed 15pts (after the French GP) in the World Championship.'

Gregor Grant, the editor of *Autosport*, tended to support that view when reflecting on the British Grand Prix. Grant wrote:

> 'I cannot understand why Stirling had to make that extra stop for fuel. Schell went through non-stop – and he certainly was not hanging about. Stirling has stated that the BRM was not quite quick enough, but a glance at the progress of the lap record makes this controversial:-

Lap 26	Moss	1m 58.6s
Lap 29	Brabham	1m 58.4s
Lap 38	Moss	1m 58.2s
Lap 39	Moss	1m 58.0s
Lap 42	Brabham	1m 58.0s
Lap 45	Moss	1m 57.8s
Lap 68	Moss	1m 57.6s
Lap 69	Moss	1m 57.0s
Lap 75	McLaren	1m 57.0s

> Now Brabham won the race by 22.2 seconds, and Moss lost about 55 seconds altogether by reason of his two stops. Therefore Stirling's actual race speed was higher than Brabham's. There will always be conjecture if Moss had been able to pursue Brabham non-stop: would Jack have been able to hold off the BRM?'

This, of course, did not take into account the fact that Moss had to decide whether or not to push Brabham hard and force a pit stop, or simply motor at a more gentle pace and perhaps face a tyre change in any case. And the refuelling, as it turned out, had been made necessary by a fault in the fuel-feed system.

But the matter refused to go away. A few weeks later, an editorial criticised Moss for continually chopping and changing cars. The dreaded word 'jinx' was mentioned.

That set the cat among the pigeons and the correspondence columns fairly crackled with indignation from Moss fans. The final word, however, went to Rob Walker, who wrote:

'I beg to disagree with certain remarks made in your Editorial regarding Stirling Moss and his choice of cars for Grandes Epreuves.'

After explaining why Moss had been forced to choose the various cars, Walker went on to say:

'It has been said that Stirling Moss is hard on a car but this is absolute nonsense and I am sure all of those for whom he has driven will tell you that Stirling takes it out of himself, not the car. People forget the times he has won with no water, no clutch, no oil pressure...'

Whatever the rights and wrongs of the various arguments neither Moss nor Walker were rid of problems with the Colotti gearbox, despite their belief to the contrary. The German Grand Prix, held on the uninspiring Avus track in the western zone of Berlin, saw Tony Brooks win for Ferrari with Moss sidelined by transmission trouble. And, to make matters worse, the entire meeting was overshadowed by the death of Jean Behra when his Porsche flew off the top of the banking during a sportscar race.

The Walker team's false dawn came when Moss won in Portugal and at Monza. They went to the final round, the first American Grand Prix at Sebring, in the belief that they had a fair chance of taking the championship from Brabham. Moss had to win and set the fastest lap; Brabham merely needed to take the one point for fastest lap. Moss claimed pole and felt confident about achieving his target. After six laps in the lead, the transmission broke.

He had lost the title yet again and, on this occasion, he would not even have the dubious honour of being runner-up. Tony Brooks, who had an outside chance of taking the championship, finished third and claimed enough points to move into second place on the table.

The US Grand Prix had been won by McLaren, the Cooper driver assuming command after Brabham had run out of fuel on the very last lap. Jack pushed the car across the line to take fourth place and the 1959 championship. And Bruce McLaren, at 22, had just become the youngest driver to win a Grand Prix. Back in Britain, the knives were out.

It was said that Moss had been guilty of all manner of crimes, ranging from indulging in too much wheelspin at the start to driving much too fast when it was not necessary. Once again this provoked another long letter from Rob Walker, the team patron explaining clearly and logically just why Moss had retired. But it was now January 1960. Another season beckoned. Would Moss finally lay the bogey to rest by winning the championship?

Jack Brabham
The first man to win a Grand Prix and a championship in a car bearing his own name. Before that, the Australian won the world title twice while driving for Cooper. Claimed the British Grand Prix on three occasions – and it would have been four had he not run out of fuel in 1970.

Handle with care

By the time the British Grand Prix came round in July, the answer was in the negative. Stirling Moss started the race – in every sense. Handling the Union Jack was about all he could manage since he had just been released from hospital. Moss was still recovering from a broken nose, broken legs and a crushed vertebra, the result of a high-speed shunt during practice for the Belgian Grand Prix at Spa-Francorchamps the previous month.

Rushing through the 140 mph right-hand sweep at Burnenville, the left-rear wheel had parted company with his car, sending Moss into the grass bank before throwing him from the cockpit. He was driving a Lotus 18, a car which would bring Moss success and grief in equal amounts.

Colin Chapman had not taken long to register that the rear-engine design was the way to go. Thus, when the 1960 season opened in Argentina, Lotus revealed their hand with the 18, christened by some as a coffin-on-wheels thanks to its box-like appearance. It was fast, but fragile.

Innes Ireland set a stunning pace in Buenos Aires but the car literally fell apart and victory went to McLaren's Cooper. Moss and Rob Walker quickly realised that the Lotus 18 was worth investigating and they took delivery of their car shortly before the Monaco Grand Prix.

Moss was impressed by the car's precision, even though it was not as forgiving as the

Cooper, and he elected to race it. Just as Moss and Walker had given Cooper their first victory in a *Grande Epreuve*, they did the same for Lotus at Monte Carlo. But the fact that the engine mounts had broken and the Coventry Climax was hanging by the skin of its teeth should have provided a warning of what was in store.

In Holland, the car behaved perfectly and Moss became a victim of tactics he was reluctant to employ. Frustrated by the continuing idle gossip which suggested that he was a car-breaker, Moss elected to abandon his policy of running at the front in favour of cruising in second place behind whoever was leading. In this case, it was Brabham and, Jack being Jack, he ran over a kerb at one stage and inadvertently flicked a piece of concrete into Moss's path. The resulting puncture meant a pit stop and a stunning drive back to fourth place.

To hell with those tactics, thought Moss. It would be back to normal at Spa. Then the axle shaft broke.

It was to be the start of a miserable weekend all round. During the Belgian Grand Prix itself, Alan Stacey was struck in the face by a bird, the Lotus driver losing control and crashing fatally. Chris Bristow was also killed when he crashed his Cooper while duelling fiercely with the Ferrari of the Belgian driver, Willy Mairesse.

By the time the British Grand Prix came round, Brabham had won at Zandvoort, Spa and Reims to hold joint-first place in the championship with McLaren. Few were willing to tip anything other than a victory for Cooper at Silverstone.

The arrival of James Clark

'Jim Clark is one of today's most brilliant newcomers, and is perfectly capable of being up in front and one must also emphasise the brilliance of John Surtees.'

Autosport, British Grand Prix Preview

Jim Clark had first come to Colin Chapman's attention when the Scot almost beat the Lotus boss at Brands Hatch. Clark, racing for the Border Reivers team, had taken delivery of a Lotus Elite shortly before the 1958 Boxing Day meeting at Brands. Relatively unknown south of the border, the sheep farmer from Berwickshire had been dismissed when it came to discussing the likely winner of the event. The pundits sat up and took notice when he led the similar car of Chapman, no mean driver himself. Had it not been for a backmarker getting in Clark's way, he would have won. Chapman made a note of the name.

Clark signed to drive for Lotus in Formula Junior (introduced in 1959), and at the beginning of 1960 he agreed to join the Aston Martin Grand Prix team. The Aston Martin effort never managed to get into its stride and Clark was free to accept the offer of a Formula 1 drive with Lotus in the Dutch Grand Prix. He would drive almost exclusively for Colin Chapman for the remainder of a brilliant career.

Lotus had also signed John Surtees, the motor-cycle world champion making the switch to four wheels with apparent ease. The new boys would support Innes Ireland in the works team at Silverstone. Brabham and McLaren, meanwhile, would spearhead the Cooper team, a third car having been hired by Lance Reventlow, a Californian whose team of front-engined Scarabs had been grounded due to a shortage of spare parts. But Reventlow would hand his car over the Chuck Daigh, designer of the Scarab.

Reventlow, heir to the Woolworth's fortune, and Daigh must have felt a little foolish with their dated design since BRM had also made the switch to a mid-engined car, the P48. There were three on hand at Silverstone for Jo Bonnier, Graham Hill and Dan Gurney. Ferrari had also begun to think about moving with the times, and a mid-engined car had made its first Grand Prix appearance at Monte Carlo. Driven by Richie Ginther, a slightly-built American, this car had been nothing to write home about, but the potential was there. Rapid strides were to be made later in the season when the 1,500cc Formula 2 engine was fitted. It was clear that this was a prototype for 1961 and the dreaded change in formula from 2.5 to 1.5 litres. For the British Grand Prix, however, Phil Hill and Wolfgang von Trips had to make do with the front-engined Dino 246.

A new name, the Yeoman Credit Racing Team, had first appeared at the end of 1959 when three brothers from the Samengo-Turner family decided to link their finance company with motor racing. Working with Alfred Moss and Ken Gregory, they ordered three Coopers for 1960, but their first full season was fraught with difficulty, Harry Schell crashing fatally during practice for the International Trophy at Silverstone, this tragedy being followed not long after by the loss of Bristow at Spa. Bolstered by a second place for Olivier Gendebien at Reims, Yeoman Credit entered the Belgian driver, along with Tony Brooks and Henry Taylor, for the British Grand Prix.

A pair of red Cooper-Maseratis were brought along by *Scuderia Centro-Sud* for Masten Gregory and Ian Burgess, while Roy Salvadori and Maurice Trintignant were hoping for better things from a front-engined pair of Aston Martins. The usual group of private entrants consisted of the Gilby Cooper-Maserati for Keith Greene, Cooper-Climaxes for Jack Fairman and Lucien Bianchi, a front-engined Lotus-Climax to be driven by David Piper, and a pair of Ferrari-engined Coopers for Gino Munaron and Giorgio Scarlatti.

Glancing down the entry list, Gregor Grant of *Autosport* was clearly not a man to stick his neck out when he wrote:

> 'Scarlatti and Munaron can be discounted. Given ideal weather conditions, it is probable that the race will be won at over 110mph, and very few drivers and cars are capable of maintaining, or even lapping at this speed. I should say that the winner of the 13th British Grand Prix will be found from Brabham, Ireland, McLaren, Brooks, Graham Hill or Phil Hill, with Gendebien, Surtees, Clark, and von Trips, as the best bets for "outsiders."*

Yes, well, that seemed to cover it.

Hill makes his mark

The one person Grant had not mentioned was Bonnier and he must have been alarmed when the Swede put his BRM on the outside of the front row. However, a glance at the lap times showed that he was almost two seconds slower than Brabham's pole position Cooper and it seemed the Australian was set for a repeat of the 1959 result at Aintree. But that did not take into account the grimly determined Graham Hill as he lined up his BRM alongside the Cooper.

Before the main event of the day, however, there was time for a spot of light entertainment. The Mini had been launched the previous autumn, and as a means of promoting this revolutionary car the Formula 1 drivers were asked to take part in a 'demonstration'. Some hope.

The Minis formed on the grid, the flag fell, and they all shot off – backwards. It was easy to detect the naughty hand of Graham Hill in the plot and, as soon as the joke had ended, the serious business began as the drivers crunched the long gear-levers into first and roared off at high speed. Four and five abreast they were all around the circuit, with Hill just managing to stay in front. The 24 cars were in less than showroom condition at the end of it. And fate was to have the last laugh on Hill.

He stalled at the start of the Grand Prix and was eventually helped on his way by an unintentional nudge from behind by Tony Brooks. All that effort during practice had been wasted, and by the time Hill had sorted himself out, Brabham led McLaren, with Bonnier and Ireland poised to bundle the New Zealander down to fourth place.

The subsequent struggle between Bonnier and Ireland allowed Brabham to make good his escape and once the Lotus driver had fought his way into second place, Bonnier was left to deal with a furious assault from Surtees, McLaren and Clark.

But all eyes were on Hill. Driving like the wind, moustache fairly bristling with rage over his stupid mistake at the start, Hill caught and passed the Ferraris as if they were standing still. By the time Hill had worked his way into seventh, the next quarry was his team-mate, Bonnier having been shoved down to sixth. On lap 19, Hill rocketed past the Swede and the chase was on.

In just two laps, he had caught and passed McLaren who, in turn, had been overhauled by Clark. That made it Brabham, narrowly leading the Lotus team of Ireland, Surtees and Clark. Hill, still 'a bit narked with myself', pressed on. Stopwatches clicked as he reeled in Clark to take fifth place. By lap 31, he was ahead of Surtees. Brabham now led Ireland by three seconds with Hill a further nine seconds in arrears. Then, with 37 laps on the board, Hill took second place from Ireland. Brabham was just five seconds ahead.

The gap see-sawed as the leaders dealt with back-markers, Ireland taking the opportunity at one stage to close on Hill and divert his attention from the leading Cooper. The BRM, though, had the legs of the Lotus and Graham pulled away as soon as the track was clear.

50 laps: Brabham led Hill by 2.5 seconds. The gap came down to 1.7 seconds at Stowe. Lap 51: Brabham led by 1.3 seconds. Lap 52: the gap was a mere 0.5 seconds. Lap 54: they were wheel to wheel. As the Cooper and the BRM roared through Abbey Curve and under the

Daily Express bridge at the end of the lap, Graham Hill led the British Grand Prix. The grand-stands at Woodcote erupted.

Brabham was not about to give up, even though Hill set the fastest lap, and for the next 30 minutes the BRM and the Cooper drivers put on a magnificent display, Brabham willing Hill into a mistake.

After 60 laps, Hill led by a scant 1.2 seconds with Surtees almost half a minute behind in third place and pulling away from Ireland and McLaren. They were the only cars to remain unlapped, Clark having pulled into the pits to attend to collapsed front suspension. Ten laps later and the leaders were ready to lap the Ferraris for a second time.

Outwardly, Hill seemed to have the measure of the world champion. The Londoner was driving with calm precision in contrast to Brabham who crouched in the cockpit, sawing at the wheel with great gusto. The tension was almost unbearable. Graham Hill was about to win his first Grand Prix – at home. But he had a wily Aussie on his tail and the brakes on the BRM were wilting; Hill had been driving flat-out for close on two hours. There were six laps to go.

Hurtling towards Copse, Hill had to make a snap decision about how to deal with two backmarkers; should he risk overtaking them and gain some breathing space, or should he fall into line – and perhaps give his pursuer the opportunity to sneak through. With a character like Brabham on your tail, there *is* no choice.

Hill went for the gap. He arrived too quickly, the brakes were not up to the task and he spun into the ditch. Dejectedly, he climbed out as Brabham, followed eventually by Surtees, Ireland and McLaren, gratefully accepted the gift of another move up the scoreboard. Hill was cheered all the way back to the pits. It would turn out to be one of his finest races and, certainly, the closest he would come to winning the British Grand Prix.

'Com'on boy!' John Cooper (centre) waits for Brabham to appear through Woodcote. The signal shows 'Placed second, minus two seconds (on Hill), six laps to go'.

'Thought I had the bugger, Sir but…' Graham Hill explains himself to Alfred Owen (leaning on the shoulder of Louis Stanley) after returning on foot to the BRM pit.

A sudden end

That made it four wins for Brabham and he put the championship beyond reach by scoring yet again in Portugal after Gurney and Surtees had both taken turns at leading before running into trouble. The race at Oporto marked the return of Moss as he moved the Lotus into second place before making a pit stop. Back in fifth place with four laps to go, he spun and stalled at the same corner where Hawthorn had almost lost the championship in 1958. Moss got going again by employing the same tactic which he had rigorously defended on Hawthorn's behalf. This time, this was no one to speak for Stirling. He was disqualified…

After that, the 1960 season and the 2.5-litre formula gradually petered out. The leading British teams boycotted the Italian Grand Prix. The organisers had decided to use a combination of the road circuit and the bumpy banking at Monza, a ploy which was seen as a means of favouring the larger and stronger Ferrari Dinos. Ferrari did not send any cars to the final race at Sebring (won by Moss in the Walker Lotus) and while the British teams tried to ignore the advancing 1.5-litre formula, work was well in hand at Maranello. The days of British Racing Green domination were over – for the time being.

CHAPTER 10

SMALL, BUT BEAUTIFULLY FORMED

He who hesitates

On or about 28 May 1961 an envelope, postmarked London Ealing W5, was delivered to Enzo Ferrari. It contained an unsigned letter offering Ferrari good wishes, with an accompanying donation of 10 shillings. Since the letter did not carry an address, Ferrari was unable to acknowledge the gift and he wrote to *Autosport* instead.

In fact, Ferrari was the last person in need of financial assistance. Had there been a Ostrich Society, c/o Head-in-the-Sand, Southern England, then any moral support would have been well-received, if undeserved.

To the surprise of many in Britain, the 1.5-litre Formula had not gone away. There had much clucking and tutting throughout the land and a serious effort was made to support the so-called Inter-continental Formula for up to 3-litre cars. This, said the pundits, was the way to go – 1.5 litres would be a disaster. There was talk of a boycott, and the movement had many prominent figures rallying to its cause. Stirling Moss, in an outspoken interview in *Motor Racing*, claimed the new formula would be less exhilarating thanks to the lack of power.

Ironically, Moss would turn out to be the one person capable of demonstrating that there *was* a substitute for horsepower; namely, the brilliance of the driver.

But, before the season got under way, the editorial and correspondence columns were filled with gloom and doom. Jack Brabham, the reigning world champion, deprecated the mandatory need for on-board starters, saying that the presence of a battery constituted an unnecessary fire hazard. And there was the general feeling that the 450 kilogramme minimum weight would prove too much for the 1.5-litre engines to cope with.

Enzo Ferrari, meanwhile, made the occasional encouraging noise about the Intercontinental Formula, knowing full well that work was continuing apace on his 1.5-litre car. It was unveiled in March 1961. And that was the beginning of the end as far as the British teams were concerned.

Sharknose

The most distinctive aspect of the Ferrari was a twin-nostril nose, from which the car, officially known as the Tipo 156, won the nickname 'sharknose.' This aerodynamic design was introduced in the interests of low drag, but the car's selling point lay behind the driver; the 120° V6 engine would have no equal during 1961.

Porsche had arrived on the Formula 1 scene with an air-cooled flat-four engine of Formula 2 origin. By now Coventry Climax and BRM had realised that the 1.5-litre Formula was here to stay and, of course, they had missed the boat.

This did nothing to alleviate the melancholy tone of most of the media prophets at home. There were valiant attempts to massage the Intercontinental Formula into life, but without world championship status it failed to carry the clout necessary to knock it beyond the status of British national meetings. By the time the opening round of the world championship arrived in May, most people had begun to abandon the up to 3-litre ship and switch their attention to the serious business of season.

The Monaco Grand Prix more or less set the pattern. Ginther took the lead in the only Ferrari to have the latest 120° V6 (Phil Hill and von Trips had to make do with older 65° versions). On the streets of Monte Carlo, however, power was not the ultimate criterion and Moss moved his four-cylinder Lotus-Climax into the lead on lap 14. He was hounded all the way by the Ferraris but Stirling made up the power deficit by dint of a virtuoso performance in a more nimble car; a 150bhp greyhound against a 180bhp carthorse on a circuit such as this. It was one of Stirling's finest races.

In Holland, however, Moss had no answer to the Ferraris, von Trips becoming the first German to win a championship Grand Prix since 1939. Another historical point of interest was the fact that all 15 starters were running at the end and not one of them had made a pit stop. The same could not be said of the next round in Belgium, almost half of the field failing to reach the finish. But Ferrari were not among the stragglers. Indeed, no one could touch them on the fast open sweeps of Spa-Francorchamps, their domination extending to fourth place and a car painted yellow for the Belgian, Olivier Gendebien. A repeat performance was expected at Reims a fortnight later.

One side-effect of the 1.5-litre formula had been the flood of non-championship Formula 1 races. The switch to 1,500cc engines had more or less wiped out Formula 2, leaving competitors without a decent secondary single-seater formula. Overlaps on the calendar led, for example, to the Naples Grand Prix being held on the same day as Monaco. And while Ferrari were humbled by Moss in the Principality they at least had the minor consolation of winning at Naples.

The car had been entered by FISA (not the international body, but the *Federazione Italiana Scuderie Automobilistiche*, a consortium of racing teams pledged to encouraging home-grown talent) and given to Giancarlo Baghetti. This was his second win in succession (Syracuse having marked a début victory) but the Milanese was expected to carry out nothing more than a supporting role when FISA were asked to bring their car along to the French Grand Prix.

Baghetti won his first world championship Grand Prix. In an amazing turn-around, all three works cars retired after running line astern at the front and Baghetti, calm as you like, slipstreamed Dan Gurney's Porsche and pulled out at the last minute to beat the American by one tenth of a second.

By now, the British editorials had changed their tune. This 1½-litre formula wasn't so bad after all. The lap speeds were, in most cases, faster than the 2½-litre formula and the racing was close. The Editor of *Autosport* practically choked on humble pie when writing the preview for the British Grand Prix.

Struggling to keep up

Giancarlo Baghetti was billed as the star of the show; three wins in three races – and only the back-up to the 'works' drivers, Phil Hill, Wolfgang von Trips and Richie Ginther. The British weather would soon burst the bubble.

Baghetti, now racing under the *Scuderia Sant Ambroeus* banner, but without the benefit of the 120-degree engine, was under the spotlight as he tried to learn the Aintree circuit during practice on Thursday. He spun during the second session, which began at 4 pm, and rain the following day meant he did not have the chance to fully recover and keep pace with Hill, Ginther and von Trips.

The one driver capable of giving them a run for their money turned out to be Jo Bonnier, the Porsche driver taking a place on the outside of the front row, and ahead of von Trips.

As ever, it was left to Stirling Moss to keep the British customers satisfied. Due to a conflict of interest between Esso, who sponsored Lotus, and BP, who supported Rob Walker, Esso had asked Lotus not to supply their latest car, the 21, to the Walker team. As a result, Moss had to make do with his trusty 18, although Alf Francis had made one or two modifications and the car had been adapted to take the latest cigar-shaped body panels from the 21. Esso's thoughts are not recorded after Moss beat the works cars and just failed to equal the time set by von Trips....

It was a typical doughty effort and Stirling had taken time out to try a couple of laps in the second Rob Walker car, the experimental four-wheel drive Ferguson P99. Powered by a front-mounted Coventry Climax engine, this innovative machine proved ideal in the wet on the Friday, Moss setting the fastest time of the day before handing the car back to Jack Fairman.

The faithful four-cylinder Climax engine was seeing Lotus (Ireland and Clark) and Cooper (Brabham and McLaren) through this lean period while belated work continued apace on the V8. BRM were in a similar 'caught with their pants down' situation, and Tony Brooks, an excellent sixth fastest ahead of Ireland and Clark, had to make do with an interim car, powered by a Climax, as had his team-mate Graham Hill.

The Yeoman Credit Coopers of Surtees and Salvadori were managed by Reg Parnell, the former racer also overseeing the Lotus 18 driven by his son, Tim. The UDT-Laystall Racing Team had converted two 18s to take 21 bodywork and their lime-green cars were driven by

Henry Taylor and Lucien Bianchi, while the 18s of Ian Burgess, Gerry Ashmore, Tony Marsh, Tony Maggs and Wolfgang Seidel helped to make Lotus numerically the strongest marque on the grid.

Cooper were not far behind, *Scuderia Centro Sud* bringing along a pair for Lorenzo Bandini and Massimo Natili; *Camoradi*, entrants of the Burgess Lotus, had a 1960 Cooper for Masten Gregory, and the promising young Welshman, Jack Lewis, was about to make his Grand Prix début in a similar car. Swelling the entry to a record-breaking 30 starters was the Gilby-Climax special of Keith Greene. But, as ever, anyone beyond the front two rows would be struggling to keep up. Unless, of course, it rained.

A wet walkover

By lunchtime on race-day, Saturday, a major department store in Liverpool had sold out of plastic macs – and the rain showed little sign of relenting. Even when there was a break in the cloud, the dilemma on the starting grid increased. There was a huge demand for Dunlop's new wet weather rubber but the tyre technicians sounded a note of caution. If the track dried out, the heat build-up would be so great that wet weather tyres would not take the punishment. Then the rain returned in greater quantities than before and that particular problem was solved.

The next obstacle for the drivers would be the unenviable task of trying to grope their way through the appalling conditions. The rear half of the field could just about make out A. V. Ebblewhite as he dropped the flag. After that, it was pot luck. Judging the corners would be a matter of memory and guesswork.

Phil Hill had the advantage of a clear track as he led von Trips at the end of the first lap, Ginther making it a red trio at the front. They took the blue Lotus of Moss with them as the rest of the field dealt with the more immediate problem of simply staying on the road, never mind thinking about trying to take on the Ferraris. There were frightening moments aplenty as the track became awash, the circuit never having being designed to cope with rain such as this. Puddles and streams formed rapidly to trap the unwary, Innes Ireland being one of the first to spin onto the grass.

Ireland resumed in 21st place but, a few laps later, Henry Taylor was not so lucky. Coming through Melling Crossing the Lotus driver lost control and smashed into some advertising hoardings. It took some time to cut Taylor from the wreckage and remove him to hospital with broken ribs. That would be the Englishman's last British Grand Prix.

Moss had taken third place from Ginther and, not long after, von Trips moved into the lead, leaving Hill to deal with the Walker Lotus. Lapping two seconds faster than Hill, it took Moss just three laps to pick his way past the American and set after von Trips.

Further back, Surtees had raised a cheer as he charged through the field, the progress of the Yeoman Credit Cooper seemingly unimpeded by a trailing exhaust, the result of a nudge from behind at the start. Officials prepared to show the black flag but a spin at Tatts prompted Surtees to make a stop and have the pipe attended to.

Moss and von Trips were evenly matched on lap times although the Lotus would close on the Ferrari under braking. There was little Moss could do except attempt to pressure the German into an error and, given von Trips's cool performance, there seemed little chance of that.

Moss was the solitary British standard bearer, Phil Hill and Ginther having kept Graham Hill at arm's length in fifth place. Indeed, such was Moss's advantage over the third-place Ferrari that he managed to spin at the exit of Melling Crossing, make a rapid recovery and continue without losing second. Von Trips, meanwhile, had managed to pull out a 10-second lead, doubtless a welcome release after the intense pressure of the previous 15 laps.

The rain had eased, and by lap 30 had stopped altogether. So had Baghetti. The Italian's heady summer came to an abrupt halt when he crashed at Waterways Corner, just after being lapped by the leader, von Trips. Moss began to reduce the gap and the rapidly drying track produced changes in the order right down the field.

Ginther reasserted himself by passing Phil Hill and the American seemed to be making remarkable progress as he closed on Moss. The lap times, however, revealed that Moss was in trouble and, when both Ferraris overhauled the Lotus before the end of lap 44, it was clear that Britain's hopes had been dashed. At the end of the next lap, Moss pulled into the pits and retired with brake failure.

Once Phil Hill had passed Ginther to take second place a few laps later, the order would

All change. Stirling Moss takes over the four-wheel drive Ferguson for a spot of development work after his Lotus had retired with brake trouble. Jack Fairman (right) looks on.

remain settled for the rest of the afternoon. Brabham's fourth place looked like being threatened by Jim Clark as the Lotus improved in tandem with the track conditions but the Scotsman was eventually sidelined by an oil leak. Salvadori was unable to prevent Bonnier from taking fifth place while Gurney caught and passed McLaren for seventh. Graham Hill had retired with a broken valve spring while Brooks, in his last British Grand Prix, was back in ninth place after a lengthy pit stop to change plugs and generally dry out the BRM-Climax. But, once he was firing on all four, the Englishman had the satisfaction of signing off with the fastest lap, a mere eight-tenths of a second outside the 2½-litre lap record.

It was final proof that the 1.5-litre formula was capable of providing quality motor racing. And the Ferrari demonstration ensured that the 1961 title would be a fight between Wolfgang von Trips and Phil Hill.

No way to win

Doubtless the merits of both drivers were discussed at length on the Webbair charter flight from Liverpool to Gatwick (return fare £8). John 'Connaught Club' Webb was now on the board of Brands Hatch Limited following a recent change of ownership, Grovewood Securities having acquired a controlling interest for an estimated £100,000. With the benefit of hindsight, cheap at the price!

Of more immediate concern to Webb, however, was the safe conduct of his charter trip by DC3 to the German Grand Prix, price £22-5s-0d (£22.25p), and a four-day package to Monza by Elizabethan aircraft for 41 guineas (£43.05p). In each case, the enthusiasts would get more than they bargained for.

The Coventry-Climax V8 was installed in Brabham's Cooper in time for the German Grand Prix. Second fastest to Hill's Ferrari in practice, Brabham hit a patch of oil and flew off the road, leaving Moss to assume the lead. The Nürburgring suited Moss perfectly and he managed to stave off a strong attack from Hill, the American then spinning down to third place when rain fell on the closing stages. His rival, von Trips, gratefully accepted second place but, on this day, no one could do anything about Moss.

Ferrari were out in force at Monza, Baghetti and a young Mexican by the name of Ricardo

Rodriguez being drafted in to support the main trio. The organisers were using the combination of the road circuit and the banking once more, but on this occasion the British had no objections and a full entry was received. A close battle was keenly anticipated.

The championship reached a terrible conclusion early in the race, von Trips and Clark colliding as the field rushed towards the Parabolica Curve. The Ferrari speared off the track, careered up a five-foot bank, struck a fencing post and then cannoned off the spectator fence itself. Von Trips was killed, along with 14 spectators.

Phil Hill won the race and, with it, the championship, but the success meant little to the sensitive American in the face of such tragedy.

Ferrari gave the final round, the US Grand Prix at Watkins Glen, a miss, leaving the stage clear for Brabham and Moss to fight a spirited battle. The Cooper and the Lotus eventually retired and Innes Ireland went through to score for Lotus.

As Ireland savoured the heady moments of victory, he was unaware that Colin Chapman would not require his services in 1962. And Moss was equally oblivious to the fact that he had just taken part in his last world championship Grand Prix.

A savage denial of talent

Stirling Moss was voted BBC Sportsview Personality of the Year. He received his award inbetween jetting back and forth to races in the Bahamas and South Africa. Then he moved across to the Tasman Series in Australasia driving Rob Walker's new Lotus 21

Moss won the final race of the series, the Lady Wigram Trophy at Christchurch, before returning to Europe for one or two non-championship races which marked the beginning of the 1962 season. While the 21 was returning by sea, Stirling would revert to the old faithful 18/21 for the Easter Monday meeting at Goodwood.

Problems with the gear linkage meant a pit stop and a charge back through the field. Having smashed the lap record and worked his way into seventh place, Moss went straight on at the approach to St. Mary's and crashed into the bank. Badly injured and concussed, he survived the impact. But his racing career ended right there. And, to this day, he does not know why he left the road. Britain was suddenly without its star performer.

There were, however, one or two likely candidates waiting in the wings. During his final races in South Africa and in the Tasman Series, Moss had come to respect the emerging qualities of greatness in Jimmy Clark.

The Coventry-Climax V8 was now fully developed and Chapman had produced the Lotus 24 for Clark and Trevor Taylor, the Formula Junior champion of 1961. Cooper would continue to run the V8 but they no longer had the services of Brabham, the Australian going off to race as an independent, first in a Lotus and later in a car of his own design. That elevated Bruce McLaren to number one driver with Cooper and he was joined by the South African, Tony Maggs. Innes Ireland had found a place at UDT-Laystall with Masten Gregory, while Richie Ginther left Ferrari to join BRM.

In fact, Ginther was not the only person to quit Maranello. In the aftermath of the Monza tragedy, the Italian team had taken a terrible lashing and Phil Hill had agreed to stay loyal. Not so members of the management – Carlo Chiti, Romolo Tavoni and the financial expert Ermano della Casa storming out after a massive argument. Unfortunately for poor Hill, no one had seen fit to warn him of the imminent row and he signed shortly before the walk-out. The reigning champion was to be partnered by Baghetti and Lorenzo Bandini, with Willy Mairesse taking over Ginther's place as chief development driver.

Meanwhile, back in Britain there had been a major row on the domestic scene following the announcement by the RAC, in the latter part of 1961, that the 1962 British Grand Prix would be held at Aintree for the second year in succession. The reason given by the Executive Committee (and not the subsidiary Competitions Committee) was that the BARC would be celebrating their Golden Jubilee in 1962. The BRDC, organisers of the Grand Prix when it visited Silverstone, were stunned. And there were ugly rumours that money had changed hands and a five-year deal had been done with the BARC and Aintree.

Politics were at play here and John Bolster made no bones about who he thought was to blame.

Bolster wrote in *Autosport*:

> '... *The members of the Competitions Committee are all well-known sportsmen and if it is true*
> *that their decision (to hold the race at Silverstone) was reversed by a handful of the Executive,*

> *grossly insulted. They should resign forthwith.*
>
> *The BARC make the lame excuse that 1962 is their jubilee year. In fact, the jubilee they are celebrating is of a non-existent club (the Cyclecar Club)...The point is, however, that though the present BARC can probably trace its ancestry back to the original Cyclecar Club, it has not the slightest interest in cyclecars and for years has done nothing to further that cause. To celebrate the jubilee of something that you have long ceased to support seems a somewhat questionable action....*
>
> *Those of us who have attended races at both circuits can, I am sure, find no superiority in the Liverpool venue, nor can we detect any advantage in the organization of a BARC event over one run by the BRDC. Many of us have been treated with rudeness and discourtesy at the meetings of one of these clubs and I'll give you one guess which it is. The BARC are quite good at running dances and they have some amusing little club meetings at Goodwood, but to give them a monopoly of running the British Grand Prix would be both wrong and absurd.'*

The major portion of the flood of correspondence which followed supported Bolster. There was even a letter from Rob Walker which displayed an uncharacteristic outburst of indignation. Walker wrote:

> *'Very many congratulations on the superb article by John Bolster....I think we must have a massed resignation from both clubs (the RAC and the BARC), as I feel that the only thing that will hurt people of their sort is taking money away from them by reducing membership....'*

The following week, *Autosport* ran an apology. Apparently the letter had been a personal one to the Editor and should never have been published....

The Lotus 25

But, like it or not, the 1962 British Grand Prix was scheduled for Aintree on 21 July. And, by then, there were other more important matters to deal with. Such as speculating on the likely winner. Never, in recent times, had a season been more open. Of the four championship races held thus far, each had been won by a different marque. Hill had won the Dutch Grand Prix in his rapid and reliable V8 BRM, this race also marking the arrival of the monocoque Lotus 25.

Showing typical flair and a touch of genius, Colin Chapman had introduced a chassis construction which spelt the end of the tried and trusted spaceframe. Chapman was looking for a more rigid structure which, at the same time, would weigh less and be more compact. Originally, there had been talk of a column gearchange but Chapman was persuaded to find more space for the more conventional shift. Clark also had trouble with the original pedal layout and the production of the car took longer than anticipated.

But it was ready for Zandvoort, and although Clark had done absolutely no testing it was a sign of things to come when he led for several laps until clutch trouble intervened.

A multiple pile-up, coupled with an engine failure for Hill, helped McLaren and Cooper win at Monaco, but the Lotus 25 really came into its own at Spa, Clark winning the first of four Grands Prix at a circuit he detested. Porsche returned from a short break while modifications were carried out to the air-cooled flat-8 and gave Dan Gurney a popular win at Rouen. The one notable absentee from the honours list was, of course, Ferrari, the current world champions continuing to suffer from all manner of problems, including industrial unrest at home. For the British Grand Prix, they entered just one car, more or less in 1961 trim, for Phil Hill.

Lola had arrived on the Formula 1 scene with neat Climax V8-powered cars for Surtees and Salvadori, the team running under the Bowmaker (formerly Yeoman Credit) banner. Clark had the only Lotus 25 available, team-mate Trevor Taylor making doing with a 24, as did Jack Brabham and the UDT-Laystall team of Ireland and Gregory. The foregoing ran the Coventry Climax V8 whereas Wolfgang Siedel had fitted a BRM V8 to his new 24. A Lotus 24 for Trintignant had been withdrawn after the Rob Walker car had been damaged at Rouen, leaving Jay Chamberlain and Tony Shelly (Lotus 18s), Ian Burgess and Jack Lewis (Coopers), Tony Settember (Emeryson) and Carel de Beaufort (Porsche) to flesh out the entry.

The weekend was all about Jim Clark and the Lotus 25. Fastest in practice by over half a second, the Scot simply left the field for dead. It was a stunning display – and a tedious race.

Surtees offered a challenge for the first few laps but then the Lola lost fourth gear. It did not

Jim Clark cocks a wheel as he sweeps through Melling Crossing. The Scot and the Lotus 25 dominated the entire weekend.

deter the motor-cycle champion however and he managed to maintain second place until the end. Any hopes the Porsche team may have had about repeating their victory at Rouen were swiftly dispelled when Bonnier stopped to attend to gearbox trouble and Gurney's clutch began to slip, dropping Dan from an early third place to ninth. And as for Innes Ireland, starting from the outside of the front row, his race had more or less ended before it had begun when a bent selector fork meant serious gearbox trouble for the rest of the race.

All of which meant McLaren was more or less untroubled in third spot. The New Zealander soon discovered that the Cooper was no match for the hobbled Lola and McLaren simply concentrated on keeping Graham Hill at arm's length. This was a disappointing race for the Londoner, his BRM showing a dislike for the number of tight corners at Aintree, and Hill was troubled for some time by Brabham. Looking like a bandit, with a handkerchief covering the lower half of his face as protection from grit carried by a stiff breeze, Brabham soon had his own problems as a chassis tube carrying hot water began to burn his right foot. Braking became a painful business and Brabham considered himself lucky to finish fifth ahead of Tony Maggs.

Clark set the fastest lap and, along the way, he had lapped Phil Hill shortly before the champion's embarrassment was eased by ignition failure. Towards the end, Clark lapped Brabham but decided against rubbing it in when he came upon Graham Hill, the Lotus driver easing off to trail the BRM to the line. It was Jim Clark's second Grand Prix win, but the commanding style of the victory made it clear there was more to come from the Scot and his Lotus.

The German Grand Prix was as captivating as the British was dull. Graham Hill, Surtees and Gurney became engaged in a ferocious battle in damp conditions, the BRM taking an excellent win just 2.5 seconds ahead of Surtees, with Gurney finishing third, 1.9 seconds behind the Lola. Buoyed by this return to form, BRM scored a splendid one-two (Hill-Ginther) at Monza. Clark, who forgot to switch on his fuel pump at the start in Germany and suffered problems in Italy, regained the initiative at Watkins Glen. A convincing win, despite the loss of his clutch for most of the 230-mile race, gave the Lotus driver an outside chance of winning the title at the final race, the South African Grand Prix at East London on 29 December.

Clark needed to win if he was to snatch the championship from Graham Hill. Clark took pole, with Hill alongside, and the Lotus led for 59 of the 82 laps. Then a retaining bolt on the distributor drive housing worked loose, allowing oil to escape. By lap 62 his race was over.

The minute Clark pulled off, Graham Hill became the 1962 world champion. But he won it in style by taking his fourth Grand Prix victory of the season – and BRM claimed the constructors' title thanks, in part, to excellent reliability. The embarrassment of Silverstone 1950 seemed another age.

Britain had won eight of the nine Grands Prix, with a Scot and an Englishman debating the title. Not surprisingly, therefore, the correspondence columns howled with indignation when BBC radio saw fit to offer just ten minutes of commentary from the final race in South Africa. There was also lively written debate on the relative merits of the championship contenders. Clark and Hill were the first to admit, however, that they had benefited from the enforced absence of Moss, now very much in evidence at the trackside and sporting a beard. There was continuing speculation that he might return to the cockpit the following season.

Moss hands over to Clark

At noon on 1 May 1963, Stirling Moss left his flat in London and went to Goodwood. There, he climbed into a competition car for the first time since his accident. It was a test session, not of the car, but of the driver.

Moss was able to handle the Lotus 19 racing sportscar with little difficulty, but he noticed the absence of the instinctive reflexes which had made him great. With hindsight, Moss now reckons he returned to the track too soon. But, later that day, he announced his retirement. His loss was ours too.

Twenty-five days later, the battle to decide who would be Britain's top driver opened at Monaco. Jim Clark and Trevor Taylor stayed put at Lotus, Graham Hill re-signed with BRM, as did Ginther, while John Surtees decide to take the offer of a contract with Ferrari, where he would race alongside Mairesse. The Lolas, meanwhile, had been acquired by Reg Parnell, who had been astute enough to take on a very promising 20-year-old New Zealander by the name of Chris Amon.

The UDT team had been taken over by the British Racing Partnership, Innes Ireland and the American, Jim Hall, driving Lotus 24s with BRM V8 engines. When Porsche withdrew from Grand Prix racing at the end of 1962, Gurney joined Jack Brabham in the two-car Brabham-Climax team and Bonnier moved to the Walker *équipe*. Cooper retained McLaren and Maggs while Graham Hill's championship-winning BRM was sold to *Scuderia Centro-Sud* for Lorenzo Bandini. If Phil Hill thought he had endured a difficult time in 1962 he jumped from the Ferrari frying pan straight into the fire by signing to drive an ATS *(Automobili Tourismo Sport)* V8 designed by Carlo Chiti. Baghetti, as number two driver for this Italian organisation, more or less signed off his brief Formula 1 career.

At Monaco, though, one or two of the minor teams would not be ready for the new season and it was the old firm of Hill and BRM who kicked off with a win once Clark had dropped out with gearbox trouble. After that, though, the 1963 season would belong to Lotus.

The front cover of *Autosport*, depicting the opening seconds of the French Grand Prix, summed it up. As the field charged towards the first corner, Jim Clark had already pulled three or four lengths ahead. During the course of that first lap, he would completely annihilate the opposition, breaking the tow to remain untroubled for the rest of the afternoon.

Victory in France made it three in a row, Clark having led from start to finish in Belgium (a mesmeric drive in the rain on a circuit which, don't forget, he disliked) and in Holland. And there was every reason to believe that he would repeat the dose at Silverstone on 20 July.

More speed

A letter to *Autosport* from Sheridan Thynne, an amateur racing driver, pointed out that there appeared to be a need for a Racing Safety Council. Thynne, later to become heavily involved with the Williams Grand Prix team, claimed that certain matters needed attention in this field. He cited, as an example, the position of the pits at Silverstone.

It would prove to be a most prescient letter when, on the day of the British Grand Prix, Christabel Carlisle lost control of her Austin Healey Sprite at the exit of Woodcote during the Sports and GT race. The car careered straight into the pit road (then without any protection whatsoever) and fatally injured Harold Cree, one of eight scrutineers on duty that weekend,

Following like sheep. As the Scottish farmer lights up his rear tyres on pole position, the rest of the field set off in hopeless pursuit of Jim Clark's Lotus.

as he walked towards Woodcote to investigate spilled oil which, ironically, probably instigated the accident. Bolting the stable door the following week, the RAC decreed that the Silverstone pits could no longer be used in their present form.

Speeds had risen sharply as the cars taking part in the supporting events rapidly reached new levels of sophistication. The Formula Junior race was won by Peter Arundell, the Lotus driver also setting the fastest lap at 106.01mph, race 17 of the 1,000cc cars lapping at an average of over 100mph. Jack Sears won the Touring Car race in a Ford Galaxie but failed to improve upon his own lap record of 94.42mph while Roy Salvadori won the Sports and GT event, the Cooper-Climax lapping at 105.58mph.

As far as the Grand Prix cars were concerned, Innes Ireland held both lap records of note; the absolute record of 1 minute 34.2 seconds (111.86mph) set in a 2.5-litre Lotus in 1960, and the 1.5-litre record of 1:35.4s recorded during the International Trophy a few months before.

In the second practice for the British Grand Prix, Clark got down to 1 minute 34.4 seconds. He was joined on the front row by the Brabham team, Gurney and Brabham being split by

Graham Hill's BRM. Brabham was making excellent progress with his latest car, the BT7, while BRM were not so impressed with their first monocoque car, which had appeared at Zandvoort. Hill and Ginther were back to the older spaceframe model for Silverstone.

Other changes included BRP's own car of monocoque construction for Ireland and the appearance of Tony Settember and Ian Burgess in a pair of Scirocco-BRMs run by an American team which had taken over the Emeryson project. Reg Parnell had expanded his entry to include a pair of Lotus 24s for Masten Gregory and Mike Hailwood, the motor-cycle world champion.

Former motor-cyclist, Bob Anderson, had switched to four wheels and a Lola-Climax, while the Swiss private entrant, Jo Siffert, brought along another Lotus 24 powered, like Gregory's car, by a BRM V8. Ian Raby had a similar engine for his Gilby special, John Campbell-Jones relied on Climax power for his Lola and the Dutch aristocrat, Count Godin Carel de Beaufort, flew the flag for Porsche in his capacity as a private entrant, some nine seconds off Clark's pace in the Lotus. The ATS team, probably to the great relief of Hill and Mairesse, withdrew their entry.

Bruce McLaren had qualified in the middle of the second row and, satisfied that the time was good enough, the Cooper team had begun race preparation before practice had ended. McLaren took himself to the inside of Club Corner to watch his colleagues at work. In his *Autosport* column, 'From the Cockpit', Bruce wrote:

'When you are in a G.P. car you haven't got time to think about the fact that you're moving fast; you're concentrating on keeping the movement of the car as smooth and graceful as possible, getting the throttle opened just that fraction quicker than last time, and keeping it open all the way when you've got it there.

At Silverstone, you concentrate on shaving the brick walls on the inside, not just an inch or two away, and you hold the car in a drift that, if it were any faster, would take you into a bank or onto the grass. You know perfectly well you are trying just as hard as you possibly can, and I know when I've done a few laps like this, I come in and think to myself, well, if anyone tries harder than that, good luck to them.

But you haven't thought about the people who have been watching. At least, I haven't anyway, but here at Club Corner the role was reversed, and I was watching.

Jimmy came in so fast and left his braking so late that I leapt back four feet convinced that he wouldn't make the corner, but he went through, working and concentrating hard. I'm sure his front wheel just rubbed the wall. I barely dared to watch him come out the other end...'

Jimmy and the Lizard 25

McLaren managed to see more of Clark in the race than planned. He takes up the story as 2 pm on Saturday afternoon approached.

'The drivers' briefing was quick and to the point The "2 MIN" board was up and my team-mate Tony Maggs was in trouble. Part of the ignition system had let us down again. So while Tony sat with arms raised to signify that he wasn't going to move, the flag was lifted and with the deafening blast and excitement of Formula 1 racing, 1963, the race was on.

I made a good start in behind Gurney and alongside Graham's BRM. But suddenly I was nearly on top of Gurney's Brabham. I assume he missed a gearchange. I swerved to miss his rear wheel and felt a bump as I touched someone else's wheel. Jimmy had made a poor start and Jack snatched the first corner in the lead with Dan and myself right on his tail and Jimmy a yard or two behind us.

For six laps we had the sort of motor racing that I haven't been in since the Formula 2 days at Brands Hatch....but Jimmy soon came through and took command of the bunch. After six short laps the song from my Climax V8 was abruptly strangled. Initially it seemed as though it was a petrol or ignition failure, but a quick glance in the mirror showed enough smoke coming out the back to screen a small-sized army. So that was that and I parked the Cooper alongside Becketts.'

As McLaren climbed from his car and came to terms with his early retirement, Gurney moved into second place ahead of his team-mate, leaving Brabham to fend off Surtees and Hill.

Bonnier, Ginther and Bandini were squabbling over sixth place and Amon was watching from a safe distance. McLaren soon got over his disappointment as he watched the leaders, Gurney and Brabham, vainly chasing Clark:

'They reminded me of a Brockbank cartoon. Jimmy came through with his mouth open, and occasionally his tongue between his teeth. The tyres were holding a tenuous grip on the road with the body and chassis leaning and pulling at the suspension, like a lizard trying to avoid being prized off a rock by a small boy. Then Dan arrived really throwing the Brabham into the corner, understeering and flicking the car hard until he had it almost sideways, then sliding through with the rear wheels spinning and the inside front wheel just on the ground.'

It was to no avail. Clark pulled inexorably away and, on lap 29, Brabham joined McLaren as a spectator at Becketts, his Climax V8 having blown up. Gurney suffered the same fate on lap 60 and that left Clark with almost a minute in hand over Hill's BRM. In fact, the Lotus driver needed the cushion since he was concerned about making his fuel last the distance.

This was a knock-on effect of the 1.5-litre formula and the need to have each race last for two hours. With the cars becoming lighter and faster each year, the race organisers had to extend the length of their races to comply with the two-hour rule. The teams could have allowed for extra fuel capacity, of course, but in this age of nimble little cars, that went against the grain. Anyway, in Clark's case, a bag tank had kinked while being filled and there were anxious moments in the Lotus pits as the final laps ticked by.

Clark completed the distance and, in fact, it was Hill who began to run out, the BRM spluttering half-way round the last lap. In a flash, Surtees was through to second place, Hill reluctantly settling for third ahead of Ginther and Bandini.

After the race, Graham and Bette Hill threw a party at their Mill Hill home in North London. Everyone was there; Clark, McLaren, Maggs, de Beaufort, Ginther, Hall, Bonnier, Moss, members of the trade, pressmen and, of course, Innes Ireland. It was, according to one contemporary report, 'an altogether bright and breezy affair, with everyone in the highest spirits'.

This was standard procedure in the sixties. And, a few months later, Colin and Hazel Chapman held another bash, also attended by the Who's Who of motor sport, at their home in Hadley Wood, Herts. This was to celebrate Jim Clark winning the championship thanks to a further victory at Monza. In fact, Clark went on to win at Mexico City and East London, making it seven in all. The Lotus had started ten Grands Prix and failed to finish just once (Monte Carlo). That made it ten Grand Prix wins for Jimmy Clark in two seasons. And the 27-year-old Scot had not yet reached his peak.

Jim Clark
World champion in 1963 and 1965 and winner of 25 Grands Prix. But mere statistics do not begin to measure the depth of his natural genius. A sheep farmer from the Border region; shy and retiring. Drove almost exclusively for Lotus. Killed in a Formula 2 race at Hockenheim on 7 April 1968.

CHAPTER 11

SOUTH TO BRANDS HATCH

'The 1964 British Grand Prix, which will be known as the Grand Prix d'Europe, will be held at Brands Hatch on 11th July.'

Autosport 31 May 1963

It was just over 13 years since the first motor race had been held at Brands Hatch. The very brief, almost incidental, announcement at the bottom of a news page in *Autosport* did not do justice to the remarkable amount of work and the total transformation of the Kent track into a venue suitable for Grand Prix racing.

Motor-cycle grass track enthusiasts first discovered this natural bowl, just off the A20 London-Maidstone road. Known as Brands Hatch ('hatch' apparently being old English for 'wattle gate') the location offered a perfect view for spectators. Motor-cyclists also took a liking to the place when a cinder track was laid out, roughly in a kidney-shape, but things became serious after the war when the innovative 500cc brigade saw the so-called Brands Hatch Stadium as a likely venue.

The 500 Club, along with a lobby of motor-cycle road racers, contributed to the £17,000 necessary to lay a tarmac surface along the circuit's one-mile length. Trees were cut down along South Bank and close by the A20 entrance, and a spectator fence erected. The first motor race, run in an anticlockwise direction, was held on Sunday 16 April 1950. The *Daily Graphic* was there to report events under the headline: 'Suicidal Car Speeds Thrilled Race Fans'.

The first race was won by Don Parker at an average speed of 61.42mph, the uphill run through Paddock Bend being particularly hard going for the little 500cc machines. Bear in mind that they did not have the benefit of the present run downhill from Druids, the circuit simply running along what we now know as Cooper Straight and swinging left at the foot of Paddock Hill.

The extension to Druids Bend, making the circuit 1.24 miles, came in April 1954 and the races were now run in a clockwise direction – Stuart Lewis-Evans winning the first in a Cooper-Norton lapping at an average of 70.06mph. Facilities, though, were almost non-existent. The paddock area was in a field on the outside of the corner which bore its name and there were just two grandstands (at Paddock Bend and opposite the startline). Otherwise, there was nothing. The track, though, had been widened and lined on the outside by spectator protection banks.

From now on, the circuit would grow in stature, attracting quality fields from the upper levels of club racing. By 1958, the lap record had been raised to 77.77mph by Stirling Moss during a Formula 2 race. Under the guidance of their go-ahead publicity officer, John Webb, Brands Hatch had taken the bold and ultimately successful step of introducing motor racing on Boxing Day and, in 1959, this event witnessed another new record. Driving a bath powered by a Vespa engine, Graham Hill lapped at a breathtaking 24mph...

The following month, permission was granted for an extension to the circuit. Leaving the existing track at Kidney Bend, dipping into the woods, sweeping through Hawthorn and Westfield Bends, plunging down Dingle Dell, rising quickly to meet Dingle Dell Corner, followed almost immediately by Stirling's Bend, the new loop rejoined at Clearways. It increased the length to 2.65 miles and, if ever a track was made for Grand Prix racing, then this was it.

Pits were built on the narrow strip between the Top and Bottom Straights, but Webb could see that if the circuit was to progress properly and make the most of the additions it would be necessary to find a large company willing to make the necessary investment.

In April 1961, Grovewood Securities Ltd announced that they had acquired the controlling interest in Brands Hatch Circuit Ltd. Shortly afterwards, Moss averaged 91mph in his Lotus 18/21 while winning the 76-lap Silver City International Formula 1 race on the Grand Prix circuit.

Negotiations to hold a Grand Prix at Brands Hatch were either held in secret or they did not merit the attention of the media. But as soon as the news of the Brands Hatch race was announced, and details of the 1964 Grand Prix of Europe released, the correspondence columns began to fill with letters on subjects which would become hoary chestnuts over the succeeding years: prices and toilets.

John Stanton, of London NW3, more or less started the ball rolling in January 1964 when he wrote to comment on the need for better facilities at British circuits in general. To which he received a serious reply from John Webb, outlining the plans of Grovewood Securities, and a rather more amusing response from Graham Peters of Chigwell Row, Essex. Mr Peters wrote:

> '*If John Stanton cannot spend an afternoon at a race meeting without availing himself of the primitive toilet facilities, I suggest that in future he tries to stop himself from getting so excited.*
> *Anyway, if he thinks Brands bad, let him try Crystal Palace. A few months ago I had the doubtful privilege of joining several hundred others engaged in the mediaeval ritual that is affectionately known as "Filling the Horse Trough." This has to be seen to be believed!'*

As the months slipped by, there was also a growing unease over the charges being levied, one or two spectators feeling that Grovewood were out to make 'big money' at the enthusiast's expense. Mr. Stanton was to the fore once more. He wrote:

> '*...I agree £2 7s 6d includes car parking and programme, nevertheless four people in a car will pay £10 on the day, as opposed to £7 10s (plus 8s for programmes) at Silverstone last year. Certainly Continental meetings are equally expensive, but this is hardly the point. In any case, one usually pays for a permanent grandstand with restaurant and toilets beneath, not a collection of planks and scaffolding...'*

Grovewood pointed out that a £100,000 investment programme included the formation of new spectator banks, the construction of a 'modern 200-seat restaurant' behind the main grandstand, the upgrading of existing catering facilities, the addition of several new bars and cafeterias, 'each with its own "Pub Sign", table enclosure, and tables with umbrellas,' the demolition of most of the old toilet blocks and the construction of six new ones, 'all equipped with handbasins, towel machines and mirrors, and some of the ladies' toilets even have make-up tables.' In addition, the Grovewood Suite, built on stilts alongside the permanent grandstand, would provide first class viewing for 'senior guests and distinguished visitors.'

Flashing warning lights were installed on the approach to Paddock Bend. Guard rails were erected to protect the pit area and the outside of Paddock Bend, while the paddock itself had been levelled at certain points and completely resurfaced. Over 100 covered 'stalls' had been erected for the teams. (These were on a slope, causing considerable difficulties when it came to filling the cars with fuel).

The bottom line, however, was the fact that all 12,400 seats on the collection of planks and scaffolding had been sold within seven weeks of the commencement of booking. And the RAC had received a full entry.

Mr. CSI comes by bus

This would be the fifth round of the 1964 world championship. Jim Clark, having won for Lotus at Zandvoort and Spa (yet again), came to Brands Hatch with 21 points. Graham Hill, the winner at Monaco, had 18; Richie Ginther (BRM) and Peter Arundell (Lotus) had 11; Dan Gurney, after finishing sixth in Belgium and giving Brabham their first Grand Prix victory at Rouen, had ten while Brabham himself had eight. John Surtees, a pre-season favourite in the Ferrari, had only managed to collect six points by finishing second at Zandvoort and retiring at the other three.

Surtees had been joined by Lorenzo Bandini, while Phil Hill had tried to return to some form of normality by signing for a full season with Cooper. Maggs had gone to *Scuderia Centro Sud* to drive BRMs with Baghetti; Taylor had found a place alongside Ireland with the British Racing Partnership's Lotus 24 (Innes driving the latest version of the BRP proper) while Reg Parnell had managed to acquire a pair of Lotus 25s (powered by BRM V8s) for his young chargers, Amon and Hailwood.

Bonnier (Rob Walker Racing), Anderson and Siffert had production Brabham BT11s while

Dan Gurney counts the bubbly; the Gov'nor looks for his share.

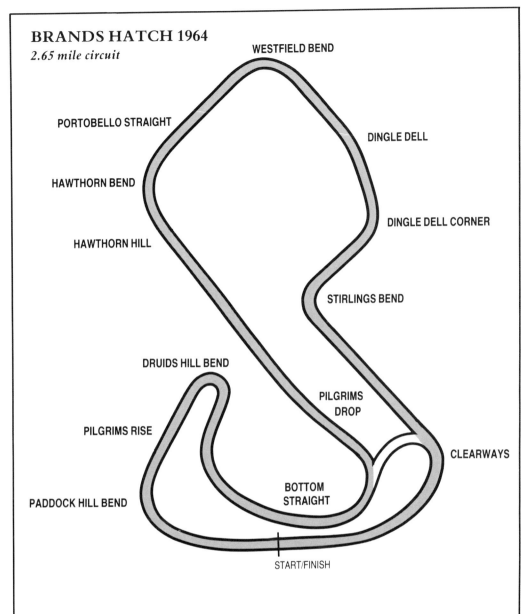

BRANDS HATCH 1964
2.65 mile circuit

WESTFIELD BEND

PORTOBELLO STRAIGHT

DINGLE DELL

HAWTHORN BEND

DINGLE DELL CORNER

HAWTHORN HILL

STIRLINGS BEND

DRUIDS HILL BEND

PILGRIMS DROP

PILGRIMS RISE

CLEARWAYS

PADDOCK HILL BEND

BOTTOM STRAIGHT

START/FINISH

John Willment Automobiles entered a Formula 2 BT10 (suitably ballasted) for Frank Gardner. There was a two-year-old ex-works BT3 for Ian Raby, a Bob Gerard-entered Cooper for John Taylor and a Lola-bodied Lotus 24 to be driven by the American, Peter Revson.

One important change to the entry list concerned Team Lotus. A most promising career for Peter Arundell had received a major set-back when the Englishman crashed heavily during a Formula 2 race at Reims. His place was taken by Mike Spence, who was allocated a Lotus 25 while Clark continued with the 1964 car, the 33. And, thinking ahead, Chapman agreed to let Jackie Stewart, then dominating Formula 3 with a Tyrrell-entered Cooper-BMC, have a trial run in the Lotus in a special 'unofficial' session after practice had finished.

By then, of course, Jim Clark had claimed pole position, even if he had missed out on the 100 bottles of champagne awarded to Gurney, the fastest driver at the end of Thursday's practice. The session had been disrupted when Trevor Taylor crashed his Lotus heavily, the BRP team replacing it with another elderly 24, the bruised and battered Yorkshireman going on to take a place on the seventh row.

Taylor was not alone in being shown up by Bob Anderson as he hustled the Brabham-Climax, running without the benefit of fuel injection, onto the third row between McLaren and Bandini. The Italian had to make do with the V6-engined Ferrari, Surtees taking the latest V8 to join Brabham on row two. The race, though, looked like being between Hill and Clark with Gurney poised to have his say if the Britons gave the American half a chance.

Talk of an estimated 135,000 spectators had, it seemed, scared most of them off, only 50,000 turning up on the day. Elaborate parking and traffic arrangements had been made but everyone reported a trouble-free run to the circuit. Hubert Schroeder, secretary of the CSI, claimed that he had made it in 45 minutes from London by – and this you will not believe – train and bus!

Threatening clouds rolled overhead but the attention of the spectators was soon diverted by the slick Brands Hatch marketing machine. A miniature Dunlop Bridge had been built over the main approach road to the stands, marquees, restaurants and shops. The best pre-Grand Prix race entertainment, however, would come on the track courtesy of Mr Jack Sears.

The start of the Ilford Films Trophy race for Grand Touring cars began in a bit of a muddle. The pole position AC Cobra of Bob Olthoff was a non-starter thanks to a heavy crash at Stirling's Bend during practice. Assuming that everyone would move forward one place on the grid, Sears, who should have been on the inside of the second row, moved his Cobra onto the outside of the front row. Heated discussions followed but, when officials started the race, all seemed to be in some sort of order.

Then they held out the black flag for Sears, a signal which he dutifully obeyed by pulling into the pits, only to find that the Clerk of the Course wished to speak to him about taking the wrong grid position. In fact, it was done as a form of penalty. The officials felt that he had, in effect, jumped the start, and rather than add a minute to his race time, it was decided to call Sears in briefly and then let him get on with his race. In any case, it might add interest to the event. It did.

Absolutely incensed by all of this, the normally equable Norfolk farmer floored the throttle of his mighty machine, shaking his fist as he went. And he shook it again at the end of the next lap. Really fired up now, Sears proceeded to give a tingling display of on-the-limit motoring as the V8 thundered round. Meanwhile, in the pits a fracas ensued as John Willment, the entrant of the Cobra and a man of a muscular disposition, felled the Clerk of the Course with one mighty blow.

Cheered all the way, Sears hurled the brute of a machine through the field. Clearly nothing would stop him this day and Jackie Stewart, for all his neatness in the leading Jaguar E-Type, had no answer to the tyre-smoking Cobra. Sears won by 4.2 seconds. All in all, an eventful race and a perfect curtain-raiser for the Grand Prix.

Classic confrontation

Brands Hatch pulled out all the stops and set a standard of pomp and ceremony for which they would become justifiably famous. The bands of the Royal Dragoons and the 1st Battalion Royal Scots marched and played. A demonstration of battle tactics involving armoured cars, helicopters, the troops of Eastern Command and the Royal Artillery gunners startled the unwary when a 25-pounder let rip just by the entrance to the tunnel. Then followed a cavalcade of historic army vehicles. Finally, a fanfare by the trumpeters of the Royal Artillery greeted the arrival of the Formula 1 cars.

Another innovation was the use of a dummy grid, where the cars would be fired up before rolling forward onto the grid proper, pausing briefly to take the start itself. Even so, this American-style procedure did not prevent Gardner from driving into the back of Siffert, the Swiss doing his best to avoid Ginther who, in turn, had been caught behind Amon, the clutch on the New Zealander's Lotus refusing to work.

Gurney made a serious attempt to take the lead by running side-by-side with Clark all the way to Druids, where the inside line favoured the Lotus and allowed Clark to lead through Bottom Bend. Gurney had the bit between his teeth and he set a new lap record as he closed on Clark again during lap two. That, however, would be the end of his challenge, the Brabham pulling into the pits to have the ignition 'black box' changed. Seeing smoke rising from the overheated box, an enthusiastic fire marshal dashed to the scene and covered everyone, including John Bolster, the BBC commentator, in foam.

Not long after, Hailwood ran wide coming through Bottom Bend and Ireland had to take avoiding action as the Lotus spun onto the grass, crushing a photographer's case as it went.

'Outa my way!' Jackie Stewart prepares to be swept aside as Jack Sears, headlights and temper blazing, powers the thundering AC Cobra towards Paddock.

McLaren's gearbox broke at South Bank Bend on lap seven when Gurney rejoined after a long delay.

Clark now had to contend with Graham Hill, and for the next two hours these two rivals would engage in a brilliant duel. On the face of it, the race was boring, since Hill would not get close enough to actually challenge for the lead. But he pushed Clark all the way, the pair of them chipping away at the lap record.

A liberal coating of oil, courtesy of Hailwood, on the track during the early laps added to their problems and Hill, his car handling better under the slippery conditions, pushed even harder. Then, as the track dried out, Clark pulled away to earn himself breathing space and time to worry about the loss of a front wheel balance weight. At no stage, however, was he more than eight seconds ahead of the BRM.

Then Hill piled on the pressure once more. The Lotus (Clark preferring to use the 25B rather than the 33) and the BRM lapped everyone bar the third-place Ferrari of Surtees who, for many laps, had held off a strong challenge from Brabham until the Australian spun. Convinced something was wrong with his car, Jack made a couple of precautionary pit stops. The mechanics could find nothing amiss and sent Jack on his way – only for the car to continue sliding unpredictably on right-handers.

It was discovered later that the tank had split, filling the undertray with fuel, which then sprayed onto the left-rear wheel as Brabham rushed through Clearways, Paddock, Hawthorn and Westfield. As the race progressed and the fuel load decreased, the problem went away and Brabham eventually worked his way past Anderson, Phil Hill and Bandini to take fourth place.

With seven laps remaining, Clark set a new lap record but Hill would not be demoralised and he gradually closed on the Lotus once more. As they disappeared out of sight for the last time, they were separated by 2.2 seconds. The gap was the same as they dived into Clearways, Clark still ahead. The eventual winning margin was 2.8 seconds. It was Clark's third win of the season and he had to work hard for it.

A drop of the hard stuff

At the end of the day, Chris Barber's jazz band, aided by Humphrey Lyttelton, took up their positions on the victory rostrum and entertained those who wished to stay behind and relax.

While spectators and officials danced into the late evening on the main straight, the drivers headed for a party held by John and Pat Surtees at their home in Limpsfield. The following day, they played the Farningham and Hartley Country Club XI at cricket, the match raising £200 for Oxfam.

Then it was off to Kingston-upon-Thames and the Contented Plaice Restaurant to celebrate Chris Amon's 21st birthday. That party raged long into the night at the famous motor racing flat rented by Amon, Hailwood, Revson and Maggs in nearby Ditton Road. Eoin Young, a freelance journalist and director of the recently formed Bruce McLaren Motor Racing Team, remembers the occasion.

'Difficult to forget it,' says Young. 'BP were making a film about how drivers filled in their time between races. We suggested that they come along to Amon's 21st. We also suggested that they pay for it; that sort of thing was unheard of in those days.

'They jumped at the chance and sent a couple of guys along with cameras. Of course, once the word got round that BP were paying, everyone turned up. The Grand Prix grid seemed to be in there.

'Halfway through the evening, the cameramen were legless; I don't think they shot more than a couple of feet of film. Certainly, they didn't shoot anything back at the flat. Which, perhaps, was just as well.

'I remember Mike Hailwood had this fireman's hat. That was filled with beer and someone offered to it Bonnier. He thought he was being asked to try it on. Which he did. I can clearly remember seeing him sitting by the fireplace, absolutely drenched. It was some party.

'At the time, it was very difficult for hooligans such as us to find a place to rent, and Amon and company had been very surprised that they had managed to get this flat. It was only later they discovered that the landlord had a sitting tenant he wanted rid of on the floor below. I think the boys unwittingly did a good job for him. The parties there were unbelievable.'

If anyone had been capable of stringing sensible words together at these hooleys, then few people would have bet on anyone other than Clark or Graham Hill winning the title. Clark had

30 points; Hill 26; Ginther, Arundell and Brabham had 11, with Gurney and Surtees tying on 10.

There were five races to go – but Clark was not destined to win any of them. Hill would score maximum points at Watkins Glen and the most significant aspect of the latter half of the 1964 season was the emergence of John Surtees as a truly world class driver.

Surtees took pole at the Nürburgring, fought with Gurney and Clark before the Brabham and the Lotus retired and then went on to finish more than a minute ahead of Hill's misfiring BRM.

The first Austrian Grand Prix, held on the bumpy runways of Zeltweg airfield, saw Surtees, Hill, Clark and Gurney retire, leaving victory to the second Ferrari of Bandini. Hill and Clark also dropped out at Monza and when Surtees won the championship took on a different complexion entirely. Things became really tense when Clark had trouble at Watkins Glen and Surtees spun down to an eventual second place while lapping a backmarker. It meant that Clark, Hill and Surtees went to the final round in Mexico each with a chance of the title.

It was a dramatic race. Clark looked set to score a dominant win when the Climax V8 seized on the last lap! Hill, meanwhile, had been hit from behind by Bandini's Ferrari, and the Italian, suddenly finding himself in second place behind Gurney, was ordered to slow down and let Surtees through and win the title.

So far, the 1½-litre era had produced championships for Ferrari (2), BRM and Lotus. Would 1965, the final year of the formula, go to Brabham, the team which had shown such promise?

Straight-laced Jim

At the end of the year, Jack had other things on his mind - like the removal of his appendix, an operation which would hinder the overseeing of production of 15 Formula 2 cars and an equal number of Formula 3 machines for his customers. The mood at Motor Racing Developments was buoyant and Brabham was happy to confirm that Dan Gurney would be staying for another season. One day into 1965, however, and Brabham was close to depression.

By the time New Year's Day had ended, he said he felt like 'throwing his machinery into the Indian Ocean at the end of the South African Grand Prix.' Both Brabhams had been plagued by mechanical trouble although, significantly, Gurney had used Goodyear tyres for the first time, Brabham remaining on the more familiar Dunlop rubber. Victory at East London had gone to the Lotus 33 of Jim Clark, who had been wearing a corset throughout because of a slipped a disc suffered a few weeks earlier while throwing snowballs at Cortina d'Ampezzo in Italy during a promotion by Ford for the Cortina. The corset did not, rivals were saddened to note, detract from his driving.

The year also began with the completion of the millionth Mini and the launching of the Townsend ferry, 'Free Enterprise 2'. The magazine Motor Racing claimed that this vessel would greatly benefit 'foreign holiday makers in general, and racing types in particular.... because it is the first car ferry built by a British owner which has both bow and stern doors.'

The next race of some importance, however, would not require the teams to go further than Brands Hatch. Following the theme set by Silverstone with their non-championship International Trophy, the Brands Hatch management introduced the Race of Champions on 13 March. And most of the heavyweight names turned out.

Gurney was on cracking form, charging through the field to finish second behind Clark in the first heat. During heat two, Gurney harried Clark to such an extent that the Scotsman made a rare error and crashed heavily at the exit of Bottom Bend. Clark was unhurt and Gurney's chances of winning were scuppered by an engine failure. Brabham then led, until sidelined by an oil leak, all of which allowed Spence to take a fortunate win in the number two Lotus.

During to clashing commitments at Indianapolis, Clark (who would score a memorable first victory for a British driver at the Brickyard) and Gurney both missed the second round of the championship at Monaco. Hill claimed his third successive win in the Principality, his new BRM team-mate, Jackie Stewart, finishing third behind Bandini's Ferrari.

Gurney's absence had allowed Denny Hulme to partner Brabham, the New Zealander finishing eighth. Brabham, meanwhile, had over-revved his Coventry-Climax V8 - built to the latest 32-valve specification - after the rev-counter had broken. Hulme was not entered for the Belgian Grand Prix (won by Clark) and Jack Brabham stood down at the French Grand Prix to allow Hulme to take over. Denny's knowledge of the difficult Clermont Ferrand circuit, gained during Formula Junior racing, was seen to be an asset and he finished an excellent fourth, victory having gone once again to Clark with Stewart repeating his Spa result by finishing second.

Flat-bloody-chat

Denny Hulme

Hulme had fitted in well with the Brabham Racing Organisation from the moment he began racing Formula Junior cars for Jack. Indeed, Denny was always around to lend a hand, and on one occasion he more than proved his worth when it came to getting the Formula 1 cars to the race on time.

'We were racing at the International Trophy one year and, in those days, we used to go home every night,' he recalls. 'On the way up on race day, Jack's transporter broke down, round about High Wycombe. I happened along in the old Ford Zodiac and I stopped to see what the trouble was. Whatever the problem may have been, it couldn't be fixed right away. So we unloaded the car off the back and Dan, who was riding in the transporter, sat in the Formula 1 car, and off we went to Silverstone - with me towing.

'This is race day, so we are going flat-bloody-chat. We get up towards Buckingham and suddenly there's a big noise. I look back and see that Dan has been fumed out by the exhaust. He's almost unconscious. Poor Dan. There was no way he could shout at us, sitting down low in the Formula 1 car. I mean, we were sideways, every which-way. Fortunately the rope hadn't been very long – certainly not long enough for him to flick off the road when he fell asleep!

'So we stop and revive him and off we go. Flat-bloody-chat again. We carve everyone up and go down the wrong side of the road all the way from Stowe School to the main gate. We've made it! Except that some guy has parked his car in the way at the gate and he won't let us through. We get all that way and this guy won't move his car.

'Time's running out and a right old shouting match starts up; I mean, if only this guy had known what we'd been through. Old Dan, he's just sitting in the racing car, half-asleep while all this is going on. Then, to cap it all, the guy causing all the trouble says he hopes our car breaks down. Anyway, we got Dan sorted out and he was on the grid in time for the race....'

There was no need for such desperate measures at the 1965 British Grand Prix, returned once more to Silverstone.

The halt and the lame

Brabham had three cars present, two BT11s for Jack and Dan, plus a BT7 for Hulme. Coventry-Climax had made 32-valve engines available to Brabham and Lotus, Clark not using his until the final practice session when he claimed pole position, beating Hill's BRM by two-tenths of a second. On the outside of the four-car front row, the second BRM of Jackie Stewart. But interrupting the display of British Racing Green, came a white car carrying the emblem of the rising sun.

Honda's plans to go Grand Prix racing had occupied the motor sporting gossip columns for quite some time during the early part of the previous year. When photographs were taken in March 1964 showing the car undergoing tests at the Suzuka circuit in Japan, the outraged motor company spoke of 'industrial spies' releasing information. It was clear from the pictures that Honda were using a transverse-mounted V12 engine and the 'spies' said it could rev to 12,000rpm.

The car first raced at the German Grand Prix later that year, the Nürburgring being the worst possible circuit for the team and their inexperienced driver, Ronnie Bucknum, to cut their teeth on. After occasional appearances during the remainder of the season, Honda returned at Monaco in 1965, Richie Ginther having been drafted in to support Bucknum. Both were entered for the British Grand Prix but Bucknum was withdrawn. Ginther, meanwhile, really stretched the V12 and no one present doubted that the V12 really did rev to 12,000rpm, if not more.

Ferrari had fielded a new flat-12 engined car for Surtees, leaving Bandini to continue with the V8, and while development may have been continuing apace at Maranello, the same could not be said of progress at Cooper. McLaren was becoming increasingly frustrated by the lack of headway but Jochen Rindt, his new team-mate, appeared to be happy to drive anything so long as it had four wheels and an engine. None the less McLaren and the Austrian qualified

ahead of the Willment and Walker Brabhams of Frank Gardner and Jo Bonnier, and the Reg Parnell Lotus 25-BRMs driven by Innes Ireland and Richard Attwood. Rob Walker had also taken Jo Siffert on board, the Swiss handling a Brabham BT11, while at the back of the grid Gregory drove the *Scuderia Centro Sud* BRM. Raby was in his Brabham BT3 and John Rhodes was allowed to start his Bob Gerard Cooper-Climax despite setting a time which was five seconds outside that recorded by the third fastest man – the supposed qualifying limit.

There was a frantic, last-minute change on race day. Brabham did not fit their 32-valve Climax until the previous evening and during the warming-up lap the V8 dropped a valve. Brabham swiftly handed his car over to Gurney.

The American barely had time to settle into the car when he was wreathed in tyre smoke as the front row powered off the line, the Goodyear-shod Honda leading the way. By Stowe, however, Clark had ducked out of the slipstream to take a lead he would not lose. This victory, his fourth of the season, was not as easy as it had seemed.

For the first 50 laps, Clark appeared to have things his own way. Hill tried hard to keep pace with the Lotus but the BRM gradually dropped back. Clark had lapped Bonnier and Gurney – fifth and sixth respectively as the tall American struggled with the discomfort of a cockpit fitted out for Jack – when the engine began to show signs of running out of oil. Clark had half a lap lead over Hill but the remaining oil was surging away from the pump on right-hand bends. As the BRM team hung out signals to urge on Hill, Clark resorted to switching off the engine and coasting through the corners!

Hill, meanwhile, had his own problems. He had been pumping his brakes since early in the race, the situation deteriorating by the lap. None the less, Hill went as quickly as he could and set the fastest lap on the final run to the flag, Clark just getting there by 3.2 seconds. The next day, incidentally, both men were racing in a Formula 2 meeting at Rouen, Clark driving for Lotus, Hill racing in a John Coombs Brabham-BRM. Clark won again.

And again and again, in the Dutch and German Grands Prix to clinch the championship with three races to run. Stewart won his first Grand Prix at Monza, Hill won at Watkins Glen but, in Mexico, Richie Ginther produced an historic first for Honda and Goodyear. Too bad the 1½-litre formula had just ended.

It had produced wonderful racing – contrary to the belief of those making a fuss at the RAC Club seven years before. Ironically, Britain had come out best at the end of it but who would dominate the next era was anyone's guess. And, as ever, the teams in green had few ideas about a suitable engine.

Blast off! Richard Ginther's shrieking Honda gets the drop on Clark (5), Hill (3) and Hulme.

The sun gets quickly on the Honda as the mechanics change plugs on the transverse V12.

CHAPTER 12

OLD HAND, NEW FORMULA

Car? What car?

There was a lot of sandbagging going on in 1965. Everyone knew that the 1½-litre era was coming to an end on 31 December. They were also aware that, the next day, Grand Prix racing would switch to the 3-litre formula, so-called because that would be the maximum permitted capacity for unblown engines. As a sop to anyone wishing to continue with 1,500cc engines, the regulations would allow them to be supercharged.

In fact, no one would take up that option since it was considered to be an uncompetitive alternative. Or, at least, it was until 1977. Then Renault wheeled out their 1,500cc turbo. But that's another story.

In fact, in 1965, there was a fair amount of story-telling taking place. In his column in *Motor Racing*, Jack Brabham wrote:

> 'Speaking for our organisation, we certainly have no plans or possibilities of going Formula 1 racing after the coming season (1965). The big problem will be the availability of engines. At the moment, there is not much sign of an engine that would be available to private teams. I think that the new F1 will have to be backed by the big firms, such as B.R.M., Ferrari and Honda. It is only manufacturers of this sort of size that will be able to take part.'

Hmmm. This may well have been the case at the time of writing but you need to bear in mind what Denny Hulme says about Brabham: 'Jack could give the impression that he was a bit vague at times. He was quite good at that, particularly with anyone who wanted to talk about money! But he knew *exactly* what he was doing and in which direction he wanted to travel.'

And Jack's travels took him to Australia and Replacement Parts Pty Ltd, a company which had built up a vast business in the southern hemisphere manufacturing automotive components under the 'Repco' brand name. Brabham had dealt with Repco before and he knew they had built a 2.5-litre engine, based on an Oldsmobile V8, for the Tasman Series. He wondered if it would be possible to take things a stage further and build a 3-litre version. After much careful consideration during the summer of 1965, Repco agreed to a Grand Prix programme. The Repco-Brabham was the first Formula 1 car to appear on the race track in 1966.

In fact, a lack of time before the start of the season forced Brabham and his partner, Ron Tauranac, to convert a BT19 chassis to accept the V8. The BT19 had been designed to take the stillborn Coventry-Climax flat-16 engine in 1965, but the project never saw the light of day. And Coventry-Climax were no longer involved in Grand Prix racing anyway since Jaguar, the new owners of the company, preferred not to commit themselves to designing a new engine for the 3-litre formula.

Meanwhile, over at Belvedere Works, just behind the shopping centre in Feltham, Middlesex, Eoin Young had been engaging in fancy footwork each time the phone rang at McLaren Racing. As Press Officer for the burgeoning sportscar team, Young had to field a growing volume of calls asking about the rumoured existence of a Formula 1 McLaren. 'No,' replied Young. 'We don't have a Formula 1 car.'

What they *did* have was a single-seater, powered by a 4.5-litre Oldsmobile engine taken from a McLaren sportscar. This had been built to assist Firestone with their tyre development programme. But Bruce McLaren also saw the car as a means of showing prospective sponsors that the team were serious and capable of producing a single seater for Formula 1. None of the callers had actually asked about that. So Young felt quite justified in telling the press that they didn't know what they were talking about. In fact, it was a field of speculative journalism in which the Kiwi would go on to make a name for himself with columns syndicated worldwide....

Bruce McLaren had long since decided that 1965 would be his last season with Cooper. He was unable to broadcast the fact since it was a sensitive issue with John Cooper, following

Brabham's departure to do exactly the same thing at the end of 1961. In the meantime, if you asked about a Formula 1 car, the answer was 'No'.

The denials became more difficult when the single-seater saw the first light of day during tyre tests, and Young was startled when a motoring magazine flopped onto his desk containing an article with more technical details about the proposed Formula 1 effort than even he knew about. But then, the nuts and bolts of racing cars never were Eoin's strong-point.

By December 1965 the first McLaren Grand Prix car, designed by a bright young lad called Robin Herd, had been unveiled. The Oldsmobile had gone. In its place, an Indy Ford V8, reduced from 4.2 to 3 litres. Bruce would do the driving, with Chris Amon as Number 2. All good keen lads, but what chance had they against the likes of Ferrari?

It was a known fact that Ferrari were working on a V12 closely related to their 3.3-litre Le Mans engine. Since the Italians seemed to be just as well organised as they had been at the start of the 1.5-litre era, most pundits saw the new car as a certain winner. Optimism was strengthened when John Surtees showed every sign of making a full and remarkable recovery from a near-fatal accident during a sportscar race at Mosport, Canada, the previous Autumn.

Bruce McLaren

He would be joined once more by Lorenzo Bandini, but there was trouble afoot with Eugenio Dragoni, the Ferrari team manager, already showing a preference for the Italian rather than an Englishman who tended to call a spade a shovel. And that's just what Surtees thought of the V12 after his first acquaintance with the car during pre-season testing. It was big, it was heavy, and the power was not quite what it should have been. Dragoni, of course, would have none of it.

Meanwhile, back at Bourne, BRM had plumped for an adventurous and technically complex H16 engine and, while this was being developed, the team would field 1.9-litre versions of the trusty V8 for Graham Hill and Jackie Stewart.

BRM had, in fact, rejected a V12 engine which had been constructed at Weslake Research in Sussex. Dan Gurney, having said goodbye to Brabham (thus leaving a permanent position for Denny Hulme), saw the V12 as a suitable engine for his own team, AAR. Originally named All American Racers when Gurney formed the operation with Carroll Shelby to tackle Indycar racing, the title of the Formula 1 effort was changed to Anglo American Racers when Gurney set up shop next door to Weslake at Rye harbour. It would take some time for the V12 to be race-ready, so as a stopgap, Gurney bought a handful of Coventry-Climax engines enlarged from 2.5 to 2.7 litres – four-cylinder workhorses which would see more than one team through the initial stages of the new formula.

Lotus had to make do with stretched versions of the Coventry-Climax V8 while they waited for the BRM H16s which they had on order. But even then Colin Chapman was looking further down the road and his search would eventually lead to the design of the Ford-Cosworth DFV. So 1966 did not promise a great deal for Chapman and the brilliant Clark, not to mention Peter Arundell, who had recovered from his injuries sufficiently to be asked back to the Formula 1 team.

Told you so

The 'experts' nodded sagely when Surtees won a non-championship race at Syracuse. But John's worst fears began to be realised when Jack Brabham claimed the International Trophy at Silverstone, the supposedly underpowered Repco V8 cross-breed beating the supposedly powerful Italian thoroughbred by seven seconds. The thought remained, however, that Ferrari would come good once the championship got under way.

When Jackie Stewart won at Monaco, that was rightly put down to the nimble V8 BRM being the ideal tool for the street circuit, and when Surtees came home first at Spa, the pundits appeared to be right after all. The Belgian Grand Prix, however, had been far from straight-foward.

It was dry as the 17 starters left the grid. Surtees was on pole and he led the field up the hill to Les Combes before swinging left to begin the gradual but very fast descent through Burnenville, Malmedy and then onto the Masta Straight. They were flat out when the road quickly changed from dry to damp – and then streaming conditions as the field ran slap-bang into a downpour.

There had been a warning – but it was in French and John Surtees was the only driver to hear the commentator mention that rain had begun to fall at Malmedy. From his experience of racing motor-cycles at Spa-Francorchamps, Surtees knew what to expect. The rest had no idea.

Cars spun every which-way, Stewart's BRM landing in a ditch, the Scotsman trapped and soaked in fuel. No one was critically injured but the 1966 Belgian Grand Prix would have a far-reaching effect on attitudes towards safety in general, and the future of Spa-Francorchamps road circuit in particular. Stewart, his collar-bone broken, would lead the campaign.

Jochen Rindt had lost control of his Cooper, now powered by a Maserati V12 engine, the heavy machine spinning like a top without coming to harm. Rindt simply engaged first gear and took off. Only seven cars completed the first lap and, three laps later, Rindt was leading. Combining his uncanny reflexes with apparent fearlessness, the Austrian fought the Cooper all the way while Surtees stalked him, waiting to pounce in the closing stages.

At least Surtees now knew a little more about the Cooper-Maserati, which was just as well since the mounting tension within Ferrari would cause him to walk out of Maranello and accept the offer of employment with the British team.

When Surtees arrived at the next round, the French Grand Prix at Reims, he was a very determined man. He put the Cooper on the front row, between the Ferraris of Bandini and Surtees's replacement, the Englishman Michael Parkes.

Surtees led into the first corner – and then the fuel pump drive sheared. The race would have belonged to Bandini but for a broken throttle cable and, as history now records, Jack Brabham became the first man to win a Grand Prix in a car of his own manufacture. It was the start of an Indian summer for the man who, as Denny Hulme had said, knew precisely where he was going even if he pretended he didn't. And the next stop would be Brands Hatch and the British Grand Prix

A rare mixture

A full colour programme was issued free of charge with admission tickets, but a small 'Practice Race Card' cost one shilling (5p). Across the cover of the programme, the 3-litre formula was heralded as the 'Return to Power.' Inside, Denis Holmes, motoring correspondent of the *Daily Mail*, the newspaper supporting the event, wrote:

> '*Around this time last year....the top men of the various teams were gloomy about the future of the world championship.*
>
> *Lack of engines suitable for the new Formula 1 was one worrying factor....Cost was another cause for alarm – £100,000 to develop a new engine from scratch – and the value of a complete Grand Prix car with engine and gearbox would leap up to around £15,000 instead of an already high £10,000.*
>
> *But today at Brands Hatch we will see motor racing of greater interest and variety than anything in the world championship for many years. Those who forecast the end of the world championship could not have been more wrong.*'

Yes, well, Fleet Street will have its way of course. If by 'variety' he meant just seven proper 3-litre cars and the remaining 13 a mixture of makeshift motors, then his preview was fairly accurate. Certainly, Holmes did not rush into print when it came to predicting a likely winner. *Autosport*, however, jumped in with both feet.

While conceding that the Brabhams were likely winners, it noted that the 'spaceframe cars are light and reliable but the Repco engine, with its comparatively humble Detroit origins, will presumably not remain competitive when the BRM H16 is fully developed.'

That prompted a swift response from Frank Hallam, General Manager of Repco-Brabham Engines in Australia.

Hallam pointed out that, in fact, the Oldsmobile crankcase was the only part of the engine which was of Detroit origin. And when it came to discussions about the BRM H16, Hallam tactfully added that, while a 16-cylinder engine should be a better bet, it was evident that a less powerful V8 appeared to be 'sufficient to cope with any contingency which has so far arisen in 3-litre Formula 1 events.'

Quite so. And Jack Brabham was about to prove that very point on the twists and turns of Brands Hatch.

Brabham and Hulme dominated practice with Gurney using his natural skills to set a remarkable time with the Climax-powered Eagle, by far and way the neatest car on the grid. Graham Hill and Jim Clark shared the second row, the reigning world champion in a new Lotus 33, but still with the Climax V8, while Hill continued with the V8 pending further development on the H16. Stewart put his V8 BRM alongside the Coopers of Rindt and Surtees on row three and you would have been forgiven for thinking that Mike Parkes had qualified a Ferrari of peculiar origin on the fourth row.

In fact it was Mike Spence, and his entrant, Reg Parnell, had been only to happy to respond to the blandishments of John Frankenheimer as the film producer flung dollars around the paddock as though they were going out of style. Frankenheimer was using the races as a backdrop for his rather dramatic and over-acted epic, *Grand Prix*, and he saw the actual Formula 1 cars as mere props.

Parnell had sprayed his Lotus 25-BRM red and Spence had donned a helmet painted in the colours of Parkes. Bonnier also had allowed his Brabham to be 'made-up' for the film and confusion was wide-spread, some of the cars even donning fake exhausts in a rather feeble attempt to resemble Ferraris, the stars of this masterpiece. Unfortunately for Frankheimer, there were no red cars present at Brands Hatch.

Enzo Ferrari was no respecter of film scripts, and when both cars (for Parkes and Bandini) were withdrawn due to industrial unrest in Italy it threw Hollywood's plans into total chaos. Then Bonnier blew up his BRM engine and that meant a switch to a Brabham-Climax and another hasty respray job and more hysterics from the producer. None the less, the Grand Prix teams were happy to relieve the silver screen merchant of his money as he attempted to maintain continuity.

McLaren arrived at Brands Hatch with his car, the M2B, powered by an Italian V8 engine built by Serenissima, the Ford engine having been declared an abysmal failure early in the proceedings. Such was the state of flux within McLaren that only one car could be made ready for Brands Hatch, and even then Bruce missed the first day of practice. As things turned out, the Serenissima would not fare much better than the Ford and McLaren shared the fifth row with Chris Irwin, a young Englishman making his debut in a third works Brabham, powered by a 4-cylinder Climax.

Rob Walker had bought a Cooper-Maserati for Jo Siffert and a similar car had been sold to a relatively unknown Frenchman by the name of Guy Ligier, later to switch his efforts to team ownership since he was not a particularly brilliant driver, although there have been moments in recent years when driving may have seemed the better option after all.

Bob Anderson now had a bright green Brabham-Climax 4-cylinder; the American, Bob Bondurant, drove a BRM V8 for Bernard White; John Taylor was entered by David Bridges in a Brabham-BRM, while near the back of the grid were two specials.

Trevor Taylor now found himself at the wheel of a perilous light green machine, known as a Shannon and built by an Irishman, Aiden Jones. This device was powered by a previously unraced Coventry-Climax V8 which had been conceived for the 2.5-litre Formula – back in 1954! The engine now belonged to Paul Emery (of Emeryson fame) and he and Jones appeared to have taken on rather too much in such elevated company. Certainly, the car looked lethal, particularly on the dip at Pilgrims Drop and it had to be said that Taylor deserved much better than this.

While the works Ferrari team may have been absent, they received token representation when J.A. Pearce Engineering, of Southall, dropped a GTO engine into the back of a neatly converted 1965 Cooper. Driven by Chris Lawrence, the car sounded nice but was very slow. Cynics suggested that it should have been left to its fate when a fire broke out near the team's transporter on the first day of practice on Thursday.

Brabham, meanwhile, had been collaring the 100 bottles of champagne for the fastest time on the first day. In fact, Jack would dominate the entire weekend.

'Yep, not bad.'

The 40-year-old who, at Zandvoort, had hobbled onto the grid aided by a walking stick and wearing a false beard, was about to show that life does indeed begin at forty. He led every lap and was never troubled.

'As far as I can recall, it was a pretty lonely race out there,' he says. 'The track was damp during the early laps and I had some pressure from Dan and Jochen, but even then I was quite comfortable. I remember having time to wonder where Denny had got to. There was no sign of him.'

Denny, in fact, had been dithering right up to the last minute over the choice of tyres to suit the conditions and it took him some time to settle into the race.

Jochen Rindt wrestles the Cooper-Maserati through Stirlings Bend as Hill, Clark, McLaren and Irwin follow.

By lap nine, Gurney was out with engine trouble. Rindt's spectacular efforts led to a quick spin which dropped him into the clutches of his team-mate. They swapped places a couple of times, Surtees then keeping second place until the track began to dry and the handling of the Cooper-Maseratis became even more lurid than before.

Hulme, on the other hand, really began to motor under these conditions and the highlight of the race would be his charge past the Coopers and onto the tail of Hill and Clark as they fought over second place. By lap 37, Denny was between the BRM and the Lotus and, two laps later, he had taken second place from Hill. The only change thereafter was a pit stop for Clark to top up with brake fluid and a subsequent climb back through the field to take fourth place. Brabham, meanwhile, had lapped everyone except Hulme.

'Yeah, it would have been nice if the Ferraris had been there,' says Jack, 'because I'm sure we would have beaten them too, particularly on that circuit. And I seem to remember there was a lot of oil about. In fact, the place seemed to be covered in oil all weekend, There were one or two dodgy motors about then... We were fortunate at the time because our Goodyear tyres were good in both the wet and the dry situations, so we weren't too worried when it was wet at the start.'

In fact, the tyre war was just beginning in earnest – and in those days teams were able to switch companies at will. BRM, Cooper and Ferrari, for instance, started 1966 with Dunlop, but when the season came to a close in Mexico City there was not a single car on the British rubber.

By then Jack Brabham had wrapped up the championship for a third time. He had won the Dutch Grand Prix, but only after a brilliant drive by Clark had been delayed by a water leak. Any thoughts that Brabham was backing into the title because of the misfortune of others were wiped out at the Nürburgring where he drove superbly in the wet to take his fourth successive victory. That more or less secured both the drivers' and the constructors' championships for Brabham.

Lodovico Scarfiotti, drafted into the Ferrari team from time to time, led nearly all the way at Monza while Jim Clark gave the H16 BRM engine its first – and only – victory when he won at Watkins Glen. To round off the late-season variety, John Surtees took the lead on the sixth lap in Mexico and was never headed, the Cooper-Maserati lapping everyone bar the new world champion.

And, in between all this activity around the world, Jack Brabham had also managed to win no less than ten races during the final season of the 1,000cc Formula 2.

'Yep, not bad,' he says. Indeed, not bad for someone who a year or so before had tried to tell us he couldn't see much future for either himself or his team.

Lotus and Ford

During 1966, Rob Walker had spent £35,000 running his privately entered team in Formula 1. The money, Walker explained in an interview at the time, had mainly come from 'the generosity of the fuel company, the tyre company, the brake companies and also by Jack Durlacher (Walker's financial partner) and starting money.' Walker considered, though, that the days of the private entrant were numbered:

'I have just spoken to Monsieur Taffe of the Monaco organisers,' he continued, 'and he hinted that there might be 16 works cars with guaranteed entries at Monaco, and at the most only two or three private entries.

'It is getting too expensive. Our costs would have been higher for 1966 if we had been starting from scratch, but over the past years we have amassed an ample amount of spares, machinery, transporter etc. But many more works teams are appearing and I don't think the organisers really want us, except to make up the field cheaply.

'Now our aim is to beat the works teams and gain some championship points, and this gives as much thrill as winning did in the old days. Our ambition is to win another world championship race.'

Rob Walker, relying on Jo Siffert and the same Cooper-Maserati, would not have much hope of that in 1967, particularly after the arrival in June of a car-engine combination which would have a profound effect on the immediate future of Grand Prix racing. Paradoxically, this car, the Lotus 49, would allow Walker to achieve his ambition the following year.

Colin Chapman had been busy at the dinner table and then the drawing board. Chapman had been asked, early in his career, to contribute the occasional article to the *Sunday Dispatch* by the paper's editor, Walter Hayes.

When Hayes became Director of Public Affairs at Ford of Britain, Chapman invited Walter to dinner and expounded his views on the need for a 3-litre Grand Prix engine. Chapman knew that Ford were in the throws of polishing their rather dowdy image. Motor sport was playing a large part in lifting the company up-market and a Ford-financed Grand Prix engine would help no end. Or, at least, that was the way Chapman saw it.

Hayes agreed. By dint of shrewd lobbying and clever political manoeuvring, Hayes got Ford to agree to commit a minimum of £100,000 towards an engine to be built by Cosworth Engineering. In fact, this deal would also include an engine for the 1600cc Formula 2 which was due to come into force.

Keith Duckworth, the 'worth' of Cosworth, was not swayed by the trend to built multi-cylinder engines. Instead, he was more impressed by the simple effectiveness of the Repco V8; it was lighter and more efficient and had better fuel consumption. Anyway, a V8 would also fit in with the plans to build a 4-cylinder Formula 2 engine. Chapman, along with his chief designer, Maurice Phillippe, got on with designing a monocoque to accept the new engine, to be known as the DFV.

Part of the deal had been to allow Lotus exclusive use of the DFV in 1967, but Ford insisted on making it freely available the following year. It was a decision which would alter the thinking behind Formula 1.

With such an engine, more or less for sale 'off the shelf', small teams would be encouraged to build their own cars knowing that they would be reasonably competitive. The strength, if not the depth, of Formula 1 would benefit as a result. And the turning point was 2 June 1967, the day the Lotus 49 appeared at Zandvoort, ready to practise for the third round of the championship.

There had been changes elsewhere within the team. After seven years with BRM, Graham Hill had joined Lotus, and he had no cause to doubt the wisdom of such a move when he put the Lotus 49 on pole with a lap which was 6.2 seconds inside the record.

Clark, having had wheel-bearing trouble during practice, was on row three – not bad considering he had not so much as sat in the car before practice began. Being a tax exile in Paris and Bermuda made life difficult for the Scot and Hill had carried out most of the testing. Graham knew all about the 400 bhp of the V8; or, at least, he knew how it would arrive in one fairly hefty lump. The DFV had great potential, but there was much refinement neeeded.

That certainly appeared to be the case when Hill led for 11 laps and then rolled to a halt, the camshaft drive broken. But Clark was beginning to feel at home now and he gradually moved forward to take the lead, one which he would not lose. It was a remarkable victory for the Ford-Cosworth V8. It was also the first of more than 150 for an engine which would be the mainstay of Formula 1 for a decade and more.

The Lotus victory at Zandvoort was very good news for Ken Tyrrell as he watched from the spectator enclosure. Now more convinced than ever that he wanted to move from Formula 2 to Formula 1, he went straight back to Surrey and ordered three DFVs, at £7,500 each, for 1968. How he would pay for them was something he would worry about later.

But an encouraging sight for Tyrrell had been a depressing one for the rest of the field. It was quite clear that so long as the Lotus 49 held together it would win.

Thus far the season had not developed a clear pattern. Pedro Rodriguez, signed by Cooper in place of Surtees (who had joined Honda) had claimed a fortunate win at Kyalami, in South Africa, while Denny Hulme had flung the Repco-Brabham around Monaco to score a well-deserved nine points. But now things were different. Once again, Colin Chapman had raised the stakes. And the next stop would be the fast sweeps of Spa-Francorchamps.

Dan's day

Dan Gurney and Weslake had finally got their act together and the Eagle-Weslake V12 had scored an impressive win at the Race of Champions. Dan loved Spa-Francorchamps and he went there buoyed by a victory at Le Mans where he had shared a Ford with the tough American, A.J. Foyt. But even Gurney had his doubts when Clark took pole.

Sure enough, the Lotus romped away. Then Clark was forced to make a couple of pit stops to deal with problems with the sparking plugs and that let Jackie Stewart into the lead. Jackie had led at Monaco in the V8 BRM until the transmission failed, but for Spa he was in the brutish H16 car. He didn't reckon the place much after the ordeal the previous year and his displeasure was heightened when BRM began to jump out of second gear. The only way was to hold the gearlever in place, a daunting task at a circuit where driving one-handed is not for the faint-hearted. But Stewart persisted even though he could not stop Gurney from sweeping past to take the one – and only – Grand Prix victory for the Eagle.

The French Grand Prix was moved to the Bugatti circuit at Le Mans, a track which used the main straight past the pits and the run over the hill towards the Esses before turning right and doubling back through the car parks. Few people were impressed by the fiddly nature of the circuit, and that also applied to the spectators, who stayed away in large numbers. At the end of the day, though, there were nine points on offer and it was Brabham who bagged them, with team-mate Hulme finishing second.

And Lotus? Both Hill and Clark had led until sidelined by mechanical problems. Few people saw anything other than a Lotus victory at Silverstone – provided the cars stayed in one piece.

A quick fix

It was a simple question of priorities. If the car breaks, you fix it. Quickly.

Distortion of the final-drive casings had caused the problems on both Lotus 49s in France. Chapman sat down in the back of the Lotus transporter and drew modifications which he then took, with the ZF gearboxes themselves, in his private plane to Germany so that ZF could put the modifications in hand immediately.

By contrast, Bob Anderson, who reckoned he had lost a possible fourth place in France when his Brabham-Climax ground to a halt, forked out 6s 6d (32½p) for a new set of contact-breaker points and he, too, was ready for Silverstone.

Lotus's troubles were by no means over. Jack Brabham had been quickest on the Thursday morning but Clark took a tenth of a second off that time in the afternoon and went quicker still on the Friday. Hill had just made sure of a place alongside his team-mate and was making his way towards the pit entrance when the Lotus suddenly turned sharp right and rammed the wall on the inside of Woodcote.

A rear radius arm had torn away from the chassis and the resulting collision with the concrete wall had torn off the radiator and a front wheel, as well as damaging the monocoque. While Clark's car was checked over for signs of a similar failure, a team of 16 mechanics prepared themselves for a 14-hour marathon to rebuild Hill's car back at the Lotus factory.

In 1967, of course, there were no such thing as garages for the teams to work in. The transporters were simply lined up behind the pits (in the case of Silverstone, reconstructed with a raised pit road following the tragedy in 1963) and the cars parked alongside. There was not even an awning to protect them from the elements and the surface was loose gravel rather than the Tarmac which is *de rigueur* today.

The pits at Silverstone, however, had a balcony and, for 30 shillings (£1.50p), it was possible to purchase a pass for the weekend and look down on teams working in either the pit lane or the paddock. For the race itself, 40 shillings (£2) would buy a seat in the Pits Grandstand.

The day's entertainment began at 10.30am with a 20-lap race for the 1,000cc Formula 3 cars. Among the 37-car entry were Brabhams for Derek Bell, Peter Gethin and Maurice Nunn; names who would go on to play a part in Grand Prix racing. Charles Lucas, driving a Lotus 41, won a typical thriller by 0.2 seconds from the Merlyn of Tony Lanfranchi.

Then followed a sportscar race. Paul Hawkins, a delightful character, had claimed pole position in his Ford GT40. He led for four laps before stopping on the far side of the circuit with a piston failure. The walk back to the pits through the cornfields gave the rough and ready Australian enough time to come up one or two choice phrases about the financial arrangements for this meeting.

The RAC had decided to scrap starting money and just pay from a prize fund, with a bonus of £4 per lap. After two day's of practice and an expensive engine failure, Hawkins was quite prepared to tell anyone who cared to listen just what he thought about earning £16 for his weekend's work.

The entrant of the winning car in the Grand Prix was due to receive the Mervyn O'Gorman

Clark follows Hill as the Lotus pair run their own race during the opening laps.

Trophy, plus £1,000, and from the outset it seemed this would go to Team Lotus. Or, at least it did, until a suspension bolt worked loose on Hill's car.

Graham had been running in close company with Clark and he limped into the pits, his left-rear wheel canted over at a drunken angle. This was quickly put right but Hill retired not long after when the DFV suddenly failed as he accelerated out of Woodcote. Clark, meanwhile, was on his own at the front and it was simply of question of his car lasting the distance. Fortunately for the 120,000 spectators, there was a thrilling contest for third place between Jack Brabham and Chris Amon.

This had been a character-building year for Chris. His future seemed assured when Ferrari offered a place alongside Bandini and Parkes for 1967. But by the time the British Grand Prix had come round, the young New Zealander was carrying the hopes of the entire Ferrari team, and everything that entailed.

Bandini had suffered the most appalling accident during the closing stages of the Monaco Grand Prix. Chasing after Hulme's leading Brabham, the Italian had clipped the chicane, the Ferrari somersaulting and bursting into flames. Bandini was trapped for five minutes in the upturned car as it lay against the straw bales lining the exit of the chicane. The rescue services were almost powerless to help. He died of his burns three days later.

Then at Spa Francorchamps, Parkes had crashed on oil dropped by Stewarts BRM, the Englishman suffering severe leg injuries which would bring his Grand Prix career to an end. And all of this was too much for Scarfiotti, coming so soon after the tragedy at Monaco. As a result, Amon was the sole representative of Ferrari at Silverstone. And the Italians were counting on him finding a way past Brabham. Easier said than done, of course.

'That race was one of the most enjoyable I ever had,' recalls Chris. 'The Lotuses were in another race, we all knew that, so the best thing to do was just forget they were there at all. I got involved in this big dice with old Jack, and I remember he was adjusting his mirrors early in the race – and one of them flew off and whistled past my head! Then he seemed to be adjusting the other one...I've never been quite sure whether he was adjusting them or trying to tear them off...

'After about 30 laps he'd lost both mirrors, and then we had a real tussle. That was a very wide car indeed, but of course afterwards he tells me he's very sorry for chopping me all over the place but his mirrors were gone and he didn't know I was there!

'I finally passed him out of Woodcote with about four laps to go. He went a bit wide there and I was able to get a run at him down to Copse. But he did a good job, I must say. After I got him I closed on Denny in the other Brabham, but there just wasn't time to catch him. I finished third.

'It was a real old-fashioned dice I had with Jack, and that was why it was so enjoyable. He was throwing everything in the bloody book at me – stones, grass, dirt, *everything!*'

Twenty-one years later and Brabham's recall of the event was still a trifle...blurred:

'You say my mirrors came off? I don't recall that particular moment but there were plenty of moments like it. If I remember rightly, I was behind somebody and the mirrors got hit by stones. And as for Chris saying I was a hard man to pass, well he wasn't so easy either!'

Clark, of course, had no such problems. He crossed the line giving the familiar thumbs-up as he led Hulme home by 13 seconds. The six points came in useful for Denny. He would go on to score maximum points at the Nürburgring and make the most of continuing problems for Lotus. By the time the 49 had found some form of reliability by winning at Watkins Glen (Clark) and Mexico (Clark), it would be too late. Denis Hulme was on his way to winning the 1967 world championship.

Silverstone, though, had surrendered completely to Clark. After the race, the entire Lotus team joined Jimmy on a tractor and trailer as they motored slowly around the circuit on a lap of honour. Spectators ducked under the barrier and climbed the earth banks to applaud the shy Scot all the way.

Little did they know it was the last time they would see their hero in Britain. Motor racing values the world over were about to be turned upside down in 1968.

Jim Clark, as the home fans remember him. The Scot takes his last public bow in Britain.

Sunday 7 April

People can usually remember exactly what they were doing on the day John Lennon was shot; they can recall their whereabouts when word of President Kennedy's assassination came through. It's the same with racing folk when Jim Clark's death is mentioned.

7 April 1968. That was the day when motor sport went into deep shock. At first, the news was confused. Reports said that Jim Clark had been killed at Hockenheim, a circuit few people knew much about. What was he doing there anyway? Why wasn't he racing in the BOAC 500 at Brands Hatch, Britain's round of the world sportscar championship? Surely some mistake. Jim Clark dead? Never.

Only when confirmation came with reports on the radio, and Michael Aspel, against a backdrop of Clark's portrait, began the evening TV news with the sombre words: 'The Scottish racing driver, Jim Clark....' did the terrible realisation begin to sink in.

Each successive detail seemed more absurd than the last. He had been racing in a Formula 2 race; lying in a lonely eighth place; the Lotus had left the road at a gentle curve; there were no obvious explanations. The only certainty was that he had been killed instantly when the car slammed broadside into a tree. The impact had been enough to rip the engine off the chassis.

159

It also tore the heart out of motor racing.

Drivers wept when news spread along the pit lane at Brands Hatch; others were stunned into silence. You could almost read their thoughts; 'if it can happen to Jimmy....'.

A few weeks later, Mike Spence was killed at Indianapolis. Then Lodovico Scarfiotti suffered fatal injuries while practising for a hillclimb at Rossfeld in Germany. Thoughts about safety – which had begun in earnest with Stewart's accident at Spa in 1966 and gathered impetus when Bandini perished at Monaco and Bob Anderson died when his car crashed into a marshal's post during testing at Silverstone – were suddenly a maximum priority. Superficial medical coverage and the paying of lip service to safety was no longer sufficient.

The iodine man

The lack of attention paid to the subject probably had its roots in the cavalier approach employed during the early days. When Charles Mortimer raced at Brooklands, in the late twenties and early thirties, there was only medical support of sorts. Mortimer recalls:

> 'The majority of Brooklands staff were fairly elderly. There was a delightful old gentleman called Walker whose main duties were the maintenance of the lavatories – and first-aid. Walker was absolutely fearless and supremely confident in all matters concerning first aid – he would tackle any injury, however serious, with an air of confidence that calmed everybody. His resources as regards equipment seemed very limited, even to us, but he made up for this by the lavish use of iodine which he seemed able to acquire in ten-gallon drums. Walker used iodine in the treatment of the most unusual injuries – but everyone survived and it was generally agreed that in the matter of first-aid, Walker knew what he was doing!'

There had been half-hearted talk of making crash helmets obligatory for the British Grand Prix at Brooklands in 1927, but when less than half of the starters wore one, the matter was quietly forgotten. Indeed, it was not until 1952 that the wearing of helmets became compulsory, although several drivers had seen sense long before that.

The need for crash helmets was answered by companies such as Herbert Johnson of New Bond Street, London – 'Hatters to the late King George VI' – who, in 1956, offered the 'H. J. Lightweight Crash Helmet' for £5 15s 0d (£5.75p) (spraying in any colour 15 shillings [75p], box and postage five shillings [25p]). These helmets, designed originally for polo players, were made of laminated canvas and gum.

The remainder of the driver's attire was up to the individual. Short-sleeved sports shirts and light cotton trousers were common place. The general belief seemed to be that if the car caught fire then you could hop out of the cockpit – assuming you had not already been thrown clear by the initial impact.

The first overalls, usually made of either silk or cotton poplin, were generally tailored for comfort and appearance rather than offering the driver any protection. Footwear ranged initially from gym shoes, through boxing boots to purpose-made driving shoes with very thin leather soles. At all times, though, drivers generally wore whatever socks they had put on that morning.

It was not until 1966-67 that serious thought was given to protection from fire. Asbestos suits had been designed for fire marshals, but after a brief trial, these were found to be too heavy and too hot for drivers to work in. The Du Pont company took an important step forward when they developed Nomex protective clothing for the flight deck crews on the US Navy aircraft carriers. The material was light and comfortable and reasonably flame resistant.

A driver was now able to kit himself out with underwear, socks, gloves, face mask and overalls which would give him some sort of fighting chance as he wriggled out of cockpits which were becoming more and more confined. In 1967, for example, Les Leston had produced overalls under the Protex brandname, the underwear and overalls selling for £15. A year later, a full set of Nomex would cost £48. And Stewart was one of the first drivers to use a full seat harness.

Driver protection was all very well, but what about the back-up at the trackside? Stewart had been appalled when it took 45 minutes for an ambulance to arrive at the scene of his accident at Spa-Francorchamps; and even then the ordeal was not over. After taking him to a first aid hut, where a rudimentary clean-up took place, it was decided to transfer Stewart to hospital. The ambulance, bouncing along the back roads, got lost. Twice.

Jim Clark sweeps his Lotus through the hoarding-free surroundings of Stirling's Bend at Brands Hatch during the 1964 Grand Prix.

John Surtees (pictured at Druids at Brands Hatch during the British Grand Prix) came into his own in 1964 and won the championship for Ferrari.

Simplest is best. Jack Brabham made the most of the new formula in 1966 with his Brabham-Repco. The Australian (main picture) heads onto the main straight at Brands Hatch on course to another win.

Inset: Jackie Stewart, recovering from the shock of Spa-Francorchamps, dives into Paddock with the BRM V8 during practice for the British Grand Prix at Brands Hatch. (Note how simple it is to read the numbers and identify the cars in 1966.)

Silverstone 1967:
Easy to see; difficult to drive. Jackie Stewart's H-16 BRM (left) parked behind the pits at Silverstone in 1967. The V8 BRM, entered by Tim Parnell for Piers Courage, is alongside.

Centre: Dan Gurney works on his Eagle on the raised pit lane.

Bottom: The beautiful lines of the Ferrari 312 are evident as Chris Amon pulls up alongside a Cooper-Maserati in the collection area.

Main picture: With there being no direct access from the paddock, through the pits and onto the pit lane at Silverstone in 1967, cars were gathered in a collection area prior to the start of practice. Jim Clark's Lotus joins the Cooper-Maserati of Pedro Rodriguez and the ex-works Brabham of Guy Ligier (no 18) whilst in the background is Silvio Moser's privately-entered Cooper.

Last shout for the privateers. Jo Siffert heads for victory at Brands Hatch in 1968 with Rob Walker's Lotus 49.

Top: *Chris Amon's Matra-Simca in the shambling surrounds of the Brands Hatch paddock, 1972 British Grand Prix.*

Above: *The style of the early seventies is clearly visible in the paddock at Brands Hatch in July 1972. Denny Hulme's McLaren has a certain fragrance about it....*

Right: *1972 was Emerson's year. Fittipaldi urges the Lotus 72 towards victory at Brands Hatch.*

The see-through screen (right) allows us to see Jody Scheckter at work with the six-wheel Tyrrell at Brands Hatch in 1976. This novel idea was soon dropped after 'little enthusiasm' was shown by the spectators.

Below: *Ronnie Peterson's wonderful style with the Lotus 72 was eventually cramped by a puncture at Brands Hatch in 1974.*

1979 saw a very popular victory at Silverstone for Clay Regazzoni (right) as he brought home the first of many Grand Prix trophies for Frank Williams.

Far right: *Tom Pryce and his Shadow: on pole at Silverstone in 1975.*

Nigel Mansell holds off Nelson
Piquet on the approach to Druids
during their superb contest at
Brands Hatch in 1986.

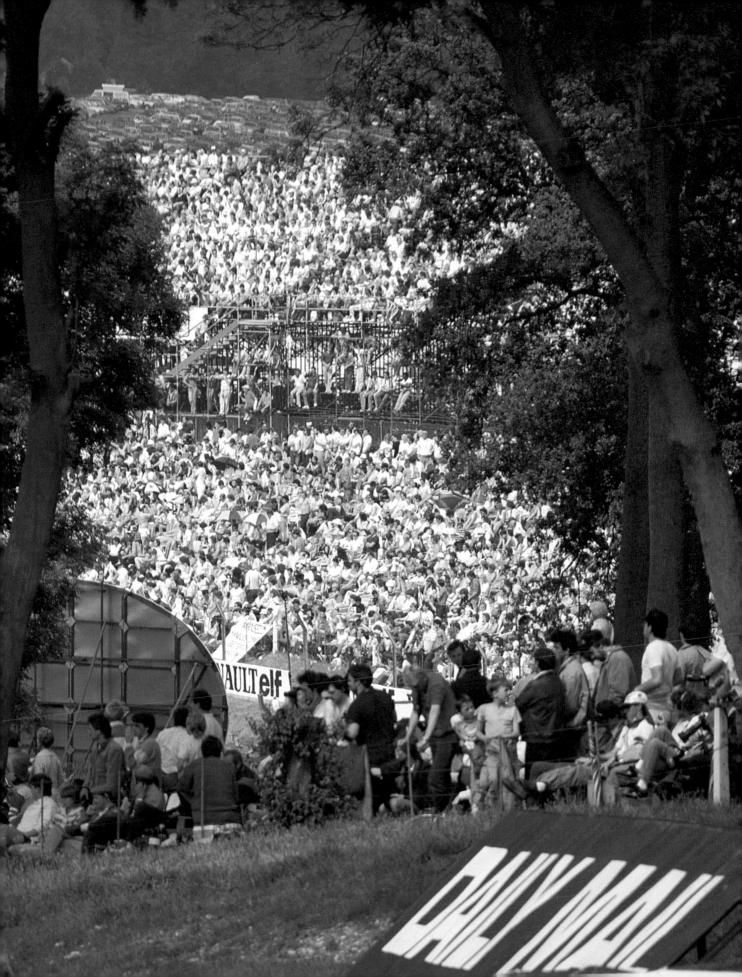

Above: *Silverstone in 1987: changed beyond all recognition. Copse is in the foreground with the runway (aka Segrave Straight) used for the first Grand Prix in 1948 running from Copse towards the top left-hand corner of the picture.*

Left: *Of all the late charges seen at Silverstone, there was none more thrilling than Nigel Mansell's dash to victory in 1987. The Englishman holds the trophy aloft while his Williams-Honda team-mate, Nelson Piquet, puts on a brave face. Ayrton Senna (right) thinks of better days ahead.*

Brands Hatch: perfect viewing for spectators (main picture).

Silverstone 1989:
The all-conquering McLaren-
Honda's of Ayrton Senna and
Alain Prost lead the field into
Copse Corner.

Enter Louis T. Stanley, an imposing figure who had become a member of the BRM team through his marriage into the Owen family some years before. Pompous and self-righteous he may have been, but he took steps to ensure that such a fiasco should not occur again. And he did it in a remarkably short space of time.

It was Stanley's idea to introduce an International Grand Prix Medical Service. This would take the form of a mobile hospital; air-conditioned, humidified and containing the very latest medical aids capable of resuscitating and stabilising patents before, if necessary, moving them on to a specialist hospital. The IGPMS would carry records of not just the drivers, but every member of the Formula 1 circus and there would be staff on board to deal with anything from minor cuts and sunstroke to fractures and serious burns.

Stanley canvassed the sport and industry for financial support, the drivers themselves contributing a considerable amount. They gave their services free at the 1967 Spring Cup meeting at Oulton Park where, coincidentally, the white articulated lorry, affectionately known as the 'Stanley Wagon,' made its public debut. It seemed everyone's problems were over. In fact, they were just beginning.

The very presence of the unit at circuits abroad was seen as indictment of the local facilities. The organisers made encouraging noises but, generally, the medical people did not want to know. At one circuit, it was parked on an inaccessible piece of waste ground some distance from the paddock. And when Bandini crashed at Monte Carlo they by-passed the unit completely.

It has to be said, however, that Mr Stanley's blustering and pontifical ways were not everyone's cup of tea. But, for whatever reason, the medical unit faded away; indeed one or two doctors maintained it was not all it was cracked up to be. Whether this was sour grapes or genuine comment is open to debate. In any case, medical arrangements would not begin to be put on a uniform and organised basis until the arrival of Bernie Ecclestone, the rebirth of the Formula One Constructors' Association and the subsequent appointment in 1978 of Professor Sydney Watkins of The London Hospital to look after the medical interests of the Grand Prix drivers.

A wing and a prayer

In 1968, however, the Grand Prix teams themselves ventured down a path of development which, at times, gave the impression they were hell-bent on self-destruction: they discovered that aerofoils had an application in Formula 1.

The phenomenon crept in gradually. There was no sign of any aerodynamic devices at the opening round of the championship, the South African Grand Prix. Interest was focused on the car entered by Ken Tyrrell and driven by Jackie Stewart. Using a chassis built by the French aerospace company, Matra, and powered of course by the Ford-Cosworth DFV, Stewart led the race briefly and then held second place for many laps before retiring with engine failure. The race at Kyalami was Jim Clark's 25th, and final, Grand Prix victory, the Lotus driver having eclipsed the previous record held by Juan Manuel Fangio

Lotus were knocked sideways by Clark's death but Graham Hill rose to the occasion magnificently by giving the team a welcome victory in the Spanish Grand Prix at Jarama, a new circuit near Madrid. And the interesting change here was that the Lotus was no longer painted in its traditional green and yellow. The car, in fact, was decked out in the colours of a cigarette packet and the team's name had been changed to Gold Leaf Team Lotus. Commercial sponsorship had arrived – not that you could have missed it.

Lotus then introduced yet another new development when a heavily revised car, sporting wings either side of the nose and a swept-up rear edge to the engine cover, appeared at Monaco. The value of this was dubious on such a tight circuit but it certainly did not prevent Hill from scoring his fourth win in the Principality.

Two weeks later, at Spa, the Ferraris (driven by Amon and a young Belgian, Jacky Ickx) had sprouted little winglets on the nose and carried an aerofoil mounted above the engine. The race went to Bruce McLaren (his orange car powered by a Ford-Cosworth) after Stewart's Matra had run out of fuel at the beginning of the last lap. Stewart made up for his disappointment by winning in Holland, but Ickx showed superb reflexes and control by giving Ferrari victory in the wet at Rouen. It was a sad day however, since Jo Schlesser, in his first Grand Prix, had died when he crashed an aircooled Honda, a new car which had been raced against the advice of Surtees, the team leader.

A haze at home. Jack Oliver leads Graham Hill during the opening laps.

Significantly, there had also been a horrifying accident during practice when a Lotus, driven by Jack Oliver, a new recruit to the team, broke in two after leaving the road at high speed. Oliver, who emerged unscathed, could offer no explanation. The finger of suspicion pointed at the aerofoils. Not one to stand still when it came to technical advancement, Chapman had mounted a wing on slender stalks which were attached to the top of the rear wheel uprights. There was no question the wing provided additional downforce. But what else besides? No one knew for sure. And they were still in place when Hill and Oliver rolled out to practice for the British Grand Prix at Brands Hatch.

The wonder of Woolworths

When Hill took pole position and Oliver joined him on the front row, it was clear that a Lotus 49 with wings was the thing to have. There had been a frantic amount of rebuilding work going on at the Lotus factory as the team prepared another car for Oliver. Not only that, but Rob Walker's mechanics were also present at Hethel as they built one of the latest cars for Siffert. (Walker had taken delivery of a new car for the Race of Champions the previous March, only to have it badly damaged against a Brands Hatch bank. Then, to cap it all, Walker's workshop had caught fire, taking with it the remains of the car and just about everything else the team possessed. Rob had got through the subsequent period by making do with a Tasman Lotus and leasing a store room from the local branch of Woolworths). The all-night effort of the mechanics was made worth-while when Siffert put the car on the second row, ahead of Rindt, who had left Cooper at the beginning of the season to join Brabham.

As for Hulme, he had gone to McLaren; Pedro Rodriguez had taken Stewart's place at BRM and the loss of Spence meant a permanent drive for Richard Attwood; Cooper had replaced Rodriguez and Rindt with Vic Elford and Robin Widdows (Brian Redman having being injured during the Belgian Grand Prix), while Matra, apart from furnishing Ken Tyrrell with a chassis, had entered their own car, powered by a raucous V12 of their own manufacture and driven by Jean-Pierre Beltoise, a plucky little Frenchman. Gurney had his Eagle, but a great driving talent appeared to be slowly wasting away on a project which had made little progress during the previous 12 months.

The privateers, led by Rob Walker of course, were reduced in numbers, just as Walker had predicted, although Bonnier was continuing with a McLaren-BRM, the car which Bruce had used towards the latter end of the previous year. McLaren had waited for the arrival of the BRM V12, an eminently more sensible unit than the H16, and that engine now powered the works BRMs as well as the Coopers and Tim Parnell's semi-works BRM, driven by the dashing Englishman, Piers Courage. Finally, the diminutive Swiss driver, Silvio Moser, had a 1966 Brabham-Repco with which he was unable to equal Jack's time set two years before. And yet, in the intervening period development elsewhere had been such that Hill had lapped almost six seconds faster than the 1966 pole.

Graham had never won the British Grand Prix, a thought which may or may not have been on his mind as he sat quietly against a trackside hoarding a few minutes before the start. More than likely, he was wondering what the weather had in store; spots of rain had placed the teams in a quandary but Lotus eventually chose dry tyres – the correct decision as things would turn out. Perhaps, though, Hill had been trying to work out just what had been going through the mind of his young team-mate.

Oliver got the jump on Hill at the start and led the pack into Paddock. For three glorious laps he stayed in front, smashing the lap record as he went. Then Hill moved ahead, with Oliver shadowing closely and Siffert not far behind. As the threatening clouds began to disappear, the three Lotuses got into their stride, with Amon hanging on in fourth place. It was soon clear that no one else would have a look in.

After 25 laps, they had lapped Rindt in 11th place but shortly afterwards a universal joint on Hill's car collapsed as he accelerated out of Druids and Oliver was leading his home Grand Prix once more. The 26-year-old from Essex appeared completely unruffled, although he was helped by the fact that Siffert and Amon were busily disputing what had become second place. On lap 44, that became a battle for the lead as Oliver went out with broken transmission.

'Looking back,' says Oliver, 'all I can remember is that it had been a very nice feeling to lead the pack. I don't remember anything about getting excited because this was Brands Hatch or the British Grand Prix; it was just a nice feeling to be out front.

'I felt quite comfortable because I was very good at Brands Hatch. It was a circuit that I seemed to perform well on; I was a bit of a Brands specialist, I suppose, and that was probably worth half a second a lap. But that's not very good, is it? What I should have been was good everywhere! The confidence level was higher there and the car was good that day.

'There had been absolutely no discussion between Graham and I before the race about who should do what. I remember, though, there was a discussion afterwards! He said I had been blowing oil onto his visor and I had been getting in the way. Anyway, when he went out, there was no argument.

'It's a bit frustrating, thinking about it now, because I could have won that race, but there you are. It was my big moment.'

Amon had led Siffert for six laps but the Swiss had responded magnificently and he happened to move back in front moments before Oliver rolled to a disconsolate halt at South Bank Bend. Amon gave chase, the Ferrari quicker through the corners, its V12 engine losing out to the DFV on the straights. Amon enjoyed throwing the car around but, beautiful as it was to watch, there was a price to be paid. By the time the race reached the final ten laps or so, his tyres were finished. Siffert won the British Grand Prix for Rob Walker, the last private entrant to do so. And a more British gentleman you could not wish to find.

The following day, the drivers presented themselves at Mersham, near Ashford in Kent, for a charity cricket match against Lord Brabourne's XI. Prince Charles, present at the Grand Prix, had agreed to play and his appearance helped raise more than £500 for the Grand Prix Medical Unit and the McIndoe Burns Unit at East Grinstead Hospital. His presence also brought representatives of the national daily press out in force but the only item of note they found worth reporting was the search for a pair of size ten cricket boots for His Royal Highness. No one cared to mention that Pedro Rodriguez, a complete novice, had taken to the field wearing a pair of black patent leather shoes. Prince Charles was out after scoring 20 runs (bowled Hill, caught McLaren – who was wearing tennis shoes and an Autolite cap).

Hill in fact had been one of the stars of the weekend. Apart from throwing a party at his cottage in Kent on the Saturday evening, he had led the singing of bawdy songs at the Farriers pub after the match. He was, on reflection, just the right man for Lotus after such a terrible start to the season.

It was understandable, therefore, that Graham had much sentimental support when the championship came down to a three-way fight between Hill, Stewart and Hulme at the final race in Mexico City. Hulme retired early, leaving the former BRM team-mates to fight it out, the verdict eventually going to Hill after Stewart ran into mechanical problems. Apart from one more win at Monaco the following year, Hill's star would be on the wane after that. The time had come for John Young Stewart, of Dumbarton, Scotland, to step forward and do battle with Karl Jochen Rindt, of Vienna. And there would be no finer example of their friendly but intense rivalry than the 1969 British Grand Prix. In fact, that race would encapsulate the entire season.

The trouble with Jochen

Jackie Stewart arrived at Silverstone on peak form. Matra had produced the MS80, a car which remains one of Jackie's favourites; not surprising 'perhaps' since he had already won with it in Spain, Holland and France. And, before that, he had claimed the South African Grand Prix in the 1968 car, the MS10. Five races and four wins (Hill, as mentioned previously, having scored at Monaco after Stewart had retired). It was an enviable record. All of which must have added to the deep sense of frustration felt by Jochen Rindt.

When he signed for Lotus at the beginning of the season, Rindt at last seemed to have a car worthy of his talent; yet here he was at Silverstone with not a single point on the board. He had been leading the Spanish Grand Prix, run on the stunning Montjuich circuit at Barcelona, when the rear wing broke, Rindt crashing into the remains of Hill's car after the Englishman had suffered a similar failure. The only positive thing to be said was that the incidents finally drew the attention of the governing body to the absurdity of high-mounted wings, which were banned almost immediately.

Then Rindt led the Dutch Grand Prix until a universal joint broke on the 17th lap. And now, to cap it all, Colin Chapman had a bee in his bonnet about four-wheel drive and his latest creation, the Lotus 63. Rindt had expressed his open dislike for the car, and when Chapman brought one to Zandvoort, the Austrian refused to even sit in it and raced his 49 instead.

This was just about the last straw as far as Chapman was concerned. Their relationship had got off to a bad start when Rindt threw a tantrum in South Africa when he learned that Lotus were running a third car for the American, Mario Andretti. The truth of the matter probably had something to do with the fact that Rindt's former boss, Jack Brabham, had switched to the Ford-Cosworth and then put his new car on pole at Kyalami! Either way, the moody Austrian was not best pleased with life.

Then, following the wing failures at Barcelona, Rindt had written an open letter to the press which said wings were dangerous and had nothing to do with motor racing. The effect this had on Chapman is not hard to imagine.

And so to Silverstone. Rindt arrived to find that he was to drive the four-wheel drive car. Worse than that, there was no alternative; Chapman had sold two 49s to Bonnier and the Rhodesian driver, John Love, leaving one as a spare car. Rindt was fit to be tied. He demanded the 49 while Graham Hill somehow persuaded Bonnier to do a swap! John Miles, who had given the 63 a brief and not very auspicious debut in France, had no choice. He would race the four-wheel drive car once more. All in all, enough drama to fill a book. And not a single Lotus had turned a wheel. Indeed, while all the fuss had been going on and the drivers were waiting for the transporter to arrive on Thursday morning, Hill had filled in his time by completing a few laps in a Brabham! Jack had broken his leg during a test session and Ickx, Rindt's replacement, had been late arriving. So Hill gave Brabham a hand. It would have been difficult to imagine Nigel Mansell doing that for McLaren in 1989 – and even more difficult to envisage Ron Dennis letting him.

When Rindt finally got down to business, the altercations in the paddock had obviously raised his adrenalin level. After a problematic first session on the Thursday afternoon, he had the car much more to his liking for the final two hours of practice the following day.

As a means of injecting further interest, the organisers had decided to give £100 to the fastest man during each 30-minute period. Stewart made sure of the first hand-out by going round in 1 minute 21.1 seconds. He was fastest again in the second session, reduced his time to 1: 20.6 in the process, and obviously felt that might be good enough for pole. That done, he then stepped into a four-wheel drive Matra, known as the MS84. Four-wheel drive was the catch-phrase of 1969; apart from Lotus and Tyrrell-Matra, McLaren had also investigated the system and produced their

Jochen Rindt – on the limit, as usual.

version, the M9A, in which Derek Bell was due to make his Grand Prix debut. There was also a four-wheel drive car built by Cosworth and entered for Brian Redman, but nothing was seen of the ugly machine at Silverstone, or any other Grand Prix.

So, while Stewart had been trying the MS84, Rindt had sorted out his gear ratios and he claimed the quickest time thus far in the third period. Stewart returned to his regular car to see if he could increase his take to £300. Just before he arrived at Woodcote on a flying lap, his team-mate, Jean-Pierre Beltoise went through and flicked a loose piece of concrete onto the racing line. Stewart hit it, punctured a tyre and that sent the bright blue car straight across the track and into the earth bank. The chassis of the MS80 was badly damaged but it had been strong enough to save Stewart from injury. He immediately hopped out and ran across to the pits to take over Beltoise's car. By this time Rindt had made sure of the fourth £100 – and pole position – with a 1 minute 20.8 seconds lap. Stewart could do little about it but the stage had been set for one of the most thrilling events in the history of the British Grand Prix.

A motor racing classic

Rindt made the best start, Stewart tucking in behind as they went to work for a scheduled 84 laps. On the first lap alone, they were more than three seconds quicker than the next man, Denny Hulme. Lap two and they had pulled out another second. The same on lap three, Stewart closing right up on Rindt. They were already destroying the lap record, both men driving absolutely on the limit from the word go.

Lap six and Stewart went round in 1 minute 22.5 seconds and snatched the lead in the process.

Then he did a 1:22.6 seconds follwed by a 22.3. Rindt responded with a 22.2. Then a 21.9. They were nose to tail again, sometimes alongside, their lap times always within a tenth of a second or so of each other. Hulme, still third, was 15 seconds behind and retreating into a very ordinary world compared to this furious activity at the front.

Stewart had been ten laps in charge when they came to overtake Beltoise, struggling along in the four-wheel drive car after giving his MS80 to Stewart for the race. There was a moment of confusion, Stewart diving to one side of the Frenchman, Rindt to the other – and the Lotus came out in front. On they went, Rindt trying to pull away, Stewart answering him with an identical lap time.

Into the thick of the backmarkers now, and still they remained tied together, neither driver letting up for a second. And so it continued until around the half-way mark when they came across a major war for fifth place between Hill, Amon, Courage (Brabham-Ford, entered by Frank Williams), Siffert (Walker, Lotus-Ford) and Rodriguez (Ferrari). Rindt made the best of it and pulled out two seconds on Stewart.

Stewart went round in 1:21.8s, his fastest so far, then did a 21.9 to nibble away at the gap. Then Rindt did a 21.9, a brief hold-up while dealing with slower cars, then a 21.9 from Stewart, followed by a 21.8 for Rindt, a 21.7 for Stewart, equalled on the next lap by Rindt who followed that with a 21.4 – Stewart going one better with a 21.3, the fastest lap of the race at an average of 129.61mph. On and on they went. They had been at it for an hour and 18 minutes. It hardly seemed possible, such was the intensity of a ferocious but exceptionally clean contest. It was utterly spellbinding.

Then Rindt rushed into the pits. The feeling of anticlimax was sudden and devastating. Spectators moved off the edge of their seats for the first time.

An end plate on the rear wing of the Lotus had come loose and was fouling the left-rear each time Rindt flung the car through the very fast right-handers. The plate was wrenched off and Rindt rejoined – 34 seconds behind his adversary but almost a minute ahead of Ickx who, in turn was 13 seconds in front of McLaren, Hill and Courage.

There was a slim chance for Rindt when Stewart's Matra began to falter slightly with a fuel feed problem, but in the end it was Rindt who would run into trouble when the pumps refused to draw the last few gallons from the tank. With six laps to go he shot into the pits for a top-up, but was so despondent when he rejoined in fourth place that he allowed Courage to slip by before waking up to the fact and taking fourth place back again on the last lap. Stewart, meanwhile, had lapped the entire field and he cruised in to take the flag. Just for good measure, Ickx ran out of fuel as he approached Woodcote but the Belgian coasted across the line, still secure in second place. One hour and 56 minutes of *racing* at an average of 127mph. It had been an absolute classic.

That victory gave Stewart 45 points. With five races to go, he had already scored seven more points than the next man, Jacky Ickx, would accumulate during the entire season. The scoring had been complicated by a rule which said the driver could only count his five best performances from the first six races and the best four from the second five. Whichever way you cared to look at it, Jackie Stewart was the best driver around as Grand Prix racing entered the seventies.

CHAPTER 14

SUCCESS, SORROW AND SAFETY

The bloody car's useless

At the beginning of the 1970 season, the novelty had not worn off. A sparkling new company manufacturing racing cars put Chris Amon on pole for the first race of the season in South Africa and brought victory for Jackie Stewart in Spain. March were looking good.

Then the truth began to dawn. At first, the criticisms were tactful. Ken Tyrrell simply said he thought the March 701 was heavy. By the time the British Grand Prix came round in July, opinion had hardened. After two days practising the Tyrrell-entered car at Brands Hatch, Stewart wrote in his diary:

> 'How are things going? Badly. The March is charging around Brands Hatch like a wild horse out of control, leaping from one side of the road to the other and knocking the hell out of me. There is nothing I can do about it. I'm just sitting there, a passenger, positive that we're out of the picture.'

Amon was rather more explicit. Climbing from his works car, after qualifying in 17th place, he sought out Robin Herd, designer of the March. 'The bloody car's useless,' fumed Amon. 'It's just a heap of shit!'

A tragic period

These were not happy times for Grand Prix racing in general and March Engineering in particular. Bruce McLaren had died the previous month while testing his latest CanAm sportscar at Goodwood. Then Piers Courage had lost his life when his de Tomaso (entered by Frank Williams) overturned and caught fire during the Dutch Grand Prix. Two major tragedies in the space of a few weeks had knocked the stuffing out of international motor racing. And now March, seen as the bright new future when they burst upon the scene in November 1969, were in deep trouble.

Formed by Max Mosley, Alan Rees, Graham Coaker and Robin Herd, March (an amalgram of their initials) had astounded everyone with their audacity. Not only were they building Formula 3, Formula 2 and CanAm cars, they would also enter a works team in Formula 1 – and make their cars available to whoever wished to buy them.

According to the eloquent Mosley, they had the financial backing. That was dependent on people actually signing on the dotted line, of course; the smiling Max knew that. But he also knew it was a seller's market. And the most important punter was the reigning world champion.

Stewart and Tyrrell had been placed in a dilemma at the end of 1969. Matra had been taken over by Simca and it had been made clear by the parent company, Chrysler, that if Tyrrell wished to continue with the French chassis-maker, then a Matra V12 would have to replace the Ford DFV. Stewart wanted to stay with the V8. But which car would they use?

Enter Max Mosley; smiling. For £6,000 they could have a March. In truth, Tyrrell had no choice. And the news that the reigning champions had thrown in their lot with March gave the operation the credibility it needed.

Certainly, it prompted Amon to sign as number one driver with the works team. Here was the perfect opportunity for the New Zealander to display his undoubted talent against that of Stewart. Besides, Chris was sick and tired of Ferrari and he had not been impressed when their latest engine, a flat-12, had given trouble during testing. In typical fashion, he moved at precisely the wrong time.

And he began to doubt the wisdom of his ways when March signed Jo Siffert as number two, and then farmed out a third car, to be run by Antique Automobiles, for Ronnie Peterson, a young Swede with a very exciting style. Each deal, of course, had its financial attractions as Mosley, still smiling, kept all the fiscal balls in the air.

Then came the final, brilliant touch. On the day that the Grand Prix car was unveiled – bang on schedule, of course – March announced that Mario Andretti, with backing from the STP Corporation, would race a 701 in the world championship. And the American was present at Silverstone on 6 February 1970 to add even more credibility to the birth of this stunning extravaganza.

By 18 July, the day of the British Grand Prix, the March Formula 1 operation had come under severe pressure as the season got into its stride. Amon's graphic description of the car went some way towards describing it.

Stewart was their top man, and he was on the outside of the third row, over a second slower than Jochen Rindt on pole position. This had been a mixed season for Rindt. He had won a stunning victory at Monaco after Jack Brabham had made a disastrous error at the very last corner. Prior to that, Chapman had unveiled the Lotus 72, a wedge-shaped car with side-radiators and torsion-bar suspension. At first Rindt kept his enthusiasm for the 72 under firm control, but once Chapman had sorted out one or two problems he won the Dutch Grand Prix with this car, although it was an empty victory for Jochen since the race claimed the life of his friend, Piers Courage.

Rindt moved to the top of the championship by winning the French Grand Prix. Going into the British round of the series, he was eight points ahead of Brabham and Stewart and, given Jackie's problems with the March, the Australian looked to be Rindt's most serious threat when he equalled Jochen's pole position time.

Ickx put his Ferrari on the outside of the front row, a feat which probably contributed to Amon's frustration with the March. The promise of the flat-12 car was underlined further by Clay Regazzoni, the Swiss setting sixth fastest time in only his second Grand Prix.

Rodriguez had scored a brilliant win at Spa-Francorchamps (the last time the road circuit would be used for a Grand Prix in that form), the Mexican's BRM (now in the colours of Yardley) holding together long enough to beat Amon to the line by 1.1 seconds, the pair of them having lapped at an average of 149.95mph. Pedro and his team-mate, Jackie Oliver, were joined at Brands Hatch by George Eaton, the wealthy Canadian paying for the dubious privilege of working for Louis Stanley.

Lotus, on the other hand, entered a third car (a 49) for Emerson Fittipaldi, a young Brazilian in whom Chapman could see the makings of a champion despite a relatively brief apprenticeship in Formula Ford and Formula 3.

'It was one of the greatest days of my life,' recalls Emerson. 'Just to be there, about to start a Grand Prix for the first time; it was the realisation of a life time's ambition. It was a dream come true for the little boy from Brazil. I remember thinking, "Now I can die a happy man."'

Fittipaldi was one of three Lotus drivers on the back row of the grid. Graham Hill, recovering from leg injuries received during the US Grand Prix at the end of the previous year, was driving a privately-entered 49 for Rob Walker while the American, Pete Lovely, was the slowest of all in his elderly 49.

Just ahead of the Lotus phalanx, John Surtees was giving his first Formula 1 car its maiden outing, the Englishman having kept his hand in by driving a McLaren while the new car was completed. As for the works McLarens, they had been trying to pick up the pieces after the shock of Bruce's death, Denny Hulme leading the way despite suffering from painful burns to his hands.

A fuel breather cap had popped open on his car at Indianapolis, the methanol catching fire, the heat shrinking the leather of his driving gloves and welding the visor to his helmet before he could bring the McLaren to a halt. He could barely hold the steering wheel of the Grand Prix car, but he was back when the team needed him most. Dan Gurney, about to finish a career which should have reaped far more than a mere four victories, was driving the second McLaren in what would turn out to be his last Grand Prix.

Not real good, is it?

The 1970 British Grand Prix would be one of the most dramatic in recent years; not a theatrical contest similar to the Rindt/Stewart epic of 1969, but a race full of interest – and surprises.

At first, everything seemed in order. Brabham led through Paddock with Ickx lining up to have a go at the turquoise car on the run up the hill to Druids. Brabham, naturally, closed the door, but Ickx kept coming. Brabham closed the door tighter still – and Ickx kept coming. With two wheels on the grass, the Belgian forced his way through on the inside and took the lead on the downhill run towards Bottom Bend. Thereafter, the Ferrari pulled away. In fact, Ickx seemed in such total command that he looked like scoring a runaway win.

Brabham, meanwhile, had his hands full as Rindt began to size up ways of overtaking his former boss. At the beginning of lap seven, Rindt made his move, the Lotus diving inside the Brabham under braking for Paddock. As they slithered side-by-side through the corner, they were suddenly confronted by Ickx's Ferrari. The differential on the red car had begun to break up, Ickx retiring at the end of the lap. Rindt was now in the lead.

The positions remained unchanged for the next 61 laps, Rindt and Brabham consistently lapping half-a-second quicker than Oliver who, in turn, was comfortably ahead of a tense battle between Hulme, Stewart and Regazzoni. It was a repeat of the psychological struggle between Clark and Hill in 1964, Rindt's every move being matched by Brabham. But whereas

'Don't ask me...' Jochen Rindt; surprised to be wearing the victory garland.

Jochen Rindt
When the mood took him – which was often – a stunning performer thanks to extraordinary reflexes. A favourite with the crowd, particularly after his battle with Stewart in 1969. Scored a lucky win in the British Grand Prix in 1970, but suffered fatal injuries a few months later at Monza. Became the first posthumous world champion.

Hill did not have enough in reserve to overtake the Lotus, Brabham was playing a waiting game. On lap 69, he decided he had waited long enough and powered ahead of the Lotus at the exit from South Bank Bend.

Brabham immediately set the fastest lap of the race. Rindt had no answer. The gap increased by around a second a lap. There were 11 laps to go. Game, set and match to Brabham. Or, at least, that seemed to be the way of it as Jack disappeared into the country for the last time, Jochen trailing along 14 seconds in arrears.

The crowd at Clearways prepared to welcome the winner. But it was the red, white and gold car which appeared first, an astonished Rindt heading for his second win of the season at Brabham's expense. Seconds later, the Brabham rolled into view with a dead engine, Jack having just enough momentum to take him to the line and claim second place. Fortunately, he was well clear of Hulme, who had inherited third after Oliver's BRM had blown up.

'I'd sooner forget that race altogether,' says Jack. 'To have a lead of 14 seconds only to lose it in the last couple of hundred yards is not real good, is it? I knew what was wrong all along.

'When the car had been started up early in the morning, it had been a bit cold and the boys put the engine onto full rich. The trouble was, nobody thought to put it back! So it ran like that throughout the race. After the start, I knew there was a problem because the car was not running cleanly out of the corners and I guessed that's what it was. Sure enough, the engine used four gallons more than it should have; there was nothing I could do.'

But this race wasn't over yet. An hour or so after the finish, Rindt's Lotus was declared illegal. Jack had won after all! Hulme, Regazzoni, Amon, Hill and François Cevert (the Tyrrell number two) would all move up one place on the points table as a result.

Chapman and his new team manager, Peter Warr, were not about to take this sort of thing lying down. The scrutineers had contended that the stays supporting the rear wing were bent and, had they been straight, the wing would have been above the legal height. Chapman proved them wrong. Rindt was reinstated after much dithering by the scrutineers, who did little for their cause by conducting their measurements on a piece of ground that was far from level.

All told, it was an unfortunate end to an excellent day's racing and doubtless Jack Brabham had a quiet word with his mechanic – a certain Ron Dennis who, ironically, would go on to set new standards in race preparation in his role as managing director of McLaren International in the 1980s.

No time to lose

After his initial doubts about the Lotus 72, Rindt's confidence soared. 'A monkey could win in this car,' he said; a statement which perhaps belittled his part in the proceedings as he went on to win at Hockenheim, the German Grand Prix having being removed from the Nürburgring after much debate over safety. A victory in his home Grand Prix – held at the Österreichring for the first time – would have assured Rindt of the championship, but his retirement postponed the seemingly inevitable until the Italian Grand Prix at Monza.

It was a weekend of extreme emotion. On the final afternoon of practice, the Austrian's Lotus suddenly went out of control under braking for the Parabolica. The car smashed into the steel barrier, the impact tearing off the front suspension and bulkhead. Rindt died afterwards of injuries inflicted by the seat-belt buckle; he had paid a dreadful price for not wearing the crotch straps which would have prevented him from being pulled further into the cockpit.

The race itself provided a heady victory for Regazzoni and Ferrari, a result which, fittingly, contributed towards Jochen Rindt becoming the first posthumous world champion.

The last time Rindt had taken the chequered flag had been two weeks before at Oulton Park, where he won a heat of the Gold Cup non-championship meeting. And the last thing British enthusiasts had seen of their dashing hero was his swift departure as he pulled up at the exit of Old Hall, climbed from the Lotus, vaulted a fence and ran across the field to a waiting plane.

This was in the days when non-championship races gave teams an opportunity to experiment with developments they might not otherwise have tried during a Grand Prix meeting. The 1970 Gold Cup, however, was deeply significant for two reasons. It marked a victory for John Surtees in a car of his own creation. And it saw the debut of the first Tyrrell Grand Prix car. In a world which thrives on rumour and gossip, this was one of the best kept secrets of all.

It had not taken Tyrrell long to work out that he would need to build his own car if he wanted to avoid a repeat of the situation he found himself in with the March 701. The Tyrrell had been designed by Derek Gardner at his home in Warwickshire, the car itself constructed behind locked doors at Tyrrell's workshop in Surrey. The motor racing world was stunned when the royal blue machine was unveiled on 17 August 1970; stunned because they knew nothing about it and stunned because the car, with its distinctive Coke-bottle shape, looked the part.

Stewart went on to prove it by setting fastest lap at Oulton Park and leading the Canadian and US Grands Prix. The Tyrrell era had arrived. Throughout 1971, the combination was usually irresistible. And nowhere more so than the British Grand Prix of that year.

Although Stewart set the joint fastest time during practice at Silverstone, pole position went to Clay Regazzoni. The Ferrari driver had recorded his best lap on the Friday morning while Stewart, only a tenth slower in that session, had to wait until the final hour in the afternoon to equal the Swiss. Not that it made much difference to how things would turn out in the race.

Regazzoni shot into the lead, followed closely by Ickx in the second Ferrari. It took Stewart just three laps to work his way to the front, and from then on he simply controlled the race as he pleased. The Tyrrell, with its Goodyear tyres, was better suited to Silverstone than the Firestone-shod Ferraris and the BRM of Siffert, who briefly held second place. Stewart was able to lap one second faster than anyone else. After 20 laps, he was 13 seconds ahead of Regazzoni. At 40 laps, the gap was 21 seconds. By lap 60 Regazzoni was out with low oil pressure and Peterson had moved the March, with its distinctive tea-tray nose wing, into second place, some 33 seconds behind Stewart. Eight laps later, and it was all over; Stewart first, Peterson second, Fittipaldi third for Lotus. The rest had been lapped. The race had lasted for a mere 91 minutes, Stewart averaging 130.48 mph.

Fortunately for the spectators, there had been other attractions. A parade of historic cars and a display by the Red Arrows had preceded the race. There was also evidence of the commercial attraction of Grand Prix racing.

Money, money, money

Hospitality areas had begun to spring up towards the rear of the paddock as Yardley, John Player, Brooke Bond Oxo and other sponsors began to scratch the surface of their association with Formula 1. And the race itself had acquired the title Woolmark British Grand Prix in deference to the International Wool Secretariat using Grand Prix racing as a means of promoting the 'Woolmark' image. And on another front, the Formula 1 Constructors' Association (F1CA) had begun to exert its collective influence when it came to discussing matters financial.

As for Silverstone itself, work continued apace. Five years previously, in July 1966, Silverstone Circuits Limited, a wholly owned subsidiary of the BRDC, had been formed to handle the commercial administration of the circuit. A Silverstone Trust had been established in 1968 in order to provide the money necessary for the acquisition of the freeholds. Everything seemed to be following an orderly pattern.

Then, later that year, the ground seemed to be cut from under the BRDC when Silverstone was listed for consideration as a possible site for London's third airport. After several worrying months, that threat passed and work resumed on establishing the circuit as a motor racing facility of the highest order.

Forty-two acres of freehold land were purchased in October 1969; a further 398 acres were bought from the Ministry of Defence in 1970 and, at the end of 1971, the final purchase of 240 acres completed the estate. Thus, the BRDC not only ran the racing, but owned the circuit as well. The RAC, as the sanctioning body of motor sport in Great Britain, continued to have its say in the organisation of the Grand Prix – sometimes with detrimental effects, as the start of the 1971 Grand Prix had proved all too clearly.

The 24 cars had rolled onto the grid, engines revved urgently, particularly the flat-12 of Regazzoni's pole position Ferrari as the Swiss began to creep forward. 'Regga' had been menacing enough to cause Dean Delamont of the RAC, the official starter for this race, to hesi-

Jackie Stewart and the Tyrrell-Ford turned the 1971 British Grand Prix into the greatest bore of all time.

tate with the Union Jack.

Regazzoni dabbed the brakes and stopped; others, watching the Ferrari rather than the flag, had begun to move forward, while at the back, Jack Oliver's McLaren was actually under way. Then he stopped – and was hit from behind, the impact knocking Oliver into the back of Graham Hill's works Brabham.

Both cars were out before the race had even started, and to make matters worse, Hill's car was more or less immobile right on the apex of Woodcote. Marshals dragged it into the pit lane just before Regazzoni led the thundering pack though at the end of the first lap. As the marshals wondered what to do next, Dave Charlton, driving an ex-works Lotus 72, swept into the pit lane and almost collided with the Brabham. As things turned out, the start had provided the most dramatic moments of the 1971 Grand Prix.

Muted celebration

Victory at Silverstone, followed by another win at the Nürburgring, more or less assured Stewart of his second championship. When the season ended with a win for Cevert's Tyrrell at Watkins Glen, it was the perfect excuse for the astute John Webb to lay on a non-championship 'Victory Race' at Brands Hatch in place of the cancelled Mexican Grand Prix in October.

There was an excellent entry and the relaxed, end of term feeling was rounded off by a perfect autumnal day. Siffert, winner of the Austrian Grand Prix two months earlier, had put his BRM on pole position but the Swiss made an appalling start. On lap 15, he crashed on the approach to Hawthorn Bend and the BRM caught fire. Siffert was dead by the time rescuers had reached him.

It was a terrible end to the year, one which had started on a sad note when Ignazio Giunti, a promising Italian who had driven briefly for Ferrari in Formula 1, had lost his life during a sports car race in Argentina. Then, just before the British Grand Prix, the immensely popular Pedro Rodriguez had been killed in another sportscar race in West Germany. Each time, the cars had caught fire.

Clearly, much work remained to be done in the field of safety although matters were not helped by over-reaction in certain quarters. In the emotional aftermath of the Siffert tragedy, Brands Hatch was immediately condemned as being far too dangerous. Indeed, fault could be found with most circuits. The difficulty lay in the fact that it was impossible to implement safety checks in the manner that is almost taken for granted today. There was no structure within the governing body to handle the problem and the growing frustration of the drivers began to lead to hasty actions which invoked resentment elsewhere. Matters would spill into print in the summer of 1972.

The Grand Prix Drivers' Association, led by Jackie Stewart, spearheaded the campaign. Stewart was not afraid to voice his opinion on the state of safety facilities at certain circuits, and top of his list was Spa-Francorchamps.

Communications between the drivers, organisers, the governing body and the press were poor and, sometimes non-existent. Confusion and misunderstanding reigned on all sides. Stewart's basic motives could not be faulted and his frustration had been heightened by the death of so many colleagues in recent years. But it was difficult at times not to feel that the safety campaigners were over-reacting even if that was not necessarily the case. All in all, international motor sport was swiftly polarising into 'traditionalist' and 'milk and water' camps at a time when everyone should have been pulling together. The subject of safety dominated the correspondence columns for months. Then John Player and Sons stepped in and threw fat of a different kind onto the fire.

Jackie Stewart
Remains a household name despite retiring at his peak in 1973, having won 27 Grands Prix and the world championship in 1969, 1971 and 1973. A gifted artist and a shrewd Scotsman who achieved his greatest success with Tyrrell. Victory in the 1969 British Grand Prix a classic of its kind.

When is a Lotus not a Lotus?

At the beginning of 1972, Colin Chapman removed the 'Gold Leaf Team Lotus' symbols and resprayed his cars in black. The 72s, with their gold pin-striping and lettering, looked sensational and, generally, they were well received.

Not so the news that the cars were to be called 'John Player Specials'. The word 'Lotus' was not to be mentioned. Worse still, Player announced that they would be sponsoring the British Grand Prix at Brands Hatch, and that the race would henceforth be known as the John Player Grand Prix.

Britain bristled with indignation. The correspondence columns went berserk. For every letter supporting the need for sponsorship, there were several vehemently against Player's heavy-handed approach. How dare Brands Hatch sell their souls? And all of this was played against a backdrop of safety fears over the circuit itself. The summer of 1972 was generally a restless time.

More outspoken than most on the subject of Brands Hatch, Jean-Pierre Beltoise expressed his views in an interview in *Competition Car*:

> *'They have spent nearly £40,000 on improving the circuit, but I must say that it is not well done. I can show you places where, if you have trouble, you can hit the guard rail at a bad angle. [There are] some places where you can hit the beginning of the guardrail. So I think it is still very bad for safety. Very bad! They have done a lot of work, but very bad work.'*

The interview was published in April 1972. Many readers may have dismissed his remarks as those of a biased, no-hope Frenchman, but attitudes changed the following month when Beltoise scored a win of consummate skill in the rain at Monaco. No one could come close to the BRM (now sponsored by Marlboro, McLaren having taken over the Yardley deal). It was an inspired drive but one which Beltoise would never repeat. He had not put a wheel out of place on a day when most people had made mistakes.

Among them was Jackie Stewart, suffering from the beginnings of an ulcer which would keep him out of the Belgian Grand Prix (run at a bland and uninspiring circuit at Nivelles), but he was back for the French Grand Prix at Clermont Ferrand, where he scored a victory at the expense of Chris Amon and Denny Hulme, both of whom had picked up punctures. Indeed, Amon's climb from eighth to an eventual third place with the Matra was one of the greatest drives of the season. Typically, though, it brought the New Zealander no closer to that illusive Grand Prix victory he so obviously deserved. Maybe he would overcome the jinx at Brands Hatch, his 73rd Grand Prix.

Emerson's title

The British round marked the half-way stage in the championship and Fittipaldi, with two wins to his credit, led Stewart (two wins) by 13 points. Hulme (one win) was third, two points behind Stewart. These three were the favourites but most people overlooked Jacky Ickx.

There was no question that the flat-12 Ferrari was one of the most powerful engines around, with a quoted 490bhp at 12,800rpm. The handling of the 312B2 left a lot to be desired however and the Belgian had only managed to score a couple of second places. At Brands Hatch, though, he put the red car on pole – a full four-tenths of a second quicker than Fittipaldi – and looked like being Ferrari's standard bearer.

Regazzoni had been injured; Andretti (racing for a full season with Ferrari) had a commitment in the United States; all of which left the way clear for Arturo Merzario to make his Grand Prix debut, the little Italian barely able to see over the wheel of the Ferrari. He qualified on the fourth row alongside Carlos Reutemann, the enigmatic Argentinian having joined Wilson Fittipaldi (Emerson's elder brother) and Graham Hill at Brabham, a team now under the ownership of B.C. Ecclestone.

Reutemann had missed much of the season thus far thanks to an ankle injury sustained in a Formula 2 race at Thruxton. Indeed, Bernie Ecclestone's team had only netted a single point, and a decent result at Brands Hatch seemed unlikely. At the end of the first lap, Reutemann was 11th and Fittipaldi 20th, with Hill sadly trailing along near the back.

At the front, Ickx was in charge and looked like staying there, just as he had done during the opening laps two years before. Fittipaldi gave chase but Stewart, meanwhile, had become stuck behind Beltoise, the Frenchman casting aside his dislike for Brands Hatch as he kept the Tyrrell at bay for six laps. Once he had found a way past, however, Stewart quickly caught the leading pair.

Jackie was at the wheel of Tyrrell 003, the car which he had used to such good effect during most of 1971. A new model had been produced but Stewart had damaged it when he slid off the track at Druids during practice. The spectators there would also receive good value for money during the race.

Brands Hatch had been blessed with three days of glorious sunshine but the downside was a rapidly disintegrating track surface, and nowhere more than at Druids. On lap 25, Ickx braked late and slid wide, Fittipaldi doing likewise. Both drivers recovered, but not before

Stewart had taken second place from the Lotus.

Then, 11 laps later, there was further activity at Druids as the leaders caught Wilson Fittipaldi and the privately-entered March of Mike Beuttler. Ickx threaded his way through but Wilson managed to ease Stewart to one side, a move which, perchance, allowed Fittipaldi junior to regain second place! It was a key moment in the race since Emerson and Jackie were soon aware that they were about to be fighting for the lead, a trail of smoke announcing the imminent departure of Ickx with low oil pressure.

Stewart now went to work on the pretender to his title, the Tyrrell closing to within a second of the Lotus. On laps 58 and 60, Stewart went round in 1 minute 24.0 seconds, the fastest laps of the race but a few tenths off the record thanks to the treacherous conditions. Indeed, there were cars littered around the circuit, the carnage having begun as early as lap three.

Andrea de Adamich had crashed his Surtees while trying to avoid the second works Lotus of Dave Walker as the Australian slowed suddenly with a loss of fuel pressure. Then Henri Pescarolo had done poor Frank Williams's limited budget no good at all by crashing heavily in the Politoys, a car built by the British team. The fact that something had broken on the car to cause the accident merely made matters worse for poor Frank.

Nanni Galli had spun off in the works Tecno; Hill had collided with the barrier at the exit of Paddock, François Cevert doing likewise with the second Tyrrell not long afterwards and, with two laps to go, Ronnie Peterson crashed into the pair of abandoned cars at the bottom of the hill when the Ford DFV on his works March suddenly cut out due to fuel starvation. Peterson had been fourth at the time, but lapped by the leaders. And in the closing stages Fittipaldi gradually eased away to put the result beyond doubt.

'A great race for me because Jackie had the pressure on all the time,' recalls Emerson. 'When you got the Lotus 72 working well at a place like Brands Hatch, it was just the most fantastic car to drive. It was one of my favourite tracks anyway – but I nearly spun off that time at Druids. I was really pleased with that win; very satisfying. And, of course that was the year of my first world championship because I went on to win in Austria and Italy. 1972 – very happy memories for me.'

At Brands Hatch, they loaded his car onto a trailer for a lap of honour. Half-way round, Emerson and Chapman discovered that the Lotus had a slow puncture – but that was immaterial by now. All that mattered to the team were the nine points and the fact they had won their sponsor's Grand Prix.

The reports the following week, however, were united in their condemnation of both the dictatorial methods employed by John Player and conditions under which the teams were working at Brands Hatch. At the end of the year, Michael Kettlewell summed up their feelings when he wrote in *Autocourse*:

> 'The people who suffered most were probably the mechanics and team personnel. The paddock area, a quarter of a mile from the pits, is on a slope and the only shelter from the elements – and thousands of spectators – is under canvas and behind barriers brought by the teams themselves. The pit road is narrow and not up to the job...
>
> On the credit side, however, Brands Hatch had more than complied with the revised safety arrangements. New guard rails and railway sleeper banking had been erected, marshals' posts resited. There were 23 extra fire points, giving a total of 65. In addition to the usual ambulances, there were six specially equipped Land-Rovers with a full range of fire-fighting equipment. All the marshals had taken part in fire-fighting training and John Player provided £1,000 worth of special helmets and visors for the 150 fire marshals.
>
> As John Player had provided £20,000 of the £110,000 budget, the Grand Prix was named after them. Most of the press either ignored Players completely or called the race the John Player British Grand Prix. The FIA's gracious bestowal of the title, Grand Prix of Europe, was wasted. Even the significance of the RAC's 75th anniversary wasn't appreciated.'

If the identity of the Grand Prix was confused and, in the succeeding years, the details of the race quietly forgotten, then the same could not be said about the 1973 British Grand Prix. It was to be another Silverstone classic – from the first lap to the last.

CHAPTER 15

WOODCOTE

Ronnie and the 72

When Ronnie Peterson joined Lotus at the beginning of 1973, it seemed the perfect place for the Swede. He had just spent three indifferent years with March, yet it had been obvious that here was a driver in the mould of Rindt; fearless and blindingly fast. The thought of Ronnie in the Lotus 72 was something to savour. And it would be interesting to see how he would compare with Emerson Fittipaldi, the reigning champion.

The season started badly for Peterson. He retired in Argentina and Brazil, and Emerson won both races. Fittipaldi finished third in South Africa and Belgium, won at Barcelona and took second place at Monaco – where Peterson claimed his first points for Lotus by finishing third. That was better than nothing and Ronnie had his home Grand Prix to look forward to. He started from pole and led every lap – until two from the end. Then he ran out of fuel and Denny Hulme won for McLaren. Poor Ronnie. He seemed doomed to failure.

On to France now and Peterson was content to hold third place while Emerson fought it out with a McLaren driven by Jody Scheckter, a bullish young South African making his Grand Prix debut in Europe. Scheckter and Fittipaldi collided with 13 laps to go – and Ronnie Peterson won his first Grand Prix. When the Swede put his Lotus on pole for the British Grand Prix, it seemed he had acquired the taste. Nothing would stop him now.

Jackie Stewart had other ideas. The Scot had, as ever, been a dominant force, collecting wins in South Africa, Belgium and Monaco to lead the championship by one point from Fittipaldi. Emerson joined Stewart on the second row at Silverstone, the Lotus and the Tyrrell being two-tenths slower than the McLarens of Hulme and Revson.

A pace car led the 28 starters for one slow lap, the field then pausing on the grid at the exit of Woodcote. No dithering this year by the man with the Union Jack. It was a clean start and Stewart slotted in behind Peterson as they rounded Copse. On through Maggotts, swinging left towards the long right-hander at Becketts. And Stewart did not appear to brake. With one sweeping move, the Tyrrell rushed alongside the Lotus and powered through the corner with such apparent ease that Peterson, caught completely unawares, was seen to shake his head in disbelief.

Hammering home the psychological advantage, Stewart drove the rest of the opening lap on the very limit. The blue car shot into sight under the *Daily Express* bridge, Stewart sweeping through Woodcote in one long, glorious drift, the Tyrrell bucking uneasily on the occasional ripple in the track surface. It was one of the most thrilling of the many superb sights that corner has produced; a classic demonstration of how to make a racing car work for you to its maximum without overstepping the mark.

It was a lesson which Jody Scheckter would have done well to note. Woodcote had been causing the men in blazers and armbands palpitations for some time now. Jody was about to write the corner into history – along with several Grand Prix cars.

Away she goes

Denny Hulme:

'Jody had driven for us for the first time at Watkins Glen at the end of the previous year. He was quick, no question about that. He was a keen young lad and, well, you needed to keep an eye on him. He was on the third row at Silverstone and, before the race, I'd had a chat with him. I just said "take it easy in the opening laps;" something like that.

'So there we are on the first lap and he comes whistling past me! So I'm right behind him and he goes charging into Woodcote and you can see it all start to happen. He runs wide, gets a wheel on the dirt at the exit and, ever so slowly, away she goes – into a big slide. Then the car shoots straight across the track towards the pit wall.

'From where I was sitting, I could see I was going to be okay because I was able to drive *behind* the accident. He went across me, from left to right, and I just shot round the back of him. Missed it all. Then I looked in my mirror and saw that all hell had broken loose.'

Scheckter had managed to reach the pit wall without being touched. The impact sent him

rolling backwards as the remaining 20 or so cars swept through Woodcote. One or two made it through but, for each succeeding driver, the warning was reduced in relation to their view of the road ahead. Then, all at once, the track was a swirling mass of wreckage. Wings, wheels, bodywork and dust flew above the pin-balling cars.

Jody Scheckter: 'I remember there had been a selection of tyres; hard and soft. We chose hard on the left because the soft ones could not live with the fast corners. But we made our decision very late and the tyres were brand new and I tried to warm them up by sliding around a little more than normal on the first lap. I reached Woodcote – and they weren't warm enough.

'I was sliding and then it just snapped round on me. I was heading towards the pit wall, but still sliding. I had full opposite lock on and I thought everything would be alright because I hadn't actually hit the wall. I thought I would be able to come off the brakes and, with the lock still on, the car would whizz round and I'd just carry on. As I tried that, the car hit the wall...

'When I looked to my right, there were cars hitting each other before they hit me. I put my head down, felt a lot of banging. Then it went quiet for a bit and I thought "time to get out of here." I looked up, only to see another load of cars heading towards me so I put my head down again.

'I jumped out and ran across to the pit wall. Phil Kerr (the McLaren team manager) said. "I'd better hide you." So he took me away and told me not to speak to anyone. I mean, John Surtees had just seen his team wiped out before his very eyes and he was soon round at our pit demanding Scheckter's head...'

Meanwhile, rescuers were attempting to cut Andrea de Adamich from his wrecked Brabham. It was the moment which ended his Grand Prix career, as Andrea recalls only too well:

'The first lap and, of course, you are busy watching the car ahead and those on your right and left and keeping an eye on your mirror. You don't see what's going on further down the track. Because the accident was so sudden, there were no warning flags and suddenly I realise something had happened. By then, it's too late. Everyone was braking, smoke everywhere, you don't know what's going on. Just try and get away from it.

'I remember very well that I saw a gap on the left-hand side and I released the brakes and aimed for it. At that very moment, Beltoise's BRM came from nowhere – but at 90 degrees to me. We collided and the BRM turned my car round and aimed me towards the outside of the track. I remember trying to lift my foot from the throttle but couldn't. The front of my car was now badly damaged and I went straight into the guardrail. Unfortunately, this rail was mounted on the wooden sleepers so there was no flexibility.

'I felt no pain at this stage. My adrenalin was very high! I switched off the engine, undid the belts, lifted myself just one centimetre, found I could go no further and sank back down into the car. And then the pain arrived. And it was a very bad pain.....'

It took 53 minutes to cut the Italian from his car, the rescuers moving carefully, surrounded as they were by 200 litres and more of fuel.

'I was conscious throughout,' says de Adamich. 'The other drivers didn't help because, naturally, when you see there are marshals there, it's best not to get in the way. In fact, I remember the only driver I did see was Stirling Moss – and he was trying to interview me...'

De Adamich suffered a badly broken right ankle and minor fractures to his left ankle. Nine cars were involved, many of them written off. He was the only driver to suffer injury. And none of the cars, now featuring crushable structures around the side of the chassis, had caught fire. Safety had come a long way in a short space of time.

There might have been more cars involved had Stewart, flat out through Woodcote at the end of his second lap, not jumped on the brakes, raised his hand and pulled up just before reaching the wreckage strewn across the track. Indeed, the one short-coming in the safety arrangements had just been demonstrated. By following the rules and showing the red flag only at the start and finish line, the officials had almost added to the chaos. After that, it would soon become the practice for crossed flags to be shown at each marshals' post as a warning of an impending stoppage.

The chaos begins as wheels and bodywork fly in the air.

Peter Revson; winner at the end of a dramatic day.

During the lull while de Adamich was cut free, Stewart walked casually past Peterson. 'Well, you know about Becketts now, Ronnie. I'll have to try somewhere else this time....' Peterson smiled weakly.

In fact, Peterson had the last laugh. An attempt by Stewart to take the lead at Stowe after the restart ended in disaster as the Tyrrell's gearbox, having given trouble during practice, chose that moment to play up. The transmission locked briefly and sent Stewart slewing onto the infield, where he narrowly missed a photographer, before ploughing into the cornfield. The resulting damage meant a long delay in the pits.

The race now developed into a four-way battle between Peterson, Hulme, Revson – and James Hunt, in a March entered and developed by Lord Hesketh's happy band of enthusiasts and poseurs. For all their levity and garden-party attitudes, the racing itself was a serious business and Hunt gave them their money's worth in a car which should have been no match for the best McLaren and Lotus could provide.

The outcome was settled when, about 20 laps from the end, a light shower coated the circuit and made the handling of the Lotus more perilous than before. Peterson backed off slightly, Revson saw his chance and snatched the lead. Hunt made one or two serious attempts to take second place from Peterson, and in so doing allowed Hulme to sweep past and take third.

For the remaining ten laps, the Lotus, McLaren and March were tied together, Hunt setting the fastest time four laps from the end. As they rushed into Woodcote for the last time, Peterson began to slide towards the grass, Hulme took a tighter line – and Hunt thought about coming between them both! In the end, the three were covered by 0.2 seconds with Revson, scoring his first Grand Prix win, less than three seconds in front. It was a thrilling end to a memorable race, one which could have had a tragic outcome. It was one of motor racing's better days in 1973.

Stewart's 27th and final victory was, appropriately, at the Nürburgring. It gave him the championship and a record number of wins. It also gave a fair indication that François Cevert was on the brink of stardom, the Frenchman following dutifully in Jackie's wheeltracks. The plan was for Jackie to announce his retirement at Watkins Glen, scene of the final race and, appropriately, Stewart's 100th Grand Prix. Cevert would lead the team in 1974.

During practice on Saturday morning at Watkins Glen, Cevert improved on Stewart's time from the previous day. Towards the end of the session, he went out once more and crashed at the very quick Esses. He was killed instantly by the violence of the impact with the guardrail. Ken Tyrrell withdrew his team and Stewart's illustrious career was over. For many, the 1973 season ended right there as well.

All change at Maranello

Who would fill the vacuum left by a driver of Stewart's calibre? Ronnie Peterson was the popular choice for 1974; others talked of Emerson Fittipaldi, due to leave Lotus and join McLaren.

Some said Jacky Ickx's move from Ferrari to Lotus would see the talented Belgian finally emerge as the man to beat. Then there was Carlos Reutemann, now number one at Brabham in a neat car designed by Gordon Murray. Few people, however, mentioned Ferrari, for whom 1973 had been a complete disaster. The 'Old-Man' now in his mid-seventies, had been ill. Without his firm grip on the tiller, the Grand Prix effort had wandered aimlessly from race to race. And one or two they didn't attend at all.

Then, in the autumn of '73, Enzo returned to his desk. He brought along a new broom with which he proceeded to sweep the factory clean. Personnel were moved around and, to oversee the Formula 1 effort and report directly to him, Enzo Ferrari brought in Luca Montezemolo, a law student who possessed an intelligence and sense of authority beyond his 25 years. Clay Regazzoni had returned to the fold after a dismal season with BRM and, when asked who he thought might be a suitable team-mate, Clay mentioned Niki Lauda, his partner there.

This fitted in with Enzo Ferrari's thinking in any case, the *commendatore* having been impressed by the way the young Austrian had kept his BRM ahead of Ickx's Ferrari at Monaco that year. Finally, Mauro Forghieri, a Ferrari stalwart, was put in overall charge of the design department and a heavily revised car, the 312-B3, was immediately on the pace. In 1973, Ferrari had missed the Dutch Grand Prix. In 1974, they dominated it. That made it two wins for Lauda but the outcome of the season was by no means clear.

Lotus had started off boldly with a radical car, but suffice to say that Peterson had resorted to the 72 to win at Monaco. At the beginning of the season, Hulme and Fittipaldi won a race apiece (Argentina and Brazil respectively) for McLaren but Reutemann had shown stunning form and winning in South Africa seemed to be the least he and Brabham deserved. Then, a new twist, as Tyrrell, nursing along two new boys, Scheckter and Patrick Depailler, found form and won in Sweden. In France, two weeks before the British Grand Prix, Peterson upset predictions once more by exhibiting his extrovert style to score a brilliant victory at Dijon.

And yet, throughout, Ferrari were increasingly seen as the team to beat, although their operation was not gelling. Sometimes it was their fault; sometimes not. The John Player Grand Prix at Brands Hatch would be a case in point.

There were 34 entries for the British Grand Prix, a situation which highlighted a long-running dispute between the teams and the race organisers. The Formula 1 Constructors' Association (F1CA) had been flexing their muscles the previous year by asking for more money. The organisers, in turn, had banded together to form Grand Prix International (GPI). Naturally, they resisted the suggestion that they should pay more to the teams at a time when safety improvements had raised their costs considerably.

GPI crumbled when, one by one, the organisers did separate deals with F1CA. Having won that battle, the teams could see the strength in their unity at a time when Grand Prix racing was becoming more popular than ever. But with so many teams wishing to participate, there simply was not enough room for them all and, due to vested interests, a solution which satisfied everyone could not be found.

Only 26 cars were permitted on the track at one time at Brands Hatch. It was suggested that a preliminary hour of practice should be laid on to weed out the slowest of the entrants who had not yet scored championship points. That proposal was rejected and, in the end, everyone was allowed to practice on the understanding that no more than 26 cars would be permitted onto the track. It was an easy rule to police since in the natural course of events the figure rarely looked like being exceeded.

As ever, the usual teams were in their usual places on the grid; on pole, the Ferrari of Niki Lauda; alongside, the Lotus of Ronnie Peterson with Scheckter and Reutemann on row two. None of them, however, had won the 100 bottles of champagne presented by the *Evening News* for the fastest lap during practice on the Thursday morning.

That case of bubbly had gone to Tom Pryce, a shy Welshman who seemed destined for greater things with the American-financed UOP Shadow team. Pryce eventually claimed a place on the third row, alongside James Hunt, Lord Alexander Hesketh's team having advanced their plans with their own car, designed by Dr Harvey Postlethwaite. Two British drivers on the third row probably helped swell the race-day crowd to 68,000 but, as far as Jackie Stewart was concerned, the British Grand Prix would be between an Austrian and a South African.

Having retired from the cockpit, Stewart was earning more than most drivers on the grid thanks to throwing himself into a hectic schedule of public relations work, and part of his operation included pre-race briefings on behalf of Elf Oil, sponsors of the Tyrrell team. The reign-

The end... and the beginning. Jody Scheckter takes the chequered flag for Tyrrell but trouble is brewing in the pit lane. The Ford Cortina course car and a steaming mob of humanity are preventing Niki Lauda from rejoining after a last-minute pit stop. Compare this with Aintree in 1955 (page 91).

ing world champion reckoned that Peterson would not be able to maintain the pace shown during practice. But Lauda would. And Scheckter would chase him all the way. It was to turn out a remarkably accurate prediction.

A new starting procedure was introduced whereby the drivers would start their engines on the dummy grid and, instead of rolling forward onto the grid proper, they would complete one lap, holding positions but being free to warm up their tyres and brakes. It was a system which worked well and one which remains in force, with one or two additional refinements, today.

Stewart must have nodded with quiet approval when Lauda completed the first lap with a two-second lead over Scheckter. Peterson was already down in fourth place, behind the Ferrari of Regazzoni, Clay having made one of his demon starts from the fourth row.

While Regazzoni kept the Lotus at bay, Lauda and Scheckter pulled away, the Ferrari appearing to have the measure of the Tyrrell. Short of unexpected trouble, the race looked like belonging to the Austrian.

The first hint of the problems which would ultimately dictate the outcome of this race appeared at the end of lap 19. John Watson, driving a works-assisted but but privately entered Brabham, pulled into the pits with a puncture. Small, flinty stones had been flicked onto the track at various places and, within a few laps, Beltoise (BRM), Pescarolo (BRM), Regazzoni, Peterson and Hill (Hill-Lola) had all stopped with similar problems. But Lauda, a steady eight seconds ahead of Scheckter, seemed untroubled.

He remained that way until about 20 laps from the end. Then Lauda began to feel the Ferrari squirm a little as he went through the left-handers. Stewart, commentating for BBC Television, spotted the trouble almost immediately. He could see the profile of Lauda's right-rear tyre begin to dip; Niki had a slow puncture.

Stewart described Lauda's predicament. Should he stop and lose the lead while changing tyres? Or should he risk making it to the finish? Lauda chose the latter.

There weren't that many left-hand corners at Brands Hatch; the gamble seemed to be paying off. Then Scheckter, sniffing victory, closed in and, with five laps to go, took the lead.

Lauda pressed on. He held second place for another two laps before Fittipaldi went by in the McLaren. Still he kept going. Smoke was beginning to curl from the edges of the tyre. Then chunks of rubber began to fly into the air. With one lap left, it was clear that Lauda would not make it and he pulled into the pits, where the Ferrari mechanics were waiting. The wheel was changed in 15 seconds. Lauda accelerated away. There were vital championship points to be won – but the organisers of the British Grand Prix only seemed interested in the winner.

The end of the pit lane was blocked as a crowd of hangers-on surged forward to see Scheckter take the flag. And, in the midst of it all, an official had backed his Ford Cortina across the entrance in preparation for the winner's lap of honour. It was a total shambles and in the middle of it, someone actually waved a red flag at Lauda, who undid his belts, climbed from the car and walked away. He was very angry. He was classified ninth.

Montezemolo filed a protest. It was thrown out by the RAC stewards and Ferrari immediately appealed to the FIA. A tibunal in Paris took eight hours to find in favour of Lauda and award him fifth place. Of course, that did not answer the question of whether he would actually have been able to complete the last lap and take fifth place had he been let out of the pits.

In any case, the extra two points made little difference to the championship; Lauda had more or less handed that to Fittipaldi after making mistakes in the German and Canadian Grands Prix. And, apparently, the Ferrari lawyers had claimed that Lauda's erratic performances had been caused by mental anguish over the Brand Hatch affair....

It was a messy ending to the 1974 British Grand Prix, one which did nothing to reduce the charges of incompetence being levelled at the RAC.

Showdown at Montjuich

Brands Hatch had come in for some stick too. There were the usual gripes about the catering charges. W.J. Wolfe, of Glasgow, wrote:

> 'I was appalled at the prices being asked for food and drink...The fruit stall was asking 8p for one apple. Two pints of bitter, one pint of lager and lime and one pint of lager came to about £1.37. That's well over 30p a pint!'

The most serious complaints, however, concerned the conditions in the sloping paddock. Spectators said that they had been prevented from seeing most of the teams at close quarters. The press severely criticised the shortage of passes for those who wanted to work and the high number available for those who didn't.

Brands Hatch replied that the Tyrrell team had received a threatening letter (subsequently reproduced in *Autosport* and mysteriously signed 'Kard'). On the advice of the police, most of the teams had been placed beyond the reach of members of the public, who were justifiably outraged, particularly after parting with £3 for a closer look. In any case, Brands Hatch explained that plans for a new paddock and pit complex had been put on ice pending the final position of a motorway due to run close by the circuit.

Silverstone was not so restricted and serious redevelopment had been put in hand over the winter of 1974-75. The pits and elevated pit road were demolished to make way for breeze block garages, a three-lane road and a substantial pit wall. And, a couple of hundred yards away, the Woodcote corner so enjoyed by drivers and spectators alike, was about to be desecrated by a chicane. There was uproar on both sides of the divide. But the job would be completed in time for the 1975 British Grand Prix.

The reason given was to prevent a wayward car, or bits of it, from flying into the grandstands. No one could argue with that. But, with the benefit of hindsight, it is easy to see that the chicane was also evidence of something other than worries about safety.

It was a sign of the growing strength of the teams. Speeds had been rising and the argument was; do you alter the cars, or do you alter the circuits? F1CA, led by Bernie Ecclestone and speaking on behalf of the teams, were adamant it should be the latter. The Woodcote chicane, and others like it, were proof that the constructors had won. The FIA had buckled completely. And so had the drivers. Their nadir had been the Spanish Grand Prix a few months before.

The Montjuich circuit, running through a park high above Barcelona, was one of the most

Jody Scheckter
Will always be remembered as the man who sparked off the spectacular accident at Silverstone in 1973, his fourth Formula 1 race. Returned the next year to win the British Grand Prix for Tyrrell at Brands Hatch. Became world champion with Ferrari in 1979 and retired at the end of the following year.

breathtaking places you could find on which to hold a motor race. In 1975, it was also one of the most dangerous. Trouble erupted when the drivers discovered that the crash barriers were not securely fastened. They quite rightly refused to take any further part in the proceedings. The officials wrung their hands in despair and muttered something about motor racing being dangerous and this circuit wasn't too bad. Now came the turning point.

The constructors, with package deals and obligations to put on a show now their prime motivation, waded in and ordered their drivers – their employees – to get on with what they were paid to do. With the exception of Emerson Fittipaldi, they did. The bargaining power of the GPDA collapsed on the spot.

The unbearable tension was exacerbated during the race when the carbon fibre mounting for the rear wing on Rolf Stommelen's Lola broke. The car became airborne, flew over three layers of barrier and killed four people standing in a prohibited area. Ironically, the incident had nothing to do with any deficiencies the circuit may have had. But Grand Prix racing never returned to the magnificent Montjuich Park. And F1CA, shortly to change its name to the Formula One Constructors' Association (FOCA), went from strength to strength.

Roadworks ahead

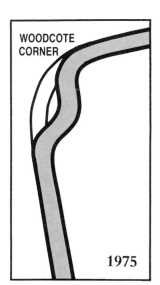

The new chicane at Woodcote Corner used at the 1975 Grand Prix.

'Bloody diabolical.' That was the typically forthright opinion of Brian Henton, one of the first drivers to try the Woodcote chicane. Mind you, Henton did not exactly get off to a good start. The bluff Midlander had been testing for Lotus at Silverstone on a day when McLaren were also present. After the lunchbreak, Fittipaldi had arranged to experiment with a makeshift version of the chicane and cones had been placed across the road at Woodcote. Unfortunately, no one passed on this news to Henton. He stormed under the bridge at close to 160mph, only to find the temporary 'deviation.' Surprisingly little damage was done....

Reactions to the chicane when it was finally built were mixed, but there was no getting away from the fact that it would be in place for the Grand Prix. A few minutes after half past eleven on Thursday 17 July, Tom Pryce officially became the first driver to use the chicane when practice began. Ironically, the Welshman was one of the drivers who mourned the passing of the old corner, but that did not prevent him from eventually claiming pole position in the Shadow; a stunning performance in such elevated company. And there was another change to the script when Carlos Pace joined Pryce on the front row.

Pace had been signed by Brabham halfway through 1974, a move which was rewarded by a home victory for him in the Brazilian Grand Prix. In fact, Pace was one of three drivers to have scored their maiden victory thus far in the 1975 season. Jochen Mass, team-mate to Fittipaldi at McLaren, found himself the winner of the shortened Spanish Grand Prix and James Hunt had outfoxed Niki Lauda to give Hesketh an emotional win in Holland. It was widely predicted that Pryce would join the elite band of Grand Prix winners at Silverstone.

Pryce was rather more circumspect. He could see that the first 12 cars on the grid were covered by exactly one second, and among their number were some heavy hitters. He knew that a good start would be vital.

He did just that – but Pace made an even better getaway to lead at the end of the first lap. The drivers had been warned that a yellow flag (no overtaking) would be displayed at the chicane first time round. After that, it was every man for himself.

At first Pace seemed to have everything under control but, gradually, Regazzoni was gathering momentum in the Ferrari. On lap ten, he took second place from Pryce and set after the Brabham. Three laps later he had caught Pace and, keen to get the job done, Regazzoni pulled off a perfectly judged pass under braking for the chicane. It was a beautiful move which startled the Brazilian. 'Regga' was clearly having one of his more flamboyant days.

Next time round he had extended his lead over the Brabham to 0.9 seconds. Then he pulled out a further half a second, repeating the process on the next lap. Then he set the fastest lap of the race. Two laps after that, he did not appear on schedule.

Dark clouds had begun to roll across the far side of the circuit. There were drops of rain at Club and Stowe. Regazzoni was one of the first to discover the rapidly changing conditions and he slid off the track, bashing the rear wing against the barrier. And that let Pryce, who had just overtaken Pace, into the lead. But for how long?

Before the start, it had been declared that the race would not be stopped in the event of rain, the wide pit lane being roomy enough to accommodate as many drivers who wished to stop and change to wet tyres should they feel the need. And it was quickly becoming apparent that they would all need to get rid of their slick tyres as soon as possible. Either that or pussy-foot through Club and Stowe each time in the hope that the rain might go away. But, if anything, it was worse and creeping up the circuit.

Pryce discovered it had reached Becketts when he spun off, the Shadow spearing though the catch-fencing, where a pole caught him a hefty blow on the helmet. Scheckter, now in second place, took note and pulled into the pits at the end of the lap to change tyres. But Pace, back in the lead again, continued. And so did Lauda, Fittipaldi and Hunt as they ran in close company with the Brabham. Then Lauda went in.

The rest gambled on the track drying out, a decision made doubtful when Scheckter came storming through on his wet tyres and passed the lot of them. But a stiff breeze ensured that the track *did* dry quickly – and Scheckter went back in for slicks! The upshot was an Englishman in the lead, Hunt staying there for eight laps before an exhaust broke and Fittipaldi took charge for the first time.

Then the rain returned – heavy this time. Suddenly cars went every whichway, half a dozen ending their race in the catch-fencing at Club; others coming to rest at various points. Fittipaldi had managed to tip-toe through and reach the pits.

'I don't remember much about the details of the early laps but I'll never forget the final stages,' recalls Emerson. 'I remember seeing that very black cloud heading towards us and I knew for sure it was going to cause trouble. Typical English summer's day; one cloud here, another one there – and this one was coming towards Stowe!

'When it arrived, it was like you had turned on the shower just over that corner; everywhere else was 100 per cent dry. As I went down Hangar Straight, I could see it. So I braked and went through the corner very slowly – in second gear, I think. I got back to the pits, put on my wet tyres and went back out. And now it was really bad down at that end of the circuit. I was aquaplaning and I knew the safest place was to stay in the middle of the track because the car could have spun off in any direction at any time.

'And now it was a curtain of rain. You could see nothing. Suddenly, I saw the back of Mario Andretti's Parnelli and I j-u-s-t missed him. Cars were off the track all over the place. I got back to Woodcote, I don't know how, saw the red flag and stopped.'

There were 11 laps to go – but it was all over. Sixteen drivers had crashed, 19 had made pit stops, seven different drivers changed the lead nine times. And at the end of it, Emerson Fittipaldi was declared the winner simply because he was leading at the end of the last lap which counted. It his last Grand Prix win.

It was a strange race in a strange season. The constructors decided not to go to Canada because the organisers would not pay the money demanded. In Austria, Vittorio Brambilla won in the wet, the Italian so elated that he promptly spun off seconds after taking the flag. Then, in September, Ken Tyrrell pulled off another coup by unveiling a car which had six wheels. A strange season indeed. The only predictable fact seemed to be Niki Lauda winning the championship for Ferrari.

But there was a terrible sting in the tail in November. Graham Hill, having announced his retirement at the British Grand Prix, was killed when his light aircraft crashed in fog. One of the sport's great ambassadors had gone. And with him went the nucleus of his talented team, including Tony Brise, a perky young driver to whom Formula 1 seemed to hold no fears in his first season.

Brise had been carrying the future hopes of Great Britain. He also unintentionally contributed to the introduction of a new word to the motor racing vocabulary.

When he spun into the catch-fencing during the British Grand Prix, his helmet had been ripped from his head. The bolt holding the chin-strap in place had broken. The helmet manufacturer said it was meant to do this; they said the bolt was 'frangeable'. And so the word passed into motor racing culture via numerous jokes. The British Grand Prix in recent years had never been short of controversy. But the 1976 event would set a new standard entirely.

Emerson Fittipaldi
Won his first world championship with Lotus in 1972 at the age of 25. Moved to McLaren with whom he became champion for the second time in 1974. Won the British Grand Prix twice but faded from the limelight after attempting to run his own team. Retired but returned to compete successfully in Indycar racing in the USA.

Graham Hill
The epitome of true British grit yet hard to believe he never won the British Grand Prix, despite being such a dominant force in the sixties. World Champion in 1962 and 1968; won the Monaco Grand Prix five times. Retired in July 1975 to run his own team; killed four months later in a light plane crash.

CHAPTER 16

THE RAT
AND THE BRAT

'The thing about 1976 is that I had to drive flat out all year; absolutely balls to the wall all the way.'

James Hunt, 1976 world champion

There is just one motor racing photograph on the walls of James Hunt's home. It pictures the Englishman, his arms outstretched, receiving a tumultuous welcome from the Brands Hatch crowd as he completes the slowing-down lap of the 1976 British Grand Prix.

He says it was the most emotional 'victory' of his career; victory in parenthesis because that win was subsequently taken away from him by the courts. And that, in turn, says everything about a season of tension, politics, protests, pure racing and near tragedy. The British Grand Prix had all of these on a glorious July day in 1976.

This was the year of the Great British Summer when the odd shower of rain was a welcome intruder. 'It's A Scorcher!' cried the front pages of the national press while, on the back pages, the sports writers whipped the British public to fever pitch. They spoke of the blond-haired hero racing for Britain and doing battle with the arrogant Austrian in the red Ferrari. It was all good stuff.

James had achieved notoriety in the gossip columns through his deeds of derring-do in 1975 with the Hesketh 308, that red, white and blue mobile bastion of British pride. But in November of that year, the Moët dried up and his Lordship called the party to order. James Hunt was without a drive for 1976 – and, by a stroke of luck, McLaren were without a driver, Emerson Fittipaldi having caught everyone on the hop by leaving to run his own team.

Hunt and McLaren would gell immediately, and when the 28-year-old with the plummy accent and rebellious ways began to win races, the media massaged their instant hero for all it was worth. The public responded with vigour

At first, though, it seemed Lauda would walk away with the championship. He won in Brazil and South Africa, finished second to his team-mate, Clay Regazzoni, at California's Long Beach (a new venue on the city's streets) and even when Hunt scored an impressive win in Spain, the nine points were taken away from him when his car was discovered to be 1.8cm too wide. Then Lauda scored imperious victories in Belgium and Monaco, and that made it 51 points to the Austrian; six to James Hunt. Talk about the under-dog! Fleet Street loved it.

There was championship stalemate in Sweden when the six-wheeled Tyrrells of Jody Scheckter and Patrick Depailler scored an historic win for the British team, but then the pendulum began to swing in Hunt's favour.

Lauda retired from the French Grand Prix – and Hunt won. Then, just before the British Grand Prix, an appeal court reinstated Hunt as winner of the Spanish Grand Prix. Now the championship table read Lauda 52, Hunt 25. It was a considerable gap but Hunt, firmly believing that the Ferrari could be beaten, took each race as it came. And there was no question that he would give his all at Brands Hatch, a circuit he enjoyed.

The names were different, but the challenge remained. Pilgrims Rise became Hailwood Hill, Bottom Bend was renamed Graham Hill Bend, Cooper Straight was the new name for Bottom Straight, South Bank Bend was changed to Surtees and the start/finish straight was renamed in honour of Jack Brabham.

And the changes were not just cosmetic. Brands Hatch had spent £300,000 rebuilding their pits and altering Cooper Straight to accommodate a new paddock to suit the latest demands of the Formula 1 teams. In addition, Paddock Hill Bend had been realigned, the 'old' track giving additional run-off. It was a timely move since the Grand Prix drivers would need all of it in the event of one of the most politically controversial accidents in the history of the British Grand Prix.

With a modified Ferrari at his disposal, Lauda won pole position by six-hundreths of a second from Hunt. Given the choice of which side of the grid he would like to start from, Lauda

James Hunt two-wheels his way along the original piece of track at Paddock. Amon's Ensign and the back of Regazzoni's Ferrari follow while Depailler's Tyrrell and the Lotus of Andretti take the more conventional line through the revised corner.

wisely opted for the left-hand side, thus avoiding the steeply cambered track which has been the bane of the traditional pole position on the right.

Mario Andretti (Lotus) claimed third-fastest time ahead of Regazzoni, Depailler and Chris Amon, now at the wheel of the underfinanced but impressively nimble Ensign. The generous odds on Amon made the New Zealander an excellent bet, but there was no doubt about the favourites. The bookmakers and the punters, however, reckoned without the influence of Gianclaudio 'Clay' Regazzoni.

Hunt spun his wheels for a brief moment at the start – but it was enough to allow Regazzoni to charge past the McLaren and launch an immediate attack on his team-mate. Lauda, having made a perfect start, was clearly not ready for this.

James Hunt: 'The mechanics had done a brilliant job but they hadn't time to complete the tracking on the front of the car and, for the first ten laps or so, it didn't feel too clever. I was never more than six seconds or so behind Niki and, as more rubber was laid down on the track, the grip increased and my car began to work better and better each lap.'

Clay at his best. He just did not appear to brake at all and then he assaulted Niki. For a brief moment I thought I had the pleasure of watching the two Ferrari drivers take each other off the road – and then I realised I was in their accident as well.'

The Ferraris tangled and spun broadside, Hunt trying to find an escape route to the left. Unfortunately Regazzoni, now rolling backwards, caught the McLaren and tossed Hunt's car onto its side, the M23 tottering before crashing back onto its wheels. Hunt's relief at remaining mobile was short-lived; the collision had damaged the steering and he motored slowly up the hill, convinced he was out of the race. Then he saw crossed 'yellow' and 'oil' flags, the sign that the race had been stopped. Now the confusion began in earnest.

Only four cars had been damaged and, of those, Regazzoni, Hunt and Amon had got going again. Jacques Laffite, driving a Ligier-Matra, had rammed the barrier on the outside of the corner. Rather than attempt to drag his car round the complete lap, Hunt stopped on Cooper Straight, just behind the pits. His spare car was wheeled onto the grid, Ferrari and Ligier doing likewise for Regazzoni and Laffite. Meanwhile, the McLaren mechanics began to work feverishly on the front suspension of Hunt's damaged car.

Out came the rule books – such as they were. The organisers said that the race would start afresh. They also said that, in order to restart, each competitor should have completed the first lap. But, in truth, no one *really* knew what the procedure should be. The crowd were getting restless; they had paid to see a motor race.

After more deliberation, it was then suggested that drivers could only use their original cars. Either way, it did not look good for James Hunt, despite mutterings from Ferrari that the race had been stopped in order to give him a second chance. (Certainly, the track had been clear enough to allow the race to continue but the Observer at Paddock Hill Bend had, quite rightly, erred on the side of caution when he called for the race to be stopped.)

Hunt, meanwhile, walked to the grid and climbed into his spare car. The crowd cheered him all the way. Then they were acquainted with the latest edict from the Stewards concerning the use of spare cars.

Slow hand-clapping quickly developed into cat-calls and booing, 70,000 fans giving voice to their feelings. This was not Brands Hatch in July; it was Wembley or Highbury on a winter's weekend. The cacophony of sound grew louder; beer cans were tossed onto the track. The atmosphere turned distinctly menacing.

'I've never known anything like it,' recalls Hunt. 'The crowd went completely hooligan. It was a fantastic feeling for me as I sat in my car to know that I had all this support; really quite incredible. And it soon became clear that the organisers were going to allow me to start because, if they didn't, they would have a riot on their hands!'

Indeed, the Stewards miraculously decided everything was in order after all since Hunt had actually been mobile when the race was stopped and now, to make matters easier, the McLaren mechanics had finished their hasty repairs to the race car.

James Hunt: 'The mechanics had done a brilliant job but they hadn't time to compete the tracking on the front of the car and, for the first ten laps or so, it didn't feel too clever. I was never more than six seconds or so behind Niki and, as more rubber was laid down on the track, the grip increased and my car began to work better and better each lap.'

At half distance, the Ferrari and the McLaren began to trade fastest laps and Hunt closed in. On lap 45, Hunt rushed up the hill to Druids and dived inside Lauda to take the lead. Lauda, struggling with occasional gear selection trouble, did not respond and Hunt pulled remorselessly away.

Hunt: 'I wanted him to fight. I was on such a high that it was important for me to really win those nine points. I didn't want him to just hand over the lead and then back off. Anyway, I was ready that day for anything he cared to throw at me.

'I loved racing at Brands Hatch; a real driver's circuit. And it's special because, being a natural amphitheatre, it's very intimate; the crowd are very close to you. And when I arrived at Clearways in the lead, the place just went mad. But you can feel the presence of the crowd, sense the emotion and the movement all the time even though you are not necessarily looking at them. It's there. And you respond to it.'

Hunt responded to the tumultuous welcome at the finish by raising both arms in the air as he took the flag. What was to follow in the hush of a court room a few months later would never take that heady moment away from him.

Win some, lose some

Meanwhile, there was racing to be done. Hunt, with the momentum of Brands Hatch behind him and the points gap reduced only marginally to 23 points, went to the Nürburgring intent on victory. Under the prevailing circumstances, anything less would be totally useless. Besides, a win at the 'Ring would be one to savour regardless of the outcome of the championship.

Again, the battle lines were clearly drawn; Hunt on pole, Lauda alongside. Less than a second had separated them during practice on this 14-mile giant of a track. As the start time approached, rain was in the air, the weather uncertain. Hunt chose wet tyres; so did Lauda. Only James's team-mate, Jochen Mass, gambled on slicks. It turned out to be the right choice.

At the end of the first lap, the majority of the field, including Hunt and Lauda, rushed into the pits to change to dry tyres. At the end of the second lap, Mass led by 29 seconds. And he knew the circuit well. This was going to be his day.

Except that there had been the most appalling accident on the far side of the circuit at an easy left-hand bend on the approach to Bergwerk. For some unaccountable reason, Niki Lauda's

James Hunt
Obsessive strength of will brought him the world championship against all odds in 1976, finishing first in the British Grand Prix being the emotional highlight of a memorable year. Won his home Grand Prix in 1977, retired in 1979 and now lends his forthright opinions to television commentating.

Ferrari had turned sharp right at the exit, cannoned off the barrier and the rock-face, burst into flames and spun into the middle of the track – where two cars hit it. In the absence of rescue marshals with proper equipment, four drivers – Arturo Merzario, Guy Edwards, Harald Ertl and Brett Lunger – waded into the blazing wreckage and dragged Lauda free. He was removed to hospital where a priest gave him the last rites.

The race had been stopped and restarted. James Hunt's subsequent win, while being deeply satisfying for the Englishman, did nothing to relieve the anguish that night as the grim news of Lauda's condition emerged. His helmet had been ripped off during the accident and he had suffered extensive facial burns and breathed in the flames. Most people fully expected to wake up on Monday morning and learn that Niki had died during the night. But they reckoned without 'The Rat's' stubborn refusal to give up.

He survived. Not only that, he was racing again within six weeks. His head heavily bandaged, Lauda returned at Monza and gathered more championship points by finishing fourth. John Watson, driving a Penske, had scored his first Grand Prix victory by winning at the Österreichring a few weeks before, but Hunt had reduced the deficit on Lauda to just two points with a victory at Zandvoort. James did not score at Monza – and neither did he score in the FIA court a few weeks later.

In the immediate aftermath of the British Grand Prix, the RAC had thrown out Ferrari's appeal against Hunt's right to take part in the race. Now came a further appeal court in Paris. James was in Canada preparing for the Grand Prix at Mosport and the McLaren case was handled by team manager Teddy Mayer – who also happened to be a lawyer. In a recent article in *Autosport*, Mayer recalled what happened:

> *'I felt that when we got to the FIA court they were just trying to make things even. They'd given us one appeal, which was Spain, and decided to give Ferrari this one.*
>
> *However, there were some witnesses who we felt perjured themselves, who had been dragged to the meeting by Ferrari. One in particular was suddenly somewhere where we all knew he hadn't been, and seeing something we all knew he hadn't seen, which was pretty funny.*
>
> *Niki had just climbed out of his deathbed and they wheeled him in all wrapped up in bandages, more for dramatic effect than anything else. Really, at that point I knew we didn't have a chance, and James would be disqualified.'*

Hunt responded in the only way he could – by driving with brilliant aggression to win both at Mosport and Watkins Glen. That made it Lauda 68 points and Hunt 65, with only the Japanese Grand Prix remaining.

The race was run in teeming rain. Lauda pulled out after two laps, saying it was too dangerous to continue. For a man whose values had been sharpened by events at the Nürburgring, no one could dispute such a brave decision. Hunt, meanwhile, raced on in the atrocious conditions and finished third. He won the championship by one point. It was a dramatic finish to a truly remarkable year. And the British Grand Prix had more than played its part.

No joy for John

If the British public were not aware of James Hunt at this point, they soon would be. But the adulation would give way to the usual sniping as the media proceeded to knock Hunt from the pedestal on which they had placed him in the first place. Not that he cared. And the less he cared, the more vitriolic the writers became until the whole process spiralled downhill into a morass of general unpleasantness.

The one accusation which could not be levelled at Hunt, however, was a reduction of his motivation in the cockpit. If anything, he was driving better than ever although the results did not reflect that. Indeed, the press were concentrating on one or two spectacular incidents – a high-flying act when he collided with John Watson at Long Beach attracting particular attention.

With the Penske team having withdrawn from Formula 1, Watson found himself with Brabham just as the flat-12 Alfa Romeo was at last becoming competitive. The Ulsterman had claimed pole position at Monaco, but victory went to Jody Scheckter at the wheel of a Wolf-Ford, a car designed by Harvey Postlethwaite and run by Peter Warr for Walter Wolf, a wealthy oil man.

If the compact Wolf outfit was the team of 1977, then the car of the year was most certainly

Niki Lauda
A legendary character and three-times world champion who had a fascinating love/hate relationship with the British Grand Prix at Brands Hatch. Almost lost his life in Germany in 1976, the year he fought tooth and nail with James Hunt for the championship, but came back to win at Brands Hatch in 1982 and 1984.

Denied yet again. John Watson and the Brabham-Alfa Romeo; eternally unlucky in 1977.

the Lotus 78, a typical product of Chapman's fertile mind as he began an investigation into the 'ground effect' phenomenon which would soon revolutionise Formula 1.

But, in the light of such novelty and newness in Grand Prix racing, no particular combination had stood out as the likely winner of the championship. By the time the British Grand Prix, the tenth of 17 races, came round, Niki Lauda (Ferrari) led Mario Andretti (Lotus) and Scheckter by one point, with Carlos Reutemann (Ferrari) not far behind in fourth place. None of the foregoing gentlemen, however, would be in the reckoning at Silverstone. The 1977 British Grand Prix was all about James Hunt and John Watson.

Two Britons on the front row of the grid attracted 85,000 fans to Northamptonshire. Hunt had taken pole position with the M26 McLaren, a car which hitherto had not shown the form expected of it. But it was Watson who powered into the lead, with Hunt, his clutch dragging badly, being pushed down to fourth place by Lauda and Scheckter.

By one third distance, Hunt had worked his way into second place and the chase was on. It took just six laps to whittle down Watson's lead, but, once he had caught the Brabham, Hunt discovered that passing it would be a different proposition entirely:

'If I remember rightly, the M26 was quicker than the Brabham through the corners but that Alfa was developing a lot of power. I was absolutely stuffed on the straight – he would just pull away. There was no way I could pass him so all I could do was pressure John and hope that he would make a mistake. And "Wattie" wasn't making many mistakes in those days.'

For 20 laps or so it was stalemate, Watson remaining in complete control. Then the Alfa Romeo began to stutter, and Hunt was leading at the end of lap 50.

John Watson: 'The Brabham had three or four fuel tanks and a couple of them weren't draining properly. The same thing had cost me a win on the last lap of the French Grand Prix a few weeks before and that was a big disappointment, I can tell you. After that, this was frustrating, but not such a shock.

'The Brabham was quite good round Silverstone and I felt sure I could win because my car had an advantage on certain parts of the circuit. James had made one or two lunges at me but he hadn't been able to get through. But I have to say that had James been in front of me, I think I would have had difficulty catching and passing him. As it was, I felt everything was under control. The car was nicely balanced and I had the speed to maintain my position. Then it just spluttered and that was that.'

Hunt reeled off the remaining 18 laps, his lead over Lauda, the champion-elect, being so great that he could reduce his pace considerably and enjoy this victory. Or, at least, enjoy it was much as Silverstone would allow.

'After winning at Brands the year before, that 1977 result just does not begin to compare in any shape or form. I have always felt Silverstone is as dull as ditch water from a driver's point of view. Okay, it is reasonably challenging because of the quick corners but it has no character, no atmosphere because the crowd are more spread out. But obviously the win was very nice because it was my first one of the season.'

The first turbo

The race was also notable for another first – the debut of the Formula 1 Renault, the first car to explore the 1.5-litre turbocharged alternative permitted by the rules. The yellow car, driven by Jean-Pierre Jabouille, qualified three rows from the back of the grid and lasted for 16 laps before creeping into the pits in a cloud of smoke, the turbocharger broken. It may not have been a particularly auspicious first race, but the arrival of the Renault turbo marked the beginning of an era which would have far-reaching political effects before turbochargers were finally outlawed at the end of 1988.

And there was one more novelty on that summer's day in 1977. McLaren had entered a third car, an elderly M23, for a young French-Canadian who had been stunning observers in North America with his remarkable car control and pure zest for driving. Gilles Villeneuve was faster than Jochen Mass throughout the weekend and he held seventh place in the early stages. But for a pit stop – unnecessary as it turned out – he would have finished in the points. McLaren, though, decided against signing him. Ferrari were more astute.

For 1978, Villeneuve joined Carlos Reutemann, who had been brought in to replace Lauda in the latter half of 1976. Then Lauda made his remarkable recovery and quickly set about showing Reutemann just whose team this was. It was not a smooth working relationship in 1977, and at the end of the year Lauda, having won the championship, left Ferrari to join Brabham. Clearly, there were one or two scores to be settled here and it all came to a head at Brands Hatch during the 1978 British Grand Prix.

British fans, always amongst the most knowledgeable and fanatical in the world.

Carlos times it right

Carlos Reutemann loved the British in general and Brands Hatch in particular. When he first came to England to race in Formula 2 in 1970, he had travelled by bus to the Kent circuit and pinched a photographer's pass in order to watch the Race of Champions from close quarters. The Argentinian returned the following July to spectate at the British Grand Prix and the emotional win for Jochen Rindt had greatly impressed him. Eight years later, he arrived in the capacity of number one driver for Ferrari but, in truth, he held out little chance of winning.

This was the year of the Lotus 79, a most beautiful device with large sidepods containing the secret of 'ground effect.' The inverted wings inside these pods helped suck the car to the track. The sure-footed handling put this car into a different class, something which Reutemann was plainly aware of.

During practice, Peterson had passed Carlos on the outside going through Surtees, the Swede flooring the throttle and leaving black streaks of rubber on the track. The Ferrari,

Carlos Reutemann
One of the most stylish performers ever to win the British Grand Prix. On a good day, the Argentinian was unbeatable; but good days were sometimes hard to find. Drove for Brabham, Lotus, Ferrari and Williams but failed to win the championship before retiring in 1982.

meanwhile, just spun its wheels and went nowhere. At the end of the day, Ronnie was on pole with Mario Andretti alongside; just what everyone had expected. After all, Andretti had 45 points to his credit and Peterson 36. Lauda was third with 25 and Reutemann fifth with 22. Appropriately enough, Lauda was on the second row with the Wolf of Jody Scheckter while Reutemann was sharing row four with Laffite's Ligier-Matra. On row three were Riccardo Patrese and Alan Jones, representing two new names, Arrows and Williams respectively, Frank Williams now beginning the serious climb from that of an impecunious entrant to a race-winning constructor.

Reutemann arrived early on race morning, declared himself pleased with the Ferrari during the warm-up, and then sat down on the infield to watch the team owners act like hooligans as they raced Ford Escorts, Frank Williams shovelling Jack Oliver aside to lead the battered cars home. The outcome of the Grand Prix, though, was easier to predict.

Sure enough, Andretti and Peterson led as they pleased. Until lap seven. Ronnie was the first to disappear, his black and gold Lotus brought to a halt by a broken fuel line. But Andretti was in easy command – until he picked up a puncture, made a swift pit stop, and retired not long after with a blown engine. Scheckter and Jones were now fighting for the lead, Jones being encouraged by the smell of leaking gearbox oil wafting from the back of the dark blue Wolf. The Australian should not have entertained such wicked thoughts; three laps later and the Williams was out with a broken drive shaft.

'Yeah, a right bastard, that was,' recalls Jones. 'I was able to stay with Jody, no problem, and this looked like being the big breakthrough for Frank after all those years. And, of course, the British would have been a good one to win. In fact that car, the FW06, should have won a race in 1978. It was a lovely car to drive, but the problem was it was about a year too late in terms of not having ground effect. It was by far and away the best conventional car, a really beautiful car. But then Mr. Chapman came along with his Lotus 79...'

Jones's disappointment was compounded when Scheckter stopped, as the Australian had anticipated, with gearbox trouble. Now Lauda leads. Patrese is second. And Reutemann third. Carlos can see no way past the excitable Italian but the cards are falling the Ferrari driver's way when Patrese suddenly pulls off with a puncture.

The Ferrari, with its Michelin tyres, is now working very well. Reutemann shaves two or three tenths of a second off the gap to Lauda every lap. Now he is right behind the Brabham-Alfa Romeo. But where do you pass Niki Lauda on such a twisting track? Reutemann patiently waits for his chance.

It comes on lap 60. The leaders are about to lap the third works McLaren, driven by Bruno Giacomelli. This is only the Italian's fourth Grand Prix. On the approach to Clearways, Giacomelli heeds the blue warning flag and moves to his left. But he is already too late. Lauda has decided to pass on the left and, in the brief moment of confusion, Lauda is forced to lift off the throttle while Reutemann sees the gap on the right, takes his chance and dives for the inside, the Ferrari clipping the grass on the way through.

As Reutemann emerges from Clearways, Lauda is alongside, to the left of the Ferrari. But Reutemann has the line for the next corner, Paddock. He takes the lead and drives flat-out for the remaining 16 laps. Lauda, momentarily disheartened, backs off but then makes a late charge, setting the fastest lap four from the end. Carlos Reutemann wins the British Grand Prix by 1.23 seconds.

Motor racing is also this

Ferrari also won the final two races of the season, at Watkins Glen and in Canada, but otherwise it was Lotus all the way. The Dutch Grand Prix was the perfect example of their dominance, Peterson dutifully following Andretti across the line. This, in fact, would be the American's final Grand Prix win and the last time we would enjoy Ronnie Peterson's extrovert style. Two weeks later at Monza, Andretti was crowned world champion but it was a joyless weekend for Mario.

Peterson had been shoved into the crash barriers shortly after the start and, at first, it seemed his leg injuries would not cause a problem. There was even talk that he would be able to drive again. Then complications set in during the operation that night. When Mario Andretti arrived at Niguarda Hospital on Monday morning, he was told that his friend had just died. Stunned and deeply saddened, the 1978 world champion uttered one brief but immortal line: 'Unfortunately,' he said, 'motor racing is also this.'

Ronnie Peterson

CHAPTER 17

A FAMILY AT WAR

If it was that easy, everyone could do it

Carlos Reutemann left Ferrari to join Lotus for 1979 and it was difficult to fault his logic. Thanks to Colin Chapman's intuitive thinking, ground effect cars were now *de rigueur*, and clearly Lotus had a head start. Apart from that, Ferrari would be struggling to make the idea work on their new car since the bulky nature of the Ferrari flat-12 engine would severely restrict the effectiveness of the sidepods.

But motor racing can, if nothing else, be a black art. The 1979 Lotus did not work – and Chapman didn't know why. But the brand new Ligier did work – and they didn't know why. Jacques Laffite and Patrick Depailler dominated the opening races in South America with such ease that the championship seemed a foregone conclusion, even at that early stage.

Then the French team began lose their edge and, the more they tried to return to full competitiveness, the more confused they became. By the time the British Grand Prix came round, Laffite and Depailler were third and fourth in the championship, behind the Ferrari drivers Jody Scheckter and Gilles Villeneuve.

The Ferrari, though, was not a brilliant car and at Silverstone it was off the pace, so much so that Scheckter and Villeneuve were back on the sixth and seventh rows of the grid. Williams, with their ground effect car, the FW07, were now setting the standards and their principal rival looked like being Renault following a splendid first win for Jean-Pierre Jabouille and the French team, appropriately in their home Grand Prix two weeks before.

Jokes about the smoking, droning turbo had long since ceased and the business of racing turbocharged engines had quickly become a political issue. It was increasingly being seen as an unfair advantage, even though the opportunity to try this particular avenue of development had been present for more than a decade. And when Jabouille put the yellow and white car on the front row alongside Jones's Williams-Ford it was a reminder of just how far Renault had come in the two years since their début at Silverstone.

But, on 14 July 1979, the French team knew they would be hard-pressed to keep the Williams in sight. Jones had never felt so confident before, as he recalls:

'That car was unbelievable. The thing about Silverstone is that you have to be really, really smooth if you want to find that extra tenth of a second in those quick corners. You have got to have a lot of commitment through the likes of Stowe and Club and FW07 gave you a great feeling of confidence. It was almost perfect. As you came out of the corner you were cheekily glancing down at your rev-counter just to see if you had managed to extract another 100 revs more. It was rare that you would have a car as good as that and I felt very positive going into the race.'

Indeed, the only question was one of reliability. Williams were still novices when compared to the likes of Ferrari, a fact Jones knew to his cost since an electrical problem had cost him the Belgian Grand Prix, a race which was subsequently won by Scheckter. For the Grand Prix at Silverstone, Williams and Cosworth decided to fit a new development engine after practice had finished. Due to problems with the fuel pump, the installation took all night. The mechanics were shattered. But the car was ready.

Tiredness was flushed away by the flow of adrenalin as the team watched Jones lead Jabouille for seven laps before the Renault began to run into tyre trouble. By half distance, the French car was gone altogether, thanks to a broken valve-spring. Jones had a 25-second lead and he reduced his revs and concentrated on looking after the car and bringing it home to a well-deserved victory. It seemed a mere formality.

Then, with 31 laps remaining, a fine spray was seen coming from the back of the Williams. A gasket on the neck of the waterpump – modified to fit the tight confines of the Williams chassis – had gone. The water temperature gauge soared and Jones drove slowly into the pits, his race over.

'I probably remember that British Grand Prix better than the one I won,' says Jones. 'I just felt so comfortable out there. Everything had come together so well. I wasn't under pressure; just cruising really. And that would have been my first Grand Prix win for Williams. It was

Alan Jones and Clay Regazzoni sandwich the Renault of Jean-Pierre Jabouille as the field rushes into Club Corner.

just a stupid little thing which let me down.'

Jones had a brief word with Frank Williams, stationed on his chair at the pit wall, shook hands with the Saudi sponsors and left. The interests of the Williams team were in capable hands.

Please, no champagne…

Looking for an experienced driver to support Jones, one who would not make superstar demands on his team, Frank Williams had chosen Clay Regazzoni, now in his 40th year. Clay fitted the bill perfectly; smiling, enthusiastic, a *racer*, but one who was never quite sure just how much he was earning. 'For me, the thing is to race,' he would say – and at Silverstone he was doing just that.

He had snatched the lead going into the first corner (Clay always seemed to have a telepathic link with the starter and he could be relied on to make a sensational getaway) and he then held third place once Jones and Jabouille had blasted past on the run down to Stowe. When Jones retired, Clay was perfectly placed to do exactly what Frank required of him. The second Renault of René Arnoux was almost half a minute behind, but just to make sure that the Frenchman had the message, Regazzoni established a new lap record.

The grandstands rose to welcome the Swiss with the bandit moustache as he took the chequered flag. They applauded for Frank Williams as much as for the driver, but Clay Regazzoni's rakish good looks and devil-may-care style had always appealed to the British.

'Yes,' he says, 'I never really understood that – but I liked it! They would paint my name on the track and things like that. I always liked racing in England, particularly Silverstone. The atmosphere was fantastic and I liked very much the people. They were very kind to me when I won.

'I was very happy that day but that win was really easy for me. Alan was so quick – of course, he had a special Cosworth engine – but he was very fast and obviously he deserved to win. That car was very competitive; the handling, very good. I could have gone faster but there was no need.

'I remember, afterwards, I could not take the champagne because this would have offended our Saudi sponsors. Frank, he say to me "no champagne on the podium," so every time they gave me a bottle, I gave it to someone else! But, later in the motor home, when everyone has gone, we drink whisky! Was a nice day, the British Grand Prix 1979....'

It would be the last win for Clay. Early the following year, his Ensign would pile into the tyre barrier at the end of straight at Long Beach. The brakes had failed and Regazzoni hit the barrier at undiminished speed; indeed, the impact was so violent that the concrete wall behind the tyres was moved back a couple of feet. Clay suffered severe spinal injuries. The rest of a previously active life would be spent in a wheelchair.

For a while, he shunned motor racing as he struggled to come to terms with the terrible reality of it all. But gradually he returned to do television commentary work and use his vast experience to describe a sport which he had served with a perfect mixture of dignity and devilment. 'Winning for Ferrari, that was always something very exciting; incredible emotion,' he says. 'But winning for Frank at Silverstone was a special thing for me.'

Alan Jones scored more Grands Prix victories than anyone else in 1979. Unfortunately, he won them all in the second half of the season. The rules said a driver could only count his best four results from each half, which meant Jones came away with fewer points than Jody Scheckter, who had won three races to Jones's four. For 1980, however, Williams would be ready from the word go. The problem was, would they have anywhere to race their FW07B? Politics were about to split Grand Prix racing down the middle.

The Great Dictator

The first hint of trouble had surfaced at the beginning of 1979. The season was barely thirty seconds old when a first-corner accident caused the Argentine Grand Prix to be stopped. Those present soon became aware of a man in a white suit, ranting and raving and blaming all and sundry: Jean-Marie Balestre, newly elected President of the CSI, had arrived.

The sporting arm of the FIA was soon to change its name to *Fédération Internationale du Sport Automobile* (FISA) and it quickly became clear that Balestre felt the teams, through their FOCA organisation, were having things too much their own way. Weak management had allowed the power of the governing body to be usurped but Balestre was intent on changing all that. FISA, he maintained, were there to govern, and that's just what they would do. Everyone took a deep breath and retreated to the trenches.

Among the many reforms introduced by Balestre in 1980 was the mandatory drivers' briefing before each race. It was a sensible idea but this particular issue would become a trial of strength. Members of FOCA (not all of the teams were part of the association) instructed their drivers not to attend the briefings at Zolder and Monaco. The drivers were duly fined by FISA, the teams refused to pay and Balestre said he would suspend the drivers' licences until the money was forthcoming. Thus, things turned nasty at the next race in Spain.

Ferrari, Alfa Romeo and Renault (the major manufacturers in Formula 1 who were afraid of repercussions in other spheres of motoring) distanced themselves from the dispute and did not take part in the race. Alan Jones won the Spanish Grand Prix, but the race was subsequently declared illegal. Now the gloves were off.

There was division between the 'manufacturers' and the 'constructors'; it almost boiled down to 'Europe' v 'England.' And when Williams thrashed everyone at the French Grand Prix, Jones took great delight in brandishing a large Union Jack while completing his victory lap. He was enjoying the moment since this win had put him back on top of the championship table regardless of the Spanish fiasco. The French, particularly Ligier and Renault who had high hopes of winning at Paul Ricard, were not amused. They would seek revenge at Brands Hatch in two weeks' time.

Further development of the ground effect principle, and the introduction of sliding skirts along the outside edge of the sidepods, had produced a phenomenal level of road-holding. And nowhere was this more pronounced than at Clearways and Paddock Hill Bend. The drivers hardly seemed to brake before flinging their cars into the corner and flooring the throttle. The greatest exponents of this so-called art were Alan Jones and Didier Pironi.

Pironi, a pupil of the French motor racing system, had joined Ligier after a period with Tyrrell. Cool and confident almost to the point of arrogance, there was never any doubt that he would be a world champion one day. He had just scored his first Grand Prix win in Belgium, a victory which he had treated as a matter of course. And with the Ligier working well, he

Gianclaudio 'Clay' Regazzoni
Most popular winner of the 1979 British Grand Prix thanks to a press-on style and an uncomplicated approach to racing. Won Grands Prix for Ferrari and Williams before suffering serious injuries at Long Beach in 1980. The Swiss now attends most races in his role as television commentator.

clearly relished the challenge of Brands Hatch as he claimed pole position. His lap average of 132 mph did not bear thinking about. Pironi's team-mate, Jacques Laffite, was almost four tenths of a second slower, and lining up behind the Gitanes-sponsored cars were the Saudia-Leyland Williams pairing of Jones and Reutemann.

Ligier were the main threat, of course, but Jones also had his eye on the white Brabham directly behind him on row three. This car, now powered by a Ford-Cosworth engine, was driven by Nelson Piquet, a crafty Brazilian who had shown excellent form in his first season with the Brabham-Alfa Romeo in 1979. Now, having won impressively at Long Beach and consistently picked up points elsewhere, Nelson was second on the championship table, three points behind Jones. Whichever way he looked, the Australian knew he had a fight on his hands.

The trouble I've caused. As Laffite swings into Surtees, the Harrier sits quietly on the infield. The guests atop the Essex bus have rearranged themselves and the paddock has returned to normal.

Blowing them all away

With the race not scheduled to start until 3pm, the Brands Hatch organisers laid on their now traditional feast of aerial performers. Among their number was Flt Lt Carvell with his Hawker Harrier, the jump-jet astonishing everyone with its versatility. But it had one trick which was not so well received. For a final flourish, Flt Lt Carvell made a high-speed pass at very low altitude. The annual *Autocourse* summed up the after-effect:

> *'There was a pause of about five seconds [after the Harrier had made its swoop], then a vicious whistling as the shock-wave shook the paddock by the throat. Hats flew in the air; umbrellas were torn inside out; tables tumbled; awnings trembled before being whipped up and over motor homes, stout metal poles flying in all directions. And then it was quiet save for nervous laughter from pale and champagne-stained guests on the roof of the Essex [sponsors of Team Lotus] double-deck bus.'*

It was just about the only excitement the Lotus people would have all season as the team slid into a trough of uncompetitiveness. Ironically, Colin Chapman's initial advantage with ground effect was being exploited brilliantly elsewhere and, whereas Lotus had dominated the early laps of the British Grand Prix on the last visit to Brands Hatch, it would be Ligier who would repeat the performance in 1980, with similarly disappointing results.

One of the more sensible acts performed by FISA and FOCA had been the staggering of the grid positions with cars no longer starting side-by-side. And to see fair play and bring unifor-mity to the most highly charged moments of the Grand Prix weekend, Derek Ongaro, a phlegmatic Englishman, had been appointed as official starter. The use of the national flag had been replaced by the more reliable system of starting lights.

When Ongaro pressed the 'Go' button, Pironi, who had carefully placed his car close to the crown of the track rather than in the dip on the right-hand side, made a perfect start and led Laffite into Paddock after Jacques had eased Jones onto the grass. At the end of the first lap, the race seemed to be as good as settled. Pironi held a two second lead and Laffite was pulling away from Jones, who had Piquet right on his tail. With each succeeding lap, the Ligiers hammered home their advantage and it was clear that Jones had no hope of keeping pace. This continued until lap 17, when Pironi began to slow.

Ligier had lost the French Grand Prix by choosing to run the wrong size of front wheel rim. They were not about to make the same mistake again, but in their haste to fit the larger rims at Brands Hatch they had not taken into account the strain imposed by the early laps when the car was full with fuel. Tiny cracks had begun to appear in the heavily-loaded front-left wheel and the first Pironi knew of it was when the tyre began slowly to deflate. He rushed into the pits at the end of lap 19.

Any hopes of a swift return were ruled out by a chaotic stop which involved changing all four wheels and recovering from a stalled engine. But at least Ligier had the consolation of seeing Laffite hold a comfortable lead. And there he stayed for another 11 laps.

Going through Dingle Dell Corner, Laffite felt the car begin to slide more than normal and he quickly worked out that his left-rear tyre was losing pressure. Passing the pits, he warned his team of an impending stop at the end of the next lap. He never got that far. The tyre suddenly failed on the approach to Hawthorn Bend, the Frenchman crashing heavily. Fortunately, he was saved by a combination of catch-fencing and a strong chassis.

As Jacques walked back to the pits, he was able to witness at first hand the stunning recovery by his team-mate. Shattering the lap record time and time again, Pironi had climbed from last to fifth place. It was a truly mesmeric drive – but one which was destined to end with a rear tyre failure, the Frenchman coming to rest without harm at Westfield on lap 64. Ligier were stunned. This had been their race without question, but the French team had paid the price for running at such a furious pace.

Jones, meanwhile, had kept Piquet at arm's length and, as he rounded Clearways for the last time, the crowd stacked high in the stands lining the corner, cheered him to the echo. It was a remarkable reception which had a lot to do with their sympathy for Jones over the Spanish débâcle.

In Spain, the organisers had somehow managed to play the Austrian national anthem but, at Brands Hatch, the Royal Artillery Band got it right. It went some way towards making up for the disappointment at Silverstone the previous year.

'Yes, I felt good about that win,' says Jones. 'As I mentioned before, nothing would really make up for Silverstone in 1979, and at Brands Hatch I had been a bit lucky thanks to Ligier being typically French and confusing themselves. But Nelson was never that far behind me and he kept the pressure on, so I had to drive hard without making any mistakes.

'Don't forget, winning the British Grand Prix in those days was really as close as I could get to winning my home Grand Prix. I lived in England for 12 years and all my friends were English. It was almost like being on home ground and it meant a lot to me for that reason.'

At the victory presentation, Jones was asked about his championship chances but he wisely refused to comment. 'Anything can happen,' he said. And it did.

A puncture cost him the lead in Germany and a silly mistake meant the loss of a certain nine points in Holland. In between, though, he finished second in Austria, a race which saw an overdue win for Renault and a gutsy drive by a young Englishman making his début in a Lotus; his name, Nigel Mansell.

In Italy, the balance swung in Piquet's favour as he won at Imola. The Brazilian and the Australian were separated by just one point as they went to North America for the final two races. The pressure was on, and it told.

Eyeing each other from the front of the grid at Montreal, Jones and Piquet managed to collide at the first corner. The race was stopped, Piquet taking his spare car for the restart. He led for 21 laps. Then the engine failed. Alan Jones, winner of the Canadian Grand Prix, was 1980 world champion with one race to go. And he won that too.

During 1980, there had been all manner of threats concerning the continuing row between FISA and FOCA. Somehow the racing survived, but it was obvious that something needed to be done if the image of Grand Prix racing was not to be sullied further in 1981. After a winter

Alan Jones
A tough, no-nonsense Australian who looked upon England as his second home and derived great pleasure from winning the British Grand Prix in 1980 – the year he became world champion. Achieved an excellent rapport with Williams, winning eleven Grands Prix for the British team.

of serious discontent, agreement was reached just ten days before the first race of the season at Long Beach. In essence, the teams agreed to do away with sliding skirts (thereby reducing the cornering speeds) while, in return, FISA would allow FOCA to keep control of their all-important commercial aspect of Formula 1. Known as the Concorde Agreement, this piece of paper signalled 'peace in our time.' But it was an uneasy peace.

Brabham were the first to exploit a loophole in the regulations. If skirts were not allowed, then the cars would need to be run close to the ground in order to make the side-pods effective in their production of ground effect. Ah, but FISA had said the bottom edge of the cars must be six centimetres (nearly 2.5 inches) above the ground and they duly measured the cars each time they came into the pits.

But they did nothing about the cars when they were out on the track. By incorporating an ingenious hydraulic suspension system, Brabham allowed their car to sink towards the track surface while travelling at speed. Then, on return at slow speed to the pits, the car would rise to the mandatory six centimetres.

Gordon Murray, the Brabham designer, was at least subtle about his rule bending. As the season progressed, rivals resorted to the simpler expedient of installing a driver-operated switch which raised and lowered the car at will. Thus, when measured in the pits, the cars were perfectly legal. But as they flashed past on the track, they plainly were not. It was a total farce. And the most ludicrous aspect was that the cars were cornering just as quickly as before.

It was a messy start to a messy season. During the first half Williams won three races and Brabham two, but the turbo Ferraris and Renaults were beginning to show their strength. Having said that, Villeneuve's victories in Monaco and Spain could be attributed to virtuoso skill in a Ferrari which was a nothing more than a crude device with a considerable amount of unmanageable horsepower.

However, victory in France for Alain Prost's Renault (his first Grand Prix win) was a more accurate barometer of the swing towards turbos. But, as far the British media were concerned, the French Grand Prix had a more immediate significance.

John Watson, now at the wheel of a McLaren which featured a beautifully crafted chassis made from carbon fibre composites, had finished a strong second. The Ulsterman was seized upon as the Great White Hope for the British Grand Prix two weeks later at Silverstone. It was to be a memorable weekend for 'Wattie,' although it got off to a bad start.

The reluctant hero

First of all, someone broke into his Golf GTi and, while he dealt with that, Watson also had to cope with the pressure associated with being 'Top Brit.' Then, once practice got under way, he found the McLaren-Cosworth was not exactly to his liking. A perfectionist in these matters, Watson described the car as having nothing in particular wrong with it – but it wasn't quite right, either. And, to cap it all, when he arrived by helicopter on race morning, an official didn't recognise Watson and stubbornly refused to let the only UK driver in the Grand Prix through gate. John didn't feel he should have to part with the £9 necessary to gain admission and the matter was eventually resolved. It could only be plain sailing from there on in. Watson takes up the story.

'The Renaults were on the front row; I was sharing row three with my team-mate, Andrea de Cesaris. In between were Piquet in the Brabham and the Ferrari of Pironi. The significant thing was that I was over a second and a half slower than Arnoux on pole, so I didn't hold out any great hopes – which is more than I can say for the media.

'The British Grand Prix always meant extra pressure – not from the race itself, but because I was racing at home, so to speak. And, at that particular race, there was more attention being focused on me than I was accustomed to. I had finished third in the Spanish Grand Prix and then second in France and I had sort of jokingly said 'Three-Two-One' – you know me; always one for the quick, off-the-cuff remark!

'I tended to prefer a more laid-back, low profile approach but that just wasn't possible in 1981 and it was something I wasn't so well-equipped to deal with. But once you get into the car, all your problems tend to disappear.

'Villeneuve, who was sharing the row behind me with Alan Jones, made an incredible start and shot past. By the end of the first lap, he was third, behind Prost and Pironi. I was down in seventh place, just behind Jones.'

Another side-effect of the need to run the cars as close to the ground as possible had been the advent of stiffly sprung suspension systems. That made the cars nervous and very difficult to drive – as Villeneuve was about to demonstrate.

Coming through the Woodcote chicane at the end of lap four, Gilles clipped a kerb which launched the Ferrari briefly. Then the rock-hard suspension took over and literally bounced the Ferrari broadside and right across the exit from the narrow chicane. The air was thick with tyre-smoke and Jones had no alternative but to plough into the catch-fencing on the outside of the track. Watson was next.

'My immediate reaction was that it meant the end of my race. All I could see was blue smoke and somewhere in that smoke were two cars, but I didn't know where. And I knew Andrea was right on my tail and I didn't know what he would do next. All I could do was slow down. But, fortunately, I was far enough behind to see a little of what was happening and maybe that prevented me from getting too involved. Andrea, as I said, was right behind me and he could see nothing. He just went straight into the fencing on my left. But, then, Andrea would, I suppose....

'I didn't go right into the smoke. I managed to stop. In fact, the engine stalled and I remembered to switch the pump on before dropping the clutch. The engine picked up – and off I went, down in tenth place.

'The car was working very nicely indeed now and I was able to line people up, plan my moves and pass them quite easily; it really was very satisfying. I just kept going as quickly as I could, and before I knew it I was third behind the Renaults. Then Prost went out with engine trouble after 17 laps – but Arnoux was still 25 seconds ahead and he looked like staying there.

'Then I could see the gap to the Renault was shrinking and I realised Arnoux must be in some sort of trouble. It was at that stage – about 15 laps to go – that I realised I might win, something I hadn't really expected. Piquet had crashed at Becketts, Reutemann was no problem, I had passed him easily. Alan Jones would have been a bigger problem but then he had got involved with Villeneuve.

'I could sense the excitement in the crowd. You could see a flutter which seemed to grow the closer I got to Arnoux. Then I could see the Renault, he was in turbo trouble, and I took the lead with eight laps to go.

'But then I remembered the last lap at Dijon 1977. I told me myself "okay, it's there, but don't pre-empt anything. Wait until the flag falls and then you can enjoy it."'

There can have been no more popular victory at Silverstone as McLaren number seven crossed the line for the 68th and final time. Even the grizzled members of the press, watching from

John Watson
Received a rapturous welcome when he won the 1981 British Grand Prix, a reception which demonstrated the high regard in which the modest Ulsterman was held. Won five Grands Prix but never fully capitalised on a graceful and fluent style at the wheel.

the Dunlop Tower, stood and cheered. James Hunt's victory had been aggressive, angry, almost tribal in its execution and reception. A win for old 'Wattie' was....nice. As for the man himself, he gingerly raised his hand – as if in disbelief.

'When I took the flag, I was totally embarrassed. Doing my lap of honour, I simply didn't understand it because the spectators were behaving in a very un-British manner. There was an incredible free flow of emotion all the way round the track and I kept wondering what I had done to deserve this. I didn't feel I had done anything over and above what I had done in previous races and yet here was this spontaneous display. I didn't know how to cope with it; I almost wanted to go away and hide. Here were 100,000 people, screaming themselves hoarse – for *me*. I'd never experienced euphoria like that in the UK before. Quite incredible.'

After that, the remainder of the season was an anticlimax for Watson – and everyone else, come to that. After Silverstone, where he finished second, Carlos Reutemann held a 17-point lead in the championship. Somehow, the occasionally brilliant Argentinian managed to fritter it away. He allowed Nelson Piquet to back into the title amid the tinsel of an appropriately artificial track in a car park in Las Vegas. That final race of the season was dominated by Alan Jones and it was the perfect way for the tough Australian to sign off from Formula 1 for the time being.

Losing sight of the objective

Jones didn't miss much at the beginning of what was to be a bewildering season in 1982. Political and personal wrangling would stretch the fabric of Grand Prix racing almost to breaking point. Boycotts and bitterness would leave their mark. And it started to go wrong before a car had turned a wheel in anger.

The drivers, angry over the terms imposed by a new FISA-inspired super-licence, locked themselves in a Johannesburg hotel room and refused to come out. Compromise was reached and the South African Grand Prix took place, but only after a day had been lost.

In Brazil, the first two finishers were disqualified over the exploitation of another loophole concerning the topping up of liquids in the car once the race had finished. Ferrari and Renault accused the British teams of cheating by running their cars under the minimum weight limit in the race and then putting matters right with this topping up process. FISA decided to make such a practice illegal, and that led to a boycott, by most of the British teams, of the San Marino Grand Prix at Imola.

Only 14 cars took part, among them the Ferraris of the Gilles Villeneuve and Didier Pironi. They had the race to themselves and Pironi won. Villeneuve was incensed. He said he had been duped by his team-mate and he swore never to speak to the Frenchman again.

He never did. Two weeks later, the brilliant French-Canadian was dead. The accident, during the final moments of practice for the Belgian Grand Prix, was the result of Gilles's iron determination to beat his team-mate and the need to keep the throttle floored while using the sticky qualifying tyres. Back off, and your chance was gone; the tyres would not be good enough for another quick lap. Villeneuve had come across a car motoring slowly in the middle of the track. In that split instant of decision making, both drivers had moved to the right.

This tragedy should have pulled politicians up short; placed their petulance and bickering in a different light. It did anything but. Gilles knew the risks, they said. The dice which he threw with such tingling virtuosity had not rolled his way for once.

At Monaco, we had a farce in three acts as successive leaders in the last two laps either crashed or stopped and the eventual winner – Riccardo Patrese – having spun, took victory without knowing it. On a new street circuit in Detroit, the reigning world champion failed to qualify – but won in Montreal seven days later where a terrible accident on the start-line claimed the life of an Italian novice.

And so it went on. By the time the British Grand Prix arrived, confusion and tension reigned. There had been nine championship races and six different winners. Among them, Andreas Nikolaus Lauda, riding the crest of an astonishing comeback.

Niki Lauda had quit motor racing on the first day of practice for the 1979 Canadian Grand Prix. He decided he didn't like it any more and walked out. Just like that. He even left his overalls and helmet on the pit counter.

For the next 18 months or so, Lauda concentrated on building up his airline. Then he visited the 1981 Austrian Grand Prix and was intrigued by the new generation of ground effect cars. Here was the sort of challenge he relished. Was it possible for a driver to make a comeback?

The only irritation for Lauda was the fact that his team-mate, John Watson, had won two races and, by the time they reached Brands Hatch for the British Grand Prix, the Ulsterman was leading the championship with 30 points. Lauda, in seventh place, had half that number. And Brands Hatch had never been kind to Lauda – witness the shambles in 1974, the nine points won in a court room in 1976 and the fumbled moment when he lost the lead in 1978. Fortunately, Niki Lauda had no time for superstition. A driver, he always maintained, makes his luck and, from time to time, he can make everything can come right. He had one of those days on 18 July 1982.

Trouble at the start of the 1982 British Grand Prix. René Arnoux's Renault tangles with Riccardo Patrese's Brabham whilst John Watson takes avoiding action in his McLaren.

Little Keke

Williams had signed Keke Rosberg, a cocky little Finn who smoked like a train and drove like the wind. He was always good value, both in the car and out. Laid-back was hardly the word. He would end a bubbling conversation by crushing a cigarette under the heel of his driving boot, strolling to his car and, within a few minutes, driving as though his life depended on it – or not, as it sometimes seemed. Practice for the British Grand Prix was a case in point.

The turbo ranks had been swollen during the previous 12 months by the arrival of BMW power for Brabham, and a Hart four-cylinder engine in the back of a car built by Toleman, the 1980 Formula 2 champions. The season thus far, however, had seen the pole positions divided up by Ferrari and Renault, the only exception being a startling performance by de Cesaris in a V12 Alfa Romeo at Long Beach.

The Ford-Cosworth, used by the likes of Williams, McLaren, Lotus and Tyrrell, had more or less been rendered obsolete in the face of the high turbo boost prevalent during practice. But mere horsepower was not enough on a driver's circuit such as Brands Hatch, and Keke Rosberg put his Williams on pole with a thrillingly aggressive performance. Lauda, meanwhile, was on row three.

Things began to go the Austrian's way when Rosberg's engine refused to start for the final parade lap. In the heat of the afternoon, fuel had begun to vaporise, and by the time a watering can had been rushed to the grid, the rest of the field had started the parade lap. Rosberg had no option but to adhere to the rules and start from the back of the grid.

Then, another stroke of luck for Lauda. Patrese, on the outside of the front row, stalled his Brabham-BMW. Arnoux, placed immediately behind the Italian, tangled with the Brabham and put both cars out. Lauda immediately found himself in second place behind Nelson Piquet. This was better than he could have hoped for.

Piquet began to pull away by about a second a lap. But there was something funny going on here. Before the start, the Brabham team had been seen furtively arranging unfamiliar equipment in their pit. The mechanics were dressed in flame-proof suits, pressurised barrels of fuel were in evidence while the cars themselves had been fitted with quick-lift jacks and modified inlets to the fuel tanks. Ovens to heat tyres had been produced overnight and a day-glo orange and white line had been drawn on the pit lane to guide the cars to a precise spot in front of the Brabham pit. It didn't need Einstein to work out that the intention was to start the Brabhams with a light load of fuel, allow them to build up a comfortable lead and then bring them in for fresh tyres and enough fuel to see them through to the end of the race.

There was nothing in the regulations which said refuelling was illegal. The question was, would the advantage gained on the track be ruled out by nervous hands during the pit stop. As Piquet pulled inexorably away, the first phase seemed to be working satisfactorily. But we never did get the answer to the key question. After just nine laps, Piquet was out with a broken pulley on the fuel metering unit. And Niki Lauda was in the lead.

The Flying Pig

The only excitement after that surrounded the progress of a young Englishman, Derek Warwick, at the wheel of the ungainly Toleman-Hart. Until this moment, the Toleman had lived up to its nick-name, 'The Flying Pig'; a car which required a lot of effort to drive but gave very little reward in return. Steady development work, however, had been sufficient to put Warwick on the eighth row of the grid and he quickly went to work on a circuit he knew intimately.

With Watson having spun out of the race while avoiding someone else's accident, the capacity crowd turned their attention to Warwick as he worked his way into the top six, the turbo power paying dividends against the Williams and Lotus Cosworths. But when Warwick reached third place, it seemed he had more than met his match as he closed on the turbo Ferrari of Pironi.

The Frenchman would be much more difficult to pass but undaunted by such minor details Warwick made a very fast exit from Clearways at the end of lap 25 and drew alongside the Ferrari as they approached Paddock Hill Bend. In full view of the grandstands lining the main straight, Warwick calmly held his ground under braking and took second place. Such an achievement for the Toleman was unheard of – and the ecstatic reception from the crowd reflected that. Lauda was 25 seconds in front. Could Warwick catch him too?

Lauda, surprised to see the name Warwick on his pit board, went just fast enough to keep the Toleman at arm's length. Then, on lap 41, the potential threat disappeared as Warwick's fine drive ended with a broken drive-shaft. With 40 seconds in hand over Pironi, Lauda eased off and finally took the victory in the British Grand Prix which had been owing to him for eight years.

Pironi looked set to take the championship but this crazy season had a further shock in store. During practice for the German Grand Prix, Pironi crashed heavily and suffered leg injuries severe enough to keep him out of racing for good. The race was won by Patrick Tambay, a Frenchman drawn from certain obscurity by Ferrari as the replacement for Villeneuve. And, for good measure, Nelson Piquet indulged in fisticuffs with a another competitor who had dared to want the same piece of track as the reigning world champion. As so it went on.

By the time the season had finished, there had been 11 different winners, no less than five of them scoring nine points for the first time. Keke Rosberg was declared world champion even though he scored but one victory, the Swiss Grand Prix – which was held in France! It had been that sort of year.

And, at the end of it, everyone saw sense. Problems were resolved, quarrels patched over, agreement reached over the technical regulations. The family was no longer at war.

CHAPTER 18

KINDLY LEAVE THE STAGE

Thoroughly fenced off

The correspondence columns were unanimous. Spectators who had parted with £6 for a Paddock Pass at the 1983 British Grand Prix had been comprehensively ripped off. There was universal condemnation of the sudden appearance of high fencing which drew an impersonal line between the insular world of the Formula 1 performers and those who paid to watch them.

This, however, was merely in keeping with the isolation policy favoured at all circuits by Bernie Ecclestone and FOCA. Silverstone had been told to put up and shut up. Besides, Ecclestone had a ready-made excuse. With refuelling, as pioneered by Ecclestone's Brabham team, now an essential part of the game, safety in the paddock and pits was paramount.

It was difficult to argue with that. The spectators had to go. And, of course, when refuelling was banned at the end of 1983, the fences remained. But whatever FOCA's motivation may have been, the heart had been cut right out of the Silverstone paddock. It was now an austere place; a location for business and commerce. And, perhaps fittingly, the 1983 Marlboro British Grand Prix was just as boring.

Discussing the rules which had come into force in 1983 was like talking about the latest fashion from Paris; skirts were out and flat bottoms were in. The final ban on side-skirts and the call for cars to have flat bottoms had been a relatively straightforward way to kill off ground effect. But designers and aerodynamicists, always searching for a technical advantage, would soon find other ways of regaining the lost downforce.

In the meantime, the new regulations had brought a return to cars which were more comfortable to drive. And the most heartening aspect was the fact that rule change had been accepted with equanimity and good grace by all concerned. Now there was another cause for concern – turbocharged engines.

There had been seven turbocharged cars on the grid at the final race of 1982; a year later there would be seventeen. The deeply entrenched attitudes of the British teams had finally caved in to the realisation that turbos were a necessary evil. And, predictably, Colin Chapman had been one of the first to make the move by reaching an agreement with Renault. That had been in

'Wattie' supporter waits for a glimpse of his hero outside the newly erected paddock fencing.

August 1982. Four months later, he died of a heart attack at the age of 54.

Lotus were devastated but Peter Warr quickly rallied the team together and continued production of the first Lotus-Renault, the 93T. It was a disastrous car. In June, Lotus hired Gerard Ducarouge (formerly with Ligier and Alfa Romeo) and commissioned him to design a new car in double-quick time. A pair of Lotus 94Ts were ready for Elio de Angelis and Nigel Mansell to drive in the British Grand Prix. But it was a close-run thing.

Mansell's car had not been completed until the day before practice began, and from the outset the Lotus was plagued by electrical problems. The mechanics spent the next night changing the engine and the ancillary components. They finished at 6am and Mansell, who was sleeping with his family in a caravan at the circuit, was roused from his bed. Other campers received an unexpected early-morning call as Mansell roared up and down the length of the paddock. Everything seemed to be in order, but when practice began, one lap at racing speeds confirmed that the electrical misfire was, in fact, still present.

By a process of elimination, the wiring loom was seen to be the culprit and a new one was placed on order. A small electrical company at Diss, in Norfolk, began working through the night, Mansell having been forced to qualify the unloved 93T in 18th place. De Angelis's new car, meanwhile, had not missed a beat and he was on the second row, alongside the Renault of Alain Prost.

On the front row, the Ferraris of René Arnoux and Patrick Tambay as the Italian team lined up to start their 354th Grand Prix. Further back, a small British team were about to make their début and the most significant aspect was not the car but the engine which powered it. Stefan Johansson of Sweden had qualified a Spirit-Honda in the middle of the grid. The turbocharged V6 engine would only last for five laps but this was to be the thin end of a very large and powerful wedge.

A lap too few

Early on Saturday, the wiring loom was completed and rushed to Silverstone in time to be fitted to Mansell's car for the warm-up. The engine ran perfectly. It was the first time Mansell had been able to drive the car in anger. Prost, meanwhile, was working out his strategy.

The Ferraris were running on Goodyears; the Renault on Michelins. Prost figured that if he was to have any chance of defeating the Ferraris then he would need to attack the red cars immediately and force Arnoux and Tambay to push their tyres to the limit. His Michelin tyres were up to the job; the Goodyears, he felt sure, were not.

And so it proved. Tambay shot into the lead followed by his team-mate, with Prost snapping at their heels. It was not long before the Goodyears began to lose grip, the Ferraris sliding more and more with each passing lap. One by one, Prost picked them off. By lap 20, the Renault was in the lead.

And Mansell was seventh! In a startling turnaround in fortune, de Angelis had got as far as lap two when a sudden belch of flame from the back of the Lotus announced his retirement. Mansell had gained eight places in the first lap but his progress was suddenly limited when a balance weight flew off a front wheel and upset the handling of the Lotus. The man with the Union Jack helmet persevered until his pit stop, where the change of tyres transformed the car and he continued his rapid progress through the field.

Indeed, the only thing which could alter the outcome of this race now was a fumbled pit stop by the Renault team as they dealt with Prost. The Frenchman duly made his stop just after half-distance and, while he was in the pits, Piquet took the lead in his Brabham-BMW. The Brazilian had yet to make his stop, of course, but there was the outside chance that if the Brabham team acted swiftly, he could mount a late challenge. The Brabham mechanics were efficient as ever, but due to an unusual lapse by the team management no one thought to inform their driver of the gap to the leader. Assuming it was a lost cause – which was far from the case – Piquet reduced his pace and concentrated on finishing second.

By Silverstone standards the reception accorded to Prost was muted as he crossed the line, the cheering and applause being reserved for Nigel Mansell as he stormed home in fourth place. Victory for Prost meant that the Renault driver was the first Frenchman to win the British Grand Prix since Robert Benoist at Brooklands in 1927. Mansell's great day had yet to come.

Prost's more immediate concern had been becoming the first Frenchman to win the world championship. Despite the fact that Prost led Piquet by six points after Silverstone, Renault would allow BMW to make impressive progress with their four-cylinder turbo. By the time the final showdown came in South Africa, Prost had no answer to Piquet's power advantage.

A large contingent of French sports writers were present at Kyalami to see Prost lose and, almost to a man, they pilloried him for it. Renault were more or less seen as the innocent party. But then they had picked up the tab for the trip. Shortly afterwards, Renault showed Prost the door. Marlboro and McLaren were waiting with open arms.

In a similar opportunist move, John Webb of Brands Hatch had seized the chance to run a Grand Prix the previous Autumn even though the British round of the championship had been allocated to Silverstone. The cancellation of the proposed New York Grand Prix gave Webb and the RAC Motor Sports Association the opportunity to lobby FISA for the revival of the *Grand Prix d'Europe* title, thus allowing Britain to side-step the regulations which prevented each country from holding more than one Grand Prix. (Imola had managed it in 1981 by holding a Grand Prix on behalf of San Marino, a tiny republic a few miles down the road, while Monza continued to host the Italian Grand Prix.)

There seemed no valid reason why Brands Hatch could not run the race. After all, they had more than proved themselves by being voted the best Grand Prix of 1982 as well as winning the *Prix Orange* for the most efficient press service that year. Another £400,000 had been spent on the circuit, and for the 1982 Grand Prix the number of grandstands had risen to seventeen, providing seating for 18,000 of the 110,000 crowd.

Small wonder that Brands Hatch won immediate approval to run the 1983 *Grand Prix d'Europe* even though they had the almost impossible task of arranging it all in ten weeks. It was an unqualified success and, to add the final touch, the September sun shone throughout and Nigel Mansell finished third behind Piquet's Brabham and Prost's Renault. After that, holding the 1984 British Grand Prix on schedule would be a doddle.

Nelson Piquet
Struck a brilliant rapport with Brabham and won the world championship with the British team in 1981 and 1983 before moving to Williams to earn his third title in 1987. Never won the British Grand Prix but claimed a victory in the Grand Prix d'Europe at Brands Hatch. Failed to maintain winning form after moving to Lotus in 1988.

More miles for your money

Whatever Marlboro and McLaren had paid for Prost, it was a snip. During 1984, the Frenchman would prove just how his latent talent had been squandered by Renault. And Ron Dennis, the McLaren boss, would demonstrate his qualities as a shrewd politician, organiser and motivator.

Right from the start, Dennis had seen the need to put together the right 'package'; in other words, two top drivers, the best chassis and the most powerful and efficient engine. He already had the excellent carbon fibre chassis; Prost joining Niki Lauda answered the question of driver strength, and as for a suitable engine, he had the solution there too.

Dennis had gone to Porsche and commissioned the German company to build a turbocharged engine. There were no strings attached. Dennis, through his business partnership with TAG (*Techniques d'Avant Garde* – a Saudi-connected corporation) would pay for the engines and they would be called TAG Turbos. Porsche would simply design and build them; there was no question of Porsche returning to Grand Prix racing.

It was a clever move because, in return, Dennis had exclusive use of engines developed by a company whose experience in sportscar racing had taught them a great deal about fuel efficiency. And that had become an increasingly important trend in 1983-84.

In 1983, fuel capacity had been limited to 250 litres – not a problem since refuelling had been allowed. But in 1984, the capacity had been reduced to 220 litres and refuelling banned. Fuel management became the primary area of development – and in simple terms, Porsche gave McLaren an engine which would run faster than any other and still have fuel to spare at the end of the race. Brabham and BMW would provide the main competition, but, in the end, the 1984 season was all about a fascinating struggle between Niki Lauda and Alain Prost. And they would dominate the John Player Special British Grand Prix.

Brands Hatch? Very nice...

When the teams assembled at Brands Hatch, Prost led Lauda by 10½ points (an unsual figure due to half points being awarded for a rain-shortened Monaco Grand Prix won by Prost). Lauda, having made an uncharacteristic error during the previous race at Dallas, Texas, knew that he had to restore the balance at this critical stage – round ten in a sixteen-race series – in the season.

Of more immediate concern, though, was Nelson Piquet in the Brabham. BMW had begun to produce engines built specially for qualifying. With up to 1000bhp available under his right foot, the Brazilian had taken pole position at four of the previous races, and he did it again at Brands Hatch. Prost was next, with Lauda a few tenths of a second slower.

The race was immediately a battle between these three, with Piquet leading for eleven laps. It had become apparent to the Brazilian, however, that he had made an incorrect choice of tyres and he dived into the pits for a replacement set. Luck was on his side.

Jonathan Palmer, driving a difficult and unwieldy RAM-Hart, crashed at Clearways. The young Englishman was unhurt but the car was deemed to be in a dangerous position. The race was stopped at the end of lap twelve. The rules stated that the drivers should take the restart in the order in which they had finished the eleventh lap. This meant Piquet was able to line up on pole position!

Prost snatched the lead this time and Lauda quickly dealt with Piquet (now running harder tyres) and moved onto the Frenchman's tail. This was the confrontation everyone had been waiting for – who was the better, Lauda or Prost? The answer to that question would have to wait. On lap 27, Prost lost third gear...then fourth... then fifth. A gearbox bearing had failed; the Frenchman was out.

Piquet gave chase but Lauda had the race under control. In any case, the Brabham–BMW began to suffer from fluctuating turbo boost and, in the closing stages, Derek Warwick moved his Renault into second place, followed by a young Brazilian of outrageous talent driving a Toleman-Hart. By finishing third Ayrton Senna made his second visit to the victory rostrum (he had taken second place at Monaco) in this, his first season of Formula 1. It was a routine he would become very familiar with in years to come.

For Lauda, the nine points meant he had closed the gap on Prost. All told, it had been a good weekend for the Austrian.

'I had my problems with Brands Hatch over the years,' he recalls, 'but I always liked racing in England. When you won there, it was always a fantastic feeling. I don't know why it was – maybe something to do with the fact that the British Grand Prix is a famous race. You know, motor racing was more or less established in England, so therefore this was a good race.

'Anyway, I liked Brands Hatch very much, particularly when I was young and didn't care about the risks! For the driver, that circuit was always a big challenge and I had always been quick at that place for some reason. But there was no question that it was dangerous, particularly when the turbos had so much power.

'But the really amazing thing for me about racing in Britain was the crowd. The people were always very nice, very polite. If you were under pressure during the weekend, they knew the right way to approach you and not just eat you up like in other countries I could mention. This was what I liked. They were very knowledgeable and they had the right....respect. British Grand Prix – a good race, no question. Always well organised. Except for 1974....'

Ten years on from that débâcle and Niki Lauda was about to win the championship for a third time. In a fight which went all the way to the last lap of the last race in Portugal, 'The Rat' claimed the title – by half a point. And the irony was that Prost had equalled Jim Clark's record by winning seven races in a season. Lauda had won five. But he had won the championship through sheer graft, guile and experience. Lauda was the first to recognise that Prost was the quicker of the two but somehow it was fitting that the Austrian's great comeback should end this way. Prost's day would come and, fittingly, it would come at Brands Hatch.

160 mph!

Having established a precedent in 1983, John Webb laid a valid claim to running Britain's second Grand Prix in 1985. His wish was granted and the October date also held the possibility of settling the outcome of the championship. And, as things would turn out, the official British Grand Prix at Silverstone would provide an adequate pointer to the way the title would run.

Until that day in July, the championship had been difficult to predict. McLaren were the first to admit that twelve wins in 1984 would be a hard act to follow and so it proved as Ferrari and Lotus-Renault provided the main competition. Michele Alboreto had won the Canadian Grand Prix for Ferrari while Ayrton Senna, who had moved to Lotus, scored his maiden victory in the rain in Portugal. But such was the varied nature of the 1985 season that Senna's team-mate, Elio de Angelis, was in serious contention for the title thanks to being declared the winner at Imola (after Prost had been excluded on a technicality) and finishing in the points everywhere else.

As the teams arrived at Silverstone, Prost held joint second place in the series with de Angelis, the pair of them five points behind Alboreto. None of these drivers, however, would provide the story of practice.

During the previous eighteen months, the Williams team had been learning to cope with the brutally powerful Honda turbo V6 and their latest car, the FW10, went a long way towards making the combination competitive. Williams had signed Nigel Mansell for 1985 and, thus far, the Englishman had shown very encouraging form when compared with his extrovert team-mate, Keke Rosberg. But Saturday 20 July would be Keke's day.

The first day of practice on the Friday had almost been washed out. Proceedings had been delayed by the late arrival of the medical air-support, the helicopter being unable to land due to the low cloud swirling around the Northamptonshire circuit. The morning was lost and official practice was a rushed affair, run on a damp but drying track later in the afternoon. It was evident that grid positions would be determined the following day – provided it remained dry.

In fact, the weather fluctuated from showers to bursts of sunshine but the all-important hour of qualifying started dry. Then after 20 minutes dark clouds rolled in. Rosberg rushed out of the pits on his first of two sets of qualifying tyres. Rain was beginning to fall as he reached Woodcote but neither the potentially greasy track nor a slowly deflating front tyre would prevent the Finn from completing the lap in 1 minute 5.967 seconds, the first time any driver had reached the 160mph average at Silverstone.

Fresh winds soon dispersed the clouds and the racing line dried very quickly. With nine minutes remaining, Piquet took his Brabham-BMW round in 1:6.249 and, not long after, Senna recorded 1:6.794. Clearly Rosberg's pole position was under threat.

Once again it was time to stub out the cigarette and reach for the crash helmet. There were five minutes left. In a stunning display of speed, reflexes and car control, Rosberg lapped the still-damp 2.932-mile track in 65.591 seconds. The crowd were on the their feet as the Williams returned to the pits. After that, the race would be an anticlimax for Rosberg.

Prost takes his turn

A misfire on an engine installed for the race meant Rosberg had to make a last-minute switch to his spare car but that did not prevent him from giving chase to Senna as the Lotus made an excellent start from the second row of the grid. These two pulled away from the rest.

Prost, starting from the second row, had made a comparatively poor getaway and it took the Frenchman until lap ten to move into third place and catch the leaders. At this point, Rosberg began to ease off since he felt his tyres would not last at such a pace. Within two laps Prost had moved into second place and he set about reducing the gap to Senna.

The closest he got was a couple of car lengths, and each time Prost looked remotely threatening Senna was capable of pulling away with apparent ease. And he was also clever enough to use the back-markers to good effect by overtaking them on the approach to a corner and putting further daylight between the Lotus and the McLaren as Prost waited his chance to pass the slower cars. Then it started to go wrong for Senna.

As he passed the pits at the end of lap 50, the Renault V6 sounded flat. Then it cleared itself – only for the misfire to return eight laps later. By now Prost was looking for a way through and the McLaren snatched the lead.

Then the Renault cleared itself once more and Senna attacked immediately, the two cars running nose-to-tail. As they rushed towards Becketts, the leaders came across Lauda's McLaren as the world champion, lying in a distant third place, slowed suddenly with engine trouble and inadvertently held up his team-mate in the process.

It was all Senna needed, the Lotus drawing alongside Prost's McLaren and regaining the lead on the run towards Stowe. He held it for almost a lap. Then the engine faltered once more. And this time there would be no remission, the Lotus coasting to halt on the pit straight, right under the noses of the shocked Lotus team.

Subsequent examination would show that a wire running from the heat sensor on the right-hand exhaust had broken. As a result, the electronic engine management system had tried to compensate and the fuel injection had caused the right-hand bank of the V6 to run rich. The Lotus had simply run out of fuel.

All of which left Prost with a clear lead since Lauda, Rosberg and Mansell had retired. Alboreto, having played no significant part in the weekend, found himself in a fortunate second place. In the end, Prost had lapped the entire field. Small wonder, then, that the man with the chequered flag

Alain Prost
Regarded by many as one of the all-time great drivers, possessing a perfect mixture of outright speed, temperament and tactics. Won the British Grand Prix for Renault in 1983 but achieved his greatest success with McLaren, winning the championship in 1985 and 1986.

became confused and waved it a lap early. Prost completed another lap, just to make sure of the nine points.

Alboreto's place helped him maintain his position at the head of the table – as did a win at the revised Nürburgring two weeks later. After that, however, Prost really got into his stride by winning in Austria, Holland and Italy. Fourth place in the European Grand Prix at Brands Hatch was good enough to bring him the title he clearly deserved.

Mansell makes it

Prost's rather subdued drive that day had been swept aside by stunning performances from the Williams-Hondas and Senna in the Lotus-Renault. Senna had led for the first half-dozen laps or so with Rosberg pushing him hard. Rosberg would claim later that Senna had been less than fair in his blocking tactics. An almost desperate lunge inside the Lotus at Surtees saw Rosberg losing control as Senna resolutely refused to give way. The Finn spun, and took the hapless Piquet with him.

The contact between the Brabham and the Williams resulted in Rosberg limping into the pits with a punctured tyre. He rejoined just as Senna, now pursued by Mansell, was passing the pits. Rosberg vented his frustration by taking his time over moving out of Senna's path and, in the resulting confusion, Mansell shot into the lead, with Senna giving chase.

For the next 66 laps, Mansell would not put a foot wrong and he won his first Grand Prix amid scenes of great emotion. The Englishman's career, for so long dogged with controversy over his ability, was about to take off in the biggest possible way.

Proving that Brands Hatch had been no fluke, Mansell went on to Kyalami and won the South African Grand Prix. Then Rosberg rounded off the season for Williams and Honda by winning the first Formula 1 race to held on the streets of Adelaide in Australia. It was a memorable Grand Prix, thanks to the unstinting efforts of the organisers – and in 1986 the Australians would be rewarded with a most dramatic climax to the championship.

The three wins in succession for Williams at the end of 1985 had automatically made the team favourites for the following season even though Rosberg had left to join McLaren in place of Lauda, who had retired for the second and final time. Williams, meanwhile, had signed Nelson Piquet.

The season got off to a terrible start for the team from Didcot when Frank Williams was severely paralysed as the result of a road accident. Fortunately for Frank, he had surrounded himself with excellent people and the team barely broke its stride on the race track.

Piquet won in Brazil; Mansell in Belgium, Canada and France. On the surface, it looked good. Underneath, the growing tension between the two drivers was threatening to seriously undermine the team's championship momentum. Brands Hatch would be the scene of a dramatic confrontation as Piquet claimed pole position with Mansell joining him on the front row.

Within 15 seconds of the start, it was all over. A drive-shaft coupling failed as Mansell snatched second gear. Motoring disconsolately up the hill towards Druids, Mansell radioed the bad news to his pit. They replied with good news. The race had been stopped.

Behind Mansell, there was chaos. As the mid-field had rushed into Paddock Hill Bend, they had been confronted by Thierry Bousten's Arrows-BMW, broadside in the middle of the road. Seven cars collided. Worse still, Jacques Laffite had been forced off the track and the Frenchman, having just started his 176th Grand Prix to jointly hold the record with Graham Hill, suffered serious leg and pelvic injuries when his Ligier rammed the crash barrier.

Unlike the confusion which had surrounded a similar stoppage in 1976, the situation was quite clear. The rules had been clarified and the race would start from scratch. There was no doubt that Mansell could use the team's spare car, but the fact that it had been set-up for Piquet did not bode well for the Englishman. But he was prepared to give it a go. The estimated 120,000 spectators, not to mention the man himself, breathed a sigh of relief.

Since he was relatively unfamiliar with this car, having only driven it briefly on the first day of practice, Mansell made a circumspect start and finished the opening lap in third place behind Piquet and the Benetton-BMW of Gerhard Berger. He remained there for two laps and then, with an impressive burst of speed, overtook the Benetton and set after his team-mate.

On lap 20, Mansell recorded the fastest lap of the race thus far and closed right up on Piquet. Three laps later, the Brazilian missed a gear as he accelerated out of Surtees. It was the error Mansell had been waiting for. The spectator enclosures erupted when he appeared at Clearways in the lead. The next phase of this in-house battle would be the scheduled pit stops for fresh tyres.

Piquet came in first. The stop took a scant 9.04 seconds. Two laps later, at the end of lap 32,

Mansell made his stop. It took half a second longer.

As Mansell booted the Williams-Honda out of the pits, Piquet was rushing towards him along Brabham Straight. Mansell's tyres had been pre-heated – put Piquet's were at working temperature and he knew he had to make the most of that fact before Mansell got into the groove once again.

Piquet attempted to move alongside as they approached Surtees but Mansell refused to be budged. They ran nose to tail for the rest of that lap and, at the end of it, Mansell employed a legitimate blocking tactic as they sped towards Paddock. It kept Piquet at bay but Mansell, holding the tighter line, had left himself open to attack on the run up the hill to Druids. Piquet wisely took the conventional line through Paddock, made the faster exit and lined himself up to take the lead.

The move would have paid off – except that Alessandro Nannini, dutifully staying on the right-hand side of the track in order to let the leaders through, was in the way! Piquet had no alternative but to back off and tuck in behind Mansell who, by now, had his tyres working perfectly. That was the last challenge Piquet would be allowed to make.

For the remaining 43 laps, the pace was unrelenting. First Piquet would establish a new lap record, then Mansell would improve on it. The gap was never more than a couple of seconds. On lap 68, Piquet made one last effort. Mansell responded instantly with another lap record. With four laps to go, Piquet realised Mansell had the measure of him.

For the second time in nine months, the entire assembly within the Brands Hatch bowl stood and cheered Nigel Mansell home. Mansell wrote in his book *Driven to Win*:

> *'I could sense the euphoria in the car. I was carried home by waves of cheering fans. The previous year at Brands had been very special, and yet this one surpassed it. It was such a hard race. I'd never had to drive at that speed so consistently. I hadn't had a fluid bottle (there had been no time to fit the drink supply to the spare car) and I was worn out at the end. I didn't feel too steady at the top of the podium, but I knew where I was all right – I was on top of the world.'*

He led Alain Prost by four points. Piquet was fourth, fourteen points behind Mansell.

Then Piquet won three races to move into second place, five points behind Mansell, but Nigel redressed the balance by winning in Portugal. He threw away an opportunity to clinch the title in Mexico when he failed to put the car in gear at the start. The pressure was mounting. With one race, the Australian, to go, Mansell still led, but Prost and Piquet were within striking distance.

With 50 miles to go, it seemed certain Mansell would take the title. Piquet was leading but second place would be good enough for the Englishman. Then Mansell's rear tyre exploded as he sped along the back straight at 180 mph. Fighting the car all the way, he brought the Williams to a halt, his race and championship wrecked. Piquet was called into the pits for a precautionary tyre change – and Alain Prost motored serenely by to win the race and become the first driver since Jack Brabham to win the title in successive years.

As Mansell made his weary way from the paddock at the end of a gruelling season, the elation of Brands Hatch seemed to be from a different age. But eight months later at Silverstone it would be obvious that he had put the bitter disappointment of Adelaide behind him.

Brands axed

The mood at the press conference in the Grovewood Suite at Brands Hatch had been buoyant. It was May 1986, and John Webb was delighted to announce that John Foulston, a motor racing enthusiast and a wealthy man thanks to his success in the computer business, had just bought Brands Hatch, Oulton Park and Snetterton from Eagle Star Holdings (the parent company of Grovewood Securities) for £5.25 million. The future of motor sport at these circuits was therefore secure, and the British Grand Prix would continue to be the financial cornerstone.

A week later, FOCA announced that they had signed a deal with Silverstone to run the British Grand Prix for five years. Brands Hatch had effectively been closed out. Mansell's momentous win in July 1986 was to be the last such event for some time.

One day in the future, the *real* reason for such an unpopular decision may be made apparent. Certainly, the excuse that continuity for Silverstone in the light of their three-year programme of expenditure was seen as a lame one in view of the willingness by Brands Hatch to do likewise. In any case, the Shell Oils British Grand Prix had been scheduled for the Northamptonshire circuit on 12 July regardless of this shock news and the teams simply got on with the business of sorting out the 1987 championship.

Goodbye Brands? Nigel Mansell and Alain Prost wait for practice to begin during the 1986 British Grand Prix meeting. With the 5-year agreement to run subsequent Grand Prix at Silverstone it seems unlikely that Formula One cars will ever return to the much-loved Kentish circuit.

The enemy within

The championship points table as the race approached showed Ayrton Senna leading Alain Prost by one point, with Nigel Mansell and Nelson Piquet third and fourth respectively. But everyone knew that this season so far had belonged to the Williams drivers since, overall, their cars were vastly superior to the Prost's McLaren-TAG and Senna's Lotus-Honda. True, Senna had used the computer-controlled 'active' suspension on his car to good effect on the bumpy streets of Monaco and Detroit, and Prost had used his experience and skill to win in Brazil and Belgium. But the Williams drivers had always been in contention. Now, as the summer reached its height, they were at war with themselves as well as the competition.

Mansell had thrashed Piquet the previous week in the French Grand Prix when he had simply out-driven the Brazilian. Stung by comments that he was past it and should retire, Piquet took the unusual step of holding a press conference to refute such speculation. And, as a casual aside, he happened to mention that he had won two world championships whereas Mansell had lost one. True – but it hurt. Piquet would pay dearly for such a remark later in the weekend.

When it came to the final qualifying session, Mansell and Piquet drove like maniacs as the Brazilian fought to retain his pole position and Mansell did everything in his power to take it away from him. In the end, Mansell spun at the entrance to a dog-leg left, a new corner introduced to contain speeds through Woodcote. Round one to Piquet.

Making the most of his pole position, Piquet held off Mansell as they rushed towards Copse on the first lap. Neither driver seemed to care that Alain Prost had out-accelerated them both and on the run through Becketts and down to Stowe, the Williams drivers would brush the McLaren aside as if it were a minor irritation, which, in a manner of speaking, it was. From here on in, the British Grand Prix would be dominated by Nigel Mansell and Nelson Piquet.

As they pulled away from the rest of the field, Mansell remained no more than three car lengths behind his rival. There seemed to be very little in it until lap 13, when Mansell began to drop back; a balance weight had become detached from the front-left wheel of his car and the resulting vibration was giving him cause for concern.

Goodyear had advised Williams that one set of tyres should last the distance but Mansell, his vision occasionally blurred by the vibration, realised he would have no alternative but to make a pit stop.

He came in at the end of lap 35 and, in 9.5 seconds, the Williams team had changed all four tyres and sent him on his way – still in second place. Stopwatches clicked all round the circuit. The gap to Piquet was 28 seconds. There were 29 laps remaining. That seemed to be that. Game, set and match to Nelson Piquet.

Then Mansell went round in 1 minute 11.968 seconds, half a second quicker than anything he had managed before. Making full use of the fresh tyres, he reeled off three or four laps at this speed. Piquet responded with a 1: 11.913 and a 1: 11.934 in quick succession.

The team, meanwhile, had examined Mansell's discarded tyres and it was clear that they would have lasted the distance but for the balance weight problem. The message was duly relayed to Piquet, thus ridding the Brazilian of any fears that he might have to stop. In any case, in the space of eight laps, Mansell had only pulled back five seconds. There was nothing for Piquet to worry about.

But Mansell had his head down now. With 12 laps to go, he was really thrashing his car and lapping consistently in the 1 minute 9 seconds region. Then, inexplicably, Piquet's tyres suddenly began to lose grip. The gap had narrowed to 11.6 seconds. There was no need for a stopwatch now; the crowd could see it for themselves.

Sniffing blood, Mansell went quicker still. With ten laps remaining, the gap was 7.6 seconds. At this rate of going; Mansell would catch Piquet before the finish.

At the end of the next lap, they were 6.5 seconds apart. Fastest lap of the race to Mansell brought the deficit down to 3.9 seconds. Then 2.0 seconds, 1.4 seconds and, starting lap 63, 0.8 seconds. The only thing which would stop Mansell now was the effect his unbelievable pace may have had on the car's fuel consumption. With each turbocharged car restricted to 195 litres, Mansell's fuel read-out on the dashboard was registering a big zero.

What the hell. No time to worry about that. Just keep going. In any case, he was too busy working out how to pass Piquet.

Mansell tailed him through Chapel Curve. Running down Hangar Straight, Piquet stayed on the right, thus blocking any attempt Mansell might make to overtake on the inside going into Stowe.

Then Mansell darted to the left and, unbelievably, Piquet did likewise. It was the oldest trick in the book and Nelson had bought the dummy. No sooner he had moved left than Mansell, hard on the power, swooped right and went for the inside line under braking, for Stowe. And all of this was conducted at around 180 mph.

Piquet made a desperate attempt to cut him off; they almost touched. But Mansell was through. Two and a half laps to go. Would Mansell's fuel last? Going through Copse Corner at the start of the last lap, the Honda hesitated – and then picked up again. He completed the last lap safely and the reaction of the crowd is not difficult to imagine. It had been a truly memorable charge by the Englishman.

On the slowing down lap, Mansell's Williams ran out of fuel at Club Corner. The car was immediately engulfed as spectators flocked onto the track. It took an aptly named Rescue Vehicle to scoop Mansell from the midst of his admirers and take him to the victory podium.

Once he had received his trophy, Mansell mounted the back of a Police motor bike for a lap of honour. When they reached the braking area for Stowe Corner, Mansell dismounted and kissed the piece of track where he had won the British Grand Prix. It had been a demon move alright; a

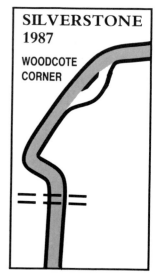

SILVERSTONE 1987

WOODCOTE CORNER

1987: The new dog-leg left after the bridge slowed the cars sufficiently to allow the original Woodcote corner – minus the chicane – to be brought back into use.

Nigel Mansell
Winner of the British Grand Prix in 1986 and 1987, each victory being a typical example of the Englishman's capacity for stunning performances. A questionable career with Lotus blossomed when he joined Williams in 1985. Twice runner-up in the championship before joining Ferrari in 1989.

highlight of his career.

But motor racing can bite back. Four months later, on a tricky piece of the Suzuka track, Mansell would kiss his championship chances goodbye by crashing and injuring his back during practice for the Japanese Grand Prix. Nelson Piquet would have the last laugh as he became world champion at that very moment while standing idle in the pits.

A matter of honour

The repercussions of the 1987 British Grand Prix would be far-reaching. Piquet, as number one driver – at least in name – felt that the team should have protected him from Mansell's advances by ordering the Englishman to hold station. On the political front, Piquet was preferred by Honda over Mansell and it is likely that the Japanese company were not impressed by the team's decision to allow their drivers to race each other at Silverstone. True, Honda had achieved their victory but, given the highly charged atmosphere between the two drivers, that race could have ended in tears and Honda could have come away with nothing.

Whatever their feelings, Honda announced two months later that they were parting company with Williams at the end of 1987 despite there being one year of the contract remaining. Both sides said the split had been amicable. Few people believed it. And those who did said the arrival of a compensatory bag of yen at Didcot had helped to heal the wounds. Like the Brands Hatch/Silverstone affair, the truth may one day be known.

For 1988, Williams would switch to a normally aspirated Judd engine. Honda would remain with Lotus and, more important, they would substitute McLaren for Williams. This had been the result of another shrewd move by Ron Dennis.

The McLaren Managing Director had been quick to realise that the Formula 1 tempo was changing. It was no longer good enough to pay for a research and development programme such as the one they were about to terminate with Porsche. The time had come for a high degree of commitment from a major manufacturer and the subsequent long term technical development.

Honda answered these requirements perfectly, and proof of that would be their attitude towards racing in 1988. This would be the last year of the turbocharged engine; they would be banned at the end of the season. But rather than wind down their development with the turbo, Honda accelerated it. In 1988, they would completely wipe the floor with the opposition and rewrite the record books – with a little help from the two best drivers around.

As a final touch to his 'package', Ron Dennis had persuaded Ayrton Senna to join Alain Prost. It was a brilliant move, one which would ensure maximum effort from both drivers throughout the season. Ironically, the one exception would be the British Grand Prix.

Wet, wet, wet

Honda Marlboro McLaren had won every race up until 10 July, 1988, but Prost led Senna by 15 points. Ayrton, however, was gradually recovering from an embarrassing set-back when he threw away nine points by crashing during the closing stages of the Monaco Grand Prix. But overall, the McLaren monopoly was becoming tedious in the extreme.

Small wonder that there was rejoicing in the press room when the Ferraris of Gerhard Berger and Michele Alboreto set the fastest times during practice. But they were under no illusions; the Ferraris had been well suited to the fast corners but everyone realised that the McLarens, on the second row, were suffering from minor handling problems. Besides, the fuel economy enjoyed by Honda (the fuel capacity had been reduced further to 150 litres) meant that they would dominate the Grand Prix – as usual. No one reckoned on the British weather intervening to produce one of the most dramatic races of the season.

It rained on race day – for the first time since Aintree in 1961. On that occasion, Ferrari had walked away with the race but the men in the red cars did not hold out much hope of repeating that result 27 years later. Even so, Gerhard Berger was intent on having some fun rather than driving cautiously with one eye on the fuel consumption read-out.

The Austrian powered off the line to take the lead and he held it despite Senna's attempts to relieve him of the place during the first lap. Seeing that Berger was not about to give up easily, Senna eased off and maintained second place, safe in the knowledge that the Ferrari could not make its fuel last if Berger continued at such a break-neck pace. Besides, Senna had noted that his teammate and rival was nowhere to be seen.

Prost had never made any secret of his dislike of racing in the wet. It was not the rain which

Ayrton Senna
Single-minded and totally dedicated to finishing first. Generally regarded as the fastest driver of his generation, victory in the 1988 British Grand Prix helping the Brazilian take his first world title and create a record of eight wins in a season.

bothered him but the patches of standing water which could pitch a car in any direction without warning. And he had not helped matters by making a poor start and becoming engulfed in the swirling ball of spray kicked up by the mid-field.

At the end of the first lap he was 11th. And it got worse from there on. After 25 laps struggling along with the back-markers, Prost called it a day and pulled in to the pits. The handling of the car had been unpredictable and he didn't feel it was worth the risk. And his decision was probably prompted in part by an embarrassing moment when he almost collided with his team-mate while being lapped.

In fact, Senna had just used a moment's hesitation by Berger as they approached Prost to wrong-foot the Austrian and take the lead. Now it was all over bar the shouting. But at least the bedraggled crowd had something to cheer thanks to their old friend Nigel Mansell.

It had been a wretched season thus far for the Englishman. True, he no longer had the benefit of Honda power but the Williams team had also been experimenting with a computer controlled 'reactive' suspension. It was fine when it worked efficiently but, according to Mansell, that was not often. Problems had been caused by airlocks developing within the hydraulic struts, prompting the car to develop a mind of its own. Three times it did this during practice on the Friday. Enough was enough. A decision was taken to convert the car overnight to a conventional suspension, and during final qualifying Mansell had taken one second off his time. There seemed little hope of the winner of the previous three Grands Prix in England repeating the dose in 1988.

Nigel Mansell was one of the few people pleased to see the rain on race day since he reckoned it would favour the drivers rather than the technical contribution made by their cars.

Passing four cars on the first lap, he began lap two in seventh place. Moving up the leader board in tow with the Benetton-Ford of Alessandro Nannini, Mansell passed the Italian to take fourth place on lap 20. Ahead were the two Ferraris with Senna, of course, leading comfortably. Mansell overtook Alboreto, but Nannini was attacking again, the Benetton passing Mansell before a moment's inattention in the treacherous conditions saw the Italian spin off without harm for the second time. Mansell was third once more.

Berger, having had his fun, was now paying close attention to his fuel read-out and his pace had dropped noticeably. On lap 50, with 15 to go, Mansell took second place knowing there was nothing he could do about Senna unless the Brazilian made a mistake. And there was little chance of that, the champion-elect driving with his now familiar blend of brilliance and skill in truly appalling conditions.

By the time the race finished, the rain had stopped and Mansell's performance had gladdened the hearts of the spectators. Mansell, his flagging morale boosted by this performance, was also able to draw some consolation from the fact that he had recently signed a contract with Ferrari.

It was exactly thirty years since a Ferrari driven by an Englishman had won the British Grand Prix at Silverstone. And, three decades or so before that, an Englishman had finished second in the very first British Grand Prix at Brooklands. The fact that Malcolm Campbell's Bugatti was nearly ten minutes behind the winner is neither here nor there. It was the status associated with finishing such a prestigious event which mattered and, in that respect, the British Grand Prix had gone from strength to strength during the intervening sixty-two years. It is a classic of its kind.

The 1988 British Grand Prix was the first rain-affected race since Aintree in 1961. At the start the Ferraris of Gerhard Berger (left) and Michele Alboreto lead into Copse, but Aryton Senna (right) was soon to display his supreme skills in the wet to win his first British Grand Prix.

227

BRITISH GRAND PRIX RESULTS

1926 · 7 August · British Grand Prix
Brooklands · 2.616 miles · 110 laps

Results

1	R. Senechal/ L. Wagner	*Delage*	4h 00m 56s	(71.61 mph)
2	M. Campbell	*Bugatti*	4h 10m 44s	
3	R. Benoist/ A. Dubonnet	*Delage*	4h 18m 08s	

Fastest lap:

H. Segrave	*Talbot*	85.99 mph

1927 . 1 October · British Grand Prix
Brooklands · 2.616 miles · 125 laps

Results

1	R. Benoist	*Delage*	3h 49m 14s	(85.59 mph)
2	E. Boulier	*Delage*	3h 49m 21s	
3	A. Divo	*Delage*	3h 52m 20s	
4	L. Chiron	*Bugatti*		

Fastest lap:
Not given

1937 · 1 October · Donington Grand Prix · Donington Park · 3.125 miles · 80 laps

Starting grid

⬆ von Brauchitsch
(Mercedes-Benz)
2m 09.4s

Rosemeyer
(Auto Union)
2m 11.4s

Lang
(Mercedes-Benz)
2m 11.2s

Seaman
(Mercedes-Benz)
2m 11.2s

Muller
(Auto Union)
2m 15.2s

Caracciola
(Mercedes-Benz)
2m 15.2 s

Hasse
(Auto Union)
2m 16.0s

'Bira'
(Maserati)
2m 25.0s

Mays
(ERA)
2m 26.8s

Howe
(ERA)
2m 26.8s

Hanson
(Maserati)
2m 27.4s

Dobson
(ERA)
2m 28.6s

Martin
(ERA)
2m 31.6s

Whitehead
(ERA)
2m 32.0s

Maclure
(Riley)
2m 35.2s

Results

1	B. Rosemeyer Auto Union	3h 01m 02s	(82.86 mph)
2	M. von Brauchitsch Mercedes-Benz	3h 01m 40s	
3	R. Caracciola Mercedes-Benz	3h 02m 18s	
4	H.P. Muller Auto Union	3h 04m 50s	
5	R. Hasse Auto Union	3h 09m 50s	
6	'Bira' Maserati	78 laps	

Fastest lap: Rosemeyer and von Brauchitsch 2m 11.4s (85.62 mph)

1938 · 22 October · Donington Grand Prix · Donington Park · 3.125 miles · 80 laps

Starting grid

⬆ Lang
(Mercedes-Benz)
2m 11.0s

Nuvolari
(Auto Union)
2m 11.2s

von Brauchitsch
(Mercedes-Benz)
2m 11.4s

Seaman
(Mercedes-Benz)
2m 12.2s

Muller
(Auto Union)
2m 12.6s

Baumer
(Mercedes-Benz)
2m 13.8 s

Hasse
(Auto Union)
2m 15.4s

Kautz
(Auto Union)
2m 18.6s

Villoresi
(Maserati)
2m 21.0s

Dobson
(ERA)
2m 24.6s

Dreyfus
(Delahaye)
2m 25.4s

Connell
(ERA)

Cotton
(ERA)

Cuddon-Fletcher
(MG)

Maclure
(Riley)

Hanson
(Alta)

'Raph'
(Delahaye)

Results

1	T. Nuvolari Auto Union	3h 06m 22s	(80.49 mph)
2	H. Lang Mercedes-Benz	3h 08m 00s	
3	R. Seaman Mercedes-Benz	79 laps	
4	H.P. Muller Auto Union	79 laps	
5	M. von Brauchitsch Mercedes-Benz	79 laps	
6	A. Dobson ERA	74 laps	

Fastest lap: Nuvolari 2m 14.4s (83.71 mph)

1948 · 2 October · RAC Grand Prix · Silverstone · 3.67 miles · 65 laps

Starting grid

Johnson *(ERA)* 2m 58.6s	Gerard *(ERA)* 2m 58.2s	Etancelin *(Lago-Talbot)* 2m 58.0s	De Graffenried *(Maserati)* 2m 57.0s	Chiron ⬱ *(Lago-Talbot)* 2m 56.0s
	Rolt *(Alta)* 3m 00.2s	Walker *(ERA)* 2m 59.8s	Parnell *(Maserati)* 2m 59.8s	'Bira' *(Maserati)* 2m 58.6s
Richardson *(ERA)*	Bolster *(ERA)*	Rosier *(Lago-Talbot)*	Comotti *(Lago-Talbot)*	Harrison *(ERA)*
	Hamilton *(Maserati)*	Mays *(ERA)*	Watson *(Alta)*	Ansell *(ERA)*
Gilbey *(Maserati)*	Salvadori *(Maserati)*	Ansell *(Maserati)*	Nixon *(ERA)*	Hampshire *(ERA)*
		Ascari *(Maserati)*	Villoresi *(Maserati)*	

Results

1	L. Villoresi	Maserati	3h 18m 03s	(72.28 mph)
2	A. Ascari	Maserati	3h 18m 17s	
3	R. Gerard	ERA	3h 20m 06s	
4	L. Rosier	Lago-Talbot	3h 22m 38s	
5	'Bira'	Maserati	64 laps	
6	Bolster	ERA	63 laps	

Fastest lap: Villoresi 2m 52s (77.73 mph)

1949 · 14 May · British Grand Prix · Silverstone · 3 miles · 100 laps

Starting grid

Gerard *(ERA)* 2m 14.4s	De Graffenried *(Maserati)* 2m 13.6s	Walker *(ERA)* 2m 13.2s	'Bira' *(Maserati)* 2m 10.2s	Villoresi ⬱ *(Maserati)* 2m 09.8s
	Harrison *(ERA)* 2m 16.4s	Etancelin *(Lago-Talbot)* 2m 15.8s	Rolt *(Alfa-Aitken)* 2m 15.8s	Parnell *(Maserati)* 2m 14.8s
Whitehead *(Ferrari)* 2m 18.4s	Ansell *(ERA)* 2m 18.0s	Abecassis *(Alta)* 2m 17.6s	Cabantous *(Lago-Talbot)* 2m 17.4s	Hampshire *(ERA)* 2m 17.2s
	Claes *(Lago-Talbot)* 2m 32.2s	Ashmore *(Maserati)* 2m 20.8s	Bolster *(ERA)* 2m 20.0s	Chiron *(Lago-Talbot)* 2m 19.2s
Salvadori *(Maserati)* 2m 29.2s	Hamilton *(Maserati)* 2m 29.0s	Baring *(Maserati)* 2m 27.0s	Rosier *(Lago-Talbot)* 2m 25.2s	Mays *(Thinwall-Ferrari)* 2m 24.6s
		Murray *(Maserati)* 2m 30.4s	Nixon *(ERA)* 2m 29.8s	

Results

1	E. De Graffenried	Maserati	3h 52m 50.2s	(77.31 mph)
2	R. Gerard	ERA	3h 53m 55.4s	
3	L. Rosier	Lago-Talbot	99 laps	
4	D. Hampshire/W. Cotton	ERA	99 laps	
5	P. Etancelin	Lago-Talbot	97 laps	
6	F. Ashmore	Maserati	97 laps	

Fastest lap: 'Bira' 2m 11s (82.44 mph)

1950 · 13 · May Grand Prix d'Europe
Silverstone · 2.889miles · 70 laps

Starting grid

Parnell	**Fangio**	**Fagioli**	**Farina** ⬦
(Alfa Romeo)	(Alfa Romeo)	(Alfa Romeo)	(Alfa Romeo)
1m 52.2s	1m 51.0s	1m 51.0s	1m 50.8s

	Martin	Cabantous	'Bira'
	(Lago-Talbot)	(Lago-Talbot)	(Maserati)

Chiron	Walker	Rosier	De Graffenried
(Maserati)	(ERA)	(Lago-Talbot)	(Maserati)

	Etancelin	Gerard	Johnson
	(Lago-Talbot)	(ERA)	(ERA)

Murray	Crossley	Hampshire	Harrison
(Maserati)	(Alta)	(Maserati)	(ERA)

	Claes	Fry	Kelly
	(Lago-Talbot)	(Maserati)	(Alta)

Results

1	G. Farina Alfa Romeo	2h 13m 23.6s	(90.95 mph)
2	L. Fagioli Alfa Romeo	2h 13m 26.2s	
3	R. Parnell Alfa Romeo	2h 14m 15.6s	
4	Y. Giraud-Cabantous Lago-Talbot	68 laps	
5	L. Rosier Lago-Talbot	68 laps	
6	R. Gerard ERA	67 laps	

Fastest lap: Farina
1m 50.6s (94.02 mph)

1951 · 14 July · RAC British Grand Prix
Silverstone · 2.889miles · 90 laps

Starting grid

Ascari	**Farina**	**Fangio**	**Gonzalez** ⬦
(Ferrari)	(Alfa Romeo)	(Alfa Romeo)	(Ferrari)
1m 45.4s	1m 45.0s	1m 44.4s	1m 43.4s

	Bonetto	Sanesi	Villoresi
	(Alfa Romeo)	(Alfa Romeo)	(Ferrari)
	1m 52.0s	1m 50.2s	1m 45.8s

Hamilton	Gerard	Rosier	Whitehead
(Lago-Talbot)	(ERA)	(Lago-Talbot)	(Thinwall Ferrari)
1m 57.2s	1m 57.0s	1m 56.0s	1m 54.6s

	Claes	Chiron	Shawe-Taylor
	(Lago-Talbot)	(Lago-Talbot)	(ERA)
	2m 05.8s	2m 00.2s	1m 58.2s

Kelly	James	Fotheringham-Parker	Murray
(Alta)	(Maserati)	(Maserati)	(Maserati)

	Parnell	Walker	
	(BRM)	(BRM)	

Results

1	J.F Gonzalez Ferrari	2h 42m 18.2s	(96.11 mph)
2	J.M. Fangio Alfa Romeo	2h 43m 09.2s	
3	L. Villoresi Ferrari	88 laps	
4	F. Bonetto Alfa Romeo	87 laps	
5	R. Parnell BRM	85 laps	
6	C. Sanesi Alfa Romeo	84 laps	

Fastest lap: Farina
1m 44.0s (99.99 mph)

1952 · 19 July · RAC British Grand Prix
Silverstone · 2.926 miles · 85 laps

Starting grid

Manzon (Gordini) 1m 55s	Taruffi (Ferrari) 1m 53s	Ascari (Ferrari) 1m 50s	Farina ⬩ (Ferrari) 1m 50s

Hawthorn (Cooper-Bristol) 1m 56s	Parnell (Cooper-Bristol) 1m 56s	Downing (Connaught) 1m 56s

Hamilton (HWM) 1m 57s	'Bira' (Gordini) 1m 57s	Thompson (Connaught) 1m 57s	Poore (Connaught) 1m 56s

Collins (HWM) 1m 58s	Brown (Cooper-Bristol) 1m 58s	G. Whitehead (Alta) 1m 58s

Brandon (Cooper-Bristol) 2m 00s	McAlpine (Connaught) 2m 00s	Moss (ERA) 1m 59s	Fischer (Ferrari) 1m 58s

Trintignant (Gordini) 2m 00s	P. Whitehead (Ferrari) 2m 00s	Salvadori (Ferrari) 2m 00s

Crook (Frazer Nash) 2m 03s	Hirt (Ferrari) 2m 03s	Claes (Gordini) 2m 02s	Murray (Cooper-Bristol) 2m 02s

Bianco (Maserati) 2m 07s	Cantoni (Maserati) 2m 06s	Gaze (HWM) 2m 05s

Schell (Maserati) No time	De Graffenried (Maserati) No time	Aston (Aston-Butterworth) 3m 28s	Macklin (HWM) 2m 08s

Results

1	A. Ascari Ferrari	2h 44m 11s (90.92 mph)
2	P. Taruffi Ferrari	84 laps
3	M. Hawthorn Cooper-Bristol	83 laps
4	D. Poore Connaught	83 laps
5	E. Thompson Connaught	82 laps
6	G. Farina Ferrari	82 laps

Fastest lap: Ascari 1m 52s (94.08 mph)

1953 · 18 July · RAC British Grand Prix
Silverstone · 2.926 miles · 90 laps

Starting grid

Fangio (Maserati) 1m 50s	Hawthorn (Ferrari) 1m 49s	Gonzalez (Maserati) 1m 49s	Ascari ⬩ (Ferrari) 1m 48s

Marimon (Maserati) 1m 51s	Villoresi (Ferrari) 1m 51s	Farina (Ferrari) 1m 50s

Wharton (Cooper-Bristol) 1m 54s	Rolt (Connaught) 1m 54s	Schell (Gordini) 1m 52s	Trintignant (Gordini) 1m 52s

Whitehead (Cooper-Alta) 1m 57s	McAlpine (Connaught) 1m 57s	Macklin (HWM) 1m 57s

Gerard (Cooper-Bristol) 2m 02s	Hamilton (HWM) 2m 02s	Bonetto (Maserati) 1m 58s	J. Stewart (Cooper-Bristol) 1m 58s

Brown (Cooper-Bristol) 2m 04s	I. Stewart (Connaught) 2m 04s	'Bira' (Connaught) 2m 04s

Crook (Cooper-Alta) 2m 07s	Rosier (Ferrari) 2m 07s	Collins (HWM) 2m 06s	Behra (Gordini) 2m 04s

Salvadori (Connaught)	Fairman (HWM) 2m 32s	De Graffenried (Maserati) 2m 09s

Results

1	A. Ascari Ferrari	2h 50m 00s (92.97 mph)
2	J.M. Fangio Maserati	2h 51m 00s
3	G. Farina Ferrari	2h 50m 12s
4	J.F. Gonzalez Maserati	88 laps
5	M. Hawthorn Ferrari	87 laps
6	F. Bonetto Maserati	82 laps

Fastest lap: Gonzalez and Ascari 1m 50s (95.79 mph)

1954 · 17 July · RAC British Grand Prix
Silverstone · 2.926 miles · 90 laps

Starting grid

Moss *(Maserati)* 1m 47s	Hawthorn *(Ferrari)* 1m 46s	Gonzalez *(Ferrari)* 1m 46s	Fangio ⬳ *(Mercedes-Benz)* 1m 45s

Salvadori *(Maserati)* 1m 48s	Kling *(Mercedes-Benz)* 1m 48s	Behra *(Gordini)* 1m 48s

Collins *(Vanwall Special)* 1m 50s	'Bira' *(Maserati)* 1m 49s	Wharton *(Maserati)* 1m 49s	Trintignant *(Ferrari)* 1m 48s

Parnell *(Ferrari)* 1m 52s	Bucci *(Gordini)* 1m 52s	Pilette *(Gordini)* 1m 51s

Gerard *(Cooper-Bristol)* 1m 55s	Beauman *(Connaught)* 1m 55s	Schell *(Maserati)* 1m 53s	Manzon *(Ferrari)* 1m 52s

Riseley-Prichard *(Connaught)* 1m 58s	Gould *(Cooper-Bristol)* 1m 56s	Whitehouse *(Connaught)* 1m 56s

Brandon *(Cooper-Bristol)* 2m 05s	Whitehead *(Cooper-Alta)* 2m 00s	Thorne *(Connaught)* 1m 59s	Marr *(Connaught)* 1m 58s

Marimon *(Maserati)* No time	Villoresi *(Maserati)* No time

Mieres *(Maserati)* No time	Ascari *(Maserati)* No time	Rosier *(Ferrari)* No time

Results

1	J.F. Gonzalez Ferrari	2h 56m 14s	(89.69 mph)
2	M. Hawthorn Ferrari	2h 57m 24s	
3	O. Marimon Maserati	89 laps	
4	J.M. Fangio Mercedes-Benz	89 laps	
5	M. Trintignant Ferrari	87 laps	
6	R. Mieres Maserati	87 laps	

Fastest lap: Gonzalez, Hawthorn, Moss, Ascari, Behra and Fangio 1m 50s (95.79 mph)

1955 · 16 July · RAC British Grand Prix
Aintree · 3 miles · 90 laps

Starting grid

⬳ Moss *(Mercedes-Benz)* 2m 00.4s	Fangio *(Mercedes-Benz)* 2m 00.6s	Behra *(Maserati)* 2m 01.4s

Kling *(Mercedes-Benz)* 2m 02.0s	Taruffi *(Mercedes-Benz)* 2m 03.0s

Mieres *(Maserati)* 2m 03.2s	Schell *(Vanwall)* 2m 03.8s	Simon *(Maserati)* 2m 04.0s

Musso *(Maserati)* 2m 04.2s	Castellotti *(Ferrari)* 2m 05.0s

Manzon *(Gordini)* 2m 05.0s	Hawthorn *(Ferrari)* 2m 05.4s	Trintignant *(Ferrari)* 2m 05.4s

Rolt *(Connaught)* 2m 06.6s	Wharton *(Vanwall)* 2m 08.4s

Macklin *(Maserati)* 2m 08.4s	McAlpine *(Connaught)* 2m 09.6s	Ramos *(Gordini)* 2m 10.6s

Marr *(Connaught)* 2m 11.6s	Salvadori *(Maserati)* 2m 11.6s

Gould *(Maserati)* 2m 11.8s	Sparken *(Gordini)* 2m 12.6s

Collins *(Maserati)* 2m 13.4s	Brabham *(Cooper-Bristol)* 2m 27.4s

Results

1	S. Moss Mercedes-Benz	3h 07m 21.2s (86.47 mph)
2	J.M. Fangio Mercedes-Benz	3h 07m 21.4s
3	K. Kling Mercedes-Benz	3h 08m 33.0s
4	P. Taruffi Mercedes-Benz	89 laps
5	L. Musso Maserati	89 laps
6	M. Hawthorn Ferrari	89 laps

Fastest lap: Moss 2m 00.4s (89.7 mph)

1956 · 14 July · RAC British Grand Prix
Silverstone · 2.926 miles · 101 laps

Starting grid

Collins
(Lancia-Ferrari)
1m 43s

Hawthorn
(BRM)
1m 43s

Fangio
(Lancia-Ferrari)
1m 42s

Moss ⬅
(Maserati)
1m 41s

Salvadori
(Maserati)
1m 44s

Gonzalez
(Vanwall)
1m 44s

Schell
(Vanwall)
1m 44s

Titterington
(Connaught)
1m 46s

Scott-Brown
(Connaught)
1m 45s

Brooks
(BRM)
1m 45s

Castellotti
(Lancia-Ferrari)
1m 44s

Gould
(Maserati)
1m 48s

Behra
(Maserati)
1m 47s

de Portago
(Lancia-Ferrari)
1m 47s

Manzon
(Gordini)
1m 49s

Flockhart
(BRM)
1m 49s

Trintignant
(Vanwall)
1m 49s

Perdisa
(Maserati)
1m 49s

Fairman
(Connaught)
1m 51s

Halford
(Maserati)
1m 51s

Villoresi
(Maserati)
1m 50s

Godia
(Maserati)
1m 55s

Maglioli
(Maserati)
1m 54s

Emery
(Emeryson-Alta)
1m 54s

Gerard
(Cooper-Bristol)
1m 53s

Brabham
(Maserati)
2m 01s

Rosier
(Maserati)
1m 59s

Ramos
(Gordini)
1m 56s

Results

1	J.M Fangio Lancia-Ferrari	2h 59m 47s	(98.65 mph)
2	Marquis A. de Portago/P. Collins Lancia-Ferrari	100 laps	
3	J. Behra Maserati	99 laps	
4	J. Fairman Connaught	98 laps	
5	H. Gould Maserati	97 laps	
6	L. Villoresi Maserati	96 laps	

Fastest lap: S. Moss 1m 43.2s (102.104 mph)

1957 20 July RAC British Grand Prix
Aintree · 3 miles · 90 laps

Starting grid

⬅ Moss
(Vanwall)
2m 00.2s

Behra
(Maserati)
2m 00.4s

Brooks
(Vanwall)
2m 00.4s

Fangio
(Maserati)
2m 00.6s

Hawthorn
(Lancia-Ferrari)
2m 01.2s

Lewis-Evans
(Vanwall)
2m 01.2s

Schell
(Maserati)
2m 01.4s

Collins
(Lancia-Ferrari)
2m 01.8s

Trintignant
(Lancia-Ferrari)
2m 03.2s

Musso
(Lancia-Ferrari)
2m 03.4s

Menditeguy
(Maserati)
2m 05.4s

Leston
(BRM)
2m 05.6s

Brabham
(Cooper-Climax)
2m 07.0s

Fairman
(BRM)
2m 08.6s

Salvadori
(Cooper-Climax)
2m 07.0s

Bonnier
(Maserati)
2m 12.6s

Gerard
(Cooper-Bristol)
2m 12.6s

Bueb
(Maserati)
3m 15.4s

Results

1	S. Moss/A. Brooks Vanwall	3h 06m 37.8s	(86.8 mph)
2	L. Musso Lancia-Ferrari	3h 07m 03.4s	
3	M. Hawthorn Lancia-Ferrari	3h 07m 20.6s	
4	M. Trintignant Lancia-Ferrari	88 laps	
5	R. Salvadori Cooper Climax	85 laps	
6	R. Gerard Cooper Bristol	82 laps	

Fastest lap: Moss 1m 59.2s (90.6 mph)

1958 · 19 July · RAC British Grand Prix
Silverstone · 2.926 miles · 75 laps

Starting grid

Hawthorn *(Ferrari)* 1m 40.4s	Salvadori *(Cooper-Climax)* 1m 40.0s	Schell *(BRM)* 1m 39.8s	Moss ⬆ *(Vanwall)* 1m 39.4s

Lewis-Evans *(Vanwall)* 1m 41.4s	Collins *(Ferrari)* 1m 40.6s	Allison *(Lotus-Climax)* 1m 40.4s

Von Trips *(Ferrari)* 1m 42.0s	Brabham *(Cooper-Climax)* 1m 42.0s	Brooks *(Vanwall)* 1m 41.6s	Behra *(BRM)* 1m 41.4s

Hill *(Lotus-Climax)* 1m 43.0s	Bonnier *(Maserati)* 1m 43.0s	Trintignant *(Cooper-Climax)* 1m 42.6s

Gerini *(Maserati)* 1m 53.0s	Bueb *(Connaught)* 1m 54.4s	Burgess *(Cooper-Climax)* 1m 45.4s	Shelby *(Maserati)* 1m 44.2s

Stacey *(Lotus-Climax)* 1m 58.8s	Fairman *(Connaught)* 1m 58.8s

Results

1	P. Collins Ferrari	2h 09m 04.2s	(102.05 mph)
2	M. Hawthorn Ferrari	2h 09m 28.4s	
3	R. Salvadori Cooper-Climax	2h 09m 54.8s	
4	S. Lewis-Evans Vanwall	2h 09m 55.0s	
5	H. Schell BRM	2h 10m 19.0s	
6	J. Brabham Cooper-Climax	2h 10m 27.4s	

Fastest lap: Hawthorn 1m 40.8s (104.5 mph)

1959 · 18 July · RAC British Grand Prix
Aintree · 3 miles · 75 laps

Starting grid

⬆ Brabham *(Cooper-Climax)* 1m 58.0s	Salvadori *(Aston Martin)* 1m 59.0s	Schell *(BRM)* 1m 59.2s

Trintignant *(Cooper-Climax)* 1m 59.2s	Gregory *(Cooper-Climax)* 1m 59.4s

Shelby *(Aston Martin)* 1m 59.6s	Moss *(BRM)* 1m 59.6s	McLaren *(Cooper-Climax)* 1m 59.6s

Hill *(Lotus-Climax)* 2m 00.0s	Bonnier *(BRM)* 2m 00.0s

Flockhart *(BRM)* 2m 00.2s	Stacey *(Lotus-Climax)* 2m 02.8s	Burgess *(Cooper-Maserati)* 2m 03.0s

Naylor *(JBW-Maserati)* 2m 03.0s	Fairman *(Cooper-Climax)* 2m 04.2s

Bristow *(Cooper-Borgward)* 2m 04.4s	Brooks *(Vanwall)* 2m 04.6s	Bueb *(Cooper-Borgward)* 2m 04.8s

Herrmann *(Cooper-Maserati)* 2m 05.6s	d'Orey *(Maserati)* 2m 05.6s

H. Taylor *(Cooper-Climax)* 2m 05.6s	Piper *(Lotus-Climax)* 2m 06.0s	Ashdown *(Cooper-Climax)* 2m 06.2s

M. Taylor *(Cooper-Climax)* 2m 07.0s

Results

1	J. Brabham Cooper-Climax	2h 30m 11.6s	(89.88 mph)
2	S. Moss BRM	2h 30m 33.8s	
3	B. McLaren Cooper-Climax	2h 30m 34.0s	
4	H. Schell BRM	74 laps	
5	M. Trintignant Cooper-Climax	74 laps	
6	R. Salvadori Aston Martin	74 laps	

Fastest lap: Moss and McLaren 1m 57.0s (92.31 mph)

1960 · 16 July · RAC British Grand Prix
Silverstone · 2.926 miles · 77 laps

Starting grid

Bonnier	McLaren	G. Hill	Brabham ⬦
(BRM)	(Cooper-Climax)	(BRM)	(Cooper-Climax)
1m 36.2s	1m 36.0s	1m 35.6s	1m 34.6s

von Trips	Gurney	Ireland
(Ferrari)	(BRM)	(Lotus-Climax)
1m 37.0s	1m 36.6s	1m 36.2s

Surtees	P. Hill	Brooks	Clark
(Lotus-Climax)	(Ferrari)	(Cooper-Climax)	(Lotus-Climax)
1m 38.6s	1m 37.8s	1m 37.6s	1m 37.0s

Gregory	Salvadori	Gendebien
(Cooper-Climax)	(Aston Martin)	(Cooper-Climax)
1m 39.8s	1m 39.4s	1m 39.2s

Naylor	Bianchi	Taylor	Fairman
(Cooper-Maserati)	(Cooper-Climax)	(Cooper-Climax)	(Cooper-Climax)
1m 41.2s	1m 40.2s	1m 40.0s	1m 39.8s

Trintignant	Burgess	Daigh
(Aston Martin)	(Cooper-Climax)	(Cooper-Climax)
1m 43.8s	1m 42.6s	1m 42.4s

Munaron	Piper	Greene
(Cooper-Ferrari)	(Lotus-Climax)	(Cooper-Maserati)
No time	2m 05.6s	1m 45.8s

Results

1	J. Brabham Cooper-Climax	2h 04m 24.6s	(108.69 mph)
2	J. Surtees Lotus-Climax	2h 05m 14.2s	
3	I. Ireland Lotus-Climax	2h 05m 54.2s	
4	B. McLaren Cooper-Climax	76 laps	
5	A. Brooks Cooper-Climax	76 laps	
6	Count W. von Trips Ferrari	75 laps	

Fastest lap: G. Hill 1m 34.4s (111.62 mph)

1961 · 15 July · RAC British Grand Prix
Aintree · 3 miles · 75 laps

Starting grid

⬦P. Hill	Ginther	Bonnier
(Ferrari)	(Ferrari)	(Porsche)
1m 58.8s	1m 58.8s	1m 58.8s

von Trips	Moss
(Ferrari)	(Lotus-Climax)
1m 58.8s	1m 59.0s

Brooks	Ireland	Clark
(BRM-Climax)	(Lotus-Climax)	(Lotus-Climax)
1m 59.0s	1m 59.2s	1m 59.2s

Brabham	Surtees
(Cooper-Climax)	(Cooper-Climax)
1m 59.4s	1m 59.6s

G. Hill	Gurney	Salvadori
(BRM-Climax)	(Porsche)	(Cooper-Climax)
2m 00.0s	2m 00.2s	2m 00.8s

McLaren	Lewis
(Cooper-Climax)	(Cooper-Climax)
2m 01.0s	2m 01.0s

Gregory	H. Taylor	De Beaufort
(Cooper-Climax)	(Lotus-Climax)	(Porsche)
2m 01.4s	2m 01.8s	2m 02.0s

Baghetti	Fairman
(Ferrari)	(Ferguson-Climax)
2m 02.0s	2m 03.4s

Bandini	Seidel	Greene
(Cooper-Maserati)	(Lotus-Climax)	(Gilby-Climax)
2m 03.6s	2m 04.2s	2m 06.0s

Maggs	Burgess
(Lotus-Climax)	(Lotus-Climax)
2m 06.4s	2m 06.6s

Ashmore	Marsh	Natili
(Lotus-Climax)	(Lotus-Climax)	(Cooper-Maserati)
2m 08.2s	2m 09.6s	2m 10.2s

Parnell	Bianchi
(Lotus-Climax)	(Lotus-Climax)
2m 16.8s	2m 18.8s

Results

1	Count W. von Trips Ferrari	2h 40m 53.6s	(83.91 mph)
2	P. Hill Ferrari	2h 41m 39.6s	
3	R. Ginther Ferrari	2h 41m 40.4s	
4	J. Brabham Cooper-Climax	2h 42m 02.2s	
5	J. Bonnier Porsche	2h 41m 09.8s	
6	R. Salvadori Cooper-Climax	2h 42m 19.8s	

Fastest lap: A. Brooks 1m 57.8s (91.68 mph)

1962 · 21 July · RAC British Grand Prix
Aintree · 3 miles · 75 laps

Starting grid

⌂ Clark
(Lotus-Climax)
1m 53.6s

Surtees
(Lola-Climax)
1m 54.2s

Ireland
(Lotus-Climax)
1m 54.4s

McLaren
(Cooper-Climax)
1m 54.6s

G. Hill
(BRM)
1m 54.6s

Gurney
(Porsche)
1m 54.8s

Bonnier
(Porsche)
1m 55.2s

Ginther
(BRM)
1m 55.2s

Brabham
(Lotus-Climax)
1m 55.4s

Taylor
(Lotus-Climax)
1m 56.0s

Salvadori
(Lola-Climax)
1m 56.2s

P. Hill
(Ferrari)
1m 56.2s

Maggs
(Cooper-Climax)
1m 57.0s

Gregory
(Lotus-Climax)
1m 57.2s

Lewis
(Cooper-Climax)
1m 59.4s

Burgess
(Cooper-Climax)
2m 00.6s

De Beaufort
(Porsche)
2m 01.4s

Shelly
(Lotus-Climax)
2m 02.4s

Settember
(Emeryson-Climax)
2m 02.4s

Chamberlain
(Lotus-Climax)
2m 03.4s

Seidel
(Lotus-BRM)
2m 11.6s

Results

1	J. Clark Lotus-Climax	2h 26m 20.8s	(92.25 mph)
2	J. Surtees Lola-Climax	2h 27m 10.0s	
3	B. McLaren Cooper-Climax	2h 28m 05.6s	
4	G. Hill BRM	2h 28m 17.6s	
5	J. Brabham Lotus-Climax	74 laps	
6	A. Maggs Cooper-Climax	74 laps	

Fastest lap: Clark 1m 55.0s (93.91 mph)

1963 · 20 July · RAC British Grand Prix
Silverstone · 2.926 miles · 82 laps

Starting grid

Brabham
(Brabham-Climax)
1m 35.0s

Hill
(BRM)
1m 34.8s

Gurney
(Brabham-Climax)
1m 34.6s

Clark ⌂
(Lotus-Climax)
1m 34.4s

Maggs
(Cooper-Climax)
1m 36.0s

McLaren
(Cooper-Climax)
1m 35.4s

Surtees
(Ferrari)
1m 35.2s

Ireland
(BRP-BRM)
1m 36.8s

Taylor
(Lotus-Climax)
1m 36.8s

Ginther
(BRM)
1m 36.0s

Bandini
(BRM)
1m 36.0s

Amon
(Lola-Climax)
1m 37.2s

Hall
(Lotus-BRM)
1m 37.0s

Bonnier
(Cooper-Climax)
1m 36.8s

Settember
(Scirocco-BRM)
1m 40.8s

Hailwood
(Lotus-Climax)
1m 39.8s

Anderson
(Lola-Climax)
1m 39.0s

Siffert
(Lotus-BRM)
1m 38.4s

De Beaufort
(Porsche)
1m 43.4s

Burgess
(Scirocco-BRM)
1m 42.6s

Raby
(Gilby-BRM)
1m 42.4s

Campbell-Jones
(Lola-Climax)
1m 48.8s

Gregory
(Lotus-BRM)
1m 44.2s

Results

1	J. Clark Lotus-Climax	2h 14m 09.6s	(107.75 mph)
2	J. Surtees Ferrari	2h 14m 35.4s	
3	G. Hill BRM	2h 14m 47.2s	
4	R. Ginther BRM	81 laps	
5	L. Bandini BRM	81 laps	
6	J. Hall Lotus-BRM	80 laps	

Fastest lap: Surtees 1m 36.0s (109.76 mph)

1964 · 11 July · Grand Prix d'Europe
Brands Hatch · 2.65 miles · 80 laps

Starting grid

Gurney	G. Hill	Clark △
(Brabham-Climax)	(BRM)	(Lotus-Climax)
1m 38.4s	1m 38.3s	1m 38.1s

Surtees	Brabham
(Ferrari)	(Brabham-Climax)
1m 38.7s	1m 38.5s

Bandini	Anderson	McLaren
(Ferrari)	(Brabham-Climax)	(Cooper-Climax)
1m 40.2s	1m 39.8s	1m 39.6s

Ireland	Bonnier
(BRP-BRM)	(Brabham-BRM)
1m 40.8s	1m 40.2s

Spence	Hailwood	Amon
(Lotus-Climax)	(Lotus-BRM)	(Lotus-BRM)
1m 41.4s	1m 41.4s	1m 41.2s

P. Hill	Ginther
(Cooper-Climax)	(BRM)
1m 42.6s	1m 41.6s

T. Taylor	Raby	Siffert
(Lotus-BRM)	(Brabham-BRM)	(Brabham-BRM)
1m 42.8s	1m 42.8s	1m 42.8s

J. Taylor	Gardner
(Cooper-Ford)	(Brabham-Ford)
1m 43.2s	1m 43.0s

Maggs	Revson	Baghetti
(BRM)	(Lotus-BRM)	(BRM)
1m 45.0s	1m 43.4s	1m 43.4s

Results

1	J. Clark Lotus-Climax	2h 15m 07.0s	(94.14 mph)
2	G. Hill BRM	2h 15m 09.8s	
3	J. Surtees Ferrari	2h 16m 27.6s	
4	J. Brabham Brabham-Climax	79 laps	
5	L. Bandini BRM	78 laps	
6	P. Hill Cooper-Climax	78 laps	

Fastest lap: Clark 1m 38.8s (96.56 mph)

1965 · 10 July · RAC British Grand Prix
Silverstone · 2.927 miles · 80 laps

Starting grid

Stewart	Ginther	Hill	Clark △
(BRM)	(Honda)	(BRM)	(Lotus-Climax)
1m 31.3s	1m 31.3s	1m 31.0s	1m 30.8s

Gurney	Spence	Surtees
(Brabham- Climax)	(Lotus-Climax)	(Ferrari)
1m 31.9s	1m 31.7s	1m 31.3s

McLaren	Hulme	Bandini	*Brabham
(Cooper-Climax)	(Brabham- Climax)	(Ferrari)	(Brabham- Climax)
1m 32.8s	1m 32.7s	1m 32.7s	1m 32.5s

Bonnier	Gardner	Rindt
(Brabham- Climax)	(Brabham-BRM)	(Cooper-Climax)
1m 33.5s	1m 33.4s	1m 32.9s

Siffert	Anderson	Attwood	Ireland
(Brabham-BRM)	(Brabham-Climax)	(Lotus-BRM)	(Lotus-BRM)
1m 34.2s	1m 34.1s	1m 33.8s	1m 33.6s

Rhodes	Raby	Gregory
(Cooper-Climax)	(Brabham-BRM)	(BRM)
1m 39.4s	1m 36.0s	1m 35.9s

*Handed his car over to Gurney just before the start.

Results

1	J. Clark Lotus-Climax	2h 05m 25.4s	(112.02 mph)
2	G. Hill BRM	2h 05m 28.6s	
3	J. Surtees Ferrari	2h 05m 53.6s	
4	M. Spence Lotus-Climax	2h 06m 05.0s	
5	J. Stewart BRM	2h 06m 40.0s	
6	D. Gurney Brabham-Climax	79 laps	

Fastest lap: Hill 1m 32.2s (114.29 mph)

1966 · 16 July · RAC British Grand Prix
Brands Hatch · 2.65 miles · 80 laps

Starting grid

Gurney
(Eagle-Climax)
1m 35.8s

Hulme
(Brabham-Repco)
1m 34.8s

Brabham △
(Brabham-Repco)
1m 34.5s

Clark
(Lotus-Climax)
1m 36.1s

Hill
(BRM)
1m 36.0s

Stewart
(BRM)
1m 36.9s

Rindt
(Cooper-Maserati)
1m 36.6s

Surtees
(Cooper-Maserati)
1m 36.4s

Anderson
(Brabham-Climax)
1m 37.5s

Spence
(Lotus-BRM)
1m 37.3s

McLaren
(McLaren-Serenissima)
1m 38.5s

Irwin
(Brabham-Climax)
1m 38.1s

Siffert
(Cooper-Maserati)
1m 38.0s

Bonnier
(Brabham-Climax)
1m 39.3s

Bondurant
(BRM)
1m 38.9s

T. Taylor
(Shannon-Climax)
1m 41.6s

Ligier
(Cooper-Maserati)
1m 41.4s

J. Taylor
(Brabham-BRM)
1m 40.0s

Arundell
(Lotus-BRM)
1m 54.3s

Lawrence
(Cooper-Ferrari)
1m 43.8s

Results

1	J. Brabham Brabham-Repco	2h 13m 13.4s	(95.48 mph)
2	D. Hulme Brabham-Repco	2h 13m 23.0s	
3	G. Hill BRM	79 laps	
4	J. Clark Lotus-Climax	79 laps	
5	J. Rindt Cooper-Maserati	79 laps	
6	B. McLaren McLaren- Serenissima	78 laps	

Fastest lap: Brabham 1m 37.0s (98.35 mph)

1967 · 15 July · RAC British Grand Prix
Silverstone · 2.927 miles · 80 laps

Starting grid

Hulme
(Brabham-Repco)
1m 26.3s

Brabham
(Brabham-Repco)
1m 26.2s

Hill
(Lotus-Ford)
1m 26.0s

Clark △
(Lotus-Ford)
1m 25.3s

Surtees
(Honda)
1m 27.2s

Amon
(Ferrari)
1m 26.9s

Gurney
(Eagle-Weslake)
1m 26.4s

Spence
(BRM)
1m 28.3s

McLaren
(Eagle-Weslake)
1m 28.1s

Rodriguez
(Cooper-Maserati)
1m 27.9s

Rindt
(Cooper-Maserati)
1m 27.4s

Hobbs
(BRM)
1m 30.1s

Irwin
(BRM)
1m 29.6s

Stewart
(BRM)
1m 28.7s

Siffert
(Cooper-Maserati)
1m 31.0s

Anderson
(Brabham-Climax)
1m 30.7s

Courage
(BRM)
1m 30.4s

Rees
(Cooper-Maserati)
1m 30.3s

Ligier
(Brabham-Repco)
1m 34.8s

Moser
(Cooper-ATS)
1m 32.9s

Bonnier
(Cooper-Maserati)
1m 32.0s

Results

1	J. Clark Lotus-Ford	1h 59m 25.6s	(117.64 mph)
2	D. Hulme Brabham-Repco	1h 59m 38.4s	
3	C. Amon Ferrari	1h 59m 42.2s	
4	J. Brabham Brabham-Repco	1h 59m 47.4s	
5	P. Rodriguez Cooper-Maserati	79 laps	
6	J. Surtees Honda	78 laps	

Fastest lap: Hulme 1m 27.0s (121.12 mph)

1968 · 20 July · RAC British Grand Prix
Brands Hatch · 2.65 miles · 80 laps

Starting grid

Amon
(Ferrari)
1m 29.5s

Oliver
(Lotus-Ford)
1m 29.4s

Hill ⬡
(Lotus-Ford)
1m 28.9s

Rindt
(Brabham-Repco)
1m 29.9s

Siffert
(Lotus-Ford)
1m 29.7s

Brabham
(Brabham-Repco)
1m 30.2s

Stewart
(Matra-Ford)
1m 30.0s

Gurney
(Eagle)
1m 30.0s

McLaren
(McLaren-Ford)
1m 30.4s

Surtees
(Honda)
1m 30.3s

Rodriguez
(BRM)
1m 31.6s

Ickx
(Ferrari)
1m 31.0s

Hulme
(McLaren-Ford)
1m 30.4s

Attwood
(BRM)
1m 31.7s

Beltoise
(Matra)
1m 31.6s

Widdows
(Cooper-BRM)
1m 34.0s

Elford
(Cooper-BRM)
1m 33.0s

Courage
(BRM)
1m 32.3s

Bonnier
(McLaren-BRM)
1m 36.8s

Moser
(Brabham-Repco)
1m 35.4s

Results

1	J. Siffert Lotus-Ford	2h 01m 20.3s	(104.83 mph)
2	C. Amon Ferrari	2h 01m 24.7s	
3	J. Ickx Ferrari	79 laps	
4	D. Hulme McLaren-Ford	79 laps	
5	J. Surtees Honda	78 laps	
6	J. Stewart Matra-Ford	78 laps	

Fastest lap: Siffert 1m 29.7s (106.35 mph)

1969 · 19 July · RAC British Grand Prix
Silverstone · 2.927 miles · 84 laps

Starting grid

Hulme
(McLaren-Ford)
1m 21.5s

Stewart
(Matra-Ford)
1m 21.2s

Rindt ⬡
(Lotus-Ford)
1m 20.8s

Amon
(Ferrari)
1m 21.9s

Ickx
(Brabham-Ford)
1m 21.6s

Rodriguez
(Ferrari)
1m 22.6s

McLaren
(McLaren-Ford)
1m 22.6s

Surtees
(BRM)
1m 22.1s

Courage
(Brabham-Ford)
1m 22.9s

Siffert
(Lotus-Ford)
1m 22.7s

Oliver
(BRM)
1m 23.7s

Hill
(Lotus-Ford)
1m 23.6s

Elford
(McLaren-Ford)
1m 23.3s

Bell
(McLaren-Ford)
1m 26.1s

Miles
(Lotus-Ford)
1m 25.1s

Beltoise
(Matra-Ford)
1m 31.2s

Bonnier
(Lotus-Ford)
1m 28.2s

Results

1	J. Stewart Matra-Ford	1h 55m 55.6s	(127.25 mph)
2	J. Ickx Brabham-Ford	83 laps	
3	B. McLaren McLaren-Ford	83 laps	
4	J. Rindt Lotus-Ford	83 laps	
5	P. Courage Brabham-Ford	83 laps	
6	V. Elford McLaren-Ford	82 laps	

Fastest lap: Stewart 1m 21.3s (129.61 mph)

1970 · 18 July · RAC British Grand Prix Brands Hatch · 2.65 miles · 80 laps

Starting grid

Ickx *(Ferrari)* 1m 25.1s	Brabham *(Brabham-Ford)* 1m 24.8s	Rindt ⌂ *(Lotus-Ford)* 1m 24.8s
	Hulme *(McLaren-Ford)* 1m 25.6s	Oliver *(BRM)* 1m 25.6s
Stewart *(Matra-Ford)* 1m 26.0s	Miles *(Lotus-Ford)* 1m 25.9s	Regazzoni *(Ferrari)* 1m 25.8s
	Beltoise *(Matra-Simca)* 1m 26.5s	Andretti *(March-Ford)* 1m 26.2s
Peterson *(March-Ford)* 1m 26.8s	Pescarolo *(Matra-Simca)* 1m 26.7s	Gurney *(McLaren-Ford)* 1m 26.6s
	Rodriguez *(BRM)* 1m 26.9s	Cevert *(March-Ford)* 1m 26.8s
de Adamich *(McLaren-Alfa Romeo)* 1m 27.1s	Amon *(March-Ford)* 1m 27.0s	Eaton *(BRM)* 1m 26.9s
	Siffert *(March-Ford)* 1m 28.0s	Surtees *(Surtees-Ford)* 1m 27.7s
Lovely *(Lotus-Ford)* 1m 30.3s	Hill *(Lotus-Ford)* 1m 28.4s	Fittipaldi *(Lotus-Ford)* 1m 28.1s

Results

1	J. Rindt Lotus-Ford	1h 57m 02.0s	(108.69 mph)
2	J. Brabham Brabham-Ford	1h 57m 34.9s	
3	D. Hulme McLaren-Ford	1h 57m 56.4s	
4	G. Regazzoni Ferrari	1h 57m 56.8s	
5	C. Amon March-Ford	79 laps	
6	G. Hill Lotus-Ford	79 laps	

Fastest lap: Brabham 1m 25.9s (111.06 mph)

1971 · 17 July · RAC Woolmark British Grand Prix · Silverstone · 2.927 miles · 68 laps

Starting grid

Siffert *(BRM)* 1m 18.2s	Stewart *(Tyrrell-Ford)* 1m 18.1s	Regazzoni ⌂ *(Ferrari)* 1m 18.1s
	Peterson *(March-Ford)* 1m 19.0s	Fittipaldi *(Lotus-Ford)* 1m 18.3s
Hulme *(McLaren-Ford)* 1m 19.6s	Schenken *(Brabham-Ford)* 1m 19.5s	Ickx *(Ferrari)* 1m 19.5s
	Cevert *(Tyrrell-Ford)* 1m 19.8s	Amon *(Matra-Simca)* 1m 19.7s
Charlton *(Lotus-Ford)* 1m 20.05s	Stommelen *(Surtees-Ford)* 1m 19.88s	Ganley *(BRM)* 1m 19.84s
	Beltoise *(Matra-Simca)* 1m 20.2s	Gethin *(McLaren-Ford)* 1m 20.10s
Surtees *(Surtees-Ford)* 1m 20.61s	Pescarolo *(March-Ford)* 1m 20.5s	Hill *(Brabham-Ford)* 1m 20.3s
	Beuttler *(March-Ford)* 1m 20.7s	Wisell *(Lotus-Pratt & Whitney)* 1m 20.66s
Bell *(Surtees-Ford)* 1m 22.3s	Oliver *(McLaren-Ford)* 1m 21.0s	Galli *(March-Ford)* 1m 20.9s
		de Adamich *(March-Alfa Romeo)* 1m 23.2s

Results

1	J. Stewart Tyrrell-Ford	1h 31m 31.5s	(130.48 mph)
2	R. Peterson March-Ford	1h 32m 07.6s	
3	E. Fittipaldi Lotus-Ford	1h 32m 22.0s	
4	H. Pescarolo March-Ford	67 laps	
5	R. Stommelen Surtees-Ford	67 laps	
6	J. Surtees Surtees-Ford	67 laps	

Fastest lap: Stewart 1m 19.9s (131.88 mph)

1972 · 15 July · John Player Grand Prix
Brands Hatch · 2.65 miles · 76 laps

Starting grid

E. Fittipaldi
(Lotus-Ford)
1m 22.6s

Ickx ⬆
(Ferrari)
1m 22.2s

Stewart
(Tyrrell-Ford)
1m 22.9s

Revson
(McLaren-Ford)
1m 22.7s

Beltoise
(BRM)
1m 23.4s

Schenken
(Surtees-Ford)
1m 23.2s

Peterson
(March-Ford)
1m 23.7s

Hailwood
(Surtees-Ford)
1m 23.5s

Reutemann
(Brabham-Ford)
1m 23.8s

Merzario
(Ferrari)
1m 23.7s

Cevert
(Tyrrell-Ford)
1m 23.9s

Hulme
(McLaren-Ford)
1m 23.9s

Oliver
(BRM)
1m 24.4s

Pace
(March-Ford)
1m 24.0s

Gethin
(BRM)
1m 24.5s

Walker
(Lotus-Ford)
1m 24.4s

Galli
(Tecno)
1m 25.1s

Amon
(Matra-Simca)
1m 24.6s

de Adamich
(Surtees-Ford)
1m 25.2s

Lauda
(March-Ford)
1m 25.1s

W. Fittipaldi
(Brabham-Ford)
1m 25.5s

Hill
(Brabham-Ford)
1m 25.2s

Charlton
(Lotus-Ford)
1m 25.6s

Beuttler
(March-Ford)
1m 25.6s

Pescarolo
(Politoys-Ford)
1m 27.4s

Stommelen
(March-Ford)
1m 26.3s

Results

1	E. Fittipaldi Lotus-Ford	1h 47m 50.2s	(112.06 mph)
2	J. Stewart Tyrrell-Ford	1h 47m 54.3s	
3	P. Revson McLaren-Ford	1h 49m 02.7s	
4	C. Amon Matra-Simca	75 laps	
5	D. Hulme McLaren-Ford	75 laps	
6	A. Merzario Ferrari	75 laps	

Fastest lap: Stewart 1m 24.0s (113.57 mph)

1973 · 14 July · John Player Grand Prix
Silverstone · 2.927 miles · 67 laps

Starting grid

Revson
(McLaren-Ford)
1m 16.5s

Hulme
(McLaren-Ford)
1m 16.5s

Peterson ⬆
(Lotus-Ford)
1m 16.3s

Fittipaldi
(Lotus-Ford)
1m 16.7s

Stewart
(Tyrrell-Ford)
1m 16.7s

Reutemann
(Brabham-Ford)
1m 17.4s

Cevert
(Tyrrell-Ford)
1m 17.3s

Scheckter
(McLaren-Ford)
1m 16.9s

Regazzoni
(BRM)
1m 17.5s

Lauda
(BRM)
1m 17.4s

W. Fittipaldi
(Brabham-Ford)
1m 18.1s

Hailwood
(Surtees-Ford)
1m 18.0s

Hunt
(March-Ford)
1m 17.6s

Pace
(Surtees-Ford)
1m 18.3s

Mass
(Surtees-Ford)
1m 18.3s

Ganley
(Williams-Ford)
1m 18.6s

Beltoise
(BRM)
1m 18.4s

Purley
(March-Ford)
1m 18.4s

de Adamich
(Brabham-Ford)
1m 19.1s

Ickx
(Ferrari)
1m 18.9s

Watson
(Brabham-Ford)
1m 20.1s

Williamson
(March-Ford)
1m 19.5s

von Opel
(Ensign-Ford)
1m 19.2s

Follmer
(Shadow-Ford)
1m 20.3s

Beuttler
(March-Ford)
1m 20.1s

McRae
(Williams-Ford)
1m 20.8s

Hill
(Shadow-Ford)
1m 20.5s

Oliver
(Shadow-Ford)
1m 20.3s

Amon
(Tecno)
1m 21.0s

Results

1	P. Revson McLaren-Ford	1h 29m 18.5s	(131.75 mph)
2	R. Peterson Lotus-Ford	1h 29m 21.3s	
3	D. Hulme McLaren-Ford	1h 29m 21.5s	
4	J. Hunt March-Ford	1h 29m 21.5s	
5	F. Cevert Tyrrell-Ford	1h 29m 55.1s	
6	C. Reutemann Brabham-Ford	1h 30m 03.2s	

Fastest lap: Hunt 1m 18.6s (134.06 mph)

1974 · 20 July · John Player Grand Prix
Brands Hatch · 2.65 miles · 75 laps

Starting grid

Peterson	Lauda ⌂
(Lotus-Ford)	(Ferrari)
1m 19.7s	1m 19.7s
Reutemann	Scheckter
(Brabham-Ford)	(Tyrrell-Ford)
1m 20.2s	1m 20.1s
Hunt	Pryce
(Hesketh-Ford)	(Shadow-Ford)
1m 20.3s	1m 20.3s
Fittipaldi	Regazzoni
(McLaren-Ford)	(Ferrari)
1m 20.5s	1m 20.3s
Depailler	Stuck
(Tyrrell-Ford)	(March-Ford)
1m 20.8s	1m 20.7s
Ickx	Hailwood
(Lotus-Ford)	(McLaren-Ford)
1m 21.2s	1m 21.2s
Migault	Watson
(BRM)	(Brabham-Ford)
1m 21.4s	1m 21.3s
Jarier	Merzario
(Shadow-Ford)	(Williams-Ford)
1m 21.6s	1m 21.6s
Brambilla	Mass
(March-Ford)	(Surtees-Ford)
1m 21.6s	1m 21.6s
Pace	Hulme
(Brabham-Ford)	(McLaren-Ford)
1m 21.7s	1m 21.7s
Hill	Gethin
(Lola-Ford)	(Lola-Ford)
1m 21.9s	1m 21.7s
Pescarlo	Beltoise
(BRM)	(BRM)
1m 22.2s	1m 22.1s
	Schenken
	(Trojan-Ford)
	1m 22.4s

Results

1	J. Scheckter	Tyrrell-Ford	1h 43m 02.2s (115.73 mph)
2	E. Fittipaldi	McLaren-Ford	1h 43m 17.5s
3	J. Ickx	Lotus-Ford	1h 44m 03.7s
4	C. Regazzoni	Ferrari	1h 44m 09.4s
5	N. Lauda	Ferrari	Awarded 5th place following enquiry
6	C. Reutemann	Brabham-Ford	74 laps

Fastest lap: Lauda 1m 21.1s (117.63 mph)

1975 · 19 July · John Player Grand Prix
Silverstone · 2.932 miles
Scheduled to run for 67 laps but results declared after 55 laps

Starting grid

Pace	Pryce ⌂
(Brabham-Ford)	(Shadow-Ford)
1m 19.50s	1m 19.36s
Regazzoni	Lauda
(Ferrari)	(Ferrari)
1m 19.55s	1m 19.54s
Scheckter	Brambilla
(Tyrrell-Ford)	(March-Ford)
1m 19.81s	1m 19.63s
Reutemann	E. Fittipaldi
(Brabham-Ford)	(McLaren-Ford)
1m 20.04s	1m 19.91s
Mass	Hunt
(McLaren-Ford)	(Hesketh-Ford)
1m 20.8s	1m 20.14s
Andretti	Jarier
(Parnelli-Ford)	(Shadow-Ford)
1m 20.36s	1m 20.33s
Stuck	Brise
(March-Ford)	(Hill-Ford)
1m 20.46s	1m 20.41s
Peterson	Donohue
(Lotus-Ford)	(March-Ford)
1m 20.58s	1m 20.50s
Watson	Depailler
(Surtees-Ford)	(Tyrrell-Ford)
1m 20.83s	1m 20.60s
Jones	Laffite
(Hill-Ford)	(Williams-Ford)
1m 21.19s	1m 21.01s
Lombardi	Henton
(March-Ford)	(Lotus-Ford)
1m 21.60s	1m 21.26s
W. Fittipaldi	Morgan
(Copersucar-Ford)	(Surtees-Ford)
1m 21.67s	1m 21.65s
Nicholson	Crawford
(Lyncar-Ford)	(Lotus-Ford)
1m 22.86s	1m 21.86s

Results

1	E. Fittipaldi	McLaren-Ford	1h 22m 05.0s (120.04 mph)
2	C. Pace	Brabham-Ford	Crashed lap 56
3	J. Scheckter	Tyrrell-Ford	Crashed lap 56
4	J. Hunt	Hesketh-Ford	Crashed lap 56
5	M. Donohue	March-Ford	Crashed lap 56
6	V. Brambilla	March-Ford	Completed lap 56

Fastest lap: Regazzoni 1m 20.9s (130.47 mph)

1976 · 18 July · John Player British Grand Prix
Brands Hatch · 2.6136 miles · 76 laps

Starting grid

⌂ Lauda
(Ferrari)
1m 19.35s

Hunt
(McLaren-Ford)
1m 19.41s

Andretti
(Lotus-Ford)
1m 19.76s

Regazzoni
(Ferrari)
1m 20.05s

Depailler
(Tyrrell-Ford)
1m 20.15s

Amon
(Ensign-Ford)
1m 20.27s

Peterson
(March-Ford)
1m 20.29s

Scheckter
(Tyrrell-Ford)
1m 20.31s

Merzario
(March-Ford)
1m 20.32s

Brambilla
(March-Ford)
1m 20.36s

Watson
(Penske-Ford)
1m 20.41s

Mass
(McLaren-Ford)
1m 20.61s

Laffite
(Ligier-Matra)
1m 20.67s

Nilsson
(Lotus-Ford)
1m 20.67s

Reutemann
*(Brabham
-Alfa Romeo)*
1m 20.99s

Pace
*(Brabham
-Alfa Romeo)*
1m 21.03s

Stuck
(March-Ford)
1m 21.20s

Lunger
(Surtees-Ford)
1m 21.30s

Jones
(Surtees-Ford)
1m 21.42s

Pryce
(Shadow-Ford)
1m 21.84s

Fittipaldi
(Copersucar-Ford)
1m 22.06s

Evans
(Brabham-Ford)
1m 22.47s

Ertl
(Hesketh-Ford)
1m 22.75s

Jarier
(Shadow-Ford)
1m 22.72s

Edwards
(Hesketh-Ford)
1m 22.76s

Pescarolo
(Surtees-Ford)
1m 22.76s

Results

1*	J. Hunt	McLaren-Ford	1h 43m 27.61s (115.19 mph)
2	N. Lauda	Ferrari	1h 44m 19.66s
3	J. Scheckter	Tyrrell-Ford	1h 44m 35.84s
4	J. Watson	Penske-Ford	75 laps
5	T. Pryce	Shadow-Ford	75 laps
6	A. Jones	Surtees-Ford	75 laps

* Subsequently disqualified

Fastest lap: Hunt 1m 19.82s (117.71 mph)

1977 · 16 July · John Player British Grand Prix
Silverstone · 2.932 miles · 68 laps

Starting grid

Watson
(Brabham-Alfa Romeo)
1m 18.77s

Hunt ⌂
(McLaren-Ford)
1m 18.49s

J. Scheckter
(Wolf-Ford)
1m 18.85s

Lauda
(Ferrari)
1m 18.84s

Andretti
(Lotus-Ford)
1m 19.11s

Nilsson
(Lotus-Ford)
1m 18.95s

Brambilla
(Surtees-Ford)
1m 19.20s

Stuck
(Brabham-Alfa Romeo)
1m 19.16s

Peterson
(Tyrrell-Ford)
1m 19.42s

Villeneuve
(McLaren-Ford)
1m 19.32s

Jones
(Shadow-Ford)
1m 19.60s

Mass
(McLaren-Ford)
1m 19.55s

Reutemann
(Ferrari)
1m 19.64s

Keegan
(Hesketh-Ford)
1m 19.64s

Tambay
(Ensign-Ford)
1m 19.81s

Laffite
(Ligier-Matra)
1m 19.75s

Depailler
(Tyrrell-Ford)
1m 19.90s

Merzario
(March-Ford)
1m 19.88s

Jarier
(Penske-Ford)
1m 20.10s

Lunger
(McLaren-Ford)
1m 20.06s

Fittipaldi
(Fittipaldi-Ford)
1m 20.20s

Jabouille
(Renault)
1m 20.11s

I. Scheckter
(March-Ford)
1m 20.31s

Schuppan
(Surtees-Ford)
1m 20.24s

Neve
(March-Ford)
1m 20.36s

Patrese
(Shadow-Ford)
1m 20.35s

Results

1	J. Hunt	McLaren-Ford	1h 31m 46.06s (130.357 mph)
2	N. Lauda	Ferrari	1h 32m 04.37s
3	G. Nilsson	Lotus-Ford	1h 32m 05.63s
4	J. Mass	McLaren-Ford	1h 32m 33.82s
5	H. Stuck	Brabham-Alfa Romeo	1h 32m 57.79s
6	J. Lafitte	Ligier-Matra	67 laps

Fastest lap: Hunt 1m 19.60s (132.603 mph)

1978 · 16 July · John Player British Grand Prix
Brands Hatch · 2.6136 miles · 76 laps

Starting grid

⇩Peterson
(Lotus-Ford)
1m 16.80s

Andretti
(Lotus-Ford)
1m 17.06s

Scheckter
(Wolf-Ford)
1m 17.37s

Lauda
(Brabham-Alfa Romeo)
1m 17.48s

Patrese
(Arrows-Ford)
1m 18.28s

Jones
(Williams-Ford)
1m 18.36s

Laffite
(Ligier-Matra)
1m 18.44s

Reutemann
(Ferrari)
1m 18.45s

Watson
(Brabham-Alfa Romeo)
1m 18.57s

Depailler
(Tyrrell-Ford)
1m 18.73s

Fittipaldi
(Fittipaldi-Ford)
1m 18.78s

Jabouille
(Renault)
1m 18.88s

Villeneuve
(Ferrari)
1m 18.99s

Hunt
(McLaren-Ford)
1m 19.05s

Daly
(Ensign-Ford)
1m 19.13s

Giacomelli
(McLaren-Ford)
1m 19.79s

Regazzoni
(Shadow-Ford)
1m 19.83s

Stuck
(Shadow-Ford)
1m 19.98s

Pironi
(Tyrrell-Ford)
1m 19.99s

Tambay
(McLaren-Ford)
1m 20.14s

Rebaque
(Lotus-Ford)
1m 20.24s

Rosberg
(ATS-Ford)
1m 20.27s

Merzario
(Merzario-Ford)
1m 20.35s

Lunger
(McLaren-Ford)
1m 20.39s

Brambilla
(Surtees-Ford)
1m 20.70s

Mass
(ATS-Ford)
1m 20.71s

Results

1	C. Reutemann	Ferrari	1h 42m 12.39s (116.607 mph)
2	N. Lauda	Brabham-Alfa Romeo	1h 42m 13.62s
3	J. Watson	Brabham-Alfa Romeo	1h 42m 49.64s
4	P. Depailler	Tyrrell-Ford	1h 43m 25.66s
5	H. Stuck	Shadow-Ford	75 laps
6	P. Tambay	McLaren-Ford	75 laps

Fastest lap: Lauda 1m 18.60s (119.707 mph)

1979 · 14 July · Marlboro British Grand Prix
Silverstone · 2.932 miles · 68 laps

Starting grid

Jabouille
(Renault)
1m 12.48s

Jones ⇩
(Williams-Ford)
1m 11.88s

Regazzoni
(Williams-Ford)
1m 13.11s

Piquet
(Brabham-Alfa Romeo)
1m 12.65s

Lauda
(Brabham-Alfa Romeo)
1m 13.44s

Arnoux
(Renault)
1m 13.29s

Reutemann
(Lotus-Ford)
1m 13.87s

Watson
(Brabham-Alfa Romeo)
1m 13.57s

Laffite
(Ligier-Ford)
1m 14.37s

Andretti
(Lotus-Ford)
1m 14.20s

de Angelis
(Shadow-Ford)
1m 14.87s

Scheckter
(Ferrari)
1m 14.60s

Rosberg
(Wolf-Ford)
1m 14.96s

Villeneuve
(Ferrari)
1m 14.90s

Jarier
(Tyrrell-Ford)
1m 15.63s

Pironi
(Tyrrell-Ford)
1m 15.28s

Tambay
(McLaren-Ford)
1m 15.67s

Ickx
(Ligier-Ford)
1m 15.63s

Mass
(Arrows-Ford)
1m 16.19s

Patrese
(Arrows-Ford)
1m 15.77s

Fittipaldi
(Fittipaldi-Ford)
1m 16.68s

Lammers
(Shadow-Ford)
1m 16.66s

Rebaque
(Lotus-Ford)
1m 17.32s

Gaillard
(Ensign-Ford)
1m 17.07s

Results

1	C. Regazzoni	Williams-Ford	1h 26m 11.17s (138.80 mph)
2	R. Arnoux	Renault	1h 26m 35.45s
3	J-P Jarier	Tyrrell-Ford	67 laps
4	J. Watson	McLaren-Ford	67 laps
5	J. Scheckter	Ferrari	67 laps
6	J. Ickx	Ligier-Ford	67 laps

Fastest lap: Regazzoni 1m 14.40s (141.87 mph)

1980 · 13 July · Marlboro British Grand Prix
Brands Hatch · 2.6136 miles · 76 laps

Starting grid

Pironi ⬦
(Ligier-Ford)
1m 11.00s

Laffite
(Ligier-Ford)
1m 11.39s

Jones
(Williams-Ford)
1m 11.60s

Reutemann
(Williams-Ford)
1m 11.62s

Piquet
(Brabham-Ford)
1m 11.63s

Giacomelli
(Alfa Romeo)
1m 12.12s

Prost
(McLaren-Ford)
1m 12.63s

Depailler
(Alfa Romeo)
1m 13.18s

Andretti
(Lotus-Ford)
1m 13.40s

Daly
(Tyrrell-Ford)
1m 13.46s

Jarier
(Tyrrell-Ford)
1m 13.66s

Watson
(McLaren-Ford)
1m 13.71s

Jabouille
(Renault)
1m 13.74s

de Angelis
(Lotus-Ford)
1m 13.85s

Surer
(ATS-Ford)
1m 13.95s

Arnoux
(Renault)
1m 13.96s

Rebaque
(Brabham-Ford)
1m 14.22s

Keegan
(Williams-Ford)
1m 14.23s

Villeneuve
(Ferrari)
1m 14.29s

Cheever
(Osella-Ford)
1m 14.51s

Patrese
(Arrows-Ford)
1m 14.56s

Fittipaldi
(Fittipaldi-Ford)
1m 14.58s

Scheckter
(Ferrari)
1m 15.37s

Mass
(Arrows-Ford)
1m 15.42s

Results

1	A. Jones	Williams-Ford	1h 34m 49.228s (125.690 mph)
2	N. Piquet	Brabham-Ford	1h 35m 00.235s
3	C. Reutemann	Williams-Ford	1h 35m 02.513s
4	D. Daly	Tyrrell-Ford	75 laps
5	J. Jarier	Tyrrell-Ford	75 laps
6	A. Prost	McLaren-Ford	75 laps

Fastest lap: Pironi 1m 12.368s (130.015 mph)

1981 · 18 July · Marlboro British Grand Prix
Silverstone · 2.932 miles · 68 laps

Starting grid

Arnoux ⬦
(Renault)
1m 11.000s

Prost
(Renault)
1m 11.046s

Piquet
(Brabham-Ford)
1m 11.952s

Pironi
(Ferrari)
1m 12.644s

Watson
(McLaren-Ford)
1m 12.712s

de Cesaris
(McLaren-Ford)
1m 12.728s

Jones
(Williams-Ford)
1m 12.998s

Villeneuve
(Ferrari)
1m 13.311s

Reutemann
(Williams-Ford)
1m 13.371s

Patrese
(Arrows-Ford)
1m 13.762s

Andretti
(Alfa Romeo)
1m 13.928s

Giacomelli
(Alfa Romeo)
1m 14.119s

Rebaque
(Brabham-Ford)
1m 14.542s

Laffite
(Talbot-Ligier)
1m 14.798s

Tambay
(Talbot-Ligier)
1m 14.976s

Rosberg
(Fittipaldi-Ford)
1m 15.165s

Daly
(March-Ford)
1m 15.189s

Stohr
(Arrows-Cosworth)
1m 15.304s

Alboreto
(Tyrrell-Ford)
1m 15.850s

Jarier
(Osella-Ford)
1m 15.898s

Borgudd
(ATS-Ford)
1m 15.959s

de Angelis
(Lotus-Ford)
1m 15.971s

Cheever
(Tyrrell-Ford)
1m 16.099s

Surer
(Theodore-Ford)
1m 16.155s

Results

1	J. Watson	McLaren-Ford	1h 26m 54.80s (137.64 mph)
2	C. Reutemann	Williams-Ford	1h 27m 35.45s
3	J. Laffite	Talbot Ligier-Matra	67 laps
4	E. Cheever	Tyrrell-Ford	67 laps
5	H. Rebaque	Brabham-Ford	67 laps
6	S. Borgudd	ATS-Ford	67 laps

Fastest lap: Arnoux 1m 15.067s (140.61 mph)

1982 · 18 July · Marlboro British Grand Prix
Brands Hatch · 2.6136 miles · 76 laps

Starting grid

Patrese
(Brabham-BMW)
1m 09.627s

Pironi
(Ferrari)
1m 10.066s

Arnoux
(Renault)
1m 10.641s

Prost
(Renault)
1m 10.728s

Daly
(Williams-Ford)
1m 10.980s

Watson
(McLaren-Ford)
1m 11.418s

Giacomelli
(Alfa Romeo)
1m 11.502s

Warwick
(Toleman-Hart)
1m 11.761s

Jarier
(Osella-Ford)
1m 12.436s

Laffite
(Talbot Ligier-Matra)
1m 12.695s

Surer
(Arrows-Ford)
1m 13.181s

Cheever
(Talbot Ligier-Matra)
1m 13.301s

Baldi
(Arrows-Ford)
1m 13.721s

Rosberg ⌂
(Williams-Ford)
1m 09.540s

Piquet
(Brabham-BMW)
1m 10.060s

Lauda
(McLaren-Ford)
1m 10.638s

de Angelis
(Lotus-Ford)
1m 10.650s

Alboreto
(Tyrrell-Ford)
1m 10.892s

de Cesaris
(Alfa Romeo)
1m 11.347s

Tambay
(Ferrari)
1m 11.430s

Fabi
(Toleman-Hart)
1m 11.728s

Henton
(Tyrrell-Ford)
1m 12.080s

Guerrero
(Ensign-Ford)
1m 12.668s

Serra
(Fittipaldi-Ford)
1m 13.096s

Mansell
(Lotus-Ford)
1m 13.212s

Mass
(March-Ford)
1m 13.622s

Results

1	N. Lauda	McLaren-Ford	1h 35m 33.812s (124.70 mph)
2	D. Pironi	Ferrari	1h 35m 59.538s
3	P. Tambay	Ferrari	1h 36m 12.248s
4	E. de Angelis	Lotus-Ford	1h 36m 15.054s
5	D. Daly	Williams-Ford	1h 36m 15.242s
6	A. Prost	Renault	1h 36m 15.448s

Fastest lap: Henton 1m 13.028s (128.84 mph)

1983 · 16 July · Marlboro British Grand Prix
Silverstone · 2.932 miles · 67 laps

Starting grid

Tambay
(Ferrari)
1m 10.104s

de Angelis
(Lotus-Renault)
1m 10.771s

Piquet
(Brabham-BMW)
1m 10.993s

Winkelhock
(ATS-BMW)
1m 11.687s

Warwick
(Toleman-Hart)
1m 12.528s

Giacomelli
(Toleman-Hart)
1m 13.422s

Johansson
(Spirit-Honda)
1m 13.962s

Alboreto
(Tyrrell-Ford)
1m 14.651s

Mansell
(Lotus-Renault)
1m 15.133s

Laffite
(Williams-Ford)
1m 15.234s

Boesel
(Ligier-Ford)
1m 15.386s

Watson
(McLaren-Ford)
1m 15.609s

Ghinzani
(Osella-Alfa Romeo)
1m 16.544s

Arnoux ⌂
(Ferrari)
1m 09.462s

Prost
(Renault)
1m 10.170s

Patrese
(Brabham-BMW)
1m 10.881s

Cheever
(Renault)
1m 11.055s

de Cesaris
(Alfa Romeo)
1m 12.150s

Baldi
(Alfa Romeo)
1m 12.860s

Rosberg
(Williams-Ford)
1m 13.755s

Lauda
(McLaren-Ford)
1m 14.627s

Boutsen
(Arrows-Ford)
1m 14.964s

Surer
(Arrows-Ford)
1m 15.135s

Guerrero
(Theodore-Ford)
1m 15.317s

Sullivan
(Tyrrell-Ford)
1m 15.449s

Jarier
(Ligier-Ford)
1m 15.767s

Results

1	A. Prost	Renault	1h 24m 39.780s (139.218 mph)
2	N. Piquet	Brabham-BMW	1h 24m 58.941s
3	P. Tambay	Ferrari	1h 25m 06.026s
4	N. Mansell	Lotus-Renault	1h 25m 18.732s
5	R. Arnoux	Ferrari	1h 25m 38.654s
6	N. Lauda	McLaren-Ford	66 laps

Fastest lap: Prost 1m 14.212s (142.23 mph)

1984 · 22 July · John Player Special British Grand Prix · Brands Hatch · 2.6136 miles · 71 laps

Starting grid

Prost
(McLaren-TAG)
1m 11.076s

de Angelis
(Lotus-Renault)
1m 11.573s

Warwick
(Renault)
1m 11.703s

Mansell
(Lotus-Renault)
1m 12.435s

Tambay
(Renault)
1m 13.138s

Boutsen
(Arrows-BMW)
1m 13.528s

Fabi
(Brabham-BMW)
1m 14.040s

Laffite
(Williams-Honda)
1m 14.568s

Cheever
(Alfa Romeo)
1m 14.609s

Hesnault
(Ligier-Renault)
1m 15.837s

Rothengatter
(Spirit-Hart)
1m 16.759s

Alliot
(RAM-Hart)
1m 17.517s

Bellof
(Tyrrell-Ford)
1m 17.893s

Piquet ⬦
(Brabham-BMW)
1m 10.869s

Lauda
(McLaren-TAG)
1m 11.344s

Rosberg
(Williams-Honda)
1m 11.603s

Senna
(Toleman-Hart)
1m 11.890s

Alboreto
(Ferrari)
1m 13.122s

Winkelhock
(ATS-BMW)
1m 13.374s

Arnoux
(Ferrari)
1m 13.934s

Surer
(Arrows-BMW)
1m 14.336s

Patrese
(Alfa Romeo)
1m 14.568s

de Cesaris
(Ligier-Renault)
1m 15.112s

Ghinzani
(Osella-Alfa Romeo)
1m 16.466s

Palmer
(RAM-Hart)
1m 17.265s

Johansson
(Tyrrell-Ford)
1m 17.77s

Gartner
(Osella-Alfa Romeo)
1m 18.121s

Results

1	N. Lauda	McLaren-TAG	1h 29m 28.532s (124.406 mph)
2	D. Warwick	Renault	1h 30m 10.655s
3	A. Senna	Toleman-Hart	1h 30m 31.860s
4	E. de Angelis	Lotus-Renault	70 laps
5	M. Alboreto	Ferrari	70 laps
6	R. Arnoux	Ferrari	70 laps

Fastest lap: Lauda 1m 13.191s (128.523 mph)

1985 · 21 July · Marlboro British Grand Prix Silverstone · 2.932 miles

Scheduled to run for 66 laps but stopped in error, one lap early

Starting grid

Piquet
(Brabham-BMW)
1m 06.249s

Senna
(Lotus-Renault)
1m 06.324s

Alboreto
(Ferrari)
1m 06.793s

de Angelis
(Lotus-Renault)
1m 07.581s

Lauda
(McLaren-TAG)
1m 07.743s

Warwick
(Renault)
1m 08.238s

Patrese
(Alfa Romeo)
1m 08.384s

Laffite
(Ligier-Renault)
1m 08.656s

Winkelhock
(RAM-Hart)
1m 09.114s

Brundle
(Tyrrell-Renault)
1m 09.242s

Cheever
(Alfa Romeo)
1m 10.345s

Palmer
(Zakspeed)
1m 13.713s

Bellof
(Tyrrell-Ford)
1m 16.596s

Rosberg ⬦
(Williams-Honda)
1m 05.591s

Prost
(McLaren-TAG)
1m 06.308s

Mansell
(Williams-Honda)
1m 06.675s

de Cesaris
(Ligier-Renault)
1m 07.448s

Fabi
(Toleman-Hart)
1m 07.678s

Johansson
(Ferrari)
1m 07.887s

Tambay
(Renault)
1m 08.240s

Surer
(Brabham-BMW)
1m 08.587s

Berger
(Arrows-BMW)
1m 08.672s

Boutsen
(Arrows-BMW)
1m 09.131s

Alliot
(RAM-Hart)
1m 09.609s

Martini
(Minardi-Motori Moderni)
1m 13.645s

Ghinzani
(Osella-Alfa Romeo)
1m 16.400s

Results

1	A. Prost	McLaren-TAG	1h 18m 10.436s (146.274 mph)
2	M. Alboreto	Ferrari	64 laps
3	J. Laffite	Ligier-Renault	64 laps
4	N. Piquet	Brabham-BMW	64 laps
5	D. Warwick	Renault	64 laps
6	M. Surer	Brabham-BMW	63 laps

Fastest lap: Prost 1m 09.886s (151.035 mph)

1986 · 13 July · Shell Oils British Grand Prix
Brands Hatch · 2.6136 miles · 75 laps

Starting grid

Mansell
(Williams-Honda)
1m 07.399s

Berger
(Benetton-BMW)
1m 08.196s

Prost
(McLaren-TAG)
1m 09.334s

Arnoux
(Ligier-Renault)
1m 09.543s

Dumfries
(Lotus-Renault)
1m 10.304s

Alboreto
(Ferrari)
1m 10.338s

Jones
(Lola-Ford)
1m 11.121s

Streiff
(Tyrrell-Renault)
1m 11.450s

Johansson
(Ferrari)
1m 11.500s

Nannini
(Minardi-Motori Moderni)
1m 12.848s

Palmer
(Zakspeed)
1m 13.009s

Ghinzani
(Osella-Alfa Romeo)
1m 16.134s

Berg
(Osella-Alfa Romeo)
1m 18.319s

Piquet ⬄
(Williams-Honda)
1m 06.961s

Senna
(Lotus-Renault)
1m 07.524s

Rosberg
(McLaren-TAG)
1m 08.477s

Fabi
(Benetton-BMW)
1m 09.409s

Warwick
(Brabham-BMW)
1m 10.209s

Brundle
(Tyrrell-Renault)
1m 10.334s

Boutsen
(Arrows-BWM)
1m 10.941s

Patrese
(Brabham-BMW)
1m 11.267s

Tambay
(Lola-Ford)
1m 11.458s

Laffite
(Ligier-Renault)
1m 12.281s

de Cesaris
(Minardi-Motori Moderni)
1m 12.980s

Danner
(Arrows-BMW)
1m 13.261s

Rothengatter
(Zakspeed)
1m 16.854s

Results

1	N. Mansell	Williams-Honda	1h 30m 38.471s (129.775 mph)
2	N. Piquet	Williams-Honda	1h 30m 44.045s
3	A. Prost	McLaren-TAG	74 laps
4	R. Arnoux	Ligier-Renault	73 laps
5	M. Brundle	Tyrrell-Renault	72 laps
6	P. Streiff	Tyrrell-Renault	72 laps

Fastest lap: Mansell 1m 09.593s (135.220 mph)

1987 · 12 July · Shell Oils British Grand Prix
Silverstone · 2.969 miles · 65 laps

Starting grid

Mansell
(Williams-Honda)
1m 07.180s

Prost
(McLaren-TAG)
1m 08.577s

Fabi
(Benetton-Ford)
1m 09.246s

Berger
(Ferrari)
1m 09.408s

Johansson
(McLaren-TAG)
1m 09.541s

Nakajima
(Lotus-Honda)
1m 10.619s

Cheever
(Arrows-Megatron)
1m 11.053s

Arnoux
(Ligier-Megatron)
1m 12.402s

Danner
(Zakspeed)
1m 13.337s

Caffi
(Osella-Alfa Romeo)
1m 15.558s

Streiff
(Tyrrell-Ford)
1m 16.524s

Capelli
(March-Ford)
1m 16.692s

Piquet ⬄
(Williams-Honda)
1m 07.110s

Senna
(Lotus-Honda)
1m 08.181s

Boutsen
(Benetton-Ford)
1m 08.972s

Alboreto
(Ferrari)
1m 09.274s

de Cesaris
(Brabham-BMW)
1m 09.475s

Patrese
(Brabham-BMW)
1m 10.012s

Warwick
(Arrows-Megatron)
1m 10.654s

Nannini
(Minardi-Motori Moderni)
1m 12.293s

Brundle
(Zakspeed)
1m 12.632s

Campos
(Minardi-Motori Moderni)
1m 13.793s

Alliot
(Lola-Ford)
1m 15.868s

Palmer
(Tyrrell-Ford)
1m 16.644s

Fabre
(AGS-Ford)
1m 18.237s

Results

1	N. Mansell	Williams-Honda	1h 19m 11.780s (146.208 mph)
2	N. Piquet	Williams-Honda	1h 19m 13.698s
3	A. Senna	Lotus-Honda	64 laps
4	S. Nakajima	Lotus-Honda	63 laps
5	D. Warwick	Arrows-Megatron	63 laps
6	T. Fabi	Benetton-Ford	63 laps

Fastest lap: Mansell 1m 09.832s (153.059 mph)

1988 · 10 July · Shell Oils British Grand Prix
Silverstone · 2.969 miles · 65 laps

Starting grid

Alboreto
(Ferrari)
1m 10.332s

Berger ⬦
(Ferrari)
1m 10.133s

Prost
(McLaren-Honda)
1m 10.736s

Senna
(McLaren-Honda)
1m 10.616s

Capelli
(March-Judd)
1m 12.006s

Gugelmin
(March-Judd)
1m 11.745s

Nannini
(Benetton-Ford)
1m 12.737s

Piquet
(Lotus-Honda)
1m 12.040s

Nakajima
(Lotus-Honda)
1m 12.862s

Warwick
(Arrows-Megatron)
1m 12.843s

Boutsen
(Benetton-Ford)
1m 12.960s

Mansell
(Williams-Judd)
1m 12.885s

de Cesaris
(Rial-Ford)
1m 13.438s

Cheever
(Arrows-Megatron)
1m 12.948s

Streiff
(AGS-Ford)
1m 14.260s

Patrese
(Williams-Judd)
1m 13.677s

Sala
(Minardi-Ford)
1m 14.643s

Palmer
(Tyrrell-Ford)
1m 14.451s

Modena
(EuroBrun-Ford)
1m 14.888s

Martini
(Minardi-Ford)
1m 14.732s

Alliot
(Lola-Ford)
1m 14.992s

Caffi
(Dallara-Ford)
1m 14.924s

Bailey
(Tyrrell-Ford)
1m 15.135s

Dalmas
(Lola-Ford)
1m 15.004s

Larini
(Osella-Alfa Romeo)
1m 15.527s

Arnoux
(Ligier-Judd)
1m 15.374s

Results

1	A. Senna	McLaren-Honda	1h 33m 16.367s (124.142 mph)
2	N. Mansell	Williams-Judd	1h 33m 39.711s
3	A. Nannini	Benetton-Ford	1h 34m 07.581s
4	M. Gugelmin	March-Judd	1h 34m 27.745s
5	N. Piquet	Lotus-Honda	1h 34m 37.202s
6	D. Warwick	Arrows-Megatron	64 laps

Fastest lap: Mansell 1m 23.308s (128.300 mph)

BIBLIOGRAPHY

Alf Francis – Racing Mechanic Peter Lewis *(The Marshall Press Ltd 1959)*

A Record of Grand Prix and Voiturette Racing (Vols 1 & 6) Paul Sheldon *(St. Leonard's Press 1987)*

A Story of Formula 1 Denis Jenkinson *(Grenville Publishing Company Ltd 1960)*

Autocourse History of the Grand Prix Car 1966–85 Doug Nye *(Hazleton Publishing 1986)*

Brabham: The Grand Prix Cars Alan Henry *(Hazleton Publishing 1985)*

Brands Hatch Mark Cole/Mike Kettlewell *(Brands Hatch Circuit Ltd 1987)*

British Grand Prix Doug Nye *(B. T. Batsford Ltd 1977)*

BRM Raymond Mays *(Cassell & Company Ltd 1962)*

Brooklands and beyond Charles Mortimer *(Goose and Son Publishers Ltd 1974)*

Brought up in England Prince Chula *(G. T. Foulis & Co 1943)*

Bruce McLaren. The Man and his Racing Team Eoin Young *(Eyre & Spottiswoode [Publishers] Ltd 1971)*

Cooper Cars Doug Nye *(Osprey Publishing Ltd 1983)*

Dick Seaman, Racing Champion Prince Chula *(Floyd Clymer 1948)*

Challenge me the Race Mike Hawthorn *(William Kimber & Company Ltd 1958)*

Champion Year Mike Hawthorn *(Aston Publications Ltd 1989)*

Colin Chapman. The Man and his Cars Gerard Crombac *(Patrick Stephens Ltd 1986)*

Driven To Win Nigel Mansell/Derick Allsop *(Stanley Paul & Company Ltd 1988)*

Faster! Jackie Stewart/Peter Manso *(William Kimber & Company Ltd 1972)*

Ferrari: The Grand Prix Cars Alan Henry (Hazleton Publishing 1984)

Fifty Famous Motor Races Alan Henry *(Patrick Stephens Ltd 1988)*

Famous Racing Cars Doug Nye *(Patrick Stephens Ltd 1989)*

Formula One: the Cars and the Drivers Michael Turner/Nigel Roebuck *(Temple Press 1983)*

500cc Racing Gregor Grant *(G. T. Foulis & Co 1952)*

Grand Prix Greats Nigel Roebuck *(Patrick Stephens Ltd 1986)*

James Hunt. Against all Odds James Hunt/Eoin Young *(Hamlyn Publishing Group Ltd 1977)*

Life at the Limit Graham Hill *(William Kimber & Company Ltd 1969)*

Mario Andretti World Champion Mario Andretti/Nigel Roebuck *(Hamlyn Publishing Group Ltd 1979)*

McLaren: The Grand Prix, CanAm and Indy Cars Doug Nye *(Hazleton Publishing 1984)*

My Greatest Race Editor: Adrian Ball *(Granada Publishing Ltd 1974)*

Nuvolari Count Giovanni Lurani *(Cassell & Company Ltd 1959)*

Power and Glory William Court *(Patrick Stephens Ltd 1966/1988)*

The British Grand Prix Richard Hough *(Hutchinson & Company 1958)*

The Chequered Year Ted Simon *(Cassell and Company 1971)*

The Grand Prix Drivers Editor: Steve Small *(Hazleton Publishing 1987)*

The Grand Prix Tyrrells Doug Nye *(Macmillan 1975)*

The History of Brooklands Motor Course William Boddy *(Grenville Publishing Company Ltd 1979)*

The Monaco Grand Prix David Hodges *(Temple Press Ltd 1964)*

Motor Racing with Mercedes-Benz George Monkhouse *(White Mouse Editions 1984)*

Grand Prix Racing, Facts and Figures George Monkhouse/Roland King-Farlow *(G.T. Foulis & Co 1964)*

Racing the Silver Arrows Chris Nixon *(Osprey Publishing Ltd 1986)*

Silverstone Peter Carrick *(Pelham Books Ltd 1974)*

Speed Was My Life Alfred Neubauer *(Barrie & Rockliff 1960)*

Stirling Moss. My Cars, My Career Stirling Moss/Doug Nye *(Patrick Stephens Ltd 1987)*

The Formula One Record Book John Thompson *(Leslie Frewin Publishers Ltd 1974)*

Periodicals

Autocourse, The Motor, The Autocar, Motor Sport, Autosport, Motoring News, Motor Racing, Motor Racing Year, Competition Car, Speed World International, Grand Prix International.